The Dangerous Man

Conversations with Free-Thinkers and Truth-Seekers – A Collection of Alternative Research

First published by O Books, 2010
O Books is an imprint of John Hunt Publishing Ltd., The Bothy, Deershot Lodge, Park Lane, Ropley,
Hants, SO24 0BE, UK
office1@o-books.net
www.o-books.net

Distribution in:	South Africa
	Stephan Phillips (pty) Ltd
UK and Europe	Email: orders@stephanphillips.com
Orca Book Services	Tel: 27 21 4489839 Telefax: 27 21 4479879
orders@orcabookservices.co.uk	
Tel: 01202 665432 Fax: 01202 666219 Int.	Text copyright Karen Sawyer 2009
code (44)	
	Design: Stuart Davies
USA and Canada	
NBN	ISBN: 978 1 84694 345 4
custserv@nbnbooks.com	
Tel: 1 800 462 6420 Fax: 1 800 338 4550	All rights reserved. Except for brief quotations
	in critical articles or reviews, no part of this
Australia and New Zealand	book may be reproduced in any manner without
Brumby Books	prior written permission from the publishers.
sales@brumbybooks.com.au	
Tel: 61 3 9761 5535 Fax: 61 3 9761 7095	The rights of Karen Sawyer as author have been
	asserted in accordance with the Copyright,
Far East (offices in Singapore, Thailand, Hong	Designs and Patents Act 1988.
Kong, Taiwan)	
Pansing Distribution Pte Ltd	
kemal@pansing.com	A CIP catalogue record for this book is available
Tel: 65 6319 9939 Fax: 65 6462 5761	from the British Library.

Printed in the UK by CPI Antony Rowe, Chippenham, Wiltshire

The Dangerous Man

Conversations with Free-Thinkers and Truth-Seekers – A Collection of Alternative Research

Karen Sawyer

BOOKS

Winchester, UK
Washington, USA

CONTENTS

The Dangerous Man

The most complete guide to what free-thinking is all about. A true 'red pill', which only looks like a book.
~ **Paul Bondarovski, *The Dot Connector* magazine**

What is genuine, what is a lie? What is real and what is false? In this remarkably incisive and honest work, the author, Karen Sawyer, in a series of fascinating interviews peels away the choking layers of disinformation, half truths and downright lies that have, almost since time began, been presented as absolute truth by those who choose to retain their grasp on power, and in some cases the nature of reality itself, by any means at their disposal.

While the reader might have their own opinions regarding individual contributors, nevertheless each and every one of them have repeatedly spoken out fearlessly and accurately against the 'big brother' state and other groups who subvert our thoughts. This book encapsulates a range of alternative opinions with a shared theme, the very survival of the human race and the planet we live on. What is written here will entertain, shock, enrage and amaze in equal part, but ultimately it is a source of hope and I thoroughly recommend it to all who seek the truth.
~ **Brian J Allan, paranormal investigator, researcher, and author of *The Heretics, Can We Now Explain The Unexplainable***

To say this book is thought-provoking is an understatement. It is exquisitely addictive. You tell yourself that you will just dip in and find yourself a couple of hours later, fascinated by the revelations with a cup of cold tea at your elbow. The book is quite simply astounding and we highly recommend you read it.
~ **Nikki Mackay, *The Witch Hiker's Guide***

Karen Sawyer set out on a fantastic journey to explore and survey the widest reaches and some of the most fearless encampments in the realm of alternative thought. She returns not only with a startling map of the territory that challenges comfortable preconceptions but a collection that crackles with interest and insight. The most dangerous mind is one that thinks for itself. This is a book to inspire the type of bravery needed to do just that.
~ **David Southwell, author of** *Secrets & Lies and Conspiracy Files*

A revolutionary book, but not in the combative sense, more in the sense of turning the wheel one more time – one more revolution. A timely narrative of the way things are and the way things may be. It is a call to us for vision and bravery.
~ **Lindsay Halton, architect and author of** *The Secret of Home*

A potpourri of hope for all our futures. Please read this and sense the wonders of freedom.
~ **David Bellamy**

Karen Sawyer has accomplished a feat unmatched by any researcher I've heard of since Paola Harris: to interview almost every famous name in the business. It's a stunning collection of authorship; a true compendium of mavericks. The Dangerous Man is both an encyclopaedia of alternative free-thought which an old hand like me can learn from, and also an introduction to the subject for someone who's just beginning their waking-up process. Karen writes with optimism and humor, as do many of the book's 33 contributors. I feel hope in its pages in a world where hope seems to be absent, and the bravado of the Illuminati's endgame is painting over every place where hope pops up.
~ **Ben Emlyn-Jones,** http://hpanwo.blogspot.com

ACKNOWLEDGEMENTS

This book has come into being because others were willing to share their insights and information with me. First and foremost, I would like to express my deep gratitude to each and every one of them for their participation and support of this project.

Special thanks: to Ellis Taylor, Neil Hague, Michael Tsarion, Neil Kramer, Nick Clements, Kevin Miller, and Paul Bondarovski for their encouragement and inspiration; to Red Ice Creations for being such a fantastic research resource; and especially to Jerry Ravel, for transcribing some of these interviews.

Thanks, too, to: Anna Dudley at Twilight Bookshop, Taryan Louise Emery-Davies, and Audrey Filer for their transcribing skills. Special thanks to my dear friend Pat Reynolds and to Martin Dowling for their dedicated editorial skills and wry sense of humor.

To all those behind the scenes: all at O Books, especially Catherine Harris, Mary Flatt, Stu Davies, and John Hunt; to Peg Booth at *Booth Media Group* who arranged my interview with John Perkins; to Franci Prowse for her tremendous help with the Cleve Backster interview; to Sally Thomas at *Mountain of Love Productions* and Margaret Horton for helping finalize Bruce Lipton's hybrid interview/article; to Zoraah Mock for helping set up my interview with Robert Menard; to Patt Bekken at *Solutions in Commerce* for arranging my interview with Winston Shrout; to Baram Blackett for his editorial suggestions with Alan Wilson's interview; to Sylvia at *Coral Castle*; to Alister Taylor at *Torchlight Publishing Inc.* for approving my interview with Michael Cremo; to Jess at TPUC for organizing my interview with John Harris, and to Richard at TPUC for getting him down here.

HUGE thanks for the incredible love and support from: Glenys and Hugh Sawyer (aka Mum and Dad); my sister Bean;

(Uncle) Andy Forrest; Kris and Chris Ashdown; Angela George; Maggie Rees; Miranda Chaloner; Katie O'Murchu; and to Vince.

Loz, Pixie, and Eocha - the future is what you make yours... make sure it's wonderful.

To everyone who seeks freedom

*

In memory of Patrick McGoohan

The most dangerous man in the world is the contemplative who is guided by nobody. He trusts his own visions. He obeys the attractions of an inner voice, but will not listen to other men. He identifies the will of God with his own heart.
~ Thomas Merton; writer and Trappist monk (1915 – 1968)

The most dangerous man, to any government, is the man who is able to think things out for himself... Almost inevitably, he comes to the conclusion that the government he lives under is dishonest, insane and intolerable.
~ H.L. Mencken; Journalist, Essayist, Satirist (1880 – 1956)

They are dangerous because there are so many of them. It is one thing to have a few nuts or dissidents. They can be dealt with, justly or otherwise, so that they do not pose a danger to the system. It is quite another situation when you have a true movement – millions of citizens believing something, particularly when the movement is made up of society's average, successful citizens.
~ William Colby; director of CIA (1920 – 1996)

Believe me! The secret to reaping the greatest fruitfulness and the greatest enjoyment from life is to live dangerously!
~ Friedrich Nietzsche (1844 – 1900)

AUTHOR'S PREFACE

A happy and healthy civilization depends on balance – a development of both the mind and the soul in unison. With this equilibrium follows *true wisdom*. If we develop one without the other, it's likely that we will become either uninformed yet 'very spiritual' individuals *or* highly knowledgeable individuals who deny their spiritual selves.

In a sense, this is an age-old battle – one that has divided the psyche of humankind for a very long time; the spiritual *vs.* the material... often described as 'the light *vs.* the dark'. If you prefer, you could describe this conflict as one between the left and right hemispheres of the brain – the left representing order and logic; and the right, creativity and intuition.

While my first book, *Soul Companions*, focused on the spirit realms, *this* book explores the physical world we are often challenged by... it is the companion of '*Companions*' in that both spirit and matter are merely expressing polarities of the One.

The Dangerous Man is a collection of information. Within these pages you will find a curious combination of mystery, anomaly, and occult knowledge within fascinating research and insights from some of the most brilliant and controversial free-thinkers of our time.

A lot of collaborative effort has been involved in bringing this project to fruition. Most of the contributions in this book have been directly transcribed from interviews; then re-worked, edited and approved with the help of the individuals themselves. A handful have been directly penned by the authors and, where this is the case, I have given them the 'by' line. As with my previous book, I then arranged them into chapters for ease of reading and flow – a difficult task, I might add, as they span many genres... each one could have gone in a variety of chapters.

1

Those who dare to expose the truth often have to overcome many obstacles and take great risks in order to share what they have learned with others. Throughout history, many great men and women with groundbreaking ideas and vision have, and continue to be, largely ignored and unacknowledged, their work suppressed. Some are ridiculed, bullied and ostracized by their peers; others 'set-up', blackmailed and, in some cases, assassinated.

New ideas are often greeted with derision and contempt because they challenge the consensual 'norm'. You name it, there are many 'experts' who claim to know it all and refuse to acknowledge anything that is at odds with the current paradigm. After all, it would cost trillions to update and replace every false textbook in existence. Perhaps this suppression of information is a covert operation masterminded by the secret Society of University Librarians (SOUL) in order to avoid buying more books? Then again, perhaps this author is secret agent 'K' working for the elusive 'J' at *O Books* – the mastermind of a worldwide organization intent on banning all current study-books to be replaced only with useful *O Books* publications?

Diversity and balance is what this book is all about. We each have the right to express our uniqueness – I believe that's the whole point of being here in the first place. The ideas and concepts presented in this book will almost certainly challenge your ability to keep an open mind, especially as some of this information appears to be contradictory. THE truth does not exist, but truth certainly does – and it is not 'out there'... it is within. Truth is not a fixed point in time – it is relative to the perception of the individual, which is likely to change.

No one individual knows 'the whole truth and nothing but the truth' because we collectively hold pieces of the puzzle. It is up to you, the reader, to put these pieces together. Some may 'fit', some may not – but it is surely better to know something and discard it than remain in ignorance. If ignorance truly is 'bliss' as they say, then why aren't more people happy?

Instinctively and intuitively you *feel* when something isn't quite right. I have believed many lies. Not only that, but I have lied to myself and others. I understand why people accept a lie on one level; because it's not at all pleasant to acknowledge that you have been duped. (Sometimes 'the truth hurts'.) Like those 'magic eye' pictures, when you are ready and willing to look beyond what is presented to you, then a previously hidden picture emerges. As Lakota Tiokasin Ghosthorse said to me when I interviewed him for my previous book, *Soul Companions*, "Real eyes realize real lies".

I have come to recognize that the accepted version of 'the truth' is often a façade for another, often secret, agenda. A secret isn't necessarily 'sinister' or 'evil' – it only becomes so when you keep that knowledge to yourself in order to manipulate and control others. If there *is* a hidden agenda in the world today, we can only speculate what it may be and who is ultimately pulling the strings.

The 'who, what, where, when and why' is of no real consequence – what *really* matters is that we individually accept responsibility for our lives, for the choices we make and actions we take. In order to do this, we need to be clued-up and savvy. We deserve to know the facts so that we may draw our own conclusions and respond accordingly.

On this planet, there exists a diverse range of individuals – of all ages, cultures and beliefs – who have the potential to transform 'life as we know it' for the better. It is time for us to make informed decisions not only for ourselves, but for the future generations that follow. The informed spiritual individual is a powerful force to be reckoned with indeed…

Just for the record, I want to make it perfectly clear that the title of this book is not gender specific. By using the term *Dangerous Man*, I am referring to *mankind* – both men *and* women. The fact

3

that I only interviewed one woman is irrelevant. In my experience, women are just as 'dangerous'... oh, yes. Never doubt it for a second.

While paying for petrol recently, I was asked what my 'number' was. *"I am not a number, I am a free man!"* I replied in jest. Patrick McGoohan's brilliant TV series *The Prisoner* is one of my inspirations for writing this book. It was way ahead of its time and has become more relevant as the years go by. In a 1977 interview, he said, *"We're run by the Pentagon. We're run by Madison Avenue. We're run by television. And, as long as we accept those things and don't revolt, we'll have to go along with the stream to the eventual avalanche."* It is my intention that this book is used to dig ourselves out of it.

Be seeing you.

Karen Sawyer
March 2009, Haverfordwest.

1

THE DANGEROUS MIND

THE DANGEROUS MIND

*It is perfectly possible for a man to be out of prison, and yet not free –
to be under no physical constraint and yet to be a psychological
captive, compelled to think, feel and act as the representatives of the
national state, or of some private interest within the nation, wants
him to think, feel and act.*

*The nature of psychological compulsion is such that those who act
under constraint remain under the impression that they are acting on
their own initiative. The victim of mind-manipulation does not know
that he is a victim. To him the walls of his prison are invisible, and he
believes himself to be free. That he is not free is apparent only to other
people. His servitude is strictly objective.*

**~ Aldous Huxley, English writer (1894 - 1963); *Brave New
World Revisited***

*Since things neither exist nor do exist,
are neither real nor unreal,
are utterly beyond accepting and rejecting –
one might as well burst out laughing.*

**~ Longchenpa Rabjampa, Nyingma Tibetan Buddhist
(1308 - 1364)**

Are your thoughts truly your own? In my previous book, *Soul
Companions*, I explored the concept that each of us is like a 'straw'
or 'tube' – that we bring ideas *through* us all the time and that
there's a fine line between 'guidance' and 'manipulation'. If you
are following strict guide-lines, whether from Spirit allies or in
the physical rules we abide by, then you are being manipulated.
This is not necessarily 'good' or 'bad'; what makes it so is the

7

inability to discern truth from fiction. In all cases, whether dealing with invisible energies or physical individuals (and you're usually dealing with both), it's important to feel what is right and true for you personally and not allow anyone to dictate what you should or shouldn't do, whether that person has a body or not!

When I hear stories about 'very spiritual people' booking tickets to Egypt 'because the crystal skulls told us to', then I hear warning bells. Manipulative entities (invisible or otherwise) are very pleasant until you say, "No"... for instance; when I tell my kids not to do something and then they go and do it anyway, then all hell breaks loose. Why? *Because they didn't do what I wanted them to do.* In a sense, whatever way you look at it, most parenting skills are manipulative in that they are all ways, covertly and overtly, of making a child do this or that, i.e: *behave*, even if they don't feel like it. Sounds familiar? All of us have 'been there' and 'done that' at some point in our lives.

Manipulation and control of others is perfectly illustrated in the Peter Cook and Dudley Moore film, *Bedazzled*. The whole film is a brilliant illustration of devious manipulation and trickery – Mr. Spiggot (the devil) wants Stanley Moon's soul so that he can win a bet with God and be restored to angelic status, and all poor old Stanley wants is the girl of his dreams to love him. *Both* characters are equally manipulative and cunning in that they will go to any lengths to get what they want.

The dangerous mind is not above manipulation by any stretch of the imagination; the difference is that it can spot it, both in itself and others. At that point of realization, it is free to make its own decisions. It has a choice what to think, where to go, and how to act based on the voice within instead of external prompting. By the way, external prompting is often confused with the voice within – if you find yourself saying 'I should', 'shouldn't', 'can't', etc., then this indicates that you've bought-into the external voice. The dangerous mind is expansive and curious; is always open to new ideas and new ways of doing things.

Picture credit: Bean Sawyer

THE MAVERICK OF MAVERICKS
David Icke

The dreamer is the dream.
~ David Icke

David Icke is a former professional footballer, journalist and television news and sport presenter who had his life transformed through a series of extraordinary 'paranormal' experiences. Since then he has spent nearly 20 years revealing the illusory nature of 'physical' reality and exposing a conspiracy to impose a global Orwellian state. What David Icke has predicted in his nearly 20 books going back to 1991 is now happening by the day.

Perhaps his most extraordinary claim is that many of the people in control of global events are human-reptilian hybrid bloodlines that have resulted from the interbreeding between humans and a reptilian race going back into ancient history.

David is author of many books, including the recent *The David Icke Guide to the Global Conspiracy (And How to End it)*.

His latest DVD is *Beyond the Cutting Edge*. Both are available through his website: www.davidicke.com.

Our experiences help us deprogram, if we use them well. Life so often presents us with our greatest gifts brilliantly disguised as our worst nightmare. I had a fear of being ridiculed and what did I experience? Being laughed at on a mega scale. I was perceived and presented as a complete nutter and, as a result, I overcame the fear and I'm no longer imprisoned by the question: 'What will other people think?'

What changed my life was simply deciding that if ever my intuition and my 'intellect' were in conflict, I would go with my intuition. You don't say and do what I say and do unless you're free from control by the intellect, which is telling you to conform and to 'stay within the box'. If I had gone with my intellect and emotions, which were screaming, *"No! Shut up!"*, then what has happened since would not have happened ... I'd probably still be saying, *"Hello, good evening and welcome to the football."* You reach a point where your intellect observes the fact that although you have some challenges if you follow your intuition it all works out in the end – and not *despite* following your intuition, but *because* of it.

Following the intuitive urge to do and say things can get you into some scrapes in the world that we live in. You're going to stand out like a sore thumb in this society. The Japanese have a saying, 'Don't be the nail that stands out above the rest, because that's the first one to get hit', but there comes a point where you become numb to the hammer because it doesn't matter anymore. It only matters if you believe it matters.

When I was a goalkeeper, I learned more about how to play in goal by the mistakes I made than the good things I did. When you make saves, you're doing it right ... not much to learn there. When you make a 'mistake', you're seeing why you did it and how you can improve on that. It's not about evolving. I don't believe that we have experiences to 'evolve'. We are already Infinite Consciousness – All That Is. The 'learning' is really the deprograming from the fake reality that we believe about ourselves and the 'world'. My passion is to understand reality and how we create it.

The Suppression of Knowledge

The famous Zulu shaman, Credo Mutwa, is a great friend and kindred spirit. What's fantastic about our friendship is that he's a jet-black South African who's gleaned his knowledge from African tradition, and I'm this guy from Leicester who used to kick a ball about for a living and presented the BBC news; and yet, despite our completely different backgrounds and life experiences, we have both come to the same basic conclusions. When we meet, it's like one consciousness meeting itself – we have an incredible rapport. He's like a library on legs and a carrier of ancient knowledge that is now returning to public awareness.

There has been a constant effort to suppress this knowledge for thousands of years – to keep people in ignorance of who they are. I mean, here we are at the so-called cutting-edge of human evolution and yet if you stop people in London, Sydney, New York or anywhere in the world and ask, *"Excuse me, can you tell me who you are, what you're doing here and where you come from?"* what will the answers be? If they don't give you a religious response, they'll say, *"I dunno, really – I've never thought about it!"* How can we see ourselves as being clever or enlightened or at the cutting-edge of understanding, when we don't even know who we are and where we've come from? I don't mean 'I am Fred Jones from London, England', but where you came from before you entered this 'world' and where you will go when you leave. Who are you? We're not encouraged to think about it and so most people don't.

To express the full magnitude of who you are is a massive challenge and most people don't even get close to it. We get locked into what I call 'computer consciousness', or 'body consciousness', and this overwhelmingly expresses itself though the five senses.

I see the human body as a biological computer that has, for example, anti-virus software (the immune system) and a central processing unit (the brain). Some cutting-edge scientists are now realizing that cells are like computer chips. DNA is a crystalline structure that works like a 'hard drive' and every time we have an experience or take on a belief, we're downloading that information into the body hard-drive. This affects the way we perceive reality if we operate on the level of body consciousness and it can be passed on to the next generation.

Society is structured to entice and attract the five senses, to hold you in that 'box'. What we bravely call education is dominated by the realm of the five-senses and is all about the 'small self'. Young people are not being awoken to the Greater Self. The brain has two hemispheres, the left side which is dominated by intellect, language and five-sense reality; and the right side which is much more 'out there' and connects into the Infinite Self.

In schools all over the world, you see the creative 'right-brain' activities like art and music all massively downgraded. The emphasis in on the left brain and thus the so-called 'education' system is turning out what I call 'left-brain prisoners' – people enslaved by the intellect and that low level of perception that we call 'thought'. The Little Self thinks, the Greater Self knows and therefore expresses itself through intuitive knowing.

The British government wants to bring in academic education for toddlers ... they want them to focus on 'left-brain' information as early as possible. Play is intuitive, spontaneous and imaginative – it's all 'right-brain' – and that's the last way they want children to develop.

Control-freaks are frightened people. When you are at peace with yourself and at peace with who you are (or at least closer to it) you don't want to control anyone – you don't want to dictate anyone's perceptions. You might say, *"Here's another way at looking at life, what do you think?"* but you're not trying to change anybody, just giving them the opportunity to change if they so choose. Those forces that are manipulating global society are the opposite of that. They want to control everything because people in fear are ill-at-ease with situations that are in constant flux. They can't deal with a lack of control.

For instance, if you go to a football match and you're not attached to the outcome, no matter what the score is, you'll have a good day whatever the result. But if you are attached to one team winning you have a completely different experience if that doesn't happen.

Given a choice, most people in that mode would want to control the game to the point where you knew the outcome, your team winning, before the game even started. This is what the forces of control are doing all the time – manipulating world events to ensure the outcome they want. This is why in their own writings they express fear of what they call 'maverick people' - those who live their lives without preconceived idea or being attached to an outcome. They go where their heart (knowing) tells them to go, and they don't know where that's going to be from day to day, even moment to moment. The manipulators are so encased with fear that they don't know how to handle the intuitive mavericks.

The fear of not-surviving is a key central motivation for these manipulators and interestingly this instinct comes from the reptilian brain, or R-complex as scientists call it. This most ancient part of the brain is also responsible for the fight-or-flight reaction to danger – where we either smack a guy or run. It's not that the manipulators are all-knowing... they, too, are in a 'box'. The way they control humanity is by putting you in a smaller box than they are in. Once you go beyond both boxes, beyond fear of not-surviving and into the understanding that we are not our bodies, but Infinite Consciousness, you realize that there is nothing to survive and there's nothing that can stop us surviving. You then lose the need to run around controlling everything. How can eternal infinite consciousness ever be in a situation where it has to survive? It might change its expression, but that's not the same as surviving.

When you study reptilian behavior, it is incredibly predictable and these manipulators are the same. What sets them apart from much of the rest of the population is lack of empathy. Empathy is vital because if I have empathy with the consequences of my actions for you, that is going to stop me doing anything that will adversely affect you. If you haven't got that empathy, you don't give a shit about bombs dropping on cities full of civilians. In some way, the genetics of these human-reptilian hybrids delete the ability to empathize and so to them anything goes. We don't appreciate the impact of genetics on behavior once we fall into body consciousness.

'Incarnating' consciousnesses has to cope with all sorts of inherited programs – physical, emotional, and mental belief programs. In the normal course of life it's very easy (and it happens most of the time) for people to go from 'cradle to grave' in body consciousness, because the implantation of our sense of reality is that we are five-sense beings. Anyone who's entered this reality with all those challenges and seen beyond it – round of applause... because that's a fantastic achievement by itself given the pressure to stay asleep.

Breaking the Shell
Some psychoactive drugs, like the rain forest plant ayahuasca, open up the channels so that you can go beyond the body-self and access levels of awareness that have a much greater fix on the nature of reality and life itself. It's not that we have to find infinite consciousness or even seek it... we *are* it. What we do is we throw emotional and mental barriers up, which create what I

symbolize as energetic eggshells that hold us in a state of fear and ignorance. We're always infinite consciousness, but we forget that and so we live as if we're not.

I took ayahuasca in the Brazilian rain forest in 2003. I was lying in the dark in a round hut in the rain forest with the guy who was running the event. I started feeling an incredible energy coming from my heart chakra, where we connect not with thought but with knowing – what some people call intuition, which is our connection to forever. This energy arced up in a half-circle and went into my head. It was absolutely gripping me. The music player started switching on and off without anyone going near it, and then three strip lights came on by themselves because of the energy in the room.

People don't realize that everything is energy – this so-called physical world, this so-called physical body, is a holographic illusory energy field. And therefore energy can interact between apparently different physical forms that are also just energy fields. We don't realize just what electrical, magnetic beings we really are.

I had some wonderful experiences that night and the following night when I took ayahuasca for the second and last time, a female voice talked to me for about five hours about the nature of reality. The voice was a part of me, because everything's part of me (you're part of me, I'm part of you – we're all part of each other... we're all everything). I was told that reality is an energetic construct, very similar to a television station. The only place that television programs exist is on the screen – everywhere else they're electrical circuits and frequency fields. We are living a highly advanced version of that, but similar in concept. We are decoding this reality all the time into what we think we're living in, in the sense of it's outside of us, when in this form it's inside of us. As even mainstream science will have to confirm, our five senses are decoding vibrational information into electrical signals that are then passed through to the brain which decodes that electrical information into the 'physical' world that we think is outside of us. In fact, it only exists inside the brain which acts as our television 'screen'. This is why quantum physics has found that while the 'physical' world is made of atoms, the atoms have no solidity. They are just pockets of energy and, overwhelmingly, 'empty' space. How can this be? Because the 'physical' is not 'physical'; it is an illusion of the decoding process.

The voice continued to tell me that infinite love – the existence of one infinite consciousness – is the only truth. Everything else is the imagination of that consciousness made manifest. It's not that we have disconnected from infinite consciousness – we can't because that's what we are. We have fallen for the delusion that the dream is separate from the dreamer. You are the dreamer and the dreamed and therefore you have control over the dream and what you experience in the dream. What the manipulators have done is to systematically reinforce, encourage and implant the belief that the dream is separate from the dreamer, because then they can control us and dictate the dream. Once we realize that, then all this manipulative, enslavement shit comes to an end. Remember, the dreamer is the dream.

Of course, the manipulators are part of us, too... but just as you're in a certain mental and emotional state, I'm in a different one, and that person over there is in another, so those who are manipulating are in a different mental, emotional and energetic state to most of those they're seeking to control. It's just a different expression of All Possibility – there are no limits, otherwise it couldn't be 'all possibility'. Once you start to come from a point of view that there are limits to possibility, you've already disconnected from infinite consciousness which is All Possibility... the infinite possibility to imagine and dream whatever it chooses. We're all in that collective dream – the imagination of the Infinite.

Because we're All Possibility, we can come in and out of this time loop whenever we want. I think that what we call the 'matrix' has multi-levels. If you don't have a greater sense of awareness, you can become addicted to this reality and the five senses, and that sets up an 'in-and-out', 'round-and-round' motion. People call that 'reincarnation'.

When I was in the ayahuasca state, I was shown a picture of humans dropping down from the sky and walking along a path across a field. As they walked, they wore the ground away and it changed from being a path to a groove in a record. The voice said, *"Is it any surprise that people look up for heaven when that is the only direction they see light?"* It also said that one of the key reasons why people are so easy to control and manipulate is because they've done it so many times before. Literally like a groove in a record, you come in and lock into the same program. You play it out again. The theme was about getting caught in the addiction to this reality.

The 'ayahuasca' had a terrific sense of humor and I was laughing through most of it. At one point, I saw this image of myself on a stage just standing there looking at the audience, not saying a word. I saw a woman in the audience nudge the one next to her in bewilderment at what I was doing. The voice said, *"You only speak words because if you didn't, the audience would be wondering* 'when the fuck is he going to start?!'". The point was that the real communication is energetic – it's not even through the voice, although that's a form of energy ... the words keep the mind occupied, but the real change is going on energetically.

Psychoactive drugs can be an effective tool for breaking down the barriers, but they can be another box, another diversion. They can help some people, but we have the ability to go 'out there' without them. I took that drug twice in Brazil and I never have since because the idea is to get 'out there' without them.

The Last Cul-de-Sac Before The Gold Mine
Whenever I think of the universe, I see a donut-shape going round and round. This shape is known by science as a 'torus'.

The apparent passage of events and experience give us the illusion of time moving forward from the past, but actually it's all happening in the same 'now'. There is only the now, the moment you are experiencing. When you think of the 'past' you are doing so in the 'now'; when you think of the future, you are doing so in the 'now'. There is only the now and thus no time. Past and future are illusions of the mind.

In this repeating cycle, approximately every 26,000 years with the precession of the equinoxes, it is claimed that the planet moves into alignment with a massive energy beam, rebalancing and realigning anything that's out of balance. Some people call this the 'photon belt'. And as you go through it, it rebalances everything, and when you come out the other side you start a new era – a 'New Age'.

It's a self-balancing system so that, because of free will and other 'variables', there is great potential to become energetically out of balance. The more out-of-balance something is, the bigger that jump is to get back into balance.

There's nothing more manipulatable than genuineness that's not streetwise, and this is why the awakening and the conspiracy have to go together. There are a lot of people in the so-called 'New Age' movement that go for the spiritual awakening but they're manipulated like crazy because they don't realize that there is a force that wants to divert them from getting there. I call the New Age the 'last cul-de-sac before the gold mine', because it was created to capture those who have rejected mainstream religion and 'science' before they see the infinite truth about themselves and reality

One of the misunderstandings that people have is that when they decide to be 'spiritual' everything is immediately wonderful. But as you wake up, what actually happens (if you really make the commitment to go for it) is that all hell can apparently break loose in your life. Things can change dramatically when you have the intent to understand who you are and the nature of life. It's not always a pleasant experience because what's happening – especially in the initial period – is the energetic fields or construct that has been creating your life up to that point suddenly changes as you change. As your inner transforms, so must the outer because one is just a reflection of the other.

What you attract into your life changes. New people and experiences appear as the physical expression of the 'old you' crumbles – relationships can break up, jobs can be lost, and sometimes financial difficulties arise... but this is just the outer expression of one energetic state replacing another. It's not that you have an experience which breaks down the 'old you' and then you become the 'new you'... it's actually an on-going journey, and the same process will unfold over and over again. It gets easier by understanding the process, because when it first happened to me I had no idea what was going on. My old life didn't just slowly disintegrate... it suddenly collapsed. You immediately think, 'I'm on the wrong path!' when you're actually on the right path. In truth, we're not on any path, but that's another story. People need not to judge the journey by each step. Just enjoy each step and the 'journey' takes care of itself. In other words; be in the now, not past or future, which are just projections of the mind.

This reality has been dominated by fear for so long that, collectively, there's an enormous amount of manipulative debris to clean up by deleting the mind programs and there is an energetic change happening now that is doing just that for increasingly vast numbers of people. This change is bringing all that has remained hidden to the surface and people are going to have to deal with the shock of what's been going on around them, individually and collectively, all these years without them realizing.

People are beginning to have the ability to perceive a much greater sense of self and the world than they could before.

Therefore, the limits on human potential are also crumbling and we're going into a great time, though a very challenging one as the forces of control seek to impose their will even more blatantly. Once you realize you are the dream and the dreamer, you can start taking control of the dream and that's the challenge we have at the moment.

The Global Conspiracy

Conspiracy research is a stepping-stone to freedom, because in order to get out of the prison cell you've first got to realize that you're in one. The major prison cell is actually the left side of the brain which deals with structure and language and sees everything as apart from everything else. Most people are prisoners of the left-brain perception and the step-by-step logical dot-connecting to expose the global conspiracy to create an Orwellian world can have the effect of unlocking the left-brain and allowing a greater sense of reality to enter human perception.

Once the left-brain can understand, using five-sense logic and interconnected information, that there is a conspiracy and it is dictating events on the planet, then suddenly the left-brain starts to open up to a greater possibility. It ceases to dismiss new perceptions by reflex action.

During my public talks, after I've presented a certain amount of factual information of a left-brain nature, there comes a point when I feel the energy in the room demonstrably change. At that point I can bring in 'out there' information and people will listen, who, if I had started with that, would have said, *"This is crazy bollocks"*.

The conspiracy side of what I do is important – but it mustn't end there. If you only focus on the conspiracy, then all you're doing is compiling more and more knowledge about your own prison. You're building another version of that prison because you're adding to the fear and the sense of powerlessness that people have. So, okay, we're in a prison cell, we're in a situation of enslavement... what do we do about it? How do we become un-enslaved?

This is an area that the vast majority of conspiracy researchers won't go into because so many edit information to protect their own belief systems, which are often very religion-based. Many people involved in conspiracy research don't want true freedom... they only want freedom for their own belief-system to replace the one they are seeking to expose. It's still about control. You would think on the face of it that this area of research would be peopled by open, honest people who desire freedom for all – and there are people like that, for sure – but it is also awash with some of the most corrupt, manipulating con-men and women you could ever meet.

The books I have written are stepping stones to a greater truth ... the nature of reality itself. Once you see the deeper levels of what we call life you realize that we need to ditch the idea that the only way to overcome something or change something is to fight it. What you fight, you become. We have people fighting for freedom and fighting for peace, which is the most extraordinary example of what George Orwell called 'doublethink'. We don't need to fight for anything. If we want freedom then we need to be free – refuse to cooperate with our own enslavement, individually and collectively. If we want peace we need to be peaceful.

We create our own reality, or allow it to be created, and the manipulators of this world want to keep us in ignorance of this. If we don't know that we're creating our reality, the manipulators can intervene in this process by implanting our sense of reality – like Bin Laden orchestrated 9/11 (absolute baloney) – and thus our sense of reality becomes our experienced reality. Put simply, if we think we are powerless and have no control over our lives, we will live a reality to match.

We need to be careful that we don't get caught in labels like 'shaman' and 'guru' and 'master', etc., because these pedestal people, as I call them, can also put people in a box. All beliefs are boxes, in fact, be it belief in Jesus, a shaman or some New Age guru. We should be looking people in the eye, not looking up at them. One 'holy man' was asked to explain the difference between a 'master' and a 'pupil'... *"Their point of observation"*, he said, and he was right.

If we can lose our sense of limitation and realize that we are the 'All', not the small, then the outward manifestation of our sense of limitation will disappear and our lives will change, often dramatically.

The great thing about this period now is that there is an energetic change happening, bringing to the surface all that has been hidden. In many ways, conspiracy-researchers are expressing that energy by bringing suppressed information to public awareness. It's a time when you cannot hide your Real Self... you can't hide your true energy. If you energetically 'feel' people, it doesn't matter what their face is doing or what their voice is saying – you 'get' them. And sometimes you don't 'get' them because you're not meant to... you're meant to experience them. I think more and more we will find that some people are not who we thought they were, and that situations are not what they appear to be.

Conspiracy research on the five-sense level is like studying a cinema screen. But that's all it is, because what's happening in this world is a reflection of a deeper reality. I want to know the source of that reflection. You can stand and scream at the screen if you don't like the movie, but it's still going to play out. You can only change it when you change the reel, so I'm heading for the projection room... whatever and wherever it is.

Photo Credit: Maria Hayes, 2009

THE PATH TO REVOLUTION
Nick Clements

Thus it can be seen that mental health is based on a certain degree of tension between what one has already achieved and what one still ought to accomplish, or the gap between what one is and what one should become. Such a tension is inherent in the human being and therefore is indispensable to mental well-being. We should not, then, be hesitant about challenging man with a potential meaning for him to fulfil. It is only thus that we evoke his will to meaning for him to fulfil.

~ **Viktor E. Frankl,** *Man's Search For Meaning*

Nick Clements is an internationally-acclaimed author, filmmaker and workshop facilitator, living in Wales. He is also a Visiting Professor at Staffordshire University.

His recent books *Creative Collaboration* and *The Ugly Duckling* deal with the potential for change that comes from creativity, and the need for rites of passage in all our lives, most especially those of young men. Nick has specialized in working in areas of high social needs since 1975, and is employed by governments, charities, corporations and local authorities to train people in the multiple uses of creativity and spirituality. He describes himself as, "a pioneer and catalyst... a man paid to be himself; so fortunate, so blessed."

Nick collaborates with many organizations; including Circle of Life Rediscovery, who enable teenagers to undertake outdoor camping experiences, and Valley and Vale Community Arts, with whom he has developed Person Centred Creativity. He is also involved in the development of links between indigenous people's teachings and Western leadership styles. Details of his work can be found on the websites:

www.soundoftheheart.com; nicholasclements.co.uk, and indigenocity.com

To be a revolutionary, you've got to understand the principles of alchemy. In the beginning there was just fire or spirit. The element of fire is immense, without boundaries in terms of time, space or dimensions. When this fire alchemically, magically, and impossibly connects to 'intention,' a piece of that amorphous light becomes encapsulated and lives within a clear container. The container is unique. Its shape and form is never the same even though this process has been performed many millions of times. The container represents the element of earth. The image I have is of a lantern – a clear glass container in which resides the spark. Magically, impossibly, and alchemically, this container is, in turn, encapsulated in a denser physical form, a body. This new form is mainly water and is nurtured in water. Impossibly, alchemically, magically, the physical form is then birthed from the water out into the physical world, into the world of air. These three are linked by a mind or consciousness, which is very akin to the element of air. So, there are four layers – mind, moving inward to the body, into soul, and then, finally at the core... Spirit.

There is an infinite amount of Spirit – out there, in here, around here, and over there. Spirit knows and remembers all incarnations, all physical manifestations of Spirit. There is a particular way of doing this on Earth... it doesn't happen randomly. For every incarnation there is an intention formed in the cauldron of possibilities, which is the fusion of Spirit and soul, resulting in the physical manifestation of a unique container in which Spirit resides. The soul is in the shape of the intention, the soul's purpose. It is not inscribed with words. This is a primordial process. In Western culture we want our soul's purpose written in big letters – i.e. '**YOU ARE A VET**'. You could spend a lifetime trying to interpret and connect to it, but you won't necessarily know what it is. If, however, you're doing your soul's purpose, if you're really doing it sweet... you will be in the flow – what more can you ask for?

In the late 70's/early 80's, I absolutely *knew* what I wanted to do. I was in tune with who I was and what I was about. I set up a community arts project, *The Pioneers*. For me, the key to this work was creativity. I use the word creativity in the widest possible sense – all the arts, crafts, storytelling, film-making, writing, imaginative play, being a fool, and so much more. We ran a multi-million pound organization. I got flown all over the world – New York, Berlin... I was a bigwig and people would look at me and go, *"Fuck, I want your job!"* because I was earning a lot of money traveling all over the world being an artist. And yet, by the late 1990's I didn't want it any more. My heart was no longer in it. People said *"You're a fool, it's a successful business – franchise it, sell it, stick at it... it's worth a lot of money."* I walked away with nothing. My original intention was never to make money... it was to accept the challenge. I now realize that I walked away because my vision of my soul's purpose had changed. I had to make hard choices and it was not an easy path. I now make my living by working with rites of passage, running workshops on masculinity and spirituality, and by writing books. Choosing these new paths brought many challenges into my life.

There are very few people who have been able to spend their lifetime working as an artist; even fewer have used creativity to serve others; fewer still specialize in working in desperate communities; and very few work with men and ritual. My path is unique and it is out of the ordinary. It sounds very different but, to be honest, it has been simple to follow and makes absolute sense to me. I've never been deterred from following it. This is the consequence of who I am, and it has its advantages and disadvantages.

I have been fortunate enough to have recognized aspects of my soul's purpose. This internal work enables me to do the external work which resonates deeply with others, and nurtures me in turn. To have got this far, doesn't mean I'm enlightened... I still flounder, prevaricate, and abuse myself. It does, however, mean I have an internal security – a maturity, which I can reach simply and effectively when I *remember*. I'm still wondering at the complexity of dimensions to the container. I'm still learning about the surfaces I can't yet see... those in the shadow and those which I am unable to see until the right time. It is an unfolding and continual process.

All of us have come with a unique intention and it would be pointless if it didn't contain challenge. We tend to forget this. If the soul's purpose was to bumble along and not take risks, then we are not learning anything. This is not why we are here. It is during the moments of challenge we become who we should be, when we remember our intention... when we remember how to be a revolutionary. The revolution happens internally out of self-love and self-awareness of what the soul's purpose is. If you know why you're here, what you're about, what your particular skills are, and who you are, then you have a job to do.

Rites of Passage

I work a lot with boys and men. There's a point in every boy's life when he needs to change. All over the world they have rites of passage for teenagers, where boys leave their mothers to go and live with the male Elders. In Guatemala, teenage boys lived with a man for a year to be taught the male language – up until that point they only knew the female language because they'd spent so much time with their mothers. What that means to me, symbolically, is that you have to be *taught* how to be a man.

I live in the South Wales valleys. I worked with ex-miners, who talked about the idea that when the young lad goes down the pit, it is a rite of passage, and the main lesson he gets taught is how to collaborate. They worked with an older man. *"This is the man who's going to save your life. He will save your life every day. Trust him."* Trust, partnership, and collaboration – what is that other than a rites of passage for men?! We've forgotten it almost completely.

Teenage groups, gangs, and tribes are searching for exactly the same thing – *trust*. They want to know their 'homeys' will look after them. If you feel insecure and you don't trust anybody, you are an isolated individual. Unfortunately, peer initiation when your contemporaries try to initiate you, is not very effective. Your peers don't know where you're going because they've never been there themselves. What rights of passage, particularly for teenagers, are about is that *you are not alone*. You need other people, you need older men. You need to collaborate. Selfishness is the behavior of an uninitiated man; humility is the sign of an initiated man.

We have this concept in our culture of 'self-made men'. Richard Branson and Alan Sugar are held up as fine examples of 'how to be'. Richard Branson didn't *make* Virgin on his own – he employs tens of thousands of people! He is *not* alone. Alan Sugar keeps saying, *"I'm a self-made man... I'm a successful multi-millionaire"*. He's *not* self-made! He has an incredibly supportive wife and family. The immaturity of uninitiated men is always focused on themselves – is always saying, *"I did this", "I'm great"* and I was the same for 20-odd years. There was an ego in my actions, and I'm not saying that's a bad thing... to be driven like that is beautiful, but at some point you have to step back from the pedestal and say, *"I depend on other people – I can't do this alone."* Then you become more mature. *Then* you become a man.

The work that I do is to challenge the concept of macho. I don't mind men being aggressive; I don't mind men being angry... I don't mind any of that, but what I will challenge is violence. The use of violence is always by the uninitiated. This needs to be dealt with during those teenage years, but because we don't have rights of passage we don't do it. If we can reintroduce rites of passage for teenagers and men at other times in their lives, then we would start dealing with our present ecological and social problems.

Rites and revolutions are immediate and very relevant to our culture. This idea that you sit at the foot of the guru for 20 years in a cave and then you become enlightened is no longer relevant. Every time you connect to your soul's purpose it creates a vacuum... nature abhors a vacuum, so it chucks the next lot in and says, *"You did really well... now have a look at this behavior you thought you were in control of."* We don't have to go on courses to do the inner-work and find our purpose and we don't need to spend thousands of pounds... it's in our DNA, it's in our blood. You are, I am, all of us are our ancestors but also those to come. They're all here *right now*. We have the knowledge... all we have to do is access it. We carry the tools and the means for positive change within us at all times.

Revolutionary Ancestors

I have a website called *The Sound of the Heart*, and the name was contained in something I wrote a while ago;

"We do not often hear the sound of our heart. For the majority of our life it trots along inside us, keeping time, being patient, loving us unconditionally, and we ignore it. Every now and then we become afraid, we accept challenge, we run hard, we are in love – something moves and shifts within and without us. In those moments we hear the sound of our heart. I seek to hear my heart."

When my heart first started to beat, it enabled the blood of my ancestors to flood into me, and they have nurtured me ever since. I am a combination of three things – my original intention, my ancestral intelligence, and the experiences I have subsequently encountered along the way. All three influence my path. My ancestral influence can only be called one thing – revolutionary, and I am proud and a fierce defender of the inheritance I have received.

On my mother's side, my great grandfather, Ramsay MacDonald, was the first Labour Prime Minister of Britain in 1924. As the illegitimate son of a fisherwoman from Lossiemouth, a tiny fishing village in the north of Scotland, he became one of the most powerful people in the world. He was brought up by his mother and grandmother who instilled into him the principles of Socialism. The coming to power of the Labour government at that time was the most radical change ever in the history of British politics. His oratory and diplomatic skills combined with the discontent and unrest throughout Britain following the disastrous First World War, led to nothing short of revolution. The establishment was terrified that the Socialists would be like the Bolsheviks in Russia. However, my grandfather was able to introduce radical bills into parliament, and established the Labour party. One story goes that two Scotsmen fell to talking on the Thames Embankment; one said he was homeless, so the other said *"Come and stay with us"*. That night, the homeless man slept at Number 10 Downing Street. That's the action of a revolutionary man.

Both my grandfathers were conscientious objectors in the First World War. To do so was to risk prison and worse. Like my great-grandfather, they opposed violence and were part of the 'pacifist' movement (a much-misunderstood word). Like them, my mother was a pacifist and socialist and she was a very talented actress.

My parents, my grandparents and my great grandparents were all revolutionaries. They were Socialists, they lived in communes, they were pacifists, and they thought 'outside the box'. My ancestors had principles – they believed in ideas, they wanted to bring about change, and they didn't mind being in the minority. Historically, such revolutionary people are normally equated with politics. I have a memory of some old person feeling my young hands and saying, *"So soft... too soft to start the revolution."* That was then, this is now...

Revolutionaries for Today and Tomorrow

We can be revolutionaries without resorting to violence or having radical political views... we can even be revolutionaries with soft hands! For me, to be revolutionary is to connect to the real meaning of the word – the spiral; to revolve, to be in motion, and open to change. It is the antithesis of being linear, stagnant or stationary. It is the opposite of maintaining the status quo. The revolution starts between our ears, inside our heads, in our back gardens, and in the high street. We are revolutionaries when we see injustice and seek to change it; when we question the established and majority view; when we perform random acts of kindness; and when we stick to our principles, despite being in the minority.

My house has a front and a back door. If I choose to go for a walk from my back door I am able to walk by a wild river, in the woods, amongst nature. During this winter, I have been watching the salmon spawning, and now the goosander are dancing and fighting for territories. The restorative and beneficial qualities of these walks are immense, easily found, and easily accessed. In contrast, when I step out of my front door I step onto a main road. This leads to another (even bigger) road upon which are shops and stores. I frequently walk out of my front door in pursuit of something I have forgotten to purchase. I walk in a very different way when I am surrounded by houses cars and people. I want to be able to walk out of my front *or* back door and for it not to make a difference – for both walks to be equally restorative and recuperative. I guess when I can do that, I'm really moving towards being a revolutionary!

Right now, we live in a society without compassion, obsessed by celebrity, material goods, and in the thrall of rampant consumerism. This has created any number of climatic, economic, and social planetary crises. If we do not start living revolutionary lives in this moment, then we never will! If we do not realize we need to think and act as revolutionaries right now, then we have failed our ancestors and we will be failing future generations to come. We need radical revolutionary thought and action everywhere. We need to challenge how we live, where we live, what is community, what is good, what is bad, what we do, how we think, how we spend money, who we talk to, who we share with – everything needs to change. It is no longer effective or right to think in the short term, to be timid, to stay in that awful job, to maintain a loveless relationship, or to ignore the reality of any of our situations.

Revolution was always about injustice. The injustice is 'within' as well as 'without'. We treat ourselves very badly, we criticize and we abuse ourselves, probably harder and more vehemently than anyone else. We need to recognize this and stop being so hard on ourselves, and recognize the paradox of working with shadow. When we work with the shadow we realize that the internal always reflects the external. For example,

I was on the freeway and there was a queue because a lane had been closed. Some bastard just drove up there really fast in a big red car – *zooooom!* There was a judgment in my head, 'I don't do that, I'm not like that, and I wouldn't do that'. What bugged me about it the most was his impatience. If someone does something that really pisses me off, I have come to understand that it's *not them*... it's a behavior that is mirroring an aspect of myself that I haven't dealt with, however saintly I think I am. In this particular case, what's funny is that I am *so* impatient... I want things NOW. All he was doing was mirroring my own impatience. As soon as I understood that, I had compassion for him and *that's* revolutionary thought, because I'm not left with prejudice. I'm not sitting there saying, *"I'm better than that bastard in that red car"* – I'm saying, *"Hey, brother... you go ahead and do it, because you're just mirroring my own impatience."* There's a silver-lining to being impatient. I would never have had the drive to achieve all those things I've achieved if I hadn't been impatient. There's always the shadow and the light... the polarities are always there. May we all recognize our own paradoxes and forgive ourselves, then we can get on with leading revolutionary lives in our own unique ways.

We are called to play the good Samaritan on life's roadside, but that will be only an initial act. One day we must come to see that the whole Jericho road must be changed so that men and women not be constantly beaten and robbed as they make their journey on life's highway. True compassion is more than flinging a coin to a beggar. It comes to see that an edifice which produces beggars needs restructuring.
~ Martin Luther King, Jr.

FALL AND RISE
Steve Taylor

*The past 6000 years have been a schizophrenic nightmare from
which we are finally beginning to awake. If my book can, in however
small a way, contribute to this process of awakening, I will be
more than happy.*
~ **Steve Taylor:** *The Fall*

Steve Taylor is the author of *The Fall: the Insanity of the Ego in
Human History and the Dawning of a New Era* (O books). Colin
Wilson has described the book as "an astonishing work" while
Eckhart Tolle has described it as "a fascinating and important
book, highly enlightening and readable." Steve is also the
author of *Making Time* (Icon) and *Waking From Sleep*, a study of
higher states of consciousness, published by Hay House in

March 2010. He teaches courses on personal development at the University of Manchester and Salford College. He lives in Manchester, England, with his wife and young children. Website: www.stevenmtaylor.com

I had a completely non-intellectual, fairly working-class Northern upbringing. As a child, I was always quite artistic and musical. I loved to go walking in nature... still do, and have always had spiritual, mystical experiences – the experience of perceiving a harmony and radiance around me, and becoming one with my surroundings. I loved to read books and write poetry, which eventually led me to study literature at university. I learned meditation and felt very drawn to Indian spirituality. One of the most powerful experiences of my life was reading the Upanishads for the first time when I was about 23. I still think of the Upanishads as my personal sacred text, which I often refer to. As I grew up, I developed an insight that there's something lacking in the way that most people perceive the world.

My book, *The Fall*, grew out of my interest in archaeology and anthropology. There's evidence to suggest that, like indigenous peoples, prehistoric people had a different view of reality – a natural spirituality, which we seem to have lost. Traditional history is based on a Victorian, colonial view, a history of progression. It's the H.G. Wells view of history – that apes turned into the first human beings, who were savages living in tribes in the forest, who then developed farming and became more civilised as they developed more technology. My view of history is an *anti-progressive* view – the idea that we've *lost* something. We have progressed in a technological and conceptual sense, but in many ways we have degenerated.

The social pathology which is so common in the world today seems to have first developed around 6,000 years ago. During this time, there was a sudden intensification of warfare and social conflict, male domination and social hierarchy. Around the same time, there were signs of increasing individuality – for example, people were being buried individually rather than communally and in different areas, so that there were large graves full of material possessions for powerful chieftain figures and small insignificant graves for peasants. Texts began to appear describing individual deeds, and there were new myths describing hero figures who triumphed against nature. I suggest that an intensification of the ego gave rise to these pathologies, creating psychological discord which expressed itself – and still expresses itself – as social chaos and conflict.

The Ego

The popular definition of the 'ego' is confusing – most people think that it's the part of you that craves attention, so you feel good when you get praise and feel bad when you're criticised. In spiritual and psychological traditions, the ego is usually seen as the sense of being an 'I' within your own consciousness – an 'I' with your own beliefs, your self-image and memories. It's the part of you which is self-conscious, that plans and makes decisions, and which has concepts and beliefs about yourself, and about life and the world. In New Age teachings, the ego is often seen as negative, but I don't think this is completely true. We *need* the ego, but it has to become much less dominant – to integrate with the rest of our being rather than dominate it. The ego has become too intense... it's taken over our whole being and monopolized our psychic energy.

Some people talk about both ancient and indigenous peoples as if they had no ego or individuality, but I don't think that's true... they obviously *did* to some degree, but it was much less dominant, much less intense than ours. Their individuality didn't separate them from nature or from each other.

Today, our over-intensified egos continually chatter away... they're never quiet, and this constant disturbance creates anxieties and worries. It means that we're never content, and creates suffering and conflict in the world around us. Society is a manifestation of what is *within* our own psyche. Because of our intense ego, we feel a sense of incompleteness and discontent, and we hanker after possessions and status in order to try to complete ourselves. We experience a sense of separation from our surroundings and feel isolated and 'walled-off' from other people. We can't easily sense their suffering, and so we become capable of inflicting suffering on others. If you naturally empathize with others then it's very difficult for you to inflict any suffering on them – to steal their possessions or to conquer them – but without empathy, it's easy. The lust for wealth and power and the inability to empathize are the root causes of warfare and of all social conflict.

Most indigenous cultures are very democratic and egalitarian and this also seems to have true of pre-historic peoples. In hunter-gatherer groups, there are checks that stop people becoming too dominant or powerful. For example, with the !Kung people of Africa, if a person becomes domineering or wants too many possessions, they take measures to ignore him, ostracize him or even eject him from the group altogether. The !Kung swap arrows before hunting expeditions, so that when an animal is killed, the credit doesn't go to the person who shot it, but to the person who the arrow belongs to. I often think we need similar checks on power in modern society – to stop competitive, status-hungry people from rising into positions of power. It's always the people who desire power the most who are the worst at using it.

Fallen Origins and Characteristics

Many archaeologists and scholars have recognised that a massive cultural shift took place in central Asia and the Middle East during the 4th millennium BC – for example, the archaeologist Marija Gimbutas, and Riane Eisler, who wrote about it in *The Chalice and the Blade*. The big question mark is *why did this change take place?* There is some evidence that environmental changes may have triggered it. James DeMeo – the geographer and anthropologist who wrote the brilliant book *Saharasia* – has shown that before 4000 BC, the whole of the Middle East, North Africa and Central Asia was very fertile – full of plants, animal life, rivers and lush grasslands. But from 4000 BC onwards, a process of desiccation began. People were forced to migrate away from their homelands, as the land became arid, animals disappeared and water sources ran dry. It's possible that this environmental change may have led to a major psychological change. People had to develop a new way of thinking, becoming more practical, more inventive. They had to develop what the scholar Owen Barfield called 'Alpha thinking.' At the same time it's possible that they had to become more selfish and compet-itive, as individual survival become more difficult. As a result, these peoples in central Asia and the Middle East developed a stronger sense of ego. What I call the Ego Explosion occurred.

In a sense though, it's not so important *how* this change occurred. The really important point is that, for whatever reason, these peoples became different from any other human beings before them. They were the first human beings who experienced themselves as separate to nature, and separate to other human beings – even separate from their own bodies, in the sense they began to look at the body as something 'other' which 'they' were enclosed within.

My main aim in *the Fall* is to describe how this intensified ego has given rise to the chaos and conflict which has filled human history, and which still engulfs the world nowadays. For example, one of the characteristics of 'the fall' was sexual repression. All indigenous people have a very open attitude to sex and towards the body – they often walk around naked. They have very open sexual relationships. Many of them don't even have terms for virginity – it's a meaningless concept to them. But the Ego Explosion gave rise to a massive amount of sexual repression and separation between the sexes, as well as a great deal of shame about the body and guilt about sex.

Monotheistic religions are also a product of the overdeveloped ego. The ego gives to rise to a basic psychological discord – an inner discontent, a sense of basic isolation and incompleteness, together with the disturbance and negativity of constant thought-chatter. I think the concept of Gods and an idyllic afterlife developed in reaction to this, as a way of providing consolation and overcoming that sense of aloneness. Even polytheistic religions were a kind of 'fall', a degeneration, because deities are separate from the world and they're always conceived as personal entities. The earliest human beings, like most indigenous cultures, didn't have any concept of God. They were aware of a spirit force that pervades all reality, or individual spirits that inhabit the air, trees and other natural phenomena, and the earth as a whole. Spirits were *not* perceived as personal entities – they were abstract forces with no individuality. But the Ego Explosion gave rise to Gods who are separate from the Earth and who can control what happens on this planet.

When the first missionaries went to America, they thought that Native Americans weren't religious because they had no churches and didn't pray. But because they saw the whole world around them as sacred, they didn't need churches. There was no gap between the sacred and the profane. Spirit was in all things, not just temples or churches.

In historical terms, time is also linked to the ego. Indigenous peoples don't have a sense of linear time in the same way that we have. They don't count the years that have passed or their age in terms of years. Many of them seem to live in a constant present, with very little concept of the future or the past, and very little concept of history. We moved from the timelessness of the prehistoric hunter-gatherer peoples into the cyclical time perception of, for example, the Mayans, ancient Greeks, Egyptians and Hindus. And then came our linear time, the concept of time as a river. One of the big problems for us is that intensified ego stops us living in the present. It fills our minds with thought-chatter about the future or the past.

The Trans-Fall Movement

Our 'normal' psyche is almost like a mold from which we have formed over generations and generations, ever since the Ego Explosion. We need to dislodge ourselves out of this mold. In a sense, that's what happens in spiritual practice – we dislodge and transcend the mold that our psyche has been in for thousands of years.

The first wave of the trans-fall movement – the re-emergence of the pre-fall characteristics – occurred around 2500 thousand years ago, with the emergence of spiritual and mystical traditions, when people began to realise that they could transcend the ego. These included Hindu spiritual traditions, Buddhism and Taoism. Later it was expressed in the mystical traditions of Islam and Christianity. In India, the ancient sages realised that through meditating and following a life of renunciation and detachment, they could gain a completely new vision of reality and gain access to a new state of well-being, transcending the normal psychological discord of human beings.

The second wave came later. I see this as an evolutionary development, which first became obvious during the latter half of the 18th Century. On a collective level, human beings started to transcend the ego – to regain a sense of compassion and empathy, and a sense of the spiritual in the world. For example, the women's rights movement began at this time, the first laws outlawing cruelty to animals, the anti-slavery movement. Cruel forms of punishment, like the pillory and branding, were abolished for minor crimes. The Romantic Movement was an important part of this too, in poetry, music and art – for example, poets like Shelley, Wordsworth, and Keats in England. It was all about regaining a sense of spiritual connection to nature.

Over the last 300 years, society has slowly become more democratic with a greater emphasis on the rights of individuals. Throughout Europe, America, and other parts of the world, there has been a powerful re-emergence of compassion and empathy – towards animals, nature, and towards people of other classes or castes, for example. More recently, there's been a massive upsurge in interest in self-development and spirituality. Over the last 50 years, especially in Western Europe and America, we've transcended sexual repression, with sexual openness and equality.

This wave has been picking up speed for centuries and is growing in force as time goes by, but the fallen psyche still controls the world and is still the main driving force of human behavior and society. Some 'fallen' characteristics may seem stronger than ever before – more materialism and status-seeking, for example – but even that may not be a bad sign. The philosopher, Jean Gebser, divided history into different phases, and believed that before each new phase begins, the main characteristics of the previous age become stronger, in resistance to the change. Before a new era begins, some of the character-istics of the old era grow more powerful.

It's easy to blame society or institutions or corporations for the state of the world, but society is really only a manifestation of the way human beings are inside. I think society has been changing gradually, as a manifestation of this inner-change. I'm all in favour of social change and protest, but I think they have to happen in parallel with inner transformation.

I'm an optimist – I think there are some really positive things happening in the world, despite all the chaos and conflict we see every day in the newspapers. But we don't have much time left. If we don't collectively shift to a new way of relating to the world soon, we could easily reach a point where we destroy ourselves as a species. This change seems to be happening too slowly. That's why we have to add our individual efforts to this natural evolutionary process. As more people develop spiritually – through meditation, mindfulness, service and other forms of spiritual practice – the effect will spread through our species. It will become easier for other people to develop spiritually, and to transcend the intensified ego. In this way, it's possible that some degree of enlightenment will spread throughout the whole human race. Instead of causing an ecological catastrophe, we will move into a new era of harmony.

DANGEROUS RELIGION
Leo Rutherford

Knowing others is intelligence; knowing yourself is true wisdom.
Mastering others is strength; mastering yourself is true power.

~ Lao-Tzu

Leo Rutherford is the founder of Eagle's Wing Centre for Contemporary Shamanism and is author of *Way of Shamanism, The Shamanic Path Workbook, The View through the Medicine Wheel* and *Adam and Evil: the 'god' who hates sex, women and human bodies* (as The Heyeokah Guru). He received his MA in Holistic Psychology from Antioch University, San Francisco, and has studied with many gifted shamans. In his work he seeks to bring together ancient techniques of shamanism and modern techniques of psychotherapy to help people of today to find their Path-With-Heart and to Walk-In-Beauty. His website is: www.shamanism.co.uk

I was born in 1935, so I grew up in the 40's and 50's. During my teenage years and very early twenties, I tried to be a good little Christian boy to my immense detriment as it meant waging war against my nature. The prevailing belief systems of that time suckered me into believing things because everybody else did (so they said!) and because I was repeatedly told it was so. It all turned out to be crap... not just religion but so many other things. It limited and constrained what could have been my life most incredibly.

The main theme of my book, *Adam and Evil*, is be**lie**f. There is a lie right in the middle of it. To be a believer is to '**be** in the **lie** for **ever**'. The moment you're a believer you're stating, "*I am brainwashed. I will not look left or right. I will not consider evidence that does not agree with me*". We have to watch those beliefs very carefully because that's where we get manipulated and used. A rigid *dis*believer is just exactly the same – it's just another set of beliefs. The greatest skeptics are usually very deep believers in their *dis*-belief.

What has been peddled to us for centuries is to 'believe this, believe that, and believe the other'. I do everything I can to neither be a believer nor a disbeliever. I try to find the path between the two, which leads me bit-by-bit through life experiences to finding out for myself, and little by little to more knowledge. Knowledge is the answer, *not* belief... belief is for people who don't know and don't want to bother to find out.

A Solar Religion

I feel strongly that religion as we've been sold it is a 1700-year-old mega-conspiracy. We've been conned. The *real* story is not about the 'son' of God, but the 'sun' God. If you look at the Jesus story in the gospels, it's merely a repeat of older Sun God stories (as I detail in *Adam and Evil* in Chapter 5: 'The Many God-Men Before Jesus). Many cultures have near-identical versions of 'Jesus' going back thousands of years, for example; Horus, Attis,

Dionysus, Mithras, Virishna, Tammuz, Attis, Buddha, and Bacchus, were all 'born' on the 25th of December because that's the first measurably longer day after the winter solstice... it's a celebration of the return of the Sun God to the northern hemisphere. They all die around Easter time, because that's the final end of winter before the new season, the annual death and rebirth of the plant kingdom. These are myths of the sun and of the cycles of nature.

Sun worship is decried by Christians, yet this is what they are worshiping... the sun/son. The 'Sun of God' is the big fire in the sky! To say that the sun is the 'sun' of God is not a metaphor... if the sun dies, we're dead. The sun is the centre of our local universe – it's our local God/father, and the earth is our local God/mother. We're totally dependent on the two – we are their children.

The ancient God-men were all understood as figureheads, but the difference is that Jesus was turned into a literal figure – a 'real' man. Now, there *may* have been a Jesus/Yeshua/Joshua, but if so, he was an ordinary human being, probably a Rabbi and a 'rebel leader' against the Romans. The creator of Christianity as it has come down to us, Saul the Jew who became Paul the Roman peddled a mythical Jesus – he had never even *met* any such person! – and, over time, the mythical and a possible real Jesus were craftily mixed-up in people's minds.

The Christ story came in at a time when some Puritanism was called for to balance the extreme licentiousness of the Roman Empire in its latter stages – but that 'wave' was not a conspiracy, it was a natural response to the utter hedonism of the late Roman Empire. Hence Jesus is the only Sun-God who never copulated. All the rest did so like mad and created loads of offspring, only Jesus was so 'pure' as to be beyond human possibility – though very useful as a figure for dominators who then could turn the populace against their own bodies and their own natures and hence disempower and dominate them more easily.

Before Christianity, the Roman Emperor Constantine was a follower of the Mithras cult – the Persian version of the same thing. He 'converted' to Christianity in order to hitch the Christians to his war-like empire-building ends, because there were more of them and they were more powerful. He then forced Christianity on the empire and it became the state religion by empirical decree, where you had to believe it *or else*... (Council of Nicaea, AD 325) The Roman Church has had immense power and they have ruined culture after culture forcing people to believe their religion. The 'Holy' Inquisition was effectively thugs in cassocks who were licensed by the church to go around torturing and killing and, most usefully, stealing the lands and property of anyone they could find a reason to condemn – rather like church-approved Nazis. They even condemned some wealthy dead people so they could 'legally' steal their property! In the case of the Cathars of Languedoc, the church saw such a threat that they wiped the whole nation out in mass genocide. So much for spirituality.

Spirituality is our connection with the Spirit-Of-All-Things – with God, Essence, Life-Force, the Universe, etc.; whereas religion is an organization... a corporation. Any religion is both corporate and cultural and, in order to harmonize a culture, seeks to have everybody believing what they are told without question and thus becoming docile and malleable.

In the beginning there may be a charismatic leader and while it's small it may do good work but then if it starts to get big... it needs more and more rules in order to organize, and, like any large organization or corporation, it's first duty is its own survival and so it inevitably becomes corrupt. There is a big difference between a shaman, who has just a few apprentices and a duty to pass on that knowledge and a bishop with a whole diocese to administer, or a guru with a whole dirty great Ashram with loads of followers and all the subsequent problems such as hierarchies that go with that.

Adam and Evil

The Garden of Eden as a myth is the idea of a 'perfect place' where all is in harmony, but a perfect place also is static – there's no growth in a perfect place and, in that sense, Adam and Eve are not awakened. The serpent is written as 'bad', but the serpent is really the 'good guy'. The serpent (earth energy) encouraged awakening while 'God' is shown to be a liar. When the Serpent said to 'eat of the tree', Adam and Eve *didn't die* like God had said they would, but their 'eyes were opened' instead.

There's something rather important that would *not* have happened if Eve had 'obeyed God' and not eaten of the 'Tree of the Knowledge of Good and Evil'. What would not have happened? *Human beings would not exist!* We would still be in the state of animal consciousness because if you haven't got the knowledge of good and evil, you haven't got self-consciousness. They only 'wake up' by eating the 'fruit of the tree' – urged on by nature, or kundalini (i.e. the Serpent) and they awaken but, of course, once you awaken you suddenly know the score… you're 'naked' in the sense that you've been ignorant and suddenly you know all sorts of things.

Incidentally, there are studies of ancient tablets that suggest there *was* a garden in E-din, somewhere up in the Lebanese mountains, where beings, possibly from elsewhere in the galaxy (the *Annunaki/ Annanage* or the 'Shining Ones') created civilization by the 'Gods' mating with the 'daughters of the earth' and created us as a slave race. This story has become mixed up with the real God, the Spirit in all things.

To say that Eve was created from Adam's rib does suggest that we are a genetically created race. Zecharia Sitchin has written 12 books principally postulating that star people came here and genetically modified the original inhabitants of Earth, and it may or may not be so. A lot of indigenous people talk about star people and UFOs… the Dogon tribe of Africa say that their ancestors came from Sirius. They already knew that it was a binary system, but *how did they know without modern technology?*

An *(Un)* Holy Trinity

The 'great' religions are all male dominated. 'The Father, the Son and the Holy Ghost'... *what an extraordinary trinity!* This trinity is absolutely central to Christianity yet it's 100% imbalanced because all the feminine has been removed. The 'Son' is in the place where the Mother should be... a balanced trinity would be 'the Father, the Mother and the Holy Spirit' – the masculine, the feminine, and the 'All-That-Is'.

A proper trinity represents the primal split of the Oneness into two – feminine/masculine, yin/yang, etc., which you find in every spiritual tradition... everywhere, that is, except in Christianity. How can people wake up while still believing in such a travesty of a trinity? Until Christianity changes the trinity to honor the feminine in its rightful place, it will remain a terminally misguided religion. How can you have a sensible universe when your worldview is completely imbalanced?

If you make God into a man then you disenfranchise all the feminine. You find this in many religions, including Christianity, Judaism, Hinduism and Islam (which is something like Christianity was around 5 or 600 years ago). All of these religions in their different ways, by turning God into a man have more or less made women into a possession of the male. The Roman Church did not consider women to possess souls until around 1540. This religious contempt of the feminine has, and continues to do, terrible things to women – justified and supported by the 'Lord's' words in the Bible, of course;

'Now therefore kill every male among the little ones, and kill every woman that hath known man by lying with him. But all the women children, that have not known man by lying with him, keep alive for yourselves.' (Numbers 31: 17-18)

Incredible! That makes 'God' into a kind of pimp!

The God-Lie

The 'God lie' has had a horrible effect on making people frightened and guilty of so many things. Nobody is good enough for God. For a start, God is promoted through the figure of Jesus as a man who never had sex with a woman, never had sex with a man, or even with himself – in fact, he never even had an erection because to have an erection he would have had to have had a 'dirty thought' and *He* was absolutely perfect. Therefore he is symbol that no boy or man can possibly live up to which means that if you believe this bunk, you're a 'sinner' just by being normal! All women are not good enough because they're not men and all men are not good enough unless they can completely squash and contain their sexuality. We all know what that does to a man! And a woman.

As I discovered researching my book, the Christian church fathers of old times hated their bodies and their natures and despised women both as an inferior species and as temptresses of their sexuality (which they took immense trouble to try and suppress).

The consequence of the myth that Jesus died for our sins, is that you give up any responsibility for your actions; you give all your power to the church, your money to the church, your soul to the church and you're half a person from then on which is very convenient for the Powers That Be. In the middle of an impoverished community you will find a rich church with 'comfortable' priests. On the earth level they collect your money; on the spiritual level they steal your soul.

Satan is a corruption of Saturn, the planet of constriction (in Astrology) where you have to face the results of your own actions. This goes hand-in-hand with the Christian belief that we don't need to do any of this psychotherapeutic shamanic self-growth work because Jesus did it all for us... we just have to believe in Jesus. God has become like Father Christmas for grown-ups who don't want to take responsibility.

Basically, 'God the destroyer' has been separated from 'God the good' to become the Devil. Destruction is a natural force, but it's not devilish.

Finding God by Losing Religion

If in the beginning there was only God, then who made the Universe and what did 'He' have to make it with? This is where the male-dominated 'Him' religions fall apart. God is the unity of all things and God can only create out of God. So where is God? *Everywhere!* All the crap out there says either you believe in God or you're an atheist and you don't believe in God. If you look at it from the ancients' point of view, both positions are ridiculous because they're both missing the point that the creator and the creation are one and the same. God is what we live in and questions as to whether there is or isn't a God are RIDICULOUS.

Speaking from a therapist's point of view of working to help people heal, I have never found anybody who is under the thrall of biblical religion to be anything other than tied up in knots inside themselves. They can't heal themselves while they're screwed-up by that religion because they're fighting their own nature in order to try to maintain their beliefs.

Because my own wounds are what led me into this in the first place, I know the landscape when it comes to helping other people with inherited beliefs and stuck emotions. As a shamanic practitioner/therapist, I do everything I can to help people to let go of guilt, blame and shame so that they can honor, own, and grow themselves. It can be a long gradual process because the beliefs are often so deeply ingrained. Another way to put that is to say brainwashed. There's no shortcut and these changes are often unsupported by family and friends who can make this process take even longer. It can be a lonely road because as you begin to take your own power back you become one of the fewer, not one of the many.

Realizing that I'd been brainwashed by everything I'd bought into believing was a big part in taking my power back from all the powers that had attempted to steal it in my lifetime. Once I did a goodly chunk of that, I could establish a personal link with Spirit.

For me, it was such a blessing coming across the Native American culture. A lot of teaching that I do is through the medicine wheel – to connect to the earth; to all that's above, below and within. Here in Britain, we don't have much of our ancestral roots and tuning-into our ancestors isn't a lot of use because they didn't have it, either – it's so far back that it's lost in the mists of time. Hence, for me, it is a great gift to be able to tune into live traditions of other cultures that haven't suffered as deeply as ours. True medicine-people recognize that human beings are human beings... anything less than that is cultural jealousy, which is very understandable, considering what our culture has done to theirs.

I see the New Age alternative movement on the whole as a shamanic revival. People are searching to understand their own relationship to Spirit. Like anything, some areas go wrong by becoming based on belief systems again. Any movement towards the light has to confront all sorts of shadows.

I strongly suggest that the (Un)Illuminati/Powers That Be (as written about extensively by David Icke and many others) are now a group of deeply worried people because they see their world control being potentially lost. They may be rich, but they're not all that clever, and I feel that the fate of things will go out of their control in 2010/11. I don't think they're engineering *everything*... there are also natural forces at play. There are natural cycles in the growing of crops, just as there are also natural economic cycles, for example. By devious cunning manipulative financial crapola, they've tried to avoid downturns, so now we're getting one very, very big massive downturn instead of all the little ones we would have had along the way. It's a human thing to avoid, evade, and deny – to try to be 'more clever than'. I feel in my bones that many things are about to change beyond recognition.

We humans have a tendency to perpetuate beliefs against our own selves. In North Africa thousands of women are genitally mutilated at puberty – by older women. Why? Tradition. In many boarding schools especially in U.K., small boys were ritually beaten and semi-tortured only to do the same thing to the next generation when they become the prefects. Why? Tradition. The (Un)Illuminati seek world control and see ordinary people akin to their slaves – just like the Anunnaki/Anannage/'Shining Ones' who may well have created us as slaves for themselves, perhaps as much as 400,000 years ago. I call this tendency – *brainwashing*. The brainwashed perpetuate on others the horrors that have been done to them. Its time to stop doing it to ourselves and wake up.

This period is a challenge to awakening. As the systems that we've collectively created break down and the lies come to the surface, things are shown to be what they really are and we can come out of the be-**lie**-(f)s. We can stop be-**lie**-ving. In that sense, the chaos that we're entering now has the potential to be very, very fruitful for our growth into truly 'human' beings.

SENTENCING A SPELL
Ellis C. Taylor

Those who don't know already (and there will be some) need to realize that today we are still fundamentally regulated by cultural devices and strictures set loose upon our forebears in the ancient world – in kingdoms such as Babylon and Egypt – several thousands of years ago. We have inherited their gods hidden in everyday language and societal control mechanisms so that in real effect, without even stepping into a temple or any occult congregation, we pay token to them every day.
~ Ellis C. Taylor: www.ellisctaylor.com/thywillbedone.html

Ellis Taylor is a 7th generation Australian who grew up in and around Oxford in Great Britain. Ellis is a lifetime multiple experiencer of supernatural phenomena and, seemingly, an incurable skeptic blessed with second-sight. His journeys to otherworlds and his meetings with their teachers have encouraged his innate disposition towards lateral thinking and a keen observation of the subtle currents and aspects of the human experience. He is also a philosopher, numerologist, painter, writer and speaker.

Ellis is author of *In These Signs Conquer: Revealing the Secret Signs an Age has Obscured, Living in the matrix ~ Another Way: Numerology for a new day,* and *Dogged Days.* He has also published an E-book, *The Esoteric Alphabet,* which is a draft, unedited manuscript of a book he has been working on for several years and is free to download from his website at: www.ellisctaylor.com.

Seriously weird things have happened to me all of my life but, because I wasn't always on my own experiencing these things, they didn't seem that strange… so I never really questioned them at the time. These sorts of things were just a natural part of our lives. I was just a normal kid. I'll tell you about one experience my mates and I had in 1961 when I was eight or nine…

There was a gang of us playing in the fields not far from where we lived. All of a sudden, there's a helicopter there… the blades are going round… we didn't see it land, and it wasn't there before. It was only about 50 yards away from us, real close. We'd never seen a helicopter before, I don't think… it was just a normal black or dark grey helicopter – not a big Chinook or anything. The door opened and these two blonde-haired guys in air force uniforms walked out (bolt upright, without the usual bending down and hair blowing everywhere) and they said, "*Howdy! Do you want to go for a ride?*" We didn't know them from a bar of soap, but we knew that they were American because of their accents. That's the last thing we can remember, any of us – we never talked about it, we never told anybody else about it, and we never discussed it. Over twenty years later, around 1983, when I was 30 or 31, I moved to a small village where I soon discovered that one of my childhood friends was living too. We arranged to go to the pub and, for some reason standing there at the bar, I remembered this helicopter incident and I asked him if he could recall it. He could, but only up to being asked to go for a ride that was all. A couple of years ago I met another of my friends and asked him… he said, "*We probably ran away, didn't we?*" Don't you think that's strange? It's the most *brilliant* thing that could have happened to any kid! Yet they couldn't remember anything much about it, and neither could I…

A Multi-Dimensional Reality

I know that this world isn't what we're told it is – there's far more to it. I know that we exist on more than one plane – we exist on several and we can communicate and interface with all of them. Many times I have seen human and non-human entities in other worlds, other dimensions, and sometimes I'm in there with them. Increasingly, I also see people shapeshifting – changing into something or someone else. For instance, I have seen people turn into reptilian-like creatures, sometimes still retaining their human face, half one thing and half another (a bit like a diamond facet, it depends upon what angle you look at them); it's an eerie spectacle and it seems that once they start 'turning' they have to finish, but there have also been occasions when people seem to vibrate rapidly and accelerate into another life-form. Some entities change into beings that look human but they're not – you can see that they're not because their eyes betray them – they are there but 'not there'. I think that the major part of them, their 'normal' state of being, is absent from this world but it depends upon the environment they're in and what it is they are seeking to attune with. Their way of moving alters too – most times they lose the 'bounce' of the human gait and begin to glide.

I'm quite sure that we've all got the ability to traverse dimensions, to walk between worlds, but some people can do it more easily than others... sometimes it just 'happens' and they may have no control over it.

Everyone's frequency pattern is specifically designed to attune with particular elements in this world and to be disharmonious with others, to varying degrees. A few are extremely discordant with our world and its inhabitants – they come from somewhere else... a dark place, a place where psychopathic tendencies have destroyed everything. These *states of being*, like locusts, destroy everything in their path and then move on. They crave it all and focus everything they do on selfish desire and accumulation driven by an unseen, but all-seeing, satanic master, '*the Darkness Invisible*'. No human can hide from this thing because no matter how corrupt a person may be they still have a soul and a soul is light. Only 'the Dark Ones' can creep in the shadows, they are 'the Shadow beings'; the *Shadows* who fall upon the light – humanity; assuming their superiority over us and this world. But the irony is that they can only exist where there is light, so why must we hide? Why do so many of us hide?

There are some among us who have a slightly modified frequency that gives an ability to walk between worlds, where their less restrained perception is able to experience and communicate with otherworlds and levels of reality. This adjustment occurs in their energy field, their aura, and is akin to genetic enhancement in DNA strains. For the very most part these humans live, and have lived, inconspicuously from one generation to the other. Gradually, with every incarnation their intermarrying enhances their abilities, as they prepare for a time when *the Darkness* will be repelled from this world.

The *Shadow beings* have long attempted to duplicate this strategy but they are bound to fail because the nature of the beast is not to cooperate but to compete and annihilate. It might be that it's a race against the clock whether they destroy themselves first or this planet.

When you know there are other life forms and other worlds, and you know this without any doubt whatsoever because you've experienced them, then you come to understand that people are being herded into believing certain things – they're told to behave in a certain way, they're told not to rock the boat... and, why not? Like I said, *why hide?* I can't and I won't just stand by and ignore something so fundamental to every human being's experience of life.

We've allowed the world to get this way – we all bear a responsibility in some way... some more than others, yeah, but we all bear a responsibility. There's a lot going on in this world that people are too frightened to stand up and speak out about, and it's purposefully designed that way. All that I'm doing is speaking my truth about what I've seen and what I know to be true. I'm nothing special – I'm just someone who's daft enough to stand up and say these things! These things are happening to *loads* of other people too who never say anything. When people honor their own experiences, then society becomes more open and a much more nurturing and valuable place to be. Eventually, we will begin to look at things in a way that's going to be far better for humanity and all of the inhabitants of this world.

Everything has an energy – everything has a life, from a grain of sand to the vast expanse of space. What a daft concept that is – 'space'... there are *loads* of other life forms that wander around here and in all the spaces in-between.

Quantum physicists can think up all their theories and do the math, but we don't have the ability to describe these things in a way that we can intellectually understand. There's always more than one explanation for everything and that's why I never have conclusions about anything. Life is beyond explanation in this reality because we view it from within an intentionally limited world. It's our perception. In a boundless realm we think we could explain everything, but every realm must have boundaries. It seems an infinitely impossible task.

En-Trances

There is a 'dark' force and a 'light' force – but it's One. You can't create anything without destroying something first. The change itself is the creation, but that destruction is looked upon as 'evil' and creation is looked upon as 'good' – we put our own perspectives on these things.

A lot of rituals are designed to open doorways for negative influences to come in and out, behaving like a turnstile. 9/11 was one of them. It was a portal event. Portals appear in many guises – they may be to other worlds and dimensions but they can also act as gateways to manipulating and changing individual and societal thought patterns. The date, the time, and the place were all put together like a recipe of energy to create that act of terror which means that anyone who is learned in the psychic arts – numerology, tarot, astrology… these kinds of disciplines – can read it.

When those towers went, I had a vision I was on one of those planes and I knew with absolute certainty that it wasn't what they were saying it was – the plane was full of people who were already dead… they'd been gassed through the air conditioning system. The plane was a coffin flying through the sky under remote-control. Since then, people like Professor Dewdney, from the University of Western Ontario, and other investigators have suggested that the planes were remote-controlled.

I have a friend who divests people of spirit possessions who thinks you should protect yourself with white light all the time. I think it's wise if you're going into a situation where you don't know what's going on to protect yourself with white light – it sounds a daft thing to do, but by doing this you create a frequency around yourself… a 'spiritual armor'. Personally, I ask my spirit allies to walk with me and if it's appropriate for me to experience whatever is there then I'm willing to do that. I don't want to block out anything just because it's strange or unfamiliar. Sometimes I've had to experience some real horrible things, and it's been hard. I don't know anybody on the 'shamanic' path who hasn't had to walk in the shadow of the darkness. They are initiations and tests but they are also lessons in how to sense such presence. I think it is really important to do this, but not to remain in it – although some people do… they fall for all the baubles it presents.

In These Signs Conquer

Symbols are the language of the unconscious mind. Some symbols have been imbued with a lot of negative power. For example, the swastika can mean many things depending on what culture it was used in – in some it symbolized the sun, in others it meant peace… there are a lot of different interpretations. It could also represent a vortex – something that spins clockwise or anti-clockwise. The media make sure that everybody continues to recognize it as the symbol of the Nazis, an evil sign. That's what the media is there for, to install and keep negativity in the minds of the population. If everybody woke up one day and decided that the swastika was going to mean something positive and beneficial in their mind it would take away much of the negative power that it has, but with such a strong symbol like that it's going to take a lot of effort to change that one. It isn't impossible though.

The subconscious recognizes (and is perhaps even strengthened by) instinctive symbols – what we're already primed with before we're actually born, and that's *the instinct to survive*… not only personally, but as a species. This is why the language symbols we use for writing down communication are based on the creative principles – the male and female generative organs, and the sperm and the egg. When people are primed with alphabet symbols their written and verbal communications are motivated and directed by a subconscious recognition of the directing (and accepting) messages from the ordained occult alphabet. Every thought propagates the program.

The visual sense is the most potent of all the physical senses in this designed reality. We're continually encouraged and programed to believe that it's about what things *look* like. There are a lot of pictures to be made out of words and a lot of ways of looking at them besides the basic dictionary definitions. Each letter is designed to influence certain parts of ones mind and once we realize that, we can become aware of what's going on around us and look more carefully at what those words are aimed at motivating us to do, and then make our decisions. I always think that once a secret is exposed, it loses a heck of a lot of power. Every tool has a positive and a negative use, and letters are just the same.

The Latin alphabet we use today was designed by adepts of one of the most powerful occult institutions the world has ever seen, the Roman Church. Alphabets create words which we *spell* – there's a spell going on there in your mind. Basically, the alphabet is a programming tool. The words might have a dictionary meaning, but words hold much more power within them than we have ever been taught. You can cause significant things to happen just with words... they can encourage people to do things and behave in a certain way. They can *sentence* you. It really is true that 'the pen is mightier than the sword'.

As soon as we go to school we are taught to repeat: a, b, c, d, e, f... da, da, da... so that our subconscious knows *exactly* what position in the alphabet any letter is. That is why numerology works. Numbers describe frequency patterns – that's what numbers are for. That's why they use binary codes when they send messages into space... it's a form of numerical language. Each letter has a vibrational value and you put those together to make a frequency pattern. A person's frequency pattern is described by their name and they will attract a like energy or frequency to it – so their partners, their jobs, where they live, their children, will all be born or named to suit their own energy field. Whatever you're called most will be the name that has the most influence on you, but your birth name will also have an influence on you, too.

I used to sit there at school and daydream. I could learn a lot more daydreaming than if I had to listen to that twit over there! Exams are only there to filter out who's more programmable and easily prone to it than anybody else – even the word 'examine' means 'to take the piss' (ex-amine). Like almost everything we are legislated to have to do, it is 'up is down' stuff – basically, the opposite of what they say. The last thing they want people to know is that this world is *fabulous!* Anything is possible... the only true limitation is what we believe. Human beings are so gifted, but the *Shadows* have set limits on us and designed what road we're going to walk down – it's really a railroad... we've got to stay on those lines. That's why newspapers have 'headlines' – to keep your head in line and tell you what and how to think and behave. For example, we're primed to think that smoking will give us cancer and that anybody who comes within range of a smoker will get cancer, too. *Bullshit!* It's never been proven. I know that the carcinogens people suck inside their bodies when they smoke aren't good for them, no doubt about that, but human beings have lived around smoke *for ever*. It's part of the human experience. We've always lived in smoky caves, smoky holes, smoky homes and environments. Anyone who under-stands anything about subliminal messages will know that cigarette advertizing using these god-awful images are priming people to die of those exact things. It's the signs on billboards and on the backs of cigarette packets that are killing people. It's all subliminal – everything we experience comes in via our subconscious and motivates something; it doesn't just stop inside your head. People die from second-hand smoke because they're *told* they're going to die from it! That's what it's designed to do. Smoke kills germs. I used to smoke and other people would be succumbing to flu everywhere yet I never got the bloody flu! I really suspect that people who smoke are not as vulnerable to the poisons *the Shadows* are trying to pump at us. They want people not to smoke so they can better succeed with whatever diabolical goals they're hoping to achieve. When has the government ever truly been interested in the health of the people?

Though they are clearly encouraging humans to rely totally upon their controlled communication system (the letters of the alphabet) – with mobile phones, computers, radio, television, newspapers et al - we can bypass this agenda to secretly govern our behavior. Words are not the only way we talk to each other.

When we listen we must listen with *all* of our senses and not just with our ears. Besides our five physical senses we have incredibly effective magical, yet denigrated, abandoned and under-used natural talents that every human can use to feel and discern truth and meaning in myriad circumstances. Magic is a huge part of the human experience. We all use it at times to communicate with, and journey to, other worlds; meet other beings, and not just otherworldly beings. We communicate mentally with animals all the time but it's only understood one way. Even the lowliest fly knows our intentions, reads our minds... we could live in a 'Dr. Dolittle world' if we wanted to.

We're just one life-form on this planet yet we're programed to believe that we're the top life form? We're told *we're* the rulers of this world, *we* decide who lives where and what tree stays there and we kill animals and we eat them and we farm them and stick them in god-awful conditions and apparently that's all right – that's 'normal' and anybody who doesn't think like that is a nutter... and I'm sorry but I don't go along with that.

*

If you want to use a symbol then use it. Why not imbue it with what *you* want it to be? It can be whatever you like – it could represent your car or a night in the pub… whatever you like, but it doesn't have to be what someone else has said it is. Any symbol you can make personal to yourself, as long as you determine what it means to you and that it doesn't matter what anybody else says. You can create your own thought patterns around any symbol, or you can create your own symbols… whatever makes you feel good, do it. When we start using symbols positively, we're in charge of ourselves – we're no longer being herded into certain ways of thinking or doing. We become conquerors.

Photo Credit: Charles L. Gilchrist

PAX MENTIS
by Kevin P. Miller

"I didn't hear about X in the news, thus X must be a delusion." Such a state of affairs is the clear measure of a society primed and ready for the execution by the government of localized atrocities that will simply 'not exist'. The lesson here is clear: with media control, the government can commit large-scale actions that 'do not exist' in the larger social mind even as thousands subjected to those actions witness them with their own eyes. Due to the media blackout, the larger society is not only ignorant of the events, but is also 'immunized' from the truth of those events because eyewitness reports are compartmentalized as 'crazy' and are dismissed without question – Truth Control 101.

~ Ian Williams Goddard

This instrument can teach, it can illuminate; yes, and it can even inspire. But it can do so only to the extent that humans are determined to use it to those ends. Otherwise it is merely wires and lights in a box. There is a great and perhaps decisive battle to be fought against ignorance, intolerance and indifference. This weapon of television could be useful.

~ Edward R. Murrow, American broadcast journalist (1908 - 1965)

If you don't read the newspaper, you are uninformed; if you do read the newspaper, you are misinformed.

~ Mark Twain (1835 - 1910)

Kevin P. Miller is an international award winning writer, producer and director whose films *Kids In Crisis, Let Truth Be The Bias, The Promised Land,* and more have won multiple international film and television awards. Miller's latest documentary, *Generation RX* was released worldwide in November 2008. Website: www.kevinmiller.com

The first lesson taught to young journalists pertains to the importance of accuracy and fairness. I developed a great reverence for these tenets at a very early age as I began to chart my course as a writer and editor of my high school newspaper in suburban Cleveland, Ohio. I recall a time when I won the first of two dozen academic journalism awards at the Cleveland Press Institute and Herb Kamm, the publisher of the Cleveland Press told an audience of 1000 people that, *"if this kid was a few years older, I'd hire him right now."*

Ah, but life has a way of guiding us, and it was not my destiny to become a conventional journalist. That dream was pretty much ruined in the aftermath of Watergate and the resignation of Richard Nixon – when a new generation of airheads and fluff reporters flooded into journalism so they could become 'stars'.

As a result, what exists today is largely 'corporate journalism', and modern newsrooms are filled with men and women who don't revere Edward R. Murrow – let alone Woodward and Bernstein. Instead, they pay homage to the whims of General Electric, Rupert Murdoch, and oh yes – the drug companies too.

In fact, journalism's coverage of health news is so far from truth and reality that it boggles the mind. This fact was omnipresent as I produced my latest film called *Generation RX*, a documentary about the proliferation of psychiatric medicine prescriptions among children and teens. Once again, I figured out that it was incumbent upon me to be one of the agitators; to perform the research and tell the whole truth about government cover-ups, collusion and the big business of medicine.

It's dangerous precisely because my films and indeed my blogs bring forth facts that those in power don't want made available to the public. For example, the first ones in line to buy my DVD were representatives of the drug companies. They cavalierly ordered a dozen or so copies of *Generation RX* on the very first day it was available so that they could examine the data and issues I raised. They employed hired guns – multi-million dollar public relations pros who are the best in the world, the very folks who brought the world a generation of deadly chemicals and drugs. They were hoisted on to an unsuspecting public, and the deaths caused by these ruthless intoxicants have routinely been explained away by the whorish cliques of paid professionals who care only about power and money.

Where Are the Truthtellers?

Years ago, I interviewed Dr. Carolyn Dean for my film called *We Become Silent,* a film about the drug companies, 'free-trade agreements', the World Trade Organization (WTO) and something called *Codex Alimentarius*. After analyzing government databases and peer-reviewed journal articles in the U.S., Dr. Dean discovered that despite published reports to the contrary, at least 784,000 people are dying annually due to modern medical interventions.

By comparison, how do the mainstream media report on annual deaths due to drugs, surgery and iatrogenic causes? Well, the media reports that the numbers of deaths lie 'somewhere between 42,000 and 106,000 annually', or nowhere *near* the numbers suggested by Dr. Dean's research.

Obviously 784,000 people killed by modern medicine is an astonishing number. But in *We Become Silent*, we also revealed that the 784,000 deaths cited in numerous studies only represent 5-20 percent of the actual deaths!

This raises a more vital question: how many more people are dying from drugs and conventional treatments? Is it 3.4 million? 7.8 million? 15.6 million? The sad fact is that the media doesn't seem very curious to discover the truth, despite the fact that this secrecy in medicine is both scandalous and deadly.

But where are the truth-tellers in journalism? Where have they gone? They are few and far between; missing in action when we need them most. It seems as if good reporters – the ones who uncover abuses by government and corporate interests – are no longer welcome in television news... and there aren't many left in print journalism either. So it is my job, as well as a few select others, to dig until we find the truth.

About a decade ago, reporters Jane Akre and Steve Wilson investigated rBGH, or recombinant bovine growth hormone. rBGH is a synthetic growth hormone found in milk and other dairy products and Akre and Wilson revealed that it was potentially harmful to humans. They were set to air a five-part series on the dangers of rBGH and were ready to expose what was lurking in the milk being fed to millions of American children.

But that's when Monsanto – the rBGH-patent holder, began to exert pressure on the TV network to kill the story. After repeatedly refusing an order by corporate attorneys to present a story 'more favorable' to corporate advertisers Monsanto, Akre and Wilson were fired. And yet no one – not NBC, CBS, ABC, CNN – would report the story.

But if the complete truth is to be told, it must be noted that the lack of integrity among corporate journalists is the real reason why the rBGH additive existed in the milk supply in the first place. The media has allowed the FDA and the medical community complete freedom from scrutiny – and the results have been deadly. So rBGH was approved by the FDA after only 30-60 days of inadequate testing and was deemed safe for humans and animals. And today, our children are drinking buckets of rBGH-laced milk.

The media's lack of attentiveness to their most solemn responsibility is the reason why thousands of products are full of genetically modified organisms (GMOs), hydrogenated oils, (universally damned decades ago by doctors), and cancer-causing dyes.

This lack of journalistic integrity is the main reason why most reporters refuse to conduct even basic research on pharmaceuticals and medical procedures, opting instead to print the 'talking points' of big medicine and big Pharma, despite the risks to tens of millions of people.

In many other professions this would be considered dereliction of duty, but in today's corporate journalism, it's just another day at the office.

It is for these reasons and more that I take the responsibility of producing documentary films very seriously. My training as a young journalist mandated that I become an excellent researcher, and since my films are often outside of the norm of mainstream journalism, facts are the prime currency I wield.

Many doctors, parents, critics, and others may not like *Generation RX* or any of my films – and that's fine with me. But if *Generation RX* helps spur the much-needed debate about the overuse of psychiatric medicines among children and teens, I will gladly take the heat from those who believe these medicines are 'a godsend'. My work is not designed to take away an individual's 'medical freedom of choice', but to help people make an informed choice about what they put into their bodies.

For all of the damning evidence I present in *Generation RX*, this film is about a pattern of deception by the federal government and drug companies regarding the dubious 'science' behind these powerful drugs. If we start the debate there, perhaps we can actually attain what my Latin teacher once called *'Pax Mentis'*, or 'peace of mind' – and accomplish something really important for this generation and the next.

After all, ideas are dangerous creations; it matters not if one is tackling poverty and the homeless, the inequity of healthcare or multinational corporations whose desire for profit threatens us all. If I'm 'dangerous' at all, it is because I was raised to question authority and conventional thinking. That's my blessing.

Pax Mentis.

$$\left(\,2\,\right)$$

DANGEROUS CREATIONS

2

DANGEROUS CREATIONS

Creativity in all its forms is only dangerous to the mindsets that want to eradicate freedom of thought and the feeling of freedom that comes through creative expression. Art in its truest sense is the vehicle by which we 'dream with open eyes', and it is the free flowing timeless connection to inner worlds that are waiting to be discovered. All art is spiritual and therefore can be deemed unacceptable, even 'dangerous', when it attempts to convey other levels of reality.

~ Neil Hague

I was a creative child, as children naturally are, and would spend hours with pocket money in hand, staring at stationery. I liked to paint, draw, write, sing and dream. I left school, my only qualifications being in English and art, and went straight to College to study art. In many ways, despite the 'formal training', these were the best years I ever spent in any educational establishment. I also got a band together, *The Flying Teatrays*, with some of my fellow students, and we had a whale of a time during these experimental years.

In my experience, art students are definitely very different to academic students; it seemed as though the rest of the college had to abide by rules that didn't apply to us. Artists have always had a bit of a reputation for being either crazy, rebellious or strange, I got the feeling that they almost expected us to be 'trouble'. We fulfilled their expectations as best we could by getting up to mischief on a regular basis; we were always larking around and we laughed a lot. I produced some wonderful work because of it.

On a basic level, my education in art taught me quite a few

things about the nature of creativity and creative people; all of us, when engaged in our work, would be in 'another world', and therefore I learned that ART comes from within. When the tutor set a project, every single one of us would create something very unique and individual. There was no 'right' or 'wrong' way to go about it; it was merely down to the personal preference of the tutor who happened to mark the work. They walked around the room occasionally, inspected our work-in-progress, and sometimes picked up a brush and would start painting over what we were doing, or would simply comment, *"I don't like that"* – to which I would always reply, *"Well, I like it!"* It became my catch-phrase; I wouldn't change anything just because someone else didn't like it that way. I realized back then that if I am not personally satisfied with my creations, then there's not a lot of point. No art tutor with a genuine interest in art could ever argue with that.

Non-verbal communication is very powerful – a look can say a million times more than one word ever could. All art has the ability to express what cannot be put into words and is thus beyond the controlling mechanism or 'spell' of words. It's another 'language' that has to be interpreted and is not always easy to understand… at times, the artist themselves have difficulty translating what it is they have painted into words. It's almost as though the communication is taking place on a deeper level that will be understood as and when the need arises. When my youngest daughter paints a picture, if I ask her what it is, she looks at it with her head on one side as if having to think about it first.

Any artistic creativity involves the imagination, which, by its very nature, can not be confined to a box because it cannot easily be defined. It just *is* what it is. Inspiration is a spontaneous process – you can't force yourself to create something wonderful or predict what it will be or when it will occur. It just *happens* as a natural result of imagining. This kind of spontaneity is the antithesis of control, so creative people are often regarded as 'loose cannons' because they can be unpredictable. They dislike routine and rarely work 9 to 5 in an office somewhere; that would be the death of them.

Music, books, painting and films are cultural muses that inspire and have a strong impact on others in the way they think and behave. We each have the ability to change the world through spontaneous, imaginative, creative expression. If you don't know how, then you can start by breaking out of your usual routines and habits in small ways; go for a stroll by the river during your lunch break instead of sitting in the canteen, call someone up 'for no reason', practice acting on impulse instead of worrying about your next move – doing and saying what you feel in the moment. When you get into it, you feel like you're 'on a roll'… life begins to effortlessly flow, aligned as you are with the source of creativity itself – with Spirit. *This* is living creatively, and 'dangerously'. It's simply, as my good friend Jerry Ravel writes in this chapter; 'Life as Art'.

EXPOSING THE UNTOLD HISTORY OF ART
Neil Hague

Great artists never paint things as they are, if they did, they would cease to be great artists.
~ **Oscar Wilde (1854 - 1900)**

I shall not rest from this great task to open the immortal eyes of man inwards.
~ **William Blake (1757 - 1827)**

Neil Hague is a UK visionary artist, authorial illustrator, speaker and writer. Originally trained in graphics and book publishing, he was one of the founders of Bridge of Love Publications in the UK. His work has been described as 'neo-shamanic' by people who have heard him talk or who have seen his art.

He was born and brought up in Rotherham, South Yorkshire

in the UK, to working class parents; and from an early age his imagination and passion for book illustration was to lead him into a career in illustration, publishing and lecturing.

Having spent the best part of the 1990's working as a book designer and later as a book illustrator, Neil went on to complete a postgraduate diploma in Narrative Illustration at the University of Brighton. During this period his work was selected for Images – the Best of British Illustration, and for the Macmillan Book Illustration Award at the Royal College of Art.

Neil has had numerous exhibitions of his visionary work in London and his paintings have appeared on book covers all over the world. He is inspired by native cultures, 'universal' symbols, archetypes and a love of nature, and often links and utilizes these sources in his own work. In his books *Through Ancient Eyes* and *Journeys in the Dreamtime*, he illustrates a personal and fascinating approach to art and image making. His tarot project and graphic novel *Kokoro*, encapsulates the story of creation with the 'themes and signs' unfolding in our reality, as we go through a major shift in consciousness at this time. Website: www.neilhague.com

When I was a kid, I used to see the days of the week in colors – Saturdays were orangey-yellow, Sundays were dark blue, Monday was pale yellow, Tuesday was light blue, Wednesday was green, Thursday was grey, and Friday was red.

My mother was involved with Spiritualist churches and held clairvoyant sessions, so I was always interested in the 'supernatural', but I didn't know what it was that I was drawing and playing around with in terms of visual imagery in those days. It's interesting that one of the first drawings I did back in the early '70's was of a dragon, as it seems to be something I've become connected to, in terms of the imagery I produce for people these days...

I probably had the idea that I wanted to illustrate books from around the age of 14, and eventually went to university to 'train' to become a designer and illustrator, but I lost interest in the commercial world in the early 1990's. A clear turning point for me came one day when I was late for work, rushing through the Central London 'rat race', and as I passed by a bookshop in Covent Garden, a book on American Indian mythology caught my eye. That morning, I forgot all about work – I bought the book, sat on a nearby bench, and started reading... There were hardly any pictures in this book, but the words conjured up very clear pictures in my mind of many different images relating to myths. From that point onwards, a seed had been planted... something emerged from within me, drawing me into the realms of the visionary, metaphysical, and transcendental work that I've been doing ever since.

Reality Rings and Memory Wheels

In my view, the history of art is nothing more than the history of the human mind and of human consciousness. That's all it is at its core. Whether somebody's debated whether or not they're going to paint a chair or a butterfly or whether they tried to express, like Picasso did, multiple viewpoints using different perspectives and angles, is really no more than tracking the human consciousness as it's evolved or as it's remembered itself.

All paintings up to about the 13th century were absolutely flat. It was very 2D and linear – from cave paintings or Egyptian hieroglyphics to illuminated manuscripts and murals on cathedral walls, there was hardly any attempt to make anything three dimensional. During the Renaissance period all this changed. There became a greater need to understand the world that we live in as a three dimensional structure through art, which was very metaphysical in some ways.

The Age of Enlightenment during the 18th century was the period where things began to change as artists focused on romantic dream imagery and figures in paintings became more immaterial. Artists like Francisco Goya and Eugene Delacroix were highly political painters but, at the same time, they refined Visionary sensibilities within painting using Romantic imagery. So, too, did the likes of Henri Fuseli, Karl Palovitch and, of course, William Blake.

At around the beginning of the 20th century there was another shift – to the likes of the Impressionists, who were attempting to understand and paint multiple of levels of reality. Artists like Georges-Pierre Seurat in France used pointillism (painting through dots) to create huge images that, when viewed from a distance, *appeared* like a colored painting but when you get up close, they're little dots… predominantly in red, green and blue. Much earlier in the 19th Century, Jean Baptiste Joseph Fourier identified the mathematical codes that would eventually become TV transmissions using *red, green and blue pixels*, initially pioneered through the art of Seurat and others. In around 1910-1913, Frantisek Kupka, a Belgian artist, was painting symbolic imagery that looked rather like crop circles, long before crop circles were even thought about. Then you have Matisse, who painted *The Dance*, which portrays five slightly abstract naked figures dancing in a circle. Later on, scientists looking at hydrogen structures and molecular structures noticed that the way in which he'd painted the figures almost mirrored the hydrogen dance of the molecule. Yet none of these artists had any understanding of these correlations… *or did they?*

Around the same time, Picasso completely threw convention out of the window – he was probably one of the greatest Western artists that ever lived. When you look at his work, you can see that he was massively inspired by Native indigenous art – African cultures, American Indian cultures, and obviously the Spanish roots that he had. He took all of the understanding of 3D objective viewing and with Georges Braque, was one of the first artists to ask, *"What about the 4th dimension? What about the 5th dimension?"* He painted different views of a woman's head –

looking at her from the side, the front, the back, and the top *all at the same time.*

In the late 19th, early 20th centuries, the Abstract Expressionists, Wassily Kandinsky and Paul Klee, who were both interested in subconscious realms, were naturally recreating petroglyphs and pictographs found in cave paintings going back thousands of years, but they were also tapping into other levels of consciousness in a Visionary way. Another wonderful artist from that period was Odilon Redon, a precursor to Surrealism, he used similar cosmic imagery within his work, as well as subconscious, Egyptian-style mythological themes.

The dawn of the 20th Century saw the desire to reformulate the close bonds between the human and the cosmos by means of symbolist imagery. Archetypes that were used in the ancient world to symbolize human imagination, emotion and the forces in nature, emerged quite naturally in the work of Edvard Munch, Paul Sérusier and Peliza de Volpedo, the latter being a leading representative of the Italian Divisionism. Images associated with the Sun, Moon, Stars and nature was focused on by the Post Impressionists and later the Expressionists, which can still be seen to influence artists today. In the 2003 exhibition by the Danish artist Loafer Eliasson called The Weather Project, giant installations that made use of light and mirrors to create the effect of an Inner Sun seemed to echo the work of the alchemist in a modern age. His work, like the Impressionists of 20th Century Europe, takes nature (the weather) as a starting point for exploring ideas about perception and reality. Obviously Eliasson's giant installations are not traditional oil paintings, but like a Van Gogh of the 21st Century, they reinforce the archetypal imagery that is at the heart of human perception. Anthony Gormley's *Angel of the North* near Newcastle on the A1 road in the UK is also a symbolic archetypal image.

Art in the 21st century has come round full-circle in my view. Our ancestors were tapping into portals into higher dimensions and the symbolism behind that, and you can see that in all sorts of areas today, especially within scientific studies. Inspired by scientists and mathematicians like Michael Faraday, and James Maxwell towards the end of the 19th century, art and science could be reunited. It's interesting that certain researchers and scientists during recent years have begun to incorporate art into their research. For example, Lizzie Burns from the Medical Research Council draws and paints to explain biochemical research. Some of these images look like inner and outer-worlds, and is very visionary.

So whether it's the sun, angels, or other imagery relating to 'stellar consciousness' and high levels of awareness… it's all part of the collective consciousness. These archetypes are now feeding back into the contemporary art we see today. I've illustrated this with an image called the *Historical Art History Time Loop*.

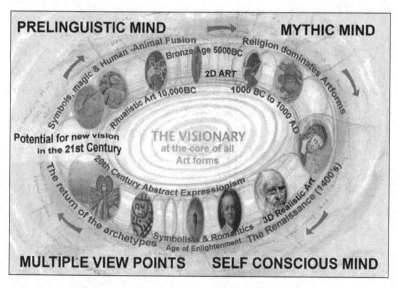

A Brotherhood of Artists

If you go back and look at the symbolism, most of the artists from the Renaissance period onwards were massively involved

in secret societies. Many painters not only worked with digni-
taries, ambassadors and high levels of society, but they also had
access to an underground stream of knowledge, which may well
explain why their art reflected tribal mythology and tribal lore.

Hieronymous Bosch, who spearheaded the Flemish
Renaissance movement was a member of The Brotherhood of Our
Lady, which was connected the Royal House of Holland and
Queen Beatrix, which still today is connected to the Order of the
Garter. His work was about the inner-worlds within worlds, he
opened up some sort of Pandora's Box. The famous triptych of
The Garden of Earthy Delights is a wonderful example – if you look
at the section that is meant to be 'paradise', there are flying
objects and other renditions relating to bird-people and other
creatures. He was somehow getting access and information that
was very much linked to African primeval stories of creation...
this coming through a Flemish painter in 15th Century Belgium?!
Bosch was obviously tapping into hidden knowledge.

Alchemical illustrators and artists, such as Robert Fludd,
Jakob Böhme and Henry Cornelius Agrippa, were also serious
secret society members. Paracelsus, the alchemist, physician, and
botanist was also very much part of this breed of alchemists
emerging at the time who inspired many artists by saying, *"The
great truth of the Universe lies within the human imagination; it is the
source, the sun and those who understand its powers are the lords of all
created things."*

Scientifically, I'm not sure how you could explain it, but I've
got an intuitive feeling that the sun is the 'projector' for this
reality – much like when you go to the movies and the film is
being projected behind you through a little hole in the wall. I
think that the alchemists knew it, and Blake and a couple of other
visionary artists were tapping into this. I think that's why these
priesthoods throughout history have worshipped the sun.

Emmanuel Swedenborg was an alchemist who inspired a
huge movement within 18th century Britain. He also inspired

many artists, including William Blake who used to visit the church of Swedenborg in London (which was the size of a small town surrounded by fields back then). Swedenborg and Blake said a lot of similar things although they came from very different backgrounds. In *The Everlasting Gospel* Blake wrote, 'The *life dim windows of the soul distorts the heavens from pole to pole and leads you to believe a lie when you see with and not through the eye'.* Swedenborg said a similar thing when he wrote, *'The eye so crude that it cannot see the small elements of nature except through a lens as everyone knows, so it is less able to see the things that are above the realm of nature like the things of the spiritual world'.* One was a scientist, one was an artist, yet they were both coming from the same viewpoint and both shared similar principles in that period of British history. Eventually, Swedenborg was ostracized and marginalized, but he was also a freemason... as far as I know, Blake wasn't; although he did believe in the coming of the 'New Jerusalem' which is something that I've looked at and touched upon in my own work.

In my view, the New Jerusalem has got nothing to do with the New World Order or our current political structures – it isn't a physical location... it's about people 'becoming' the New Jerusalem within their hearts. Although many artists generated imagery relating to religious symbolism and inner-worlds, Blake was trying to elevate Christianity to a higher level through the 'true teachings' that he felt were more important than the Church itself – he revered the teachings of Jesus and shunned the orthodox hierarchy within the Christian religion. He said that, *"If the doors of perception were cleansed, man would see everything as it is... infinite".*

In contrast, a lot of painters from the Renaissance period were involved in what we call the 'death cults' – an obsession with the inevitable slow walk towards death... the fact that the body dies and everything has its time, which was basically an obsession with the three dimensional world that we engage in through the five senses, or the part of the world that decays.

Many years ago, there was a documentary made by the British painter David Hockney called *Hidden Knowledge*. He revealed that, more often than not, many of the Renaissance paintings were created using lenses and cameras to get a prefect rendition of an image that was then reflected by a mirror onto a canvas or a wall, which was then re-painted (traced) to look beautifully photographic. The Italian Renaissance was almost a discovery of the self and of the world within 3D form through the under-standing of linear perspective. The movement was spearheaded by the likes of Leonardo Da Vinci who was said to have been a grand master of the Priory of the Sun (Sion) in recent years. There are so many paintings containing crosses and skulls. One painting called *The Ambassadors* by Hans Holbein, who was a painter for the aristocracy of Europe in the 16th century. He was very connected to the Order of the Garter and the Order of St Michael along with the Royal bloodlines of the Holy Roman Empire and the Jesuits. Within this painting, there are all kinds of instruments relating to astrology and freemasonry, but the inter-esting factor in this painting is the distorted skull, which suggests that it could have been made through the use of lenses/camera obscuras. If you go and stand in front of it in the National Gallery in London, you'll notice that you have to stand at a certain angle to be able to see it out of its amorphous state. If you stand and look at it from the front it's distorted, but when you view the painting from a certain angle at the side, you see the image for what it truly is. It's been distorted, quite possibly by using a mirror or a lens. The other interesting thing about that painting is that in the top left-hand corner there's a very small crucifix hidden behind the curtain.

In Rennes-le-Château in France, you can also see the same iconography of the skull and the cross over the entrance to the church – it crops up all over the place. These brotherhoods knew that the truth about Rennes-le-Château is the true symbolism behind the Christian religion, well... *all* religion, really. The artists rendering those symbols knew the true meaning behind the 'cult of the dead' and its opposite, 'the god of Life'. The imagery associated with the skull (including the Halloween pumpkin-head) is another symbol for the death cults that are still using archetypal imagery in many festivals, music, art forms and cinema to this day.

Even though many contemporary artists haven't recognised the fact that they're tapping into the 'bigger picture', what's interesting is that the 'Sensational art' movement over the past twenty years also has an obsession with death cults. You can see it in a whole range of artist's work, for example; Damien Hirst recently encrusted a skull with thousands of diamonds, entitled *For the Love of God*. He made diamonds look worthless, which they are, really.

In recent years, the brothers Jake and Dinos Chapman were tapping-into subconscious worlds with their miniature sculptures showing hell and the underworld, but that's no different to a paintings in monasteries all over medieval Europe (along with the Mexican art of the Aztecs) all depicting the *Danse Macabre* (Dance of the Dead). So there's a correlation of archetypes going on, but it's not necessarily recognised by the academic world.

The inner, hidden history of art, for me, is like a river that runs underneath the surface, like an underground stream full of symbols and codes and information that taps into the higher levels of human divine consciousness. As the artist and poet Cecil Collins wrote in his book *The Vision of the Fool*: '*Images derive from the Fountain-head of human life, the heart, the solar center, ancient memories in the blood and the polarity of the fire of the spirit*'.

The Art Establishment (Right/Left Brain stuff)

An important thing to remember is that we're all artists. As Picasso said, "*All children are artists – they just forget when they grow up"*. Eric Gill said a similar thing, *"What we want is more people expressing themselves creatively – not an elite few expressing themselves"*. Basically art is about understanding who you are.

True spiritual art is more interested in the worlds beyond this world – the infinite worlds that live forever. The key to open the doors into those other worlds is the one that they're trying to take out of the kids at school in all forms and facets... the imagination. We are all natural born daydreamers – kids and babies daydream naturally, as do some adults. I do it all the time if I'm sitting in some sort of meeting – I'm 'off' within five minutes... I've gone. I can't stand the bloody things!

I was at a presentation in London this year at the D&AD Conference and one of the heads of a very well known design group in London opened his lecture by saying, *"Give the art schools back to the dyslexics"*. This is a good point, because what these kids are and what these kids can do in terms of creative ability is often 'out of this world'. Just because some kids can't sit still, they can't be structured or put into a box or a pigeon hole, or they can't perform within the left-brain structure, *immediately* they're diagnosed as being dyslexic or they're diagnosed with ADHD or something else, when in actual fact there's probably nothing wrong with them! It's just the fact that they're more right-brain orientated and they can't help that. After all, it's an important part of the nature of the human spirit to be right-brain orientated and merely to use the left-brain to structure ourselves within this five sense world.

Anything from doodling through to serious drawing is so important from an early age because it allows a person to develop their own form of communication in this world – of language and understanding. This should be as important in the curriculum as Maths and English... *not* just an activity that's only done for two hours a week, or merely to keep the kids entertained!

Like I say, since the 80's, art has very much had a

Sensationalist focus, which has become a movement in itself. In my view, it's the 'X-factor' movement of the art world, which is not saying that these painters and artists aren't talented... they often are; but there is a lack of spirit and celebration of the ancient archetypes that relate to infinite consciousness and a whole stream of other symbols found in 'Outsider art'. So, you can get away with anything – like nailing elephant shit to a canvas as Chris Ofili did in recent years – as long as you've marketed yourself and become a 'name'. Unless you're slicing animals in half and encasing them in formaldehyde or even building a full-size tent and wheeling it into the Tate Britain, there's a lack of understanding of the true meaning of what art could do and how it could free us. To a certain extent, what Damien Hirst and other contemporary artists are saying is that, *'The general public doesn't understand art'*. Quite rightly so... they *don't*. What they do understand are film, cinema, and literature... but when it comes to the real healing aspect of art and the real spiritual nature of art, it's been lost in a whole pile of elitism and academic self-righteousness.

It's no different to the Dada and Surrealist movements in the 20th century. Salvador Dali was a classic because he realistically painted broken landscapes and dreamlike landscapes based on modern day regular objects such as clocks, in order to offend the bourgeois system, the state. They understood realism but they didn't understand what on earth he was painting.

William Blake and the Genius Within

The Royal Academy of Art was pioneered by several people in around 1768, not least a chap called Sir Joshua Reynolds. He was the head of the Academy when Blake was a young man. The main theme was portraiture based on self-analysis and the 'cult of the individual'. Portraiture was highly important to the art establishment, academia, and the aristocracy – mainly due to the lack of photography. Blake was a very gifted and talented artist but he was also not part of that academic league, that elite structure. Blake was shunned by the art establishment and so, as a rebuke, he sent the Royal Academy a portrait of a *Ghost of a Flea*. It's a very small, beautiful painting – basically, it's the image of a reptilian-looking gargoyle figure standing on a stage carrying a blood bowl. Up in Scotland at the time, there was a doctor called Samuel Johnson, who was just making discoveries into the phenomena of biting midges – they weren't fleas in that sense but, interestingly, if you look closely at a biting midge under a microscope, it looks very human. For me, Blake was tapping into his visionary capabilities, because that microscopic scientific knowledge wasn't available at that time, yet he was picking up on the collective information or knowledge that certain insects could have a 'persona', which has cropped-up since in alien abduction and extraterrestrial themes. Blake's painting was the portrait of a flea in another dimension. He tapped into this slightly reptilian imagery in another of his paintings – a semi-self portrait called *The Man Who Taught me to Draw in my Dreams*, I think there's this general theme with very visionary based artists and painters – they are tapping into 'stellar consciousness'… and other levels of consciousness that are contained within our DNA.

Even though Blake was hounded by the art establishment of his time, which was obsessed with proportion and figures often represented in classical and or religious iconography, he had the ability to intuit and connect with non-linear worlds in the midst of a very staunch kind of elitist academic Britain which is exactly the same today – when it comes to painting and fine art in general, nothing has changed apart from technology and the media. There's still the same elitism. Blake's imagination offended the establishment of that period in 18th century Britain and he was never rewarded and awarded the prestige he should have been given for his ability at his time – in other words, he was way ahead of his time.

The academic world will only teach you how to be commercially successful as an artist. Students who want to be Fine Artists often say, *"I've realized there's no work in fine art"* – of course there's not! Fine Art was created *by* the elite structures *for* the elite structures. It's nothing more than that. To be a fine artist, you've got to have money and connections. Today, Visionary Artists are crying out for patrons. There was a period when art was totally funded by the Church and State, who dictated exactly what the artist should create. A good example of this and the secrecy of the brotherhood of artists is the idea that Leonardo da Vinci was probably responsible for the Turin Shroud... there's no solid proof, but there's a good chance that he was involved in creating it when you look at the background to his connections and what he knew (ahead of his time). Other patrons were around the 1920's and 30's, when the banking institutions commissioned Diego Rivera, the Mexican Social Realist Muralist, to paint murals for the Rockefellers in America. And often through art, patrons, artists, politicians, and Priesthoods mix in secrecy as they did in the ancient world.

Art schools and colleges across the world are totally and utterly saturated by control through money and funding criteria. And even though there are some wonderful people working in schools and colleges at different levels, it ultimately comes back to money. Even in the early days when art schools like the Academy were being pioneered, money wasn't so much of an issue because it was a different time. Schools were created by the elite structures to turn the farming communities into working class fodder for political agendas, basically. They've done a good job of it, and look where they're leading us now...

In my workshops, I try to get students to look at other ways in which we can work with the right-brain, rather than the left-brain which dominates the world that we live in. Sometimes students don't understand the freedom that comes with it and will stand in front of their blank canvas or stare at a blank sheet of paper like rabbits caught in car headlights, because they've not been *told* what to create. *"I don't know what to do next"*, you know?

Over the years, there have been times when I've woken up in the morning, I've put something on the easel and I've meditated for a while or just 'switched off' and tuned-in, and what comes through is completely without any agenda. They don't teach that at art school or in *any* school when it comes to art, because in order to do that they would have to look at many other levels of themselves.

The Outsider and Visionary Artist

Somebody who has had little or no formal art training, who paints from within is seen as an Outsider Artist. A Frenchman – Jean Philippe Arthur Dubuffet, coined outsider Art as a phrase in the early part of the 20th century. He was an academic artist who believed that everybody has an inherent ability to recreate, visualize, and paint imagery sourced from within, without any formal training. The Outsider movement was very much based on the principles surrounding the Native or aboriginal under-standing of art. Where as 'Insider Art' or the elitist world of fine Art, especially in Britain, often concerns itself with mediocrity and academia combined. The majority of Outsider Artists you can translate as being budding Visionary Artists within themselves.

William Blake was a true British Visionary and I don't think there's been anybody like him since. A Tate exhibition poster once stated that, 'Whether artists know it or not, most of them were inspired by Blake' – and they were, actually. If it wasn't for the likes of Blake, we wouldn't have graphic novels and the kind of visionary illustration that we see today. In fact I would go as far as saying that Illustration today is the pathway to recovering the art of the visionary. Blake, in my view, was a pioneer of Outsider Art, although he wouldn't have understood the term. He would probably have seen himself as a poet, a writer, a visionary and an artist. Blake's art was a meeting ground between neo-romantic shamanism and the lost symbolism found in religious iconography at the edge of a very new world that was emerging at the time of the Age of Enlightenment.

Visionary art concerns itself with what we cannot see – with other worlds that are not necessarily connected with this world. The 16th century Italian physicist Giordano Bruno was a scientist but he was also a Dominican priest who really challenged the authority at the time. He was talking about astrophysics 400 years before 'astrophysics' even became a term. Bruno also talked about 'Reality Rings and Memory Wheels', where everything that could possibly exist exists at the same time. This is the 'non-local effect', which means that all dimensions interface within the same space. The visionary artist was fascinated by this concept even though they didn't have the scientific language of today to describe it.

A painting of a wonderful still-life, of flowers or a bowl of fruit, and copying or imitating it meticulously is not necessarily Visionary art. There is an element of Visionary within it but, more often than not, the artist doesn't necessarily see the Visionary capabilities within their own work. Visionary art is something that would look to the energy and the spirit and the unseen worlds *beyond* these things.

Even though Vincent Van Gogh painted inanimate objects in his own environment as well as painting nature and people, a certain energy flowed through his work and appeared within the energetic style in which he painted that said very much about his other levels of being – the other levels of the 'Russian doll'. Van Gogh was one of those 'wounded shaman' figures. He's been described by the academic world as Van Gogh the 'Post Impressionist' who did this and went there and was a preacher and then shot himself. That's a very linear history of a man who was very much influenced by other levels of reality! Not once do you hear any mention of him being a shaman. When Van Gogh painted *Starry Night*, he was looking at the movement of stars and the luminosity of celestial bodies. When you look at that painting, you can see a hell of a lot of movement and spiral structures. It wasn't until about 100 years later that they actually discovered stars *do* form spirals of light in space...

The Visionary artist tries to find ways of expressing other levels of understanding that relate to human consciousness. Consciousness manifests itself in many ways... it's rather like a Russian doll structure – with the 'little me' in the middle of the Russian doll that the majority of people would recognize as themselves by looking in the mirror. When you go beyond that world, you get into the subconscious level of yourself, then into the superconscious and dreamstates which is another level of yourself, and *then* consciousness beyond those worlds *as well*. Within all of those different vibratory fields are endless amounts of forms and entities and other things that we tap into which are connected to our DNA structures as well as a myriad of other life-forms that float around in the ocean of infinite consciousness.

The ability to tap into different levels of reality as an artist is no different to tapping into the inner-strength and inner-well of source and potential within ourselves. This is rather like taking a crystal and holding it up to the light and twisting it. All the different surfaces refracting in the light are like multiple viewpoints of different dimensions, each one representing facets of consciousness but they all relate to the crystal and the light – they all come back to that one object. I think each of us are like crystals... we are beacons of light. When you tap into art from a visionary point of view, it really does open you up to other levels of reality.

Cecil Collins, who taught fine art at St. Martin's School of Art between 1951 and the late 70's, wrote in his papers and dissertations about the artist in society and the 'theatre of the soul' and the vision of the fool. All these different symbols and archetypes he said would re-emerge again in the time that we are living in.

He believed that art students have to get back to the archetypes to understand the true nature of reality and the true nature of the human soul. Basically, what Collins was saying is that the repression of the world of archetypes by the mechanical, logical and over-rationalised organisation of our society has led to their reappearing in precisely in the place where you'd expect to find them reappear – in the realm of psychology and in the zone of the unconscious mind. This is why these things are coming back to the surface as we try and understand what the mind is about.

There's a chapter in a book I wrote years ago now, *Through Ancient Eyes*, called 'The Spider Inside' inspired by the creation stories of Grandmother Spider found in Native cultures. I don't go with the idea of 'the web of life' being a wonderful thing necessarily, because the spider at the centre of the web creates the web for it's own reason... to catch its prey. If you replace a spider with a giant symbol of the 'one mind' (because there *is* only one mind... there aren't individual minds) the mind in itself will always enslave us in the web like the spider does. To get beyond the web, we have to get in touch with this spider imagery within ourselves. True art relates to receiving your own visions – *not* being given visions by the outside world, which are part of the structure imposed on us by the metaphorical spider.

When you hear the word 'television' you know you're looking at somebody else telling-you-a-vision. We need to look at the metaphor of the creative views of our own life force and that's what the spider positively represents in that sense. As Duane Elgin wrote, *'There is no one who can take our place. Each of us weaves a strand in the web of creation. There is no-one who can weave that strand for us. What we have to contribute is both unique and irreplaceable. What we withhold from life is lost to life. The entire world depends on individual choices'*. The purpose of art, in my view, is individual choice and the freedom of movement and of expression in terms of being able to create our own reality or 'weave our own web', and to tap into the other levels that can help us do that.

Ten years ago, I painted some images of people holding hands around the earth called *Free Spirits*. This kind of symbology, the images of people linking and going around the earth, is a profound image in as much that it's about connecting with other levels of reality beyond the realm of the web – the earth reality. Art is a vehicle for a means of either bringing healing or awakening the soul so when I paint a picture, when I make my art, there is a unique energy and other levels of reality and consciousness coming through me and into the work, which will then give off an energy field to those that see and or absorb the imagery through their own eyes.

There was an artist many years ago called Peter London who wrote a book called *No More Secondhand Art – Awakening the Artist Within*. He said, '*When you connect with the spirit with your own personal web, to create art drawn from within is to access our internal*

power of our own and also to uncover and all-but-forgotten original primal self'. Art connects with the primal mind initially, but if you're really truly trying to know yourself your visionary capabilities will exceed the mind and you'll tap into other levels of understanding that come through a portion of the mind but they enhance the heart more than anything else.

There are two types of artists I've come across – one is a 'wounder'... that's someone who pierces the thin veneer of the veil, they punch a hole through the web that keeps us from seeing what we really need to see ... *bang!* And they say, *"Look at this!"* you know, it's kind of like, *"Bloody hell! I'd never thought of that before."* But you can't keep staring into the hole for ever... that's what happens to some people in the conspiracy movement. Nor can you stare at other areas of reality and actually worship them as though that's the only thing there is, which you see within 'New Age' movement to a certain extent. Once the hole is open, once the wound has been created, there has to be a way of *healing* that wound – this is what the other type of artist does; consoles and offers healing. This is what I've been trying to do with my art work... it's a form of cathartic healing.

David Icke said something about my work which is quite lovely; *"...the language of an open and highly creative mind. You look with your eyes, but he speaks to your heart"*. And that is what I'm interested in. For me, this is what art is about – it's about speaking first your mind, then speaking your heart.

L-R: Henrik and Fredrik Palmgren

OBSERVING · EXPLORING · BEING HERE NOW
Henrik and Fredrik Palmgren – Red Ice Creations

Every kind of ignorance in the world all results from not realizing that our perceptions are gambles. We believe what we see and then we believe our interpretation of it, we don't even know we are making an interpretation most of the time. We think this is reality.
~ Robert Anton Wilson (1932 - 2007)

We don't see things as they are, we see them as we are.
~ Anaïs Nin (1903 - 1977)

He who lives in harmony with himself lives in harmony with the universe.
~ Marcus Aurelius (121 - 180 AD)

Henrik Palmgren is a filmmaker, radio host, website editor, musician and a researcher into the esoteric, occult and conspiratorial. He has been running the website redicecreations.com since 2002 and has continuously expanded into new forms of media and new areas of research. Henrik lives on the west coast of Sweden where he was born in 1979. He has a background in music, art, media and has been interested in the mysteries since an early age. After 9/11, 2001 he developed the passion and dedication to help spread information and research to a larger audience on a wide variety of subject matters, many of which are covered on *Red Ice* and in the film productions of *Blue Fire Film*. He works closely together with his brother Fredrik on many projects, who is the producer of *Red Ice Radio* and the *Red Ice* live webcasts. Fredrik acts as an advisor to redicecreations.com and contributes sporadically with writings to the website. He is also involved in the creative process surrounding the Blue Fire Film projects.

Fredrik is a self taught musician, artist and writer. He has been keeping one eye open and one eye closed ever since the September 11th event that also sparked his interest in the occult, conspiracy research and spirituality.

Blue Fire Film have produced the DVD documentary film series *Architects of Control* together with researcher Michael Tsarion.

Websites:

www.redicecreations.com

www.architectsofcontrol.com

www.bluefirefilm.com

www.henrikpalmgren.com

The idea that something is incredibly wrong in our world and that something needs to be done about it, basically spawns from this initial question: "Why does the world look the way it does?" We really have no idea what the heck is *really* going on or the purpose of it, and I think that we should never be so bold as to say that we know exactly why we're here or what the reasons are. If we continue the search with an open mind, we might be able to learn something along the way...

On one level, we are basically being ruled by a ruthless class of inbred psychopathic killers. But every time we discover another conspiracy, it's evidence that they are *not* in full control of the entire planet or the geopolitical game. What we discover is merely their *attempt* to control everything. Whether they are either too sick to know what they are actually doing, or they have a totally outlined plan – for me, it is still very much open to debate.

I started off the radio show sometime in the spring of 2006 because of my own curiosity – to be able to talk with people and sort out for myself what the heck is going on. It's a mix of a personal interest in the information and a passion for the knowledge... it's fascinating and it's a thrill doing it. Christopher Moors asked me to be a correspondent on his show on BBS Radio, then ended up asking the fellers who handled the station if I could have my own show and that's the way it came about – I was *asked* into it, so that was pretty interesting. After a time, we realized that there were a lot of people tuning-in and listening to this, and there is a responsibility that comes with that.

How to decide who to interview has always been very much intuitive. In some cases, you might be uncertain about someone you interview, but that doesn't mean that it's wrong to do the interview or to have that information. It's always up to the individual listening to interpret the information and decide for themselves if it works in their own worldview. I think that it's always good to hear someone that you *don't* agree with, because that helps define your own opinions. Occasionally I might criticize someone on some point or whatever here or there, but never across the board – I respect their opinion and they should be able to speak it.

I think it's a part of the learning experience to be able to question *everything*, even in the Conspiracy realm. Who is putting out *that* information? Can you trust *those* people? I hope that those listening are able to make this intuitive discernment and judgment for themselves. I think it's a big mistake to hand over your own sense of responsibility and judgment to someone else.

Confusion is good for the individual. Because of the large amount of information on the web, we get confronted with this dilemma of the madness before our very eyes. Can *this* be the way it is, or can *this*? I think it's hard to pin down what exactly is going on – although there is a structure to it, the fine details are changing all the time. Basically, it's up to you to sort this out – you realize you can't trust anyone but yourself. There *are* no rules and leaders when it comes down to the individual. I'm skeptical of all kinds of authority, be it the alternative *or* the mainstream historian. In many cases it's just more interesting to listen to the alternative historian – it opens your mind a whole lot more, but it's also necessary to keep an eye on the propaganda.

Too many people are criticizing the mainstream media without actually realizing that we rely on reporters out there doing the work that they do so that we can personally interpret it. Without reporters, the alternative media wouldn't exist.

Although it would be good if the mainstream touched upon controversial topics more often, you can't use the same outlet to solve problems that have been created by the very people behind the propaganda. The remedy has to come from another level – from a passionate blogger or someone who has their own website, radio station or TV channel, or what have you. I think it's still basically down to the individual person observing the mainstream saying, "I've had enough of this... I want to look at something else." When they turn away from the mainstream they will automatically empower the alternative sources.

The internet has had an incredible impact on this type of information and how fast it can be spread around the globe, but we should use it with caution. Too many people are just sitting in front of their computers and they're so incredibly immersed in all of this. It can become an escape from reality. If all you do is study how rotten everything is in the world, sitting in front of your 'black window to the world' – the computer screen – and nothing of the natural world of beauty comes into your life, that's when it comes obsessive... it becomes too much. The important thing is to *explore* the universe, instead of just being immersed in unveiling and unraveling the incredibly complex world that the human created – the conspiratorial world. There always needs to be a balance. You have to face yourself, your decisions – do you want to sit in front of the computer and be paranoid?

Paranoia *is* part of life and it's an important stage in the research phase. I don't think it's all that bad to look over your shoulder every now and then. Having a certain level of suspicion makes things a bit more interesting, but at the end of the day I wouldn't take it so seriously. It *is* serious, but it's not *that* serious. When you wake up to the realization that the guys trying to control the world are actually very, very tiny in their mindset and very fearful, then you realize that you don't have to be afraid. They *aren't* that big and scary. They're trying to portray themselves as these all-powerful masters but, like the wizard behind the green curtain, they're really terrified individuals. Obviously, on a materialistic level they are very powerful but I think there's a spiritual component that overrides that, so there's no reason to be paranoid.

It's important to laugh, to be close to humor, to nature – to have balance so that you can realize what's *really* real... that this is just man-made, this paranoia, conspiracy and control. I'm not afraid of the paranoia because I know what *is* important. You only have to take a walk in the woods or the park sometime, or take your shoes off... basically, turn off the computer now and then.

Red Ice actually started as an art project way before it became a news site and radio show. If you have the intent of goodwill and a good heart and you're trying to spread a message in the best way you can, I think that art is perhaps *the* best way to communicate something to convey an important message. It's all about how we are being perceived by others. A flower presents itself very beautifully and if it didn't do that it wouldn't attract the bee, basically. That's why so many multi-national million-dollar corporations spend so much money on how things look on the surface – they know how to package it to sell the message. Things can be dramatized *too* much of course – we know that the media uses symbols, images and music to manipulate... within films, for instance, they play on your emotions, so you're drawn into it in that way.

People are afraid to use certain symbols – like the 'eye of providence', for example – but I think that's a huge mistake. People miss out when they have that attitude. Just because these bad, evil scumbags have got their hands on it, it doesn't belong to them... it's for everybody. We should take the symbols back – empower ourselves with them. Just because someone is showing one eye on a movie cover, doesn't mean the Illuminati's behind the movie – it *could* mean that but then again it might *not*, so we have to make that judgment for ourselves.

Many of these guys 'at the top of the pyramid' are using the same forces or themes as nature – they're emulating nature because they know that if they would go outside that realm, their manipulation wouldn't work and that's why we have to become savvy to it. We have to become smart and observe how they're playing us in order to escape from it.

People have accused us of being masons because we use some of these symbols and themes ourselves on the website. For example, we very much resonate with some of the more ancient aspects and mythologies surrounding the central theme of polarities. Too many people think that it's just about the Hegelian dialectic, and resort to the conspiratorial idea that once you begin working with two opposites that that means something bad, but it's quite the contrary. It's a 'constant' in nature – it's one of the laws, if you will, of how things work in this particular universe at this particular time.

If it weren't for the very balanced temperature on the planet, life would basically not exist. The basic idea behind calling the website *Red Ice Creations* is that through the correct or the proper aspect of both hot and cold elements, if you reach a good medium in the temperature wonderful things can arise. What determines one or the other is the observer of it. Is it red or is it blue? Is it hot or is it cold? It's up to you, the viewer or the listener engaged in the information, to decide. That's why it's an appropriate theme or backdrop to what we're doing.

The idea of balancing is so important because if you lean too much on the right or left side, basically you are going to fall over! If you become too logical, rational, and structured and your thinking is too 'square', too 'boxed-up', then you're going to lose the plot and won't realize that there's so much more to the world. Conversely, if you're too dreamy, you'll just float away with the internal world and you're not going to see what's happening in the structure of the world around you. Logic needs to be balanced with spirituality in order to attain this. Like the ancient chemical/alchemical wedding, you can be observing the one or the other side but it isn't until you incorporate *both* that something incredible happens. It's the same thing with the left and the right hemispheres of the brain... you can attain a kind of harmony within yourself when these polarities, these opposites, aren't fighting over your attention. On the path of self-discovery or the spiritual journey that we're on, although there are many paths to take within it, each path is very narrow and in order to stay focused and centered, you need to have a balance between both sides.

We're really at a crossroads right now. If the technological infra-structure of the global control system falls into place – we're talking about everything from RFID chips, ubiquitous

computing, biometric scanners, surveillance cameras everywhere, and what have you – that doesn't necessarily mean that
we'll be living in a global fascist dictatorship, but the supporting
infrastructure will be in place and that's a very dangerous
situation. The planet could be turned into a 'prison planet', and
in order to avoid that situation we have to begin to *do something*
about it. We need to wake up enough to realize that we haven't
lost the game – we're not totally under the control of these fellers.
There's another perspective to this as well as a spiritual aspect
that means that we can take back the power into our own hands
instead of handing it away to all these lunatics all the time,
because that's what we're doing right now. Then no-one will be
able to control us, at least on an individual level.

There is still freedom in the world that can be utilized. You
can pretty much spend your life doing what you want to do if
you're smart enough and passionate enough about it. Once
you've begun your journey of self-discovery and discovery about
the world, I think you have to continue it and there's no turning
back. I don't think that nature, or the spirit or force of the
universe is going to allow you back into the illusion. You can't do
what Cypher did in *The Matrix* – to go back into the lie.

To be spiritual is to be *within* the spirit, or in-spiration or in-
spiritualization – working with the muse of the universe. On one
level, you're giving up a little bit of your ego in order to work
with the higher forces of the universe, and you become a conduit
– something flows through you, but you're also still yourself. A
lot of people want to defeat the ego or get rid of it instead of
balancing and using it. To tie this in with the conspiracy, this is
something that they are very happy to utilize – they talk about
the unity and the unification of everything and although that
sounds very good and wonderful on the surface you can also
question if spirituality can be used for nefarious purposes. If we
give up too much of ourselves, we might become like the insect
hive – we're not human anymore, basically. Oneness is there all

the time. We don't have to achieve it or make it happen or strive for it – we just have to relax and tap into it.

I think that the times that we are living in have affected the idea of community. The largest community is already in place – the universe. It's right there and we don't need to divide ourselves into smaller and smaller groups. I feel that community is a form of compartmentalization, where you are actually blocking yourself off from the outside world. The state is a community, in a way, and we can look at that and see that it has pros and cons. Every individual is a community – like a cell within a bigger body, regulating its own journey... but if it weren't for the body or all the rest of the cells, that individual cell wouldn't exist or even be there. We need to support each other, but we also need to remember that we are *already* part of the 'universal' community and start working together, instead of the constant warring that's going on. I think that it's important that people with like mind get together and do something. Spontaneous community is wonderful... putting on a conference, a festival, what have you.

The Red Ice website should be more like a hub than a community – where people can go to learn something interesting and open their eyes to something that they might not have been aware of before. We try the best we can to gather information, talk with researchers, and make this knowledge accessible. The work we do here is a *little* part of the big picture, but definitely not *the* big picture. It changes slowly as we change. Things are falling into place all the time and opportunities open up that we never thought would be possible. The synchronicities are there... our 'job' is to keep up with them. You can't fight synchronicity.

THE ORION CONSPIRACY
Seb Janiak

The only new things are those which have been forgotten
~ www.theorionconspiracy.com

Born in 1966, not far from Paris, Seb Janiak has explored innumerable fields; from graphic designer and photographer, to music video director, producer and short film director.

He started out 'customizing'; first surfboards, then motor-bikes (*"specializing in tanks and helmets"*, he explains). Drawing, his other passion, then led him to the work of icono-clastic illustrators such as Giger, Soroyama and Foss, whose detailed and original imagery fed his imagination. After a friend showed him the first Paintbox programs, Seb became a post-production graphic designer. During 1987-1990's, his work was bolstered by a special photo editing technique that he perfected himself and named *Digital Matte Painting*. This enables the insertion of one or more photos into another to produce strikingly realistic images. His exhibition *Paris from*

2044 to the Present brought together many images using this photo editing technique.

In 1991, he got his first album cover commission; for *Nina Hagen*, by personal request from the artist, no less! *Daft Punk* then asked him to organize the photographs for the launch of their second album. At the same time, Seb became interested in portraits and in fashion photography. The most prestigious magazines courted him – *The Face, Harper's Bazaar, Vogue, Detour, Details, Glamour*, to name but a few.

In 1993, the music video exploded onto the scene. Seb has since become one of the principal producers of music videos stamped 'Made in France'; producing *Soul-Soul* and the subsequent classic *J'Appuie sur la Gachette (I Pull the Trigger)* for rap artistes *NTM*. Over the years, Seb has also worked with TLC, *Method Man, Janet Jackson* and *Robbie Williams*.

A few years after joining *Bandits* in 1994, the best-regarded production company of its time, he founded his own audio-visual production company, called '99' (the name is inspired by the sci-fi cult classic *The Rock Machine* by Norman Spinrad) and, joined by *Seb Caudron, Tomkan, Xavier Denauv* and *Armen*, has created a new artistic family for himself. A recent collaborative project is a DVD entitled *Vanity 9*, with musical assistance from close friends such as *Howie B, DJ Mehdi, Crydamour, Jess & Crabbe*, and some of the finest talents of French house music.

Seb's first short film entitled *The Orion Conspiracy*, has had more than 450,000 viewers since its online release. Website: www.theorionconspiracy.com

My father is an airplane pilot, so ever since I was a child I have looked at the sky and asked myself a lot of questions about it. When I was 15 years old, I saw a light, like a star, in the sky at night. At first, I thought it was a satellite because it was moving at almost the same speed, but suddenly the light stopped, reversed and turned 45 degrees. (I saw this a second time, when I was older, about 25). I was very curious about what I had seen and I wanted to understand how it could be possible, so I started to accumulate information about UFOs and other subjects. 20 years later, I decided to sort out this big mess of an archive I had, and an idea slowly developed in my mind to make a movie about it.

I have been a director and photographer for fifteen years. I knew that nobody in France would finance this kind of project, so I had to find a way to do it by myself with people who trust in me.

I spent one year writing the screenplay based on around 600 pages of facts and ideas that I had. Finding a link between all the subjects I had researched wasn't easy because I couldn't include everything, so it was quite a challenge for me to create a clear and simple dialogue for the movie. I spent another year preparing the shoot and filming and editing the final film, which was a very nice experience.

I have always been very frustrated that we never see anything interesting about UFOs or life outside earth on TV or in the media. These subjects have been completely abandoned by respectable scientists, and by other people who have the gift and the talent to bring us many insights. There are a lot of clever people who are now very dedicated to these subjects and they're doing some great work but they would never allow anyone like that on TV; the door is only open for stupid people who don't present any kind of risk. There's too much censorship, that's the problem, and there's no balance... too much bullshit and not enough serious research.

We are never told the whole truth – just a little bit of food for thought... enough to make us happy. They write a story and if the story works then they give it to the public. Nobody has access to real facts, so anybody can tell any kind of story. It's just a question of reading between the lines and having access to good information.

I don't want to prove or convince people of anything – people can believe what they want. I'm not a scientist or a journalist... I'm just an artist.

The Bigger Picture

Many people feel a connection with the cosmos; we look at the stars and we feel a connection with them, though we don't understand why. The real place of the human being is to be part of the cosmos – a human being is very big, is very large in his mind and his consciousness... so why are we so small-minded? Everything is possible in this universe. Anything that the mind can imagine could exist.

Charles Hoy Fort, who wrote *The Book of the Damned* in 1919, spent his life collecting newspaper articles and other information about 'weird stuff' that nobody can explain. People are scared of what they cannot explain, so they prefer to think these things don't exist, or that they're not true. They can live more peacefully like that.

The universe was not created in peace. I don't believe in peace; I believe in balance. Everything we can see in nature, in ourselves, or in the universe is a fight between negative and positive or 'dynamic duality'.

We tend to forget where we came from. We think we know that this universe came from a big explosion we call the 'Big Bang' – but even if it's not really like that, this universe had to start somewhere 13 billion years ago. It took that time to create a human being, that's how I see things – it couldn't go faster or slower.

Everything started with the light; the photon. Because of the speed of light, what we see in front of us is *almost* in 'real time' but it's actually already passed – when you look at the sun, it's the sun from 10 minutes ago... if you look at the stars in the cosmos, some of them are already dead.

Light is a vibration but, because the universe is more and less dense in certain places, it could be that this light slows down or accelerates in some parts of the universe. Because the speed of light is not constant, it is possible that some galaxies or planets are many thousands of years before or after ours. This is why it is easy for me to imagine that other civilizations are more advanced or are less advanced than ours. It's very logical that if civilizations are able to travel around in space they would want to know more and would want to discover other planets like we ourselves want to. The structure of Sidonia and the 'face' on Mars are very interesting, but not surprising. I believe that a lot of civilizations have visited our solar system.

When you start to understand how the universe works, you know you are not alone at all. Life exists everywhere in the universe. It's a fact. I don't need somebody to prove it with mathematics, photography, or video... I already know inside me that it exists.

The Orion Conspiracy

Although I think there are both physical and multi-dimensional UFOs, *The Orion Conspiracy* tells the story of UFOs made by man. We have more physical proof of those, so there is more footage, more images, and therefore more of a story to tell. I chose Orion in particular because it is connected to the Egyptian pyramids and also with freemasonry. I wanted to make the title more intriguing and mysterious.

Some of the photos in the movie I 'took' from the army and other official sources, but pretty much all the images I used are accessible on the web. As soon as you put a photo or a video on the net, you have to accept the idea that these could be used by someone else. You have to play the game or you don't put it on the internet. I had been collecting these images for about ten years – I never thought I would ever use them and make a film using the images, so in many cases I couldn't even

Credit: The Orion Conspiracy

remember where I had got the image from in the first place! This is why I released the movie for free – I didn't want to make any commercial profit in case I infringed any copyright.

Some photos came from people I know. Other photos were ones I 'built' and retouched myself to better illustrate the story my character is telling. I created the moon images, of course! I would love to have had the real ones... I had a lot of descriptions and amazing stories. I'm an artist so I didn't have any problem creating what I didn't have.

I don't know if the giants are real photos, and I don't know if the photos of the craft in the ice are real – they look both real *and* fake, so I don't know. You need to be a good graphic artist, of course, but the technology is very advanced today to allow you to manipulate any kind of still or moving image fairly easily. If, as a single artist with no budget, I am able to create a few images, then what could a big organization with a billion-dollar budget and a crew of a few thousand people who are very talented create?

It was my intention to show a lot of images in a very short space of time, because when you show only one or two pictures it could be fake – but when you show the whole story with a lot of different images, it confuses people. By the end of the movie, they don't know what to think... It's far more interesting to tell a story in such a way that it isn't easy for people to tell if it's true or not. It forces people to think for themselves.

I know that my movie has been shown to some military government officials – the chief of the army was very pissed because he wanted to know why his service had a photo of the secret B2 bomber, for example, so it's very funny how even the highest people in some structure like the army or the government don't have a clue what is true or not! I was happy about that.

Everybody tries to sell you something on the UFO issue – I don't know why. There are many egos within the research community who all fight for their own truth, but nobody has the truth. It's very stupid to be that serious and angry about something for which you don't have proof, and I have a lot of fun playing with that. People should be more relaxed and open until we know what's really going on.

I think it's good to be curious and open-minded, but it's more important to use your brain and be a good judge. When I read the comments that people have made about my movie I'm very amazed – there are people criticizing and people defending my movie. I'm happy this movie is creating a reaction... whether it's bad or good is not important. For me, what matters is that people are starting to think differently. I wanted to make a movie that would open people's minds.

The main character and narrator in the movie is called Francois Rousseau (played by Feodor Atkine) – a government official who is in charge of secret knowledge. When a new president or a new prime minister is in charge I'm sure that they get briefed on, and have access to, this secret information. The idea behind *The Orion Conspiracy* was to put a camera in one of those meetings and to show what could happen.

One of the first things Rousseau mentions in the movie is the 'theory of the four moons', which is based on a theory from a German guy called Hans Hörbiger, who spoke of four moons and the four evolutionary cycles on earth. G.I. Gurdjieff also talked about these moons and he named them. I thought it would be interesting to tell this story. Nobody knows if it's true or not – nobody has any proof, so why not think everything is possible instead of thinking nothing is possible?

We live a very amazing world with amazing technology that nobody even knows about yet. People think their cell phones or their computers are 'top technology', but they don't begin to imagine that technology today is very, very advanced. The military have always been between 20 and 50 years in advance of anything in the public arena.

The life of Nikola Tesla is very interesting. I'm not sure if he was connected to the Philadelphia experiment or not, as it says in the movie, but everything else we know about him I think it's safe to say is true. The guy was a genius – he found a way to harness free energy from earth, but to make free energy in that time was not a very good idea...

Hitler was very fascinated by esoteric knowledge. The most secret organization of the Third Reich was called the '*Ahnenerbe*' – they searched for a connection between the German race and the Indu-Arian race because they were supposedly connected to some mysterious secret civilization from Atlantis or from Mu. You can see a little piece of this story in Spielberg's first *Indiana Jones* movie.

One exciting story that I didn't mention in the movie is the story about the comet Shoemaker-Levy (SL9) that hit Jupiter in 1994. The official story is that the comet had exploded into 20 pieces, but someone leaked some information saying that the U.S. had been testing a new anti-matter bomb on Jupiter. Allegedly, they couldn't test it on earth – it was too powerful. Jupiter is eleven times the size of Earth, so I don't understand how the pieces of this comet, which were no bigger than one or two kilometres, could create an explosion four times bigger than earth... it's very strange.

HAARP is also mentioned in the movie as the 'ace' in the conspiratorial plan of the story. Amazingly, the Russians built a system like this 20 years before the Americans did – you can see some photos of it on the website of French scientist Jean-Pierre Petit. It's totally true; we have the technology to send a voice directly to your mind and you will be the only one who can hear it, because they can target very precisely – they hit some structure in your brain and you can hear that voice by vibration, like a remote vibrating system. This 'micro wave' technology is actually very old – people have known about it for 30 years, at least.

Another technology exists whereby using lasers and satellite, they can create a hologram in the sky or anywhere on earth. They really can make balls of light appear in the sky, or UFOs – just like the story I told in my movie! They have been able to do that for ten years *at least*. They could make the face of Jesus appear in the sky if they wanted to, and if you coupled that with this voice vibrating system... they could manipulate a lot of people at the same time very effectively. It's a scary thought.

The subjects I covered in my movie could make me paranoid, or think very dark thoughts about the future – but they don't... they show me how just about anything and everything is possible.

PSYCHIATRY ALMOST DROVE ME CRAZY
Paul Levy

The world today hangs by a thin thread, and that thread is the psyche of man.
~ Carl Jung

The gigantic catastrophes that threaten us today are not elemental happenings of a physical or biological order, but psychic events. To a quite terrifying degree we are threatened by wars and revolutions which are nothing other than psychic epidemics. At any moment several millions of human beings may be smitten with a new madness, and then we shall have another world war or devastating revolution. Instead of being at the mercy of wild beasts, earthquakes, landslides, and inundations, modern man is battered by the elemental forces of his own psyche. This is the World Power that vastly exceeds all other powers on earth.
~ Carl Jung

In 1981, Paul had a life-transforming spiritual awakening that almost killed him. A spiritually-informed political activist, Paul is a healer who is in private practice. He has developed a vehicle to help people wake up to the dreamlike nature of reality that he calls 'Awakening in the Dream Groups'. These are circles of people awakening to the dreamlike nature of our experience who are connecting with each other so as to deepen our shared discovery of how we can collaboratively help each other to wake up in the dream together. Paul is the author of *The Madness of George W. Bush: A Reflection of our Collective Psychosis*, in which he integrates his insights in dreaming, psychology, and spirituality with events unfolding in the world's body politic. A visionary artist, he is creating an 'Art-Happening Called Global Awakening'. Paul's website is at: www.awakeninthedream.com

My father was a sociopath – he was very sick, but he was undiagnosed. As an only child, I was the recipient of his murderous rage whenever I would try to separate and express my true self. It was very traumatic. This abuse created an enormous wound in me. Even though I was academically accomplished, I quickly figured out that I couldn't figure my way out of this suffering with my mind. The only thing that made me feel better in any way was by going inwards and becoming an observer to what was happening. So for many hours on end I just began to watch, and that's what meditation is.

After about a year of doing this, what happened as a result of this whole dynamic was that, in essence, I had a spiritual awakening by going inwards so deeply. One day, while sitting in meditation I got hit by an actual internal 'bolt of lightning' that ignited inside of my brain, just for a nanosecond. It's clear to me now that I was so deeply traumatized and I went so deeply inwards, that I accessed something so powerful that it almost killed me. I wasn't prepared for it and I almost wasn't able to contain what I was accessing. I went into such an incredibly expansive state that physically 'impossible' stuff began happening in my life on a regular basis – 'stuff' that we would normally call 'miracles', 'stuff' that could only happen in dreams...

I was acting so unlike my ordinary, conditioned self, that a friend took me to a hospital, thinking I was having a nervous breakdown. I was sitting in the waiting room of the first hospital I was brought to – a hospital in San Francisco – when, all of a sudden, I had the realization that I was doing something and that I should pay attention... rather like driving a car, when you realize, 'Oh, wow... how did I get here?' and you start paying attention to the road. The experience was like that. I was actually in my body and I was walking, *but* what made the situation highly unusual was that *I was walking through a wall.* Was my physical body still sitting in the chair in the waiting room while I was astrally projecting? Or did my whole body, the whole universe, turn to light and become transparent? – I don't know. All I know is, phenomenologically speaking, my subjective experience was that I was walking through a wall. After a little while, they took me by ambulance to Highland Hospital in Oakland, California to institutionalize me, because they were convinced I was having a nervous breakdown.

What is interesting is that about a decade later, a Tibetan Buddhist book written by Geshe Gendun Lodro was published, and the title was: *Walking Through Walls.* Basically, the book explains that when you begin to recognize the dream-like nature of things, you will be able to walk through walls – not in a metaphorical sense, *but in actuality.*

When I arrived at Highland Hospital, I got out of the ambulance and they led me onto the psychiatric ward, into the lounge with the other psychiatric patients. I was in a totally expansive state, feeling completely awake and filled with Spirit – like I was on the cutting edge of the 'Big Bang'... completely enthusiastic and filled with love. And in that room, I saw a blind woman. Her eyes were totally opaque. Without even thinking, I found myself going up to her and I started saying these words, *"All you have to do to see is open your eyes and look."* It was as if I was playing a role in a deeper drama, and these were the lines I was given to say, and so I said them. Over the course of about a minute, she regained her sight – her eyes became normal, healthy eyes. And at that very moment, as if it were choreographed, they took me into another room where I spent the night – strapped-up on a table. At that point, I *knew* without a doubt that I was having a spiritual awakening. It couldn't have been more obvious from my point of view.

The next day, they unstrapped me and put me in a room with a desk and chairs, and the only other person in the room was the now ex-blind woman. She just sat there looking at me, not saying a word… just smiling from ear-to-ear. All of a sudden, my heart chakra just 'blossomed' (in Buddhism this is called the thousand-petalled lotus). Then I realized; her eyes were *physically* fine, but her inner emotional self wasn't psychologically letting herself look. Somehow, that had manifested as blindness and somehow, in whatever clairvoyant way, I had tuned-into that and had been dreamed up by her and got drafted to playing the role in her waking dream to say my lines, because she was at that point of being ready to heal. As soon as I realized that, she said the only words that she had ever said to me, as far as I know… *"Aren't you going to answer the phone call from Roy?"* That's my father's name. Within ten seconds, a nurse came into the room and said, *"Paul, your father's on the phone."* My parents had just found out that their only child had been put on a psych ward. Over time, the psychiatric community's support and complicity with my father's abuse destroyed my family, because, tragically, my parents totally bought into the medical diagnosis from the mainstream psychiatric point of view and, in the end, my parents both passed away convinced, with the psychiatrists blessing, that their only child was totally crazy. Even though I was telling them, *"Look – I'm in books, I teach, I have a private practice, I give lectures,"* etc., my mother, before she passed away, reflected: *"Paul, that's all just your hallucinations."* My parents had an incentive to solidify me as being sick, however, for if they stopped seeing me as sick, they would have to look at the abuse I was pointing at in the family, which was too overwhelming and painful for them to look at.

I didn't care at all that I was in the hospital, because I had so 'let go', but my doctor, who was in charge of me, reflected back, *"You have to convince me that you're not crazy, or I'm going to keep you here for a really long time."* When he said that, I thought about it for a second, and realized I didn't want to spend a long time in the hospital, so I began talking about all the problems I was having with my father. And he let me go. He said, *"Well, you're obviously not crazy."* I spoke with him the next week, and he shared with me that if I was truly crazy, I wouldn't be able to fluidly step into my normal state on a moment's notice like I did.

At that point in my life, my father was just 'Dad', who I loved and wanted to heal this problem with. I wasn't aware that he was a world-class psychopath – and I'm not just exaggerating. His sister, his only sibling, died a month after he died and, before they both passed away, she said to me, *"Paul, d'you know who Hannibal Lecter is?"* Hannibal Lecter from the film *The Silence of the Lambs* is symbolic of the incarnation of evil. *"Well, Paul, that's the sort of person your Father is"*. It didn't surprise me to hear her say this, because I was the recipient of such incredible, crazy-making energetic abuse. She told me that when he was younger, before I was born, he did something, *"So horrible, so terrible"*, that their parents died broken-hearted because of it. She then said it was so horrible and so terrible that she would never tell me what it was, and she never did... taking the family secret with her to the grave.

What I've learned is that when somebody does something dreadful and they don't deal with it – don't feel the remorse, confess, or come to terms with it consciously – they then split off from their own sin, guilt, shame and darkness and project out their shadow. They are so disassociated from it that not only do they lie, but they begin to believe their own lies while actually unconsciously acting out the very thing they did in a disguised form. They become an unwitting instrument for evil – a conduit for the darker powers to enact themselves. My father embodied that dynamic of projecting his own shadow, not dealing with his own darkness, and believing his own lies, and he then acted out this horrible, terrible thing and I was the recipient of it. It wasn't physical abuse… it was emotional, energetic abuse – a total mind-fuck.

The following year, a number of similar, out of the ordinary, miraculous, dreamlike experiences continued to happen (even way more extreme than those I have already mentioned) and because I wasn't able to channel the experiences in a culturally sanctioned way, I kept getting thrown in psychiatric hospitals. I had stepped out of all of the conventions of what was 'acceptable' in society and, of course, it completely threatened and freaked people out. Unfortunately, I was out in the world and wasn't in a safe 'container'. I was repeatedly told, *"Oh, you're mentally ill."* Every psychiatrist was saying I had a manic-depressive illness, and that I would have this for the rest of my life, yet it was so obvious to me from where I was sitting that I was having a spiritual awakening. I was just reflecting back to them that they were totally wrong, that I wasn't a manic depressive at all, which of course just confirmed to them how crazy I was by the fact that I would have the temerity to disagree with them!

One of the things that I point out in my work, and I would debate anybody on this, is that there is a component of the psychiatric community that's completely mad. I experienced that first-hand. Psychiatrists really believe that what they see is objectively existing and separate from themselves, which is to say they are not tuned into the actual dreamlike nature of reality. They aren't aware that they're actually influencing and invoking the very reality that they're both participating in and reacting to as if it objectively exists in concrete form, separate from themselves. Being in the role of the 'authority', they misuse their power to the extent they project out their own craziness and their own shadow, which is a way of avoiding their own unconscious darkness, and they have the perfect receptacle in the patient to carry their own shadow. The whole system set up in collusion with Big Pharma gives doctors the role of holding the power, and this has destroyed a number of people's lives. Because the person having the spiritual emergency is in such a vulnerable state, to be pathologized by an authority figure can literally invoke sickness, as if being put under a spell. Once the person manifests as ill, this then only confirms to the psychiatrist the seeming objective truth of their diagnosis, which only serves to solidify their viewpoint of seeing the patient as ill – in a diabolically self-perpetuating feedback-loop. It's the nature of a self-fulfilling prophecy.

As somebody who has deep experiential insight into the horror and abuse of the 'mental health' community, I feel a great responsibility into really trying to articulate and shed light on what plays out. How many other people are having these spiritual awakenings, these 'emergencies', and are misdiagnosed? Psychiatry is so stone-age and primitive that they don't have the recognition of this phenomena.

Although being hospitalized in itself is very traumatic, I was fortunate in that I was able to get out of the psychiatric system relatively quickly and to continue my spiritual awakening. Within a year, I met my Tibetan teachers. Many great Tibetan Lamas and spiritual practitioners from Burma and Tibet are like family to me now... I've known them for so long.

I started my private practice in 1993, as I realized, after years of integrating my trauma, that the ordeal was revealing something to me that would be potentially beneficial for other people. To people who are reading this thinking, *"Oh, he's still crazy"*, I would like to add that, in a dream come true, I now have psychiatrists who send me clients, consult with me, or study with me in my groups. In addition, people all over the world study my work.

The Non-Local Field

'Non-local' is a physics term that means that it's not bound by normal rules of space and time. The 'field' is a higher dimension – although it's atemporal, it informs itself through the third dimension of space and time, playing itself out and drafting people through their unconscious blind-spots to become its instrument.

We've dreamed-up the 'field' in an acausal, nonlinear way – but the 'field' is simultaneously dreaming *us* up to dream *it* up... so it's a circular process, but it's not 'out there', separate from us. We all experience the 'field' every moment of every day, 24/7. In addition to dreaming up the field, we are all being dreamed up by the field. We are all expressions of the level of consciousness, or lack thereof, in the field. If we continue to remain unconscious, our situation will continue to incarnate in a destructive way... the evidence is all around us. If we add consciousness to the dreamlike nature of our situation, however, we can creatively channel it in a *constructive* way, which is what an artist does.

There's a psycho-spiritual disease in the soul of humanity (in my book, I call this 'Malignant Egophrenia', or ME disease for short) that pervades the underlying 'field'. It's in any one of us in potential at any moment, so it's actually a 'field' phenomenon expressing itself throughout the whole field of consciousness. Potentially, each one of us can individually fall prey to it, to the extent that we 'fall asleep' and become 'absorbed' into and act out our unconscious. One of the main points of this is that it can't just be dealt with in a collective way; each individual has to deal with their own awareness by opening their heart, integrating their shadow, and responsibly working on healing their wound(s).

Any one of us doing that non-locally affects the entire universe, as we are all connected! When enough of us do this and connect with each other, we snap out of the illusion that we exist separately and recognize the existing state of affairs – that is, we're interconnected and interdependent. That's the expansion of consciousness. Then we can really get in-synch with each other and change the waking dream in a way that is more grace-filled and serves the whole, which is to say 'everyone'.

When you discover that we are not these isolated, discrete entities, but we're actually in a seamless way interconnected with the greater 'field' – whether it be the 'field' of our family system, our community, or collective species... whatever it is, you discover that we're all oracles for the 'field'.

My experience really taught me about the non-local 'field' of consciousness animating and informing everything in our world, both individually, within families, in the community, and in the greater body of politics. When you try to bring consciousness to this non-local 'field', the shadow aspects in the field, which are reflections of darker parts within ourselves actually have a resistance to being illumined. There's a deeper process that's unfolding – not just in the microcosm of any family, but also in the macrocosm of the greater human family, the collective body politic on this planet. It's like the reiteration of an inter-nested fractal which is manifesting in the different dimensions of our experience, both personally as well as collectively. When I tried to shed light on the abuse that my father was enacting, the whole 'field' – not just my mother and the rest of my family and friends, but *even the mental health system itself* configured to protect my Father. Then *I* was the one who became demonized, *I* was the one who got pathologized, and *I* became the identified patient. I never would have believed this had I not experienced it first hand myself.

If something is happening in the 'field' – for example, if you're part of a family system and there's an unconscious element present that the parents aren't dealing with, then the kids generally tend to get dreamed up and 'act out' that unconscious element. If you think of the family system as our community, our nation, our planet, or our universe – however much you want to enlarge the circle – what you discover is that we are always picking up unconscious unhealed or unresolved energies that are in the greater 'field'. The problem occurs when we personalize them or identify with those energies instead of just acknowledging we're actually instruments... that something's coming *through* us.

That's what makes somebody an artist or a shaman – that they're able to creatively express what's moving them, what's animating them, and give shape and form to it in a way that communicates it to other people... then consciousness has been added. That's the process of beginning to alchemically transmute the energy, so that it doesn't just act itself out unconsciously through the field.

The Shamanic Archetype

The shaman is a symbol of the primordial healer in all of us. The thing about the shamanic archetype is that it gets constellated by one's emotions being disturbed – and if our emotions aren't disturbed by what's playing out in the world right now, *then we truly are disturbed!*

The way I see it, we all suffer from a collective psychosis. We're a species in trauma, continually re-enacting this trauma on ourselves and others. Through enacting our trauma, something is being shown to us that could potentially expand our consciousness... it all depends if we actually have the recognition of what the revelation is, in what we're acting out unconsciously. When we get wounded, we can either become really screwed-up or the wound can be the catalyst for this deepening of our awareness. It's really like the classic quantum phenomena – whether light manifests as a wave or a particle depends how you observe it.

To become a shaman is not something that you decide to do – you don't become one by going to graduate school or taking a week of workshops. Traditionally, the shaman is 'called' by Spirit – but, on the other hand, I would challenge anyone who says we're not *all* potential shamans-in-training, because we are *all* being called by Spirit to connect deeply with ourselves. If someone rejects the 'call' of the deeper process and says, *"No, I don't wanna do that. It's uncomfortable. It's not what I want to do for my life"*, then they can become really sick, go crazy, or even die... but as soon as they assent to it, then they are in co-operation with Spirit and will be supported.

The way that calling typically happens is through deep suffering which, to the Western world, often looks like a nervous breakdown. Though a shamanic initiation looks like a nervous breakdown, it is an experience of a far different order, as the psyche is dis-integrating towards a higher integration, as if a new inner 'constitution' is being written. The shaman descends into the underworld, into the unconscious, which is the place of 'death, demons and madness', but it's all initiatory because the darker forces are just aspects of your hologram. We're full-spectrum holograms – we're light, dark, and all the colors in-between, and we have to integrate and own that.

The archetype of the wounded healer is that through our wounding we can potentially get our gifts, *but only if we go through it*... we can't avoid it.Having gone through that ordeal, that initiation, the shaman is then able to come back into the world with a gift for the tribe, community, and fellow beings. This is essentially what exactly happened to me. Like everyone, I am a work in process, continually deepening my healing and integration.

Awakening in the Dream

This world is like a dream, in that there's nothing objectively or independently existing separate from our own consciousness... the entire dream is just aspects of your being. What's playing out in the world is an actual reflection of the very process that's happening deep inside of us, and to have that recognition is to wake up in the dream. Because what is a dream but one's internal psyche just externalized? It's a reflective process.

What's playing out in the world is speaking in symbolic form, because the language of dreams is symbols. In symbolic form it's a reflection expressing this process going on deep inside of you. When you realize that, then all of a sudden your whole point of reference has changed – it's shifted and expanded. The boundaries between the inner and the outer, between the dream and the waking, between spirit and matter, and between 'Self' and 'Other' all dissolve. Spirit then takes the form of matter; spirit *materializes* and matter becomes *spiritualized*. The opposites merge.

The 'Self' and 'Other' boundary is really interesting because instead of me thinking I exist here in my skin-encapsulated-ego, separate from you 'out there'... yeah, on one level of reality, there's clearly a separation between you and me, but on a deeper, more fundamental dimension of our 'Selves', we're in relationship with the whole rest of the universe. You can't define me in isolation except by how I'm related to every part of the universe – *that's* the interconnectedness, the interdependence; that's the part of us that's transcendent to the separate Self.

What 'awakening in the dream' is all about is that we become instruments for Spirit. It's exactly what Christ was saying when he said, *"Ye are gods"*. It's exactly that. It's beyond the notion of past or future and, when you study this as a dream in the atemporal domain, what you recognize is and what I point out in my book is that we've already 'woken up'... *we've already become enlightened*. What's playing out in our third dimension of space-time, is the medium through which the realization that this has already happened outside of time becomes actualized. But the thing is, we need to recognize what's happening. That's why the highest, most advanced form of Buddhism, called 'Dzogchen', basically says, *'There's nothing to purify, there's nothing to transform, and you don't have to become enlightened; all you have to do is recognize that you can never be separate from your enlightened nature'*. Once you have that recognition, just don't get distracted, don't forget, and don't 'fall asleep'!

If I go to sleep tonight with an unhealed wound, I'm going to dream-up my unhealed wound in my dreams, for a dream is nothing other than a projection of my inner process. In just the same way, if I have an unhealed wound in my life, I'm going to connect-the-dots on the waking ink blot and dream up my unhealed wounds in the form of my life, in the form of relationship problems, etc. Almost everybody's doing it, unwittingly re-creating their wounds... thinking that the problems are 'out there'.

Whatever is manifesting in your life – first off, it's part of you that you're dreaming-up to manifest in that particular way. By recognizing and adding consciousness to the underlying, non-local 'field' (which animates and inspires what is happening in your life), you work with what arises in the field in a way that it becomes both transmuted and you help free-up the energies that are bound up in the compulsive recreating of the trauma.

If you're in that night dream and you have the recognition that you're dreaming, that's one thing. But if you're in that night dream, and if you have the recognition that you're dreaming *and* you connect with others who are in the dream who have also have attained lucidity, *then* you actually can put your lucidity together – you can begin to help each other to discover that this dream we're in is not even separate from our own consciousness. We're having a mass shared dream right now. It's manifesting in a problematic and in a limited way because that's the way we've been conditioned to dream it, based on fear and trauma and separation. When you bring people together who are having that insight, they discover that they can actually put their lucidity together in a way that can change the dream – when a group of people become lucid in the dream together and 'conspire to co-inspire' each other to greater heights of lucidity, that's what I call an 'in-phase dreaming circle'.

The whole of humankind – all six and a half billion of us – can become an in-phase dreaming circle when we have the recognition that not only are we not separate, but we're all on the same side. We can put our energy together to create a win-win situation for all of us. The energetic expression of that is compassion. People ask me, *"How can you wake up in a dream?"* One way is to cultivate compassion... it non-locally affects the whole universe and it will increase your lucidity. True compassion is itself the expression of lucidity.

The Madness of George W. Bush

George Bush was completely taken over by his unconscious. A pathological aspect of his psyche took him over, co-opting all of the healthy parts into its service. He was an incarnation, and therefore a revelation, of this particular pathological aspect of the unconscious. When someone is possessed by and identified with an archetype of the collective unconscious, they become inflated and a certain sense of a charisma comes through somebody who's so taken over – they can also entrance other people's unconsciousness. Carl Jung said that the greatest danger in our world right now, and the greatest danger to our species, is to have millions of people fall into their unconscious and fall into a collective psychosis.

Anything you are unconscious of has to approach you from outside yourself because you split off from it, you project it out, and it gets dreamed up in, as and through your life. When you study dreaming, you can see that that's the way dreaming works. People who are waiting for the return of the Messiah to come from *outside* of themselves... *that's* insanity. We're so disassociated and split off from our true selves that we then project it out as being some sort of alien, as being some sort of 'Other'. It's almost like the Self, which is so intimate to us, but we're not acquainted with it so it can only approach us from outside as a form of 'Other'. That's what's psychologically underlying the whole alien phenomena.

Encoded in the whole dynamic of collective psychosis is something being shown to us in the form of a revelation. Just like in trauma, the pathology of the trauma is the repetition compulsion – you're continually trying to heal from the trauma, but the nature of trauma is such that in the way you're trying to heal, you're actually creating the very trauma you're trying to heal from. When a group of people reinforce each others' unconscious madness (think of people who were supporting Bush), there's a self-reinforcing impenetrable field which gets conjured up around them, whereby not only is any sort of consciousness resisted, but also gets perversely turned around and pointed out as the demon, so it becomes like a self-perpetuating, negative feedback-loop that resists consciousness. So, in trauma, you're actually unwittingly creating the very thing that you're trying to heal from, and it's crazy-making. But also encoded in that dynamic of the repetition compulsion is it's own re-solution. It's like something is trying to complete itself, something is trying to heal and liberate itself. It's the same thing with collective psychosis – something is being shown to us that we desperately need to know to 'wake up', to expand our consciousness. If we don't recognize it, then we're going to continue to destroy ourselves. If enough of us recognize what's being revealed, we as a species can help each other to 'wake up'… That's the deeper dreaming process that animates what's playing out on the world's stage.

The source of what is 'playing out' on the world stage is the human psyche. The human psyche is the origin of the underlying dynamic that's really animating the shadow projection which is at the bottom of the havoc we are wreaking on the world and each other. Jung really tried to shed light on this darkness and called this shadow projection 'the lie'. He said, *"One doesn't become enlightened by imagining figures of light, but by making the darkness conscious."*

The unconscious is 'non-local' and when we see it being acted out in others it activates your own psyche and triggers a resonant unconscious energy in yourself... you can't stay 'neutral', detached, or passive. In the same way, when most people see the evil out there, it activates and inflames this resonant dark energy within *themselves*... whether it's righteousness or indignation, for example. If you can metabolize and integrate what gets triggered in you, then you're able to consciously relate to the darkness in the world in order to deal with that manifestation of the unconscious.

Because it all operates through the shared collective unconscious of the human psyche, if people aren't able to integrate what gets triggered in them by the unconsciousness in the collective 'field', this reinforces and supports and *feeds off and back into* the unconscious. This 'acts out' en-masse on a global scale to the extent that we are no longer individuated beings; we become part of the herd. Without dealing with what's been activated in ourselves, we then try to destroy the external 'threat'... like George Bush trying to rid the earth of 'evil-doers', which is an impossibility. Then he unwittingly becomes an instrument for the darkness to act itself out through him, which is just another form of insanity.

We're at a time in our history where the inner process that's happening deep inside the 'collective soul' of our species, is manifesting in, as, and through the external world. So, people who are just doing spiritual practice and are not engaging in the world – on the one hand, if people are genuinely called in that way, that's beautiful. But so many people that I know are doing spiritual practice as a way of being in avoidance or escaping fully participating in the world. I know a lot of spiritual practitioners who just want to say their prayers and mantras, believing that if they just get themselves in order, then the whole world will reflect that back. There's truth to that on one level, but they're absorbed in their own narcissism because they don't realize that their inner process is actually manifesting as the outer world. The most effective way to work on your inner process is to combine your inner work with being actively engaged and participating in life and be in the outer world. Paradoxically, the seemingly outer world is the medium by which we can all really transmute our inner processes.

Another big mistake that a lot of spiritual people make is that they split-off from and marginalize 'darkness', or 'evil'. They don't want to put their attention on it because that will feed it. That's true from one point of view, but avoiding the issue and not dealing with it will also feed it. It's very important to *acknowledge* it, and then you can simply choose not to give it your attention. It's like we're tracking a beast... we have to understand the nature of the beast we're dealing with.

In my work, I talk about the incredible importance of being a spiritually-informed political activist, which combines spiritual wisdom and political activism. The typical political activist can become very angry and project out their own shadow – for example, Bush or whoever it is becomes demonized, and then they're unwittingly doing the very thing that Bush is ultimately doing, which is projecting out their own darkness. When you project out the shadow and you then try to destroy the person who's carrying your shadow, you actually become consumed by the very shadow that you're projecting. *Well, who is Bush?* He's not separate from any of us – he's a reflective aspect of that part of us that's crazy and ignorant. We've all dreamed him up in embodied form to potentially have the recognition of that part of ourselves. You could even say that Bush is an incredible bodhisattva, because he's playing that role to help us to awaken.

Here in the U.S. and probably in the whole world, we've all been in trauma over Bush and that whole administration that, on one level, it's great that Barack Obama has mobilized and catalyzed all this hope for change. Obama is seemingly much more open-hearted, good-natured, bright, and articulate – his rhetoric is beautiful and he's saying all the right words, but talking the talk is very different from walking the walk. A lot of Obama's advisors are the same old ex-Clinton people, and there are no anti-war people in his cabinet. In addition, the economic advisors he has appointed are the very same people who created the economic meltdown in the first place. Also, he supported the 700 billion dollar bailout, which was one of the biggest criminal heists in history – he's supported the patriot two act, the FISA bill, and on and on. So there are many red flags with Obama.

The U.S. government has been taken over for quite a number of years – there's been a coup, both economically and politically. The powers-that-be that are animating the U.S. government are not serving the interests of the people, but are self-serving. In my opinion, one doesn't get into the office of the President of the United States without being in the pocket of the powers-that-be... of corporations. When you look at who are financing him, it's the same people who financed Bush and Cheney – Goldman Sachs, etc., so his hands are tied in the sense that the central banks are the ones who are really dictating events. A friend of mine, Catherine Austin Fitts, who is in the realm of finances talks about how Obama is the perfect person for the powers-that-be to consolidate their winnings.

But the *real* point is, *who is Barack Obama?* If this is a dream, he's not separate from any of us... so we have a *huge* responsibility for how do we dream him up.

The War on Consciousness

You could say there are military, political, or economic wars but, fundamentally, there's a war on consciousness being played out through the medium of the human psyche of the collective unconscious. The darkness being played out could never continue if enough people become awake. It all depends on us… if we have the recognition of what's being shown to us.

For the powers-that-be, their worst nightmare is for us to add consciousness to what's happening. When light floods into a situation, what's the manifestation of that? All of a sudden you begin to see the darkness. Anything that's not light becomes visible. The very fact that evil is 'coming out of the closet' and is becoming more and more visible – *that itself* is an expression that light is nearby.

The propaganda, particularly in the United States these days, is unbelievable. The darker powers are controlling and influencing the mainstream media so much, that they are able to 'manage perceptions', just like in Germany during World War II. A lot of good people supported Hitler – they actually thought that he was their leader who was helping them; but because they didn't see the pathology that Hitler was channeling, they non-locally became an instrument for the propagation of that evil through the 'field'. They became unwitting instruments in the greater 'non-local' field of consciousness that actually empowered the destructive quality of evil to play itself out. Even people who were reacting against him were supporting the evil in the field *just as much*, because reacting against the darkness as if it is something outside of themselves is feeding it.

When there's abuse being acted out in the 'family' system, the only way that the abuse can continue to be perpetrated is if people are complicit and enable the abuse – either by supporting it or being silent. If anybody sees what's going on and says, "No!", then the abuse can't continue to happen. Only the real spiritually-informed political activist is able to be of some benefit.

The 'Art-Happening' Called Global Awakening

Jung always uses the following example to explain the formation of symbols in the unconscious; it's like when you have a solution of water and you keep on adding grains of sugar and they keep dissolving until it reaches the saturation point and you add one more grain of sugar – then it crystallizes into a whole crystal. He explains that this is like the formation of a symbol in the unconscious – so any one of us 'waking up', or integrating our shadow, or self-reflecting, or opening our heart, could be the grain of sugar that catalyzes a whole awakening in our species.

Each and every one of us is a creative genius, both potentially and in actuality, but the problem for some of us is that we unknowingly use our intrinsic brilliance to imprison ourselves. We have incredible power to co-create reality moment-by-moment with each experience, but we become entranced by our own genius in a way that binds us and limits us. What is a dream but your own reflection? Whatever viewpoint we hold, the dream, being a reflection, will shape-shift and offer whatever seemingly objective evidence we need to confirm our solidified point of view in a way which entrances us. Because it's manifesting 'out there', we have all the evidence that we need to justify and confirm our fixated point of view that however the dream is manifesting is separate from us. It becomes a self-fulfilling prophecy. This is one of the underlying processes that keep us asleep. We have such incredible power and such influence on how we actually invoke our reality.

Thus we can change the world by changing our point of view. Then we can access in real-time, in the present moment, our genuine place of power, which is simply to wake up in the dream and to recognize the nature of our situation... that there's nothing 'out there' that's separate from your own consciousness.

When people who are having that realization come together and connect with each other, then they can put their lucidity together and change the world – completely and empirically...

that's not New Age 'woo-woo'.

It's clear that the solution to our world's crisis right now is an expansion of consciousness, which *has* to happen within the individual, but when we discover our interconnectedness then we realize that we can connect with each other in a way that activates our collective genius. That's why the last chapter of my book, *The Madness of George W. Bush: A Reflection of our Collective Psychosis*, is called 'Art-Happening Called Global Awakening' – because an artist is not just somebody who paints or draws... there are infinite mediums we can use to express our inner experience. That's profoundly important because we are creative beings, yet so many of us in our 'sick' culture are disconnected from creativity. We are *all* dreamers and artists whose canvas is this universe. We can create this 'Living Art-Happening' where more and more of us will 'wake up' and put our lucidity together to change the dream – and that's true evolution. That's what this whole thing is about. As an artist, that's what I'm trying to bring into the world.

THE DIONYSIAN ARTIST – LIFE AS ART
Or Living the Life of the Imagination
by Jerry Ravel

Art teaches nothing – except the significance of life.
~ Henry Miller

*I am convinced that however black the picture may be, a drastic
change is not only possible but inevitable.*
~ Henry Miller

**Jerry Ravel is a film-maker and lives atop a cliff in South West
Wales.**

No matter how dark times have seemed on this earth there have
always been creators who have declared themselves *on the side of
life* - the genuine artists, mystics, poets, rebels and iconoclasts
who have attained a supreme, positive, and noble vision of life,
and who have attempted to communicate that vision to us in

their philosophies, writings, and works of art. In relatively recent times we have had the likes of William Blake, Rimbaud, Nietzsche, DH Lawrence and Henry Miller, to name but a few.

Even as the human world seems to be robbed of its meaning and value, and we are plunged into a nihilistic nightmare, the few creative, visionary types have sprung up and, in defiance of the times, have sung their songs of affirmation and joy. This is testimony of course to the authentic human spirit - to the holy spirit of life itself. And nothing, it seems, can thwart it, destroy it, or keep it down. Life requires its highest expression, and it is through the genuine artists and mystics that this is attained.

I suppose that the visionary, life-affirming types are - to those who wish to keep humanity locked in the ego-based, false, materialistic world – the most dangerous. They are dangerous because they recognize no authority other than their own inner conscience, their own will. They are not fooled by the lie of civilization. They have afforded humanity a glimpse of a totally different approach to, and understanding of life - one that has nothing to do with politics, greed, material wealth, orthodox religion, or power over others; a glimpse of something other than the mundane reality, the negative reality, necessary to those who need to control humanity in order to maintain their relative and parasitical form of 'power'. These men of spirit and integrity have pointed the way to something else altogether – to freedom and fulfillment: to Life.

The visionary artists have all had a prophetic strain running through their work, and have intimated, in their own way, what Dylan Thomas once referred to as the *electric promise of the future.* The visionary artists have been beacons in the darkness, lighting the way to a new world, a new reality, an a-historical high dimension of magic, wonder and incredible poetic beauty. And perhaps, as some people seem to be suggesting, this is what the transition we are undergoing is really about: a movement from a reactive mode of life – really a mode of death – to a creative one.

We can certainly hope so.

There is, of course, a growing awareness now, among those who are awakening, of the creative nature of consciousness, of the unity of inner and outer, of the correspondence between the psyche and the 'external' world, and of the dream-like nature of reality. Even certain scientists have had to acknowledge that consciousness affects the outer world, that all things are interconnected. The mystics, the poets, the shamans – they've always known it, of course. 'The world,' as Henry Miller put it, 'is the mirror of the state of your soul.' And I think that the German poet, Novalis, once wrote that the world is the symbolic picture of the spirit.

*

The overriding theme that I've focused on for the past twenty years or so is the vital relationship between art and life, the creative essence of life. An understanding which began in the early nineties - a period of illumination and self-discovery, when the doors of my perception were cleansed and I saw the world aright. Prior to that I had worked for ten years in dead-end, sometimes hellish jobs. My years at school were pretty awful too, especially the last three. I rebelled and left without a single qualification, and I never wanted to see a book again – if that's all books had to offer. My 'teachers' did a pretty good job. That was my purgatory, I guess: school and work.

But after years of feeling lost in an alien world, I broke free and began to find myself, as they say. I moved to London for a year in '89 and browsed in bookshops for the first time, and I found myself attracted to books with titles like *The Rebel, The Outsider, The Trial.* I watched continental films at late-night cinemas and went to the theatre occasionally. I walked out of one job, because after being reprimanded for something rather trivial, the boss had said that I didn't come to work for me, but to make him rich – little gnome of a guy who wore special elevator shoes to make him appear taller!

I then spent a month in the garden of the house I was sharing and read the complete works of Oscar Wilde, and some Kafka and Camus – this, I found, was infinitely preferable to working. I returned to the Midlands, locked myself away in my attic bedroom, and read. This was the beginning of a wonderfully enlightening, intellectual and imaginative journey for me. I found books that expressed a sense of life, a love of life. I became a member of a film workshop in Birmingham and took a course in 16mm film production. One night a guy approached me and asked me if I could write. I said, "Yes," even though I had no idea whether I could or not. He had an idea for a short film – well, not so much an idea but three characters and a diary, which wasn't much to go on. He wanted to direct. Could I write something for him? I acquired an old typewriter and started work on the script. It was a quite a painful process, learning to write.

The script was about a writer writing a script, and the basic idea was that you didn't quite know where the writer's real life ended and where his imaginative life began. As the story progressed things became increasingly mixed up. Characters were killed in one scene and alive in the next. We had no budget to speak of, but big production values. We had a murder scene in a five-star hotel, and another murder scene on the Severn-Valley (steam) Railway – we managed to get a carriage for a whole day for a hundred quid. We had a hard-boiled private investigator from the 1940's turning up in present-day England, and the writer was a heavy drinker whose wife was having an affair with his agent. (Or was that something to do with the writer's previous incarnation?) It was full of clichés and very tongue-in-cheek. The film didn't turn out all that brilliant, on account of some of the direction and some of the acting, but we were all beginners, and the making of it was a very special and magical time, and I learned a lot. It was wonderful to be doing something independent and creative, after ten years of mind-numbing, meaningless work.

While writing that script, and making that film, I began to instinctively grasp the connection between imagination and life.

After a trip to New York in 1991, I decided that I would quit work forever, return to London, and study philosophy. My first essay was on Plato – and the question was: *Does Plato have good reasons for regarding the Forms as the true objects of knowledge?* I wrote a competent academic essay. But I instinctively felt there was something wrong with this idea of a transcendent realm of Forms, of immutable, eternal Ideas – Plato had placed all the *value* beyond the world. The highest form is the *Form of the Good* and like the other Forms, can only be apprehended by the intellect. The world of our perception is but a world (a 'cave' in Plato's metaphor) of mere reflections and shadows, a shadowy reflection of the 'true' world. I wrote, I suppose, a semi-poetic conclusion: As long as we dream of something higher than this world, something higher than ourselves, we will continue to do ourselves an injustice. We should leave the cave of metaphysical illusions and enter into the world and begin to live. It is seeing for the first time, and in a sense for the last time. You realize that one day all the world's lights will be suddenly shut off forever, and for that they shine even more brightly, even more intensely. You thereby discover the highest of all values – it is simply Life itself.

I hadn't got to Nietzsche at that stage, but the lecturer had commented: *"I like the Nietzschean conclusion."* I could see that in Plato there was a negation of life – even if at the time I couldn't articulate it in those terms. And Plato, really, is the beginning of Western philosophy, the values and ideals on which our false culture and civilization have been built, and is the philosophical counterpart to Christianity – as Nietzsche wrote: '*Christianity is Platonism for the people*'. He also wrote that '*Anyone who not only understands the word "Dionysian" but understands himself in the word "Dionysian" has no need for a refutation of Plato, or Christianity, or Schopenhauer, he can smell the decay…'* I guess I had a good nose for these things.

When I began to study Nietzsche later the same year, I found for the first time, a philosophical standpoint that really made sense to me and helped me to elucidate what I'd begun to understand instinctively. Through Nietzsche, I began to clarify that we have had a metaphysic, a metaphysical world-view, that has negated life by setting up a transcendent realm, a beyond. This world in comparison to the 'true world' is, at best, a poor copy and art an even poorer copy of a copy. With Christianity, the same thing applies - we have a transcendent God, who alone is perfect and unblemished and Good, together with the idea of a heaven hereafter. Life itself is nothing more than a state of purgatory, poised between heaven and hell, and has no intrinsic value. And we, mere mortals, are tainted with original sin. We are guilty from birth; sex is but a filthy abomination, and over everything hangs the threat of eternal damnation – if we don't abide by the 'thou shalt nots', if we don't have 'faith' enough, and if we don't ask for forgiveness once or twice a week, we will surely burn in the fires of hell after we die. Nice, eh? You can see how this whole metaphysic and 'morality' has deeply wounded the human psyche, and has prevented us from living naturally, in harmony with the cosmos, and from attaining our true divine Selfhood.

Nietzsche was a supreme psychologist and he divined that Christian morality was founded in resentment, envy, malice, what he called *ressentiment.* He saw very well that Christianity was a condemnation of life, born of a hatred of life, a decadent religion. He saw that the Greeks in their heyday had revered and honored life, had celebrated the mystery of life, and that the decadence had begun with Socrates and Plato - who represent the birth of the 'theoretical man'. It's what DH Lawrence called *mental-spirituality,* the pale ghost-like intellectualism of the West. The mind deified, divorced from the body and the senses, rationality over the instincts – 'Rationality is...a force that undermines life'.

Nietzsche is perhaps the most misunderstood and misinterpreted of all the philosophers. The academics, not surprisingly, never seem to 'get' him. His philosophy is fundamentally a counter to the problem of Western nihilism. When he said that *'God is dead'*, he meant that He – God – had died in the hearts of his contemporaries. 19th century atheistic, materialist science had overcome Christianity. Both, however, were versions of what Nietzsche referred to as the 'will to truth' - *'Will to truth is the impotence of the will to create'* - and in a sense science, atheism, is the inevitable successor to Christianity. The value placed on truth by Christianity and philosophy had finally forbidden the 'lie involved in the belief in God'. Thus with the belief in a transcendent realm denied by scientific 'truth', we are left with nihilism pure and simple. Now that no one is sitting on God's throne, so to speak, life is simply bereft of any value or meaning.

To counter nihilism, he posited a formula for the affirmation of life. What he called – in honor of the Greek god of ecstasy and intoxication - the *Dionysian formula* - which he said is the highest formula of affirmation attainable. It means affirming life, this life for all eternity – to say Yes to the *eternal recurrence* of this earthly life, even with all the personal pain and suffering. *'...how well disposed,'* he asks in *Beyond Good and Evil*, *'would you have to become to yourself and to life to **crave nothing more fervently** than this ultimate eternal confirmation and seal?'*

In *Thus Spoke Zarathustra*, Nietzsche provides a clue to the state of consciousness that experiences and desires eternity:

O man! Attend!
What does deep midnight's voice contend?
'I slept my sleep,
'And now awake at dreaming's end:
'The world is deep,

'And deeper than day can comprehend.
'Deep is its woe,
'Joy—deeper than heart's agony:
'Woe says: Fade! Go!
'But all joy wants eternity,
'Wants deep, deep, deep eternity!'

The affirmation of life is not, therefore, an intellectual decision arrived at through a process of reasoning – but comes via a *profound* and ultimately *joyous, ecstatic* experience. The same thing, pretty much, was also stated in the *Upanishads*, in the *Chandogya Upanishad*:

> *Where there is creation there is progress. Where there is no creation there is no progress: know the nature of creation.*
> *Where there is joy there is creation. Where there is no joy there is no creation: know the nature of joy.*
> *Where there is the infinite there is joy. There is no joy in the finite.*

The above sums up Nietzsche's position very succinctly. Note the connection between creation, joy and the infinite. Nietzsche essentially was an artist, a visionary artist. In his first book, *The Birth of Tragedy*, he stated that *'Art is the true metaphysical task of mankind'*. And: *'The world is eternally justified as an aesthetic phenomenon'*. Art for Nietzsche – and this is something that Henry Miller reiterated – is not the goal, is not an end in itself, but *the means to life*. Miller said that if art doesn't lead to realization, it defeats itself. It is through creation, by means of heightened activity, that the connection to eternity, to life, to *reality*, is established. As Miller said: *'This is the great discovery'*. It is one road to the infinite, to an a-historical, a-temporal vision of the eternal in the here and now – to a state of pure lucid awakened *being*. In this state of heightened awareness, the artist lives purely in the moment, outside time, beyond culture and civilization.

After I finished my philosophy course, I got deep into Henry Miller, and it wasn't long before I became aware of the parallels between him and Nietzsche. Miller's 'autobiographical romances', the *Tropics*, and the *Rosy Crucifixion* trilogy, chart his journey of self-liberation and self-realization by means of his writing. In a way, Miller is Nietzsche's philosophy lived out. And whereas some of the lives of Miller's predecessors (Rimbaud, Nietzsche, Lawrence) ended tragically, Miller 'made it', went through to the end. After a definitive spiritual experience in Greece, and upon his return to America, he said that he attained a state of grace – this is while the Second World War was kicking off, by the way – and that he had to be careful what he wished for, for no sooner had he wished for it than it was granted him. He finally settled in Big Sur, on the coast, and had a little writing shed perched on the edge of a high cliff. Miller proved, I think, that no matter how bad times get, it is still possible to live joyously, to live life on your own terms. As Miller said in *The Wisdom of the Heart*:

> Strange as it may seem today to say, the aim of life is to live, and to live means to be aware, joyously, drunkenly, serenely, divinely aware. In this state of god-like awareness one sings; in this realm the world exists as poem. No why or wherefore, no direction, no goal, no striving, no evolving. Like the enigmatic Chinaman one is rapt by the ever-changing spectacle of passing phenomena. This is the sublime, the a-moral state of the artist, he who lives only in the moment, the visionary moment of utter, far-seeing lucidity. Such, clear, icy sanity that it seems like madness. By the force and power of the artist's vision the static, synthetic whole which is called the world is destroyed. The artist gives back to us a vital, singing universe, alive in all its parts.

Miller died at the age of 88, and in some of the photos of him in his later years you can see the light and joy shining through his eyes. When he was in his eighties, he wrote: *'The accomplished artist is one who sees a masterpiece with every turn of the head'.*

Essentially, the creative process pertains to the self, or rather to the Self, to *growth*, to the expansion of the self, which is what Nietzsche ultimately means by 'will to power' (i.e., nothing to do with political 'power'). Miller likened the self to an onion and said the process of self-realization is a matter of peeling off the layers. The first time you peel off a layer it's extremely painful; the second time still painful, but a little less so, and so on, and so on, until finally, he says, *'there is only the darkness yielding before the light'.*

Through art, through creation, then, the self is expanded, and that expansion is mirrored in the external world. That dimension of the visionary moment is, in a sense, the realm of *art* – 'the world exists as poem'. The world becomes perfect, as a mirror of your own perfection. Both Miller and DH Lawrence suggested that a time will come when art in the cultural, museum sense of the word won't be needed. Life itself will be lived on that higher plane, *as art*. The truly great writer, Miller said in this regard, doesn't want to write, he wants the world to be the place where he can live the life of the imagination. And in his deeply insightful book, *The World of Lawrence*, he writes:

> In this remarkable and poignant exposition of Cézanne's failings, Lawrence states most eloquently and penetratingly the problem of his own life and work. **It is the problem of creating a new world wherein art itself will no longer be necessary, wherein men will not need to live vicariously through the artist, but each man, as he says, would create that world of art which is the living man, and each man would achieve that piece of supreme art, his own life.** [My emphasis]

Only then, when each human being becomes the artist of their own life, will they be living according to their true humanness – through the divine imagination.

I am re-reading a little Miller again for the first time in a few years and, viewing it from the context of the strange and unprecedented times we're living in, I am struck by how often he alludes to the demise of Western civilization, to a period of transition, to the dying of the old world and the birth of the new. The new world being one where we are completely alive, that is, truly human. It is because the majority of human beings are not fully alive that wars are possible. Any man or any woman who has come to themselves, to consciousness, who is awake, fully alive, would find it impossible to intentionally kill or harm another human being. There's a natural, spontaneous 'morality' that comes with the state of wakefulness – you don't need rules or laws to tell you that killing is wrong. You understand, from the standpoint of aliveness, the sanctity of life. Violence in our world, and this is something John Lash points out in his book, *Not in His Image*, is partly due to the nihilism of the monotheistic religions. Miller himself had the good sense not to get involved in the war – and a man of his caliber never could get involved in anything as ignominious as a war, it goes without saying. So in the world of the true human, which Miller represents, of course – wars would cease altogether.

This was Miller's vision, and the vision of other prophetic writers like him, some of whom he writes about in his essays – that inevitably a change has to come, that the new world, 'the kingdom of MAN', somewhere along the line, is assured. Even now, given what's transpiring on the planet at the moment, we can still think that that world is a long way off. But then again, with all the talk about a 'dimensional' or 'vibrational' shift, the fact that people are waking up like never before, who knows? Who knows what we're coming to, and what the 'end of history' really means for us?

It can be seen, in relation to the unfolding 'dark agenda', that many people are coming to a lucid comprehension of their innate humanness. For perhaps the first time in our long woeful history, people are beginning to imagine a world based on compassion and co-operation, instead of division and competition, on abundance instead of scarcity and lack. People are writing about a post-money world and are able to imagine what that would mean for us. If everything begins in imagination then this is really an encouraging sign, isn't it?

Can we dare to imagine a world where all men and women are indeed the artists of their own lives, conscious of their own sovereignty and creative power? A world where no man abuses or exploits another? We can, of course. This will come when we move from a world that is governed by the ego and is based on 'having' – to a world based on *being*. The answer to the problems we face on the planet lie, essentially, with our consciousness. If we can begin to understand that life is an end in itself, that it is its own reward, that it doesn't need any form of idealism to justify it or explain it, that we need no political ideologies to make it work right, if we can get back to an understanding of the inherent value and meaning of life, and put ourselves back in intuitive relationship with the creative cosmos – then you're looking at a different world, a new world, that is most definitely not a 'new world order'. But a human and a humane world as it should be, and as I believe with Miller, one day – it will be.

A man like Miller, who has realized himself, that is to say, realized his divinity, and has lived on that higher plane of reality has an unshakeable faith in the meaning, the goodness, the simplicity, nobility and holiness of life. For an artist like Miller the essence of life is 'eternal play and creation'. And I can imagine nothing more glorious, nothing more wondrous than that. To honor the divine mystery of life, in the eternal present moment, is everything – is heaven on earth. Let that be our goal. Let that be our destiny. As Miller said, *'We are living on the edge of the miraculous'*...

3

DANGEROUS SCIENCE

DANGEROUS SCIENCE

When a true genius appears in this world, you may know him by this sign; that the dunces are all in confederacy against him.
~ **Jonathan Swift, author of** *Gulliver's Travels* **(1667 - 1745)**

The most exciting phrase to hear in science, the one that heralds new discoveries, is not Eureka! (I found it!) but rather, "hmm.... that's funny...."
~ **Isaac Asimov**

There are many ways to perceive the world or the solution to any problem; not all of these are necessarily 'scientific'. It is a peculiar characteristic of those who are fond of proof and data to become blind to anything that contradicts their cherished statistics. To remain open to the possibility of anything other than the evidence that it and other esteemed respected peer-brains in their field have gathered becomes impossibility. Sadly, this beautiful mind then becomes unable to do the exploring that it was so enthusiastic and passionate about doing in the first place. At worst, it considers itself, with its intellectual capacity of genius, to be superior to its 'uneducated' peers.

A scientific mind is expansive and exploring, with an exceptional ability to find out how things work, 'figure it all out', and then put it into a logical context that it can further understand and develop. This mind, with its complicated equations, mathematical formulae, calculations, facts, graphs and charts, functions in a very specialized way that, unless balanced, can become vainly obsessed with its own rationale. This logical part of the mind wants unquestionable proof of everything and will dismiss anything that it can't. But scientists weren't always like that... they used to call themselves 'natural philosophers' until the word 'scientist' was first coined in the 19th century by William Whewell – an English polymath, scientist, Anglican priest, philosopher, theologian, and historian of science.

Those were the days when scientists often studied the ancient occult discipline of alchemy, which was both a philosophy *and* a practice. It is generally accepted that the basics of modern chemistry derive from alchemy. I would like to propose that alchemy is the basis of *all* science as we know it today. It seems to me that what has happened is that there was a schism within alchemy, whereby the practical and the philosophical divided. It is natural that any observant and curious mind would want to study both science *and* spirituality, yet the fine dividing line between the two has grown from a splinter to a wedge over the centuries. Thus they have become polar opposites; the dogma existing within both science and religion equal in measure. Today, most 'respectable' scientists won't touch anything remotely esoteric with a bargepole. Likewise, many a vicar would balk at the idea of tea and muffins with Richard Dorkins.

The word 'science' comes from the Latin *scientia*, from *scire*, which means 'know'. The Oxford English Dictionary defines science as, *'the intellectual and practical activity encompassing the systematic study of the structure and behavior of the physical and natural world through observation and experiment.'* Interestingly, the word 'experience' derives from 'experiment' – the root of both words being *experiri*: 'to try and/or test'. By definition, then, knowledge is something that is gained from observation and experience.

In order to fully experience anything there is a need to be daring – to step courageously, and sometimes foolishly, into the unknown. The true scientist is not someone in a starched white coat with clipboard in hand – true scientists are mavericks and dangerous pioneers, adventurers and explorers; pushing boundaries to the limit and experimenting (experiencing) life, willing to try anything, and willing to observe... with an open mind.

Incredibly, such individuals seem to be either missing from or marginalized in history books and science lessons – take Nikola Tesla, 'the forgotten father of technology', for example. Of course, we're all taught about Tesla at school, aren't we? No? *Why not?!* He was perhaps the greatest inventor the world has ever known. He introduced the world to the basics of robotics, computers, missile science, satellites, microwaves, remote control, solar power and invented mains electricity (the alternating current), the electron microscope, and fluorescent lighting. In 1896, Tesla lit 200 lights *without using wires* over a distance of 26 miles, using his massive Tesla Coil. He also made the world's largest water-powered generator by using the Niagara Falls to power a whole town. Tesla worked with radio-frequency electromagnetic waves and it was he – *not* Marconi, who invented the radio in 1892. How could it be that such a genius was totally unacknowledged in his lifetime, and would spend his final days feeding pigeons in his hotel room? He once said that *"One day, man will connect his apparatus to the very wheel work of the universe... and the very forces that motivate the planets in their orbits and cause them to rotate will operate his own machinery."*

Wilhelm Reich, who discovered a physical biological energy in all living matter that he called 'orgone', met a similarly tragic fate (minus the pigeons). Alan Caldwell writes of him in his article, '*Dr. Wilhelm Reich: Scientific Genius – or Medical Madman?*';

'*During his life, Reich was portrayed as a mad psychiatrist and scientist who advocated free love, abortion, communism, and a multitude of other so-called perversions. The medical establishment regarded him as quack who tried to dupe the public into believing he had a cure for cancer. Eventually the U.S. government took legal action to suppress Reich's research, and the closing years of his life were filled with tragedy. Persecuted and hounded by the government, he was finally sacrificed on the altar of science.*

Perhaps it is time to take another look at Reich's discoveries and his dream to harness orgone energy for planetary healing. Rather than automatically placing Reich in the trash bin of medical science, he might eventually prove to be the most inventive and far-sighted physician-scientist of the twentieth century.'

Reich's discovery of orgone was, essentially, the alchemical principle of *'hieros gamos'* (or transmutation through sacred union) of spirit and matter, science and magic. We see this today within quantum physics – its observations of reality transcend space, time, and other constants to realize that the spiritual and the material worlds are not separate after all.

Science has returned full spiral, to a deeper understanding of how mysterious and magical life truly is.

A KINSHIP WITH LIFE
Cleve Backster

To those who wonder why I feel such confidence, as one person who has experienced the indifference of many scientists to this field, I can simply state that such high resistance to new ideas does not concern me. I have a truly wonderful ally: Mother Nature.

~ Cleve Backster

In addition to having been an observer of human psychophysiology tracings since 1948, starting in 1966 and continuing to date, Cleve Backster has conducted extensive research related to observed electrical responses in plant life and at a cellular level in other living organisms. His research into what has been called "The Backster Effect" has attracted world wide attention. His work was featured in the bestselling book, *The Secret Life of Plants*, by Tompkins and Bird, and another book *The Secret Life of Your Cells*, by Robert Stone. Mr. Backster has completed his own book on his biocommunication research called *Primary Perception – Biocommunication with Plants, Living*

Foods, and Human Cells. **This work includes detailed descriptions and charts of his 36 years of discoveries including nonlocal instantaneous communication between human cells in vitro and the donor. For a DVD of Cleve Backster's lecture given at Foundation for Mind Being Research and to order his book, see www.primaryperception.com**

Like any young man, I experimented with what was in my environment. As a kid, I helped the beavers build a dam and made a swimming hole. Many times I overcame my fear of heights by lighting fire to my pants and diving off of the high dive, with the focus that the fire would be put out before I got burned. It was an early version of establishing psychological set. You can't be afraid of heights if your pants are on fire. I was also into hypnosis back in high school, before there were many books on the subject. I used to hypnotize my friends and give them post hypnotic suggestions. It worked from day one...

I was raised in a religious household with my father who was the superintendent of a Sunday School for thirty years. I attended this Sunday School and church for fourteen years as a Presbyterian, without missing. Then, to do a comparison test because I was already thinking scientifically and away from the home environment, I allowed fourteen years to pass without going to Sunday School; I didn't notice any particular difference, so then I forgot about the whole thing.

My interest in hypnosis in the earlier years made me think that religion may be autosuggestion. If someone thinks someone is praying for them and lets them know it, it's pretty good stuff. I didn't criticize people who were into that sort of thing, but I wasn't buying it. I was what you'd call an agnostic who never took the trouble to be an atheist.

In the early 70's I visited Findhorn where they were growing huge vegetables in sandy soil, would talk to the bees, and it was considered normal to communicate with Nature. In the book,

Kinship with All Life by J. Allen Boone, he describes vividly his interaction with a famous dog, Rin Tin Tin, and with flies and all kinds of animals. Ancient Hinduism embraces this. I was invited to a meeting where I was the only person there who was not a Swami. We were discussing 'polygraph' and one of them said to me, *"You mean 'folly-graph', don't you?"* Those people were very aware of the importance of my research. Luther Burbank, J.C. Bose, and George W. Carver were also very tuned-in. Every one of them has contributed a great deal to humanity through listening to plants.

I had looked to science for a reality check in regard to such things as prayer and meditation, which is the very heart of spirituality and found no reality check there. Also, with plants, there was nothing in the known electromagnetic spectrum that could account for these phenomena, and so by inference they did not exist. After calling all these scientists in during the initial observations, I found that things were occurring that could not be explained by them. Even though they couldn't place it in the body of knowledge, I had to call it something; and Primary Perception was born. Observing plants and cells was only the beginning – I coined this term to describe a very fundamental communication that appears not only to occur with plants, but at the cellular level in animal life, including humans. I define it as: 'The vehicle of communication – the invisible, unrecognized 'field' that interconnects all species and life forms, whereby biocommunication can occur'. Primary Perception is distinct from extra sensory perception (ESP) in that it occurs *before* the human specialized senses of taste, touch, hearing, sight and smell, plus the psychic senses. It is likely going on all the time.

I was almost in shock by the idea that this unseen communication could be happening all the time. As everything that is used for good can also be used in the opposite direction, I could see how implanted ideas could easily compete with our normal sense of truth. It wasn't just the power of suggestion like a lot of people said, *"Well, you got to know they're doing it to you."* Well, I don't think you do.

Scientific Perception

My scientific research as related to the more conventional use of polygraph instrumentation dates back to 1948 and includes thorough familiarity with the 'scientific method'. It should be understood that I do not mistake my insatiable curiosity and an abundance of high quality observations as 'scientific proof'.

The only reason I used the polygraph was because it was handy. I only used the GSR (Galvanic Skin Response) portion, where a low current of electricity is sent through a pair of electrodes, and the instrument records decrease or increase in the electrical resistance of whatever is attached. In the pathway of resistance of, say, from one human finger to another, you have a source that involves millions of cells that are each capable of discharge, of leakage from their internal function, in the microvolt range. It adds to the electrical signal you are putting through, and you think you may have a drop in resistance, but you are actually picking up electricity on the way. With the GSR, there is a set amount of electricity and you look to see how much comes back, and you see how much resistance there was in the pathway. A decrease in resistance would be an upward swing of the pen, the way the polygraph is wired. That upward swing is supposed to be an indication of emotional surge due to the secretion of perspiration. Actually, I think it is caused by millions of cells discharging and the leakage of the electricity in the microvolt range that combines with the set electrical signal. It's a completely alternative explanation that would tie into the idea that these cells are producing the surges. It may have little or nothing to do with the autonomic nervous system. There may be an alternative communication system.

Over a period of years with hundreds of observations, I could see that my thoughts as the experimenter were being picked up by the plants that I studied. This was not 'a discovery' in as much as merely using my common sense. Once I saw that this kind of communication existed, I was then tied into the experiment rather than being 'the impartial scientist'.

I got an award from the U. S. Psychotronic Association for service in the field on July 20, 1991 – the same year that Marcel Vogel, who did a lot of work with crystals, got an award for service post humus. He was the first person with any kind of credentials that supported my work. He started out to disprove my research and then with a course he was teaching, found that there was merit. In Prague, at the Psychotronic Association, I was chairman of a section; he was my co-chairman. He felt he could actually influence the development of crystals with his mind. He also used leaves separated from the plant and, with his mind, supposedly caused them to live or die.

I have never been into torturing plants, but you can attach electrodes to a detached leaf and often the reactions correlate with what the plant is going through. But again, whatever you plan or expect is going to happen with these things, you may actually prevent them from happening. On February 2, 1966, my thought of burning that plant was with the full intention of doing it. It responded accordingly. I got the point right then and there. I didn't need to go ahead and burn it.

When we are monitoring plants, yogurt or cells, and the session is interrupted by a phone call, suddenly everything is spontaneous – the person on the phone has no planned inter-action. When you are structured; planning what you want to say in order to sound intelligent, then you are already communi-cating ahead of time. If you have pre-established opinions, etc. you are killing the spontaneity. When two people are debating one another and one of them thinks of a point to make that will 'one-up' the other, that's when we see a huge reaction. In the follow-up, when they actually speak the words they earlier thought, there is not much reaction at all. This is based on hundreds of hours of observation.

Over a long period, I noticed that communication is apparently released by the imagery prior to the speech – at the very moment you have that 'spark' of a thought, something that is later communicated or acted upon. Primary perception is the vehicle that responds to those moments. I was once interviewed by David Frost, the British television presenter. He was trying to be funny and he kept bugging me by asking how I could tell if a plant was a boy plant or a girl plant. When he mentioned lifting up the leaf to look, well, the one attached to the polygraph went wild! It was very amusing.

This is not easy to prove scientifically as spontaneous events cannot be planned, making repeatability of any experiment impossible. If I could, I'd expedite the development of the in-progress portable device. It's a combination of a camcorder and a reaction meter that when coordinated, would record the reactions of plants or cells and provide a replay. Once you have that, you really have something. You could record spontaneous events without having to pay too much attention to instrumentation.

With an accumulation of independent, high-quality observations to date, I feel strongly that negative thinking is directly in contact with millions of cells in the body, bypassing the nervous system. We should certainly be very mindful of the quality of our thoughts. I once gave a lecture, and the negative thinking was so heavy, that we went through three light bulbs for the slide projector, one after the other blinking out, until they finally got one that hung in there long enough so I could show my slides. I have no idea if somebody was trying to sabotage it psychically or if it was old bulbs. I joked about it, and said, *"Boy, you people must not want to hear what I have to say!"* Most of the university invitations I had were very positive, but I remember that one.

Those indoctrinated with western religions and science would have problems accepting my research. They side-step it and focus on all these rules of science. It's the so-called 'science with proof' that draws people away from even trying to see what is there. A great example was an event that happened when I was lecturing in 1973, at the University of Michigan. They were doing some research with flat worms there, and had obtained a big bucket of them from the slaughter house where they'd been extracted from the stomach of cows. The worms have a very simple nervous system yet seem to be able to do all kinds of interesting things. They had some hooked up to a meter with some electrodes, and they'd try different stimuli. They had a tape recorder showing the signal and an oscilloscope that showed there was something happening. On the other side of the lab, I noticed a beaker full of these worms under the counter. Without saying anything to them, I picked it up and shook it. They got a huge reaction on the tracing from the worm in the test tube, so they were looking all over for something that had caused it. They assumed there had to be loose wires or an electrical short, or some physical cause. When I showed them what I'd done, they simply could not accept it, since there was no physical connection between the tested worm and the worms in the beaker I found. They were looking to see if they could pass information along via the food from some trained worms to another generation, assuming it was through the olfactory system, taste buds, chemical messengers, etc. I tried to tell them the information was all passed along directly. But when people are so caught up in 'being a scientist', they often screw-up their perception of things they ordinarily would be very impressed by.

As individuals, mainstream scientists will often say very interesting things to me like, *"You've changed my whole life!"*, but as a collective group, they act like protectors of the faith. They won't go out on a limb because it could affect their grant requests that have to go by review committees made of up of established, conventional scientists.

When some of my work was included in the popular scientific

Nova television series, the episode called 'The Green Machine', we demonstrated biocommunication with some friendly bacteria in yogurt. We had two samples of yogurt, and would feed some nutrient to one sample. The other electroded sample, which was not being fed, would show excitation as if it were saying, *"Where's mine?"* A biology professor, Dr. Charles Brandt, who was a professor at San Diego State, actually demonstrated this interaction on camera during two separate occasions. He talked to the bacteria in the yogurt and said, *"Okay, you guys, I'm going to give you something nice to eat! You hungry?"* and the electroded one reacted with enthusiasm. When they filmed the show, they made me leave the room because they thought I would use psychokenesis on the yogurt to make the pens move. I was told afterwards that he had done this twice on film, which is really great coverage. All the cameras were right there, recording his communication with the bacteria, correlating perfectly with the feeding. When the footage went over to England for the editing, I think that was just a little too far-out for them. So much really good information is kept from the public. Whether it was getting the professors and the kooks mixed up, I don't know... the idea was *I'm* the far-out one, and *they* are supposed to be the academic body of knowledge!

Primary Perception

I never postulated that plants have emotions... only that they responded, faintly or not. Jagadis Chandra Bose demonstrated emotionality in trees and plants a long time ago, in the early 1900's. The Easterners were way ahead of us. He talked about emotionality in plants, especially the event of death, and used very sensitive equipment which he invented. With his 'cresco-scope', he used a beam of light hitting a mirror and the tremor of the plant would move this mirror and magnify the tremor. Bose treated trees like human patients undergoing surgery; one account reports that he put a tent over a tree and used chloroform before moving it, and then revived it after it was transplanted. It seemed to suffer less stress. Bose was into the emotionality of plants, and found ways to show their happiness, or unhappiness. He didn't get into the remote communication idea, but he did show that plants seem to reflect what is going on in their immediate environment.

On one occasion, a Canadian botanist, a lady, came to my office. I'd tried out my equipment before she arrived and I was getting a nice, fluid reaction from each of the plants on hand. But when she came in, every leaf attached to the electrodes just showed me a real flat, wandering pattern, which I've learned is the plant equivalent to going into shock or fainting. I asked her if she did anything to hurt the plants she worked with, and she replied, "*Hurt them? My dear, I roast them to get their dry weight!*" Each of them recovered a while after she left, then showing me a strong reaction capability.

Time and time again, plants have shown an affinity to sexuality. In *The Golden Bough* by Frazier, there are many myths about the ancient rituals where they use sexual activity at a certain time of the year and it is said to excite the trees, the orchards, and the crops, and make the yield better. I believe that was the source of rituals associated with crops, sexuality, and the earth. When I moved to San Diego, my first lab location was adjacent to an apartment complex with only a few feet between the two buildings. As I conducted most of my research late at night, I was curious about certain huge reactions on my long-term plant recordings. I later connected the timing of these reactions as just preceding the exiting of military service-aged men from an apartment next door, rumored to have some 'evening business girls' as tenants.

When I saw that plants seemed to react to emotional surges, I was motivated to re-think what is causing physiological reactions in humans. The traditional psycho-physiologist tends to credit these changes to the sympathetic portion of the autonomic nervous system. This theory is often referred to as the 'fight-or-flight' syndrome, based upon the body's reaction to threats to its well-being. I am not seeing that. In fact, there is just the opposite of 'fight-or-flight'; with typical reaction patterns during a polygraph examination, the rate of breathing often slows down or becomes more shallow. There is often an inconvenient short-term rise in blood pressure. Many times the heart rate briefly slows and exhibits less amplitude. All these things are the opposite of what you should see with the 'fight-or-flight' concept.

Before I obtained the electroencephalogram (EEG) equipment, I was trying to figure out how to test animals with the GSR. The problem was to get them to hold still long enough in order to attach any kind of electrode. I used to have a Doberman Pincher named Pete in my office. He could trigger plant reactions by interacting with humans. Pete was pretty good at sitting upon command, so I put the GSR contact electrodes that would ordinarily go on the fingers of humans, one on each side of his mouth, between the cheek and the gums. As soon as I said to him, *"Where's the kitty-kitty?"* the GSR tracing went right off the scale!

If we are to learn from J. Allen Boone's work with his dog, Strongheart, we have to accept there is a lot more going on in these so-called 'lower' forms of animal life in many respects. A friend of Boone's from the desert said, *"If you want facts about a dog, always get them straight from the dog, and if you want opinions, get them from the humans."* That's what he did. He 'interviewed' the dog over a long period of time. One of the big secrets that Boone learned is that you don't talk down to animal life just because it happens to be at a different place in the hierarchy; you talk *across* to it. If you learn to talk across to anything, up to and including ants and insects, termites and flies, and anything else, you can influence them with expectations. If you expect them to do nasty or irritating things – like landing on your nose or food

– they do. If you stop expecting that behavior, they'll stop doing it.

While I was in my office reading *Kinship With All Life*, I couldn't put it down. This rarely happens to me. When I got to reading about Freddie the Fly, I had never noticed whether we had flies or not in the office, but a fly came into the scene. I started to try the little things that he was talking about. I couldn't get the fly to land on my finger, but he did land on my hand. I put sugar and water down so he could eat from that. I was getting into a trial mind link, like thinking to him, *"Don't worry about it. I'm not going to hurt you."* The fly was in and around the area, would stand there and wash his wings off, looking at me unafraid. I finally got tired and stayed in the lab's back area, got up the next morning, and when I came out, my secretary said, *"A fly came in here and landed on this desk, right here."* I asked, *"What did you do?"* She said, *"I squashed it, of course!"* I felt badly for the fly, but I didn't know how to reprimand her for it.

Plants can easily receive messages from us, but we don't have that ease, although I've had some people visit who were fairly psychic who felt that they could. If someone senses the plants' alarm, they are likely sensing a radical change. There was a man, a chiropractor I believe, named Periakis, who would diagnose patients by having people sit next to a plant and watch the aura of the plant. He could see when he was touching on subjects that would be important in working out their problems. Once the word got out that he was doing this, he'd always deny it, because he was bombarded with so many enquiries and doubts. This is something to pursue with more research.

Mother Nature is way ahead of human perception. The thought/intent is perceived immediately, while the conscious mind and human speech is lagging behind and is basically ignored. I worked with Ingo Swann back in New York. The light from the sun takes 11 minutes to hit the earth. When sun spots kick up, they create a lot of disruption in our communications.

He was able to tell the researchers at Stanford Research Institute when it was happening in the sun, and about 11 minutes later, they would hit here. That's so important, and yet people make believe it doesn't exist.

My work has tuned me into the Gaia principle; which is to get back into attunement with planet Earth, and to stop doing all the screwed-up things we do to damage her. This principle is built on biocommunication, from the atoms and cells to the manifest components of earth, who communicate with each other in order to self-regulate. You develop a 'green thumb' when you accept that you are in touch with a living thing, and that it is in touch with you. We must continue to observe and pay attention.

'NEW-EDGE' BIOLOGY: A View From Outside the Box
by Bruce H. Lipton, PhD

*We are living in exciting times, for science is in the process of
shattering old myths and rewriting a fundamental belief of human
civilization. The belief that we are frail, biochemical machines
controlled by genes is giving way to an understanding that we are
powerful creators of our lives and the world in which we live.*

~ Bruce H. Lipton, PhD

Bruce H. Lipton, Ph.D. is a cellular biologist and former
Associate Professor at the University of Wisconsin's School of
Medicine in the U.S. His pioneering research on cloned stem
cells at Wisconsin presaged the revolutionary field of epigenetics – the new science of how environment and perception
control genes. His later research at Stanford University's School
of Medicine revealed the nature of the biochemical pathways

that bridge the mind-body duality.

Bruce is the bestselling author of *The Biology of Belief: Unleashing the Power of Consciousness, Matter and Miracles* and co-author, with Steve Bhaerman, of *Spontaneous Evolution: Our Positive Future (and a way to get there from here).*

For more information, visit: www.brucelipton.com

When I was very young and people offered me spiritual advice, even at that youthful age I recognized that most of those people's lives in no way matched the advice they were providing. In seeking truth I could rely on, my young mind sought science as a trustworthy source – since a truth in science on this side of the world was the same truth on the other side of the world, regardless of one's religious preference. So I gravitated to science and was subsequently programmed with the belief that living organisms are biological robots controlled by genes... that 'life' was all about physical mechanisms and chemistry.

In graduate school in 1968, I began culturing and studying the lives of individual stem cells. In my research, I would isolate a single stem cell and put it in a tissue culture dish. The cell would divide and, subsequently, its two daughter cells would divide and form four cells. This process of mitosis occurred over and over again until there were thousands of cells in the culture dish. What was unique about these cultures was that all the cells in the dish were derived from the same progenitor cell – in other words, all the cells were genetically identical. I split up the population and inoculated the cells into three new culture dishes. In each dish I fed the cells with a slightly different growth medium, changing some of the chemical constituents. For cells in culture, the growth medium represents the cells' environment.

In one dish the cells formed muscle, in the second dish the cells became bone and in the third dish the cells differentiated into fat cells. The primal question: *"What controls the fate of the* cells?" The answer: *"The environment controls the fate of cells".* Since all cells were genetically identical at the start of the experiment, the only thing that was different among the culture dishes was the cells' environment. These findings were a total contradiction to the scientific story I had learned and was, at that time, teaching medical students... the belief that genes controlled life!

*

Outside of the body and in my cell cultures, human cells live independently like free-living amoebas. Single cells are intelligent organisms and most cells have every functional system that is found in a human body. For example, cells have digestive, respiratory, nervous, reproductive, musculoskeletal, excretory and even immune systems. Cells are functionally equivalent to miniature human bodies and they are intelligent and capable of surviving on their own.

When the population of cells in the culture dish reaches a certain density, cells inherently strive to form harmonious communities. The cells spontaneously form cooperative colonies that inevitably create complex tissue structures. When living in isolation, every cell interprets and responds to environmental conditions by using its own innate intelligence. However, when cells assemble into community they no longer behave as independent citizens. In community, cells defer from initiating behaviors based on their personal environmental perceptions and rely upon the collective awareness of the group to guide their lives. In functioning as a coherent community, cells acknowledge and respond to the group's collective wisdom, which I refer to as the organism's 'central voice'. The perceptions and judgments of the central voice control the behavior and genetic expression of cells in the communal organism.

The insights offered by my cultured cells radically transformed my awareness on the nature of life. My research led me far outside the box of conventional science and into a 'new-edge' science, based on fractal geometry, quantum physics and the new science of *epigenetics*, sciences that deal with invisible energy forces, information fields and the power of the mind in controlling life.

As emphasized in my book, *Spontaneous Evolution: Our Positive Future (and a way to get there from here)* co-authored with Steve Bhaerman, I had come to realize that humans are the equivalent of 'cells' in an evolving larger super-organism, humanity. However, the evolving 'body' of humanity is currently suffering from an autoimmune (self-destructive) disease in which its communal cells are attacking one another. Civilization's current misperceived beliefs about who we are and why we are here are so toxic that they're destroying the human 'cells' that comprise humanity. Interestingly, most human illness today also represent variations of autoimmune disease and are an apparent physiologic reverberation of the dysfunctional patterns currently influencing civilization. A healing opportunity is upon us and it is dependent on civilization coming to the realization that every human 'cell' is as important to humanity's survival as is every cell in our own body.

While unicellular organisms (such as the amoeba) live as independent 'agents', cells in multicellular organisms, from worms to humans, cooperate in community as interdependent agents. By definition, participants in a community agree to work together toward a shared vision. A community functions when each individual betters their own life by contributing to the betterment of the community, the standard practice of systems that live by the credo: 'One for all, and all for one'. When community members stop cooperating, the community begins to dysfunction and eventually breaks down. The new science reveals that health and coherence of an organism or organization is dependent upon the communal wisdom that provides the system's central voice.

In Search of the Central Voice

With a scientific understanding of the nature of the central voice and its mechanism, we would be endowed with the ability to control our own biology and health. In an effort to understand how living organisms work, conventional biologists disassemble plants, animals and their cells to study their molecular components in quest of the central voice. Employing the philosophical principle of reductionism (which is taking something apart and studying the pieces to see how it works), the insights offered by biomedical science led to the creation of the medical model – a belief that humans are biochemical machines controlled by genes.

It was found that cells and bodies are primarily constructed from a family of over *150,000* complex protein molecule building blocks. Proteins create the physical body and provide for its behavior. Like parts in any machine, protein molecules break down over time and have to be replaced. In an amazing intellectual breakthrough, scientists found that segments of DNA molecules, called genes, were the equivalent of blueprint patterns used to manufacture the body's complex protein molecules.

Since proteins provide the character or traits of an organism, and genes are required to synthesize these proteins, DNA genes were assumed to be the molecules that 'control' the character of life. The primacy of genes in the unfoldment of life is based upon one of science's most fundamental and cherished principles, The *Central Dogma*. As defined by Francis Crick, co-discoverer with James Watson of the genetic code, *The Central Dogma* describes the flow of information in biological systems: DNA > RNA > Protein.

Accordingly, genetic DNA blueprints that encode the structure of the proteins determine the traits of the organism and are therefore considered as the source of life. The protein patterns encoded in the DNA are translated into RNA molecules. The short-lived RNA versions of DNA genes represent the actual molecular templates used in assembling proteins. Proteins, the final product derived from the DNA, collectively form our bodies and provide for our behavior.

The prevailing medical model, based on this dogma, emphasizes that the character and quality of human life is derived from DNA programs comprising our genome. Our strengths, such as artistic or intellectual abilities, and our weaknesses, such as cardiovascular disease, cancer or depression, represent traits that are presumably preprogramed in genes. Thus we tend to perceive life's attributes and deficits, as well as our health and our frailties, as merely a reflection of heredity DNA blueprints.

Since, as far as we know, we did not pick our genes, and since we cannot change our genes, the belief that genes 'control' our lives implies that we are 'victims' of heredity. This philosophy of biological victimhood fosters the idea that both dis-ease and disease represent an inherent inability on the part the body to heal itself, and that remediation relies upon outside sources, such as medical intervention and the administration of drugs.

Interestingly, the word dogma means: *a belief based upon religious reasoning rather than scientific fact.* Astonishingly, as a foundational pillar of modern science, *The Central Dogma* is, officially, a religious belief – for it is a hypothesis that was assumed to be so correct it was never experimentally evaluated. My own stem cell studies presaged a radically new understanding that is now emerging at the frontiers of cell science... *genes do not control biology!* The new hereditary science that emphasizes how environmental information controls gene activity is known as epigenetics.

While research scientists are working with the new science of epigentics, the outdated belief that genes 'control' life is still emphasized in current biology courses, textbooks and mass media. 'New-edge' science completely undermines the beliefs enshrined in the Central Dogma and removes a foundational pillar from biological science. When the newly formulated concepts of science are integrated into mass consciousness, they will profoundly change the course of human civilization, for we will come to learn, that rather than being victims, we are actually masters of our lives.

The most recent evidence that challenged the role of genes in controlling life came from the results of the Human Genome Program. According to the conventional medical model, a human would need to have in excess of a 150,000 genes to provide for its physical body and behavior. However, the results of the project revealed that the human genome (the library of genes needed to make a human being) contained only 23,000 genes. The missing genes are stark evidence that the medical model's assessment that genes control life is totally flawed.

In fact, research from almost a century ago, long before the relevance of DNA was even understood, revealed that genes did not 'control' biology. In those early days of cell research, many experimenters enucleated cells (a process of removing a cell's nucleus, the cytoplasmic organelle that contains the DNA genome). For many organisms, enucleated egg cells can divide and form a blastula – an embryological stage consisting of forty or more cells. The resulting embryonic cells possess neither nuclei nor genes. These enucleated, gene-less cells can survive for two or more months while maintaining strict regulation over their life processes. Enucleated cells travel through their world seeking food, digesting it, and excreting wastes, while simultaneously breathing, avoiding toxins and socializing with other cells – all without the necessity of having genes. If enucleated cells possess no genes, then *what* 'controls' their behavior?

Remember those proteins, the molecular building blocks comprising the body's cells? Well, proteins express a unique behavior – they can change their shape. The protein's shape-shifting ability is the secret to life! The significance is that in changing its shape, a protein moves... in so doing, it expresses behavior. Cells harness the forces of moving protein molecules to generate the behavioral functions that characterize living systems. The complexity of life is derived from the orchestrated activity of the body's protein movements, which collectively provide for respiration, digestion, muscle contraction and the many other functions needed by living organisms.

However, proteins only change shape in response to specific activating signals from the environment, which in this usage, means the whole Universe. Protein behavior-eliciting signals range from the physical signals, such as chemicals and drugs, to invisible, non-material energy signals, such as electromagnetic vibrational frequencies. The important conclusion is that the behavior of a cell, as represented by the collective activity of its proteins, is a reflection of, and directly connected to, activating environmental signals.

The public has been lead astray by an invalid scientific assumption – the belief that genes control life by turning themselves 'on and off'. The truth is that genes are simply molecular blueprints and, as such, have as much conscious awareness as an architect's printed blueprints... they cannot 'activate' themselves. Scientifically, they are not self-emergent, meaning they cannot self-actualize. So the profound question becomes, *"How are genes controlled?"*

As biologists found over a century ago, a cell's hereditary information is stored in structures called chromosomes. A chromosome is a strand of DNA, a sequence of genes encased in a sleeve of protein molecules. In order to read the gene's blueprint, the DNA strand must be freed from its protein sleeve and the genes exposed. To reveal a gene, the regulatory proteins comprising the chromosome's sleeve must change their shape and detach from the DNA. What causes a protein to change shape? Environmental signals! So what ultimately 'controls' gene activity? The environmental signals that alter the shape of the chromosome's proteins!

These findings reveal that environment signals perceived by the cell are responsible for controlling behavior (as represented by their influence on the movement of proteins) and regulating gene activity (by their controlling the shape of chromosomal proteins). As the cell 'sees' its world, its perceptions activate both behavior and gene activity. The brain is the organ whose function is to receive and respond to environmental perceptions. Obviously, the gene-containing nucleus is not the brain of the cell, since enucleated cells survive for months with out nuclei or genes.

My research revealed that the brain of the cell is the cell membrane, the equivalent of the cell's skin. The outer and inner surfaces of the cell's membrane are lined with antenna-bearing receptor protein molecules. Cell receptors are molecules that are functionally comparable to our eyes, ears, nose, taste, and touch organs – receptors on the surface of our skin that monitor environmental signals and provide cells with an awareness of their world. Specific environmental signals cause 'complementary' membrane receptor proteins to change their shape. The protein's movement in response to an environmental signal acts as a switch that engages the cell's systems to make an appropriate response to environmental stimuli. As a cell moves through its environment, signals in the environment influence and shape the cell's behavior and genetic activity.

Source of Self

In pursuing the philosophy of reductionism, scientists took cells apart down to the last biochemical pieces and discovered that the difference between individual human beings was determined by a set of protein receptor antennas built into the membrane surface of our cells. A sub-population of these identifying receptors, called appropriately enough, self-receptors, play an important role in medicine. Though every human shares identical cell types and a common anatomy, each human is a distinct individual defined by their particular set of self-receptors. These personal identity receptors are the reason why the immune system of the recipient will reject tissue and organ transplants from other people, whose cells possess their own unique combination of self-receptors. In understanding the nature of self-receptor activity, my attention was diverted from the protein's physical mechanism as a receiver, to investigating the signals that activate those protein receptors.

Quantum physics reveals that these receptor proteins respond to invisible moving energy forces that comprise what is called 'the field'. Unfortunately, conventional biology does not acknowledge these energy fields, since it is a discipline based on Newtonian physics – a science that emphasizes only the material physical realm. Medical science still perceives of the body as a mechanical device and ignores the role of the energy and invisible forces that quantum physicists now recognize as the primary factor in shaping the physical universe. Operating from a Newtonian perspective, medical science is 80 or more years out of date!

The self-receptor proteins act as antennas that 'read' specific information from the environment. While the notion of 'self' is associated with the *physical* receptor, what is more important is the signal that activates these receptors. Self-receptor signals actually represent information 'broadcast' by the environment.

The physicist's definition of the invisible moving forces that impact living organisms is the same definition that is used to define the concept of Spirit. An interesting thought to ponder is, *"If a cell dies and the self-receptor antennas degenerate at death, does that mean that the broadcast signal formerly received by these receptors stops?"* Consider the analogy of a TV set receiving a broadcast show through its antenna. If one is watching a TV show and the picture tube breaks, we say the TV is 'dead'. If the TV is dead, did the broadcast die too? To find the answer to that question, one would get a new TV, plug it in, turn it on and then 'tune' it to the station… violá, the show is still there!

I realized that my personal identity is represented by an information 'broadcast' derived from the environment, a signal I receive through my unique set of membrane self-receptor proteins. This insight suggests that if I physically die, my identity is still an energy broadcast in the field. If in the future, an embryo shows up with the same set of self-receptor antennas that I now possess, my 'show' will be back on the air but playing through a new body. The significant point is that our true identity is the broadcast, not the 'television'.

Lamarck vs. Darwin

Conventional neo-Darwinian theory (the modern molecular version of Darwin's theory) suggests that humans gradually evolved through millions of years of random mutations of their genes, the DNA blueprints that 'control' life. Two consequences derived from these Darwinian notions are, 1) There's no purpose to humanity – we evolved by accident; and 2) The theory emphasizes we're 'victims' of our heredity.

Jean Baptiste de Lamarck, who published the first scientific research on evolution 50 years before Darwin, offered a greatly different story on the origin of species. Lamarck's primal hypothesis was that the biosphere is one living community – every organism is part of the family of life and every organism is contributing to the survival of every other organism in the biosphere. He believed that an organism's biology and heredity were influenced by its communication and interaction with the environment. He recognized that organisms and the environment simultaneously evolve with each impacting the development of the other.

The Darwinian world of the 'survival of the fittest' horror that we live in – a life based on a struggle for existence, the proverbial dog-eat-dog world – is in total contrast to the world described by Lamarck. He recognized that the process of evolution is not based on competition, but is driven by communal cooperation.

Taken together, these two Lamarckian insights mean that

evolution was not an accident. Organisms, including humans, got here because they fulfill a role in maintaining balance and harmony in their environment. All species, including humans, evolve as cooperative complements of their environment. Considering that human behavior is now destroying the environment that provided for our origins, we are in the process of setting the stage for our own extinction.

Over the centuries, both science and religion have provided the same erroneous conclusion that human origins were not connected with the biosphere or natural environment. Judeo-Christian belief offers that God added humans to the planetary mix pretty much as an 'afterthought', following His heroic effort in the creating the Earth and the Heavens. Evolutionary biologists suggest that humans arose simply as a consequence of the random shake of genetic 'dice' and are therefore here 'by accident'. Both the religious and scientific beliefs concerning origins disconnect human civilization from Nature.

In 1809, Lamarck wrote that the biggest problem humanity would face is that it will become disconnected from Nature... and that's exactly what has happened. The biosphere is a complex community and exists because of the harmony of its species. When an organism in a community causes an imbalance that disturbs that harmony, Nature eliminates the disruptive element. And guess what? Nature is responding to the presence of disharmonizing 'detached' human beings as being the equivalent of infective viruses and germs that are destroying the biosphere. Nature is now confronting civilization with a wake-up challenge – either humanity learns to live in harmony with Nature, or she will assure that we'll become extinct.

Human behavior may not have caused global climate change and the other crises that threaten our survival, but we are certainly responsible for aggravating those problems. For example, by decimating the forests we are destroying the planet's respiratory system – Nature's mechanism that filters, cleans, and purifies the air we depend upon for our existence. With all of our accumulated intelligence, we have been unaware of some fundamental insights necessary for our survival. This is especially true in regard to the recent science that reveals that human evolution was not driven by genetic accidents... we evolved as an integral and supportive component of the matrix of life, the biosphere. As Native Americans have informed us for generations, *"We are here to tend the Garden."*

Mind Over Matter

In cell communities consisting of small numbers of cells, each cell is able to effectively read and respond to environmental signals. However, in larger communities, cells in the middle of the crowd are unable to efficiently communicate with the prevailing external environment, so their behavior may not be in harmony with what is going on in their world. This problem was resolved by creating a higher order of communal organization. Instead of each cell carrying out all of its own survival-requiring tasks, cells in larger cell communities became more efficient by expressing specialized functions.

Through the process of differentiation, specialized cell types such as skin cells, heart cells, bone cells, muscle cells and nerve cells, among 250 other cell types evolved from common progenitor (ancestor) cells. Each cell type contributes a specialized service supporting the survival of the community. For example, the nerve cells, which are incidentally, derived from an organism's skin, evolved to read and interpret environmental signals and then organize and coordinate the activities of the internalized cells so as to support life-sustaining responses.

Humans are born with a genetically preprogrammed set of life-sustaining perceptions, instincts, already installed in the nervous system. Instincts are perceptual behavioral programs provided by nature through the genome. From mid-gestation onward, developing human brains are wired for 'learning' – the creation of new perceptions from environmental experiences. 'Learned' perceptions are collectively attributed to the influence of nurture.

As you are undoubtedly aware, not all learned perceptions are necessarily accurate. Many perceptions we hold about the world are incorrect. Consider for example, the perception that genes 'control' biology. As we now know, this notion is a misperception. The point being that learned perceptions may either be correct or incorrect. Consequently, acquired 'perceptions' may accurately be referred to as beliefs, since we only assume that what we 'learn' is truth. Since perceptions control behavior and gene activity, then it is logical to conclude that in humans, beliefs control biology.

A Strong Case for Driver Education

The new perspectives on human biology conflicts with conventional thinking by acknowledging that our beliefs, rather than our genes, control life – Oh, ye of little belief! Since we can change our beliefs, humans are endowed with the ability to change their behavior and gene activity. Rather than being victims of heredity, we are primarily victims of our misperceived beliefs.

We should keep in mind that there are, indeed, individuals whose health is negatively impacted at birth by faulty genes and chemistry. When diseases affect these individuals, we can attribute them to pre-existing genetic and biochemical defects. These genetically-impaired individuals represent less than 5 percent of the population. This means that 95 percent of humans possess an adequate genome that should provide them with a healthy, happy and productive life.

Conventional medical doctors still adhere to the medical model, which envisions human disease to be derived from a fundamental frailty of the body's physical-chemical mechanisms. Complementary and energy medicine practitioners operate with the belief that the body is endowed with an innate recuperative power that allows it to heal itself without the use of drugs or surgery. Consequently, complementary medicine focuses on the role of environmental energy fields, rather than the genes, as the influential factor that controls life. The effectiveness of complementary healing modalities is that they support, and do not interfere with, the body's own innate healing abilities.

The new insights into how perceptions control biology is fundamental for all healing, for it recognizes that when we change our perceptions (beliefs) we send totally different messages to our cells enabling them to effectively reprogram their expression. When a mind has a thought or perception, that mental vision is 'broadcast' to all of the body's cellular residents. It is as if our cells are all tuned-in to see the TV news of the day. Our eyes are the camera, our thoughts the voice of the anchorman. Our cells are concerned with what we see because they depend on our perception for their lives. Our joys are their joys... our fears are their fears.

In regard to controlling the behavior and fate of the cellular population, the mind's central voice is the equivalent of a dictator. Based on our developmental experiences, our mind can be a benevolent dictator or through negative programming, become a rash, ruthless tyrant that can actually destroy the body's community. In general, the allegiance of our cells is so committed to the central voice that they will die if they are told to do so.

However, the system communication is not a one-way broadcast. When we experience emotions and symptoms, these represent communications forwarded from the cell population to the awareness center of the mind. A 'benevolent' central voice is attentive to such communications and will try work with the cells to ease their burden. In contrast, when a tyrannical central voice overrides the cells' innate intelligence in responding to the world, its actions will undermine the health and happiness of the body's cellular citizens.

When the mind perceives that the environment is safe and supportive, cells are preoccupied with growth and maintenance of the body, keeping us in a state of health. Perception of survival-threatening situations causes cells to forgo normal growth functions and adopt defensive, protection postures. The body possesses two fundamental protection systems. The adrenal system mobilizes the musculoskeletal system, specifically the arms and legs, for 'fight or flight' defenses against external environmental threats. In contrast, the immune system is designed to protect the body from internal environmental threats posed by viruses, bacteria, toxins, parasites and cancerous cells.

Bodily energy reserves during a protection response are distributed to *either* the immune *or* adrenal systems, based upon the source of the perceived threats. If there is a perceived threat in the external environment, the body's energy flow is directed to the arms and legs – the first line of defense. Think of it this way... if you have a bacterial infection and are also being chased by a saber-toothed tiger, how would you proportion the distribution of your system's energy? Personally, I would give it ALL to the adrenal system and get the hell out of there! Servicing the growth and immune systems would be irrelevant if you're eaten. Physicians take advantage of this adrenal system's suppression of the immune system by injecting stress hormones into patients who receive tissue or organ transplants. The stress hormones suppress the immune system and prevent rejection of the foreign graft.

While our biology readily accommodates brief (acute) bouts of stress, prolonged or chronic stress is debilitating. The energy demands of prolonged protection response interfere with required body maintenance, leading to dysfunction and disease. It is particularly relevant when perceived threats are from the external world – the higher levels of stress hormones not only shunt growth, they deactivate the immune system functions, opening the door for infectious diseases and cancer.

The perceptions of life we hold in our minds control our growth and protection behaviors. The mind resembles the driver of a vehicle. With good driving skills, a vehicle can be maintained and provide good performance throughout its life. Bad driving skills generate most of the wrecks that litter the roadside or fill our junkyards. Employing good 'driving skills' in managing our behaviors and in dealing with our emotions and perceived stresses should offer a healthy, happy and productive life. In contrast, inappropriate behaviors and dysfunctional emotional management, like a bad driver, stresses cellular 'vehicles' and interferes with performance and provokes a breakdown.

Are you a good driver or a bad driver? Before you answer that question, realize that there are two separate minds contributing to the body's controlling central voice. The *(self-)* conscious mind is the 'thinking' you... it is creative, expresses free will, and is the source of your desires, wishes and aspirations. Its supporting partner is the subconscious mind – a database of programmed reflexes and learned perceptions. Though some of its programs are derived from genetics *(instincts, nature)*, the vast majority are acquired through our developmental learning experiences *(nurture)*. In our conscious creative mind we may consider ourselves as good drivers... however, self-sabotaging or limiting behavioral programs in our subconscious may unnoticeably undermine our efforts.

The subconscious mind is *not* a seat of reasoning or creative consciousness; it is primarily a stimulus-response device. It has no sentient entity in it. When an environmental signal is perceived, the subconscious mind reflexively activates a previously programed behavioral response... no thinking required. The subconscious mind represents a programmable autopilot that can navigate the vehicle without the observation or awareness of the conscious mind. When the conscious mind is dreaming into the future, reviewing the past or solving problems, behavior is controlled by previously recorded programs in the subconscious mind.

The dual-mind system's effectiveness is defined by the quality of perceptual programs stored in the subconscious. Essentially, the person who taught you to drive molds your driving skills. For example, if you were taught to drive with one foot on the gas and the other on the brake, no matter how many vehicles you own, each will inevitably express premature brake failure because of faulty driver education. Diseases that run in families, once thought to be due to genetics, are now found to be 'learned' pathologies, passed from parent to child.

If our subconscious mind is programed with inappropriate behavioral responses to life's experiences, then our sub-optimum 'driving skills' will contribute to a life of crash and burn experiences. Cardiovascular disease, the leading cause of death, is directly attributable to stress-induced mismanagement of bodily functions. During our first six years of life, the subconscious mind is programed with fundamental perceptions or beliefs that we acquire from observing the behaviors and attitudes of parents, siblings, peers and teachers. Did your early developmental experiences provide you with good models of behavior to use in the unfoldment of your own life?

The insidious part of the autopilot mechanism is that subconscious behaviors are programed to engage without the control of, or observation by, the conscious self. Since 95 percent of our behaviors are under the control of the subconscious mind, we rarely observe them or much less know that they are even engaged. While your conscious mind perceives you are a good driver, the unconscious mind, which has its hands on the wheel most of the time, may be driving you down the road to ruin.

As we become more conscious, and rely less on subconscious automated programs, we become the masters of our fates rather than the 'victims' of our programs. Conscious awareness can actively transform the character of our lives into ones filled with love, health and prosperity by its ability to rewrite limiting perceptions (beliefs) and self-sabotaging subconscious behaviors.

Sitting at the Feet of Our Elders

The new science reveals that organisms shape their genome and species evolve as a direct consequence of their interactions with their environment. Recognizing the importance of the environment in evolution and in genetics leads us to a completely different understanding of the origins and purpose of life. Our existence is not a random accident, but a carefully choreographed event that takes into account the balance of the biosphere. We are ignoring our in-built stewardship of that biosphere by 'going it alone', and recklessly and radically changing our environment.

Our hubris threatens our survival as surely as the heroes in Greek tragedies were undone by their arrogance. We were evolutionarily designed to complement our environment, not to 'lord over' it. Radically changing the environment risks creating a future where we will no longer 'fit'. Instead of complementing our environment we may completely undo its complex balance, causing it to collapse.

Leading edge scientific research returns us to our aboriginal roots, which stressed the belief that humans are one with Nature. Aboriginal people recognize and honor the "spirits" of the air, the water, the rocks, the plants and animals, and most importantly, the spiritual nature of themselves. Fortunately, many of the lost traditions of our forefathers are still available in the few remaining aboriginals that inhabit our planet. Native Americans, African tribes, South American Indians and Australian Aborigines still hold the secrets of how to live in harmony with the planet.

The lessons of the new science, teach us that we have the power to change ourselves, and our planet, using the power of our minds. Of course, we can't just snap our fingers or read a book to effect change... we have to undo the self-defeating and planet-disturbing programing our parents (and their parents before them) inculcated into our subconscious minds. Let us tear down the false walls our programs built between one another and the environment in which we live! Our fate is inextricably tied up with the fate of our global neighbors and all the species in this world. Newly emerging science will enable us to change our beliefs so that we can join with other like-minded evolutionaries to save our world from destruction and return us to the Garden that has always been here.

AIDS: A DOCTOR'S NOTE ON THE MAN-MADE THEORY
by Alan Cantwell, M.D.

Alan Cantwell is a dermatologist and scientific researcher in the field of cancer and AIDS microbiology. For more than 40 years Dr. Cantwell has been a cancer researcher who believes that cancer is caused by bacteria, not viruses. For the past two decades his research also points to AIDS as a man-made disease. There is probably no other physician on the planet whose cancer and AIDS publications are as controversial.

He is a graduate of New York Medical College, and studied dermatology at the Long Beach Veterans' Administration Hospital in Long Beach, California. He was a member of the Dermatology Department at the Southern California Permanente Medical Group in Hollywood from 1965 until his retirement in 1994. He lives in Hollywood, California, with his partner of 31 years and their five cats.

In 1984 (the year HIV was identified) his best-selling book *AIDS: The Mystery and the Solution* was published, showing the presence of cancer-associated bacteria in this disease. And in 1990, *The Cancer Microbe: The Hidden Killer in Cancer, AIDS, and Other Immune Diseases*, was published documenting a century of vitally important and suppressed research into the bacterial cause of cancer. His most recently published book is entitled *Four Women Against Cancer*. His other two books, exclusively on the subject of man-made AIDS, are *AIDS & The Doctors of Death*: An Inquiry Into the Origin of the AIDS Epidemic; and *Queer Blood: The Secret AIDS Genocide Plot*. His book *Queer Blood* won the Benjamin Franklin Book Award for literary excellence in 1994.

All these titles are available from Aries Rising Press, PO Box 29532, Los Angeles, CA 90029, USA. Website: www.aries-risingpress.com

Science, as we know it, has become increasingly 'dark', as scientists continue to discover all sorts of new ways to kill mass numbers of people and other living things with chemical, biological, and nuclear warfare.

When AIDS officially began in 1981 the public was told that anal sex, drugs, and homosexuality were at the root of the new 'gay plague'. The first cases were all young, predominantly white, and previously healthy homosexual men from Manhattan who were dying mysteriously from 'gay pneumonia' and 'gay cancer' in the form of Kaposi's sarcoma. The association with homosexuality was so remarkable that the disease was initially termed GRID ('gay-related immune deficiency'). To this day, gays are still blamed for the spread of AIDS into the U.S. population.

When the disease first broke out, a new virus was suspected, but officials reassured the general public there was nothing to worry about. Of course, the health experts were wrong. Today, most of the world's AIDS cases are heterosexuals. The AIDS virus (HIV) can be transmitted vaginally and one does not need to be a drug abuser, a promiscuous person or a homosexual to contract AIDS.

The Green Monkey Theory

Where did HIV originate? Prominent cancer virologists and government epidemiologists have theorized that HIV originated in African green monkeys. Purportedly the monkey virus 'jumped species' and entered the black population. From there it migrated to Haiti and Manhattan. After the virus entered the black heterosexual population in the late 1970's, it rapidly spread to millions of blacks because of transfusions with HIV-infected blood, dirty needles, promiscuity and genital ulcers – or so the experts said.

Not all scientists believe the official monkey story, although it is rare to find people who express this view publicly. Proponents of the AIDS conspiracy theory believe that AIDS has nothing to do with green monkeys, homosexuality, drug addiction, genital ulcerations, anal sex or promiscuity, but that it has to do with scientists experimenting on blacks and gays: in short, AIDS is genocide.

Despite the general acceptance that HIV came from monkeys and the rain forest, there is no scientific evidence to prove that HIV and AIDS originated in Africa. What *is* true is that the first AIDS cases were uncovered in the U.S. in 1979, around the same time that AIDS cases were discovered in Africa. In addition, no stored African tissue from the 1970's tests positive for HIV. And scientists have a hard time explaining how a black heterosexual epidemic centered in Africa could have quickly transformed itself into a white homosexual epidemic in Manhattan.

The Gay Hepatitis-B Vaccine Experiment

Conveniently lost in the history of AIDS is the gay Hepatitis-B vaccine experiment that immediately preceded the decimation of gay Americans. A 'cohort' of over a thousand young gays was injected with the vaccine at the New York Blood Center in Manhattan between November 1978 and October 1979. Similar gay experiments were conducted in San Francisco, Los Angeles, Denver, St. Louis, and Chicago, beginning in 1980. The AIDS epidemic broke out shortly thereafter.

The experiment was run by Wolf Szmuness, a Polish Jew born in 1919. He was a young medical student in eastern Poland when the Nazis invaded the country in 1939. His entire family perished in the Holocaust. When Poland was partitioned, Szmuness was taken prisoner and sent to Siberia. After the war, Szmuness was allowed to finish medical school in Tomsk in central Russia. He married a Russian woman, had a daughter, and in 1959 was allowed to return to Poland where he became an expert in hepatitis.

According to June Goodfield's account of his life in *Quest for the Killers*, Szmuness defected from Poland with his family in 1969, arriving penniless in New York with $15 in his pocket. Through scientific connections he found work as a laboratory technician at the New York Blood Center. Within a few years he was given his own lab at the center and was also appointed Professor of Public Health at Columbia University. By the mid-1970's, Szmuness was a world authority on hepatitis, and was invited back to Moscow in 1975 to give a scientific presentation. As a defector he was terrified to set foot back in the Soviet Union, but his colleagues assured him he would have the full protection of the U.S. State Department. His return to Russia was a scientific triumph.

In the late 1970's, Wolf Szmuness was awarded millions of dollars to undertake the most important mission of his life: the Hepatitis-B vaccine experiment. Szmuness specifically wanted to use gay men to avoid 'serious legal and logistical problems'. For his study he did not want monogamous men, or men with lovers;

he chose only healthy, young, responsible, intelligent, and primarily white homosexuals. The experiment was costly and he didn't want any uncooperative or hard-to-find gays messing up his experiment. Involved in the experiment were the Centers for Disease Control, the National Institutes of Health, the National Institute of Allergy and Infectious Diseases, Abbott Laboratories, and Merck, Sharp & Dohme. Szmuness' experiment was hugely successful, and his vaccine was hailed as having tremendous global implications.

The Gay Plague

The links of the gay experiment to the outbreak of AIDS are obvious to anyone who wants to see the connection. Three months after the experiment began, the first cases of AIDS reported to the CDC appeared in young gay men in Manhattan in 1979. The first San Francisco AIDS case appeared in that city in September 1980, six months after the Hepatitis-B experiment started there. In June 1981 the AIDS epidemic became 'official'.

Were gay men given experimental vaccines contaminated with the AIDS virus? The government says no, but government agencies have a long history of covert and unethical medical experimentation, particularly with minorities. Was it simply a quirk of nature that a virus 'out of Africa' would suddenly decimate the most hated minority in America?

Why did the U.S. government choose Wolf Szmuness, a Soviet-trained doctor and a recent American immigrant to head this dangerous experiment? Goodfield, who has written the definitive account of the Hepatitis-B experiment, claims Szmuness had a painful life. Confined as a political prisoner in Siberia during World War II, he was repeatedly interrogated and beaten by the Russian KGB for refusing to cooperate in spy activities. When he could not be broken, they warned him, *"Say nothing of this to anyone, but remember. We will reach you anywhere in the world. No matter where you go, no matter where you try to hide, you will never be out of our grasp."*

The experimental Hepatitis-B vaccine was primarily manufactured by Merck. However, during the experiment Szmuness was concerned about possible vaccine contamination. Goodfield writes, *'This was no theoretical fear, contamination having been suspected in one vaccine batch made by the National Institutes of Health, though never in Merck's'.*

After the Hepatitis-B experiment ended, Szmuness insisted that all 13,000 blood specimens donated by gay men be retained at the Blood Center for future use. Due to space requirements, it is highly unusual for any laboratory to retain so many old blood specimens. When asked why he was keeping so many vials of blood, Szmuness replied, *"Because one day another disease may erupt and we'll need this material."* Several years later, when this blood was retested for the presence of HIV antibodies, government epidemiologists were able to detect the 'introduction' and the spread of HIV into the gay community.

A few months after the Hepatitis-B experiment began at the Center, the first AIDS cases began to appear in gay men living in Manhattan. And the retesting of gay blood at the Blood Center proved that HIV was first introduced into the gay population of New York City sometime around 1978-1979; the same year Szmuness' gay Hepatitis-B experiment began.

Was Szmuness psychic in his prediction that a new disease would appear in the gay community? Or did he actually know or suspect that a new, deadly virus was being introduced into the gay volunteers? Unfortunately, the answers to these questions can only be surmised. In June 1982, Szmuness died of lung cancer.

The African Origin of AIDS

Was HIV introduced into millions of Africans in the late 1970's during the smallpox vaccine eradication programs sponsored by the World Health Organization? It is known that animal and human cells harbor all sorts of viruses, including viruses not yet discovered, and animal tissue cell cultures are often used in the manufacture of viral vaccines. Therefore, the possibility of vaccine contamination with an animal virus is a constant danger in the manufacture of vaccines.

Despite the most meticulous precautions in production, contaminating animal viruses are known to survive the vaccine process. For example, during the 1950's, millions of people were injected with polio vaccines contaminated with SV-40, a cancer-causing green monkey virus. Such vaccine contamination problems are largely kept hidden from the public. Yet in spite of the known danger, drug companies and physicians always pooh-pooh any suggestion that AIDS could have arisen from animal virus-contaminated vaccines. Animal cancer viruses are also contained in fetal calf serum, a serum commonly used as a laboratory nutrient to feed animal and human tissue cell cultures. Viruses in calf serum can be carried over as contaminants into the final vaccine product.

The problem of vaccine contamination by fetal calf serum and its relationship to AIDS is the subject of a letter by J. Grote (*Bovine visna virus and the origin of the AIDS epidemic*) published in the Journal of the Royal (London) Society of Medicine in October 1988. Grote discounts the green monkey theory and questions whether bovine visna contamination of laboratory-used fetal bovine serum could cause AIDS. Bovine visna virus is similar in appearance to HIV.

Millions of African blacks are reportedly infected with HIV. This large number could never have been infected by the simple act of a monkey virus 'jumping' over to infect one African in the late 1970's. If that were the case, why don't we now have millions of AIDS cases in the U.S.? One logical explanation for the millions of Africans infected is that the vaccines used in the World Health Organization's mass inoculation programs were contaminated. Was the contamination accidental or deliberate? It is well-known in vaccine circles that the vaccinia (cowpox) virus used in the manufacture of the smallpox vaccine works well in genetic engineering. Charles Pillar and Keith Yamamoto, authors of *Gene Wars: Military Control Over the New Genetic Technology*, state: *'Researchers have been able to splice genes coding for the surface coats of other viruses, such as influenza, hepatitis, and rabies into vaccinia virus DNA. The result: a 'broad spectrum' vaccine with a coat of many colors.'*

In 1985, the Russians caused an international furor by claiming that AIDS was caused by experiments carried out in the USA as part of the development of new biological weapons. Responding to this Soviet accusation, Pillar and Yamamoto admitted that, "although no evidence has been presented to support this claim, manipulating genes to defeat the body's immune system is quite feasible."

In *Magic Shots*, Allan Chase claims that during the years 1966-1977, the WHO utilized *'200,000 people in forty countries – most of them non-doctors trained by seven hundred doctors and health professionals from over seventy participating countries – spent $300 million, and used forty million bifurcated vaccinating needles to administer 24,000 million (2.4 billion) doses of smallpox vaccine.'*

On May 11, 1987, The London Times, one of the world's most respected newspapers, published a front-page story entitled: 'Smallpox Vaccine Triggered AIDS Virus.' The story suggests that African AIDS is a direct outgrowth of the WHO smallpox eradication program. The smallpox vaccine allegedly awakened a 'dormant' AIDS virus infection in the black population. Robert Gallo, the co-discoverer of HIV, was quoted as saying, *"The link between the WHO program and the epidemic is an interesting and important hypothesis. I cannot say that it actually happened, but I have been saying for some years that the use of live vaccines such as that used for smallpox can activate a dormant infection such as HIV (the AIDS virus)."* The Times story is one of the most important stories ever printed on the AIDS epidemic; yet the story was killed and never appeared in any major U.S. newspaper or magazine.

Despite covert human experimentation, vaccine contamination problems, and the genetic engineering of new and highly dangerous viruses, the medical establishment ignores the AIDS bio-warfare issue. For example, in the prestigious British Medical Journal (May 13, 1989), Myra McClure and Thomas Schultz wrote a paper on the 'Origin of HIV' and quickly disposed of the idea that AIDS is connected to germ warfare. They simply state: *'Lack of supporting evidence precludes serious discussion of such a bizarre hypothesis. This review deals with the theories on the origin of HIV that are scientifically plausible.'*

Thus, medical science ignores evidence suggesting AIDS originated as a secret experiment. Most physicians and microbiologists steadfastly hold on to the illogical and improbable green monkey theory of AIDS. And the major media remain silent, often dismissing the bio-warfare theory as communist propaganda of the most malicious sort. Forgotten is the connection between the National Academy of Sciences and the military bio-warfare establishment in the development of biological weapons for mass killings.

Creation of a Super Germ

A decade before the first cases of AIDS, Dr. Donald M. MacArthur, a spokesman for the U.S. Department of Defense, told a Congressional Hearing that a 'super germ' could be developed as part of a U.S. experimental bio-warfare program. This genetically engineered germ would be very different from any previous microbe known to mankind. The agent would be a highly effective killing agent because the immune system would be powerless against this super-microbe (Testimony before a Subcommittee of the Committee on Appropriations, House of Representatives, Department of Defense Appropriations for 1970, dated July 1, 1969). A transcript of this meeting on 'Synthetic

Biological Agents' records the following comments of Dr. MacArthur:

1. All biological agents up to the present time are representatives of naturally occurring disease, and thus are known by scientists throughout the world. They are easily available to qualified scientists for research, either for offensive or defensive purposes.

2. Within the next 5 to 10 years, it would probably be possible to make a new infective microorganism which could differ in certain important aspects from any known disease-causing organisms. Most important of these is that it might be refractory to the immunological and therapeutic processes upon which we depend to maintain our relative freedom from infectious disease.

3. A research program to explore the feasibility of this could be completed in approximately 5 years at a total cost of $10 million.

4. It would be very difficult to establish such a program. Molecular biology is a relatively new science. There are not many competent scientists in the field, almost all are in university laboratories, and they are generally adequately supported from sources other than the Department of Defense. However, it was considered possible to initiate an adequate program through the National Academy of Sciences — National Research Council (NAS-NRC). The matter was discussed with the NAS-NRC, and tentative plans were made to initiate the program. However, decreasing funds in CB (chemical/biological) research, growing criticism of the CB program, and our reluctance to involve the NAS-NRC in such a controversial endeavor have led us to postpone it for the past two years. It is a highly controversial issue and there are many who believe such research should not be undertaken lest it lead to yet another method of massive killing of large populations... Should an enemy develop it, there is little doubt that it is an important area of potential military technological inferiority in which there is no

adequate research program.

Were AIDS and other so-called 'emerging viruses' such as Ebola and Marburg, created in bio-warfare laboratories during the 1970's? During the 1970's, the U.S. Army's bio-warfare program intensified, particularly in the area of DNA and gene splicing research. Renouncing germ warfare except for 'medical defensive research', President Richard Nixon in 1971 ordered that a major part of the Army's bio-warfare research be transferred over to the National Cancer Institute (where HIV would be discovered a decade later by Gallo). That same year, Nixon also initiated his famous War on Cancer, and offensive bio-warfare research (particularly genetic engineering of viruses) continued under the umbrella of orthodox cancer research. Cancer virologists learned to 'jump' animal cancer viruses from one species of animal to another. Chicken viruses were put into lamb kidney cells; baboon viruses were spliced into human cancer cells; the combinations were endless. In due process, deadly man-made viruses were developed, and new forms of cancer, immunodeficiency, and opportunistic infections were produced when these viruses were forced or adapted into laboratory animals and into human tissue cell cultures.

As predicted by the bio-warfare experts, new cancer-causing monster viruses were created that had a deadly effect on the immune system. In one government-sponsored experiment reported in 1974, newborn chimpanzees were taken away from their mothers at birth and weaned on milk obtained from virus-infected cows. Some of the chimps sickened and died with two new diseases that had never been observed in chimps. The first was a parasitic pneumonia known as Pneumocystis Carinii pneumonia (later known as AIDS); the second was leukemia.

Monkey Business

Almost two decades after the first U.S. AIDS cases were diagnosed, most people still believe the government's green monkey story, and AIDS educators continue to teach that HIV originated in Africa. However, a few cracks in the monkey theory have appeared in print.

A story entitled 'Research Refutes Idea That Human AIDS Virus Originated in Monkey,' appeared in the Los Angeles Times (June 2, 1988). In the process of decoding the genetic structure of the monkey virus and the human AIDS virus, Japanese molecular biologists discovered that the gene sequences of the two viruses differed by more than 50%, indicating absolutely no genetic relationship between the green monkey virus and HIV. The Japanese investigators specifically criticized Myron Essex and Phyllis Kanki of Harvard Medical School, who 'discovered' a second AIDS virus in African green monkeys that was widely heralded in the media. Essex and Kanki's 'second' AIDS virus was later proven to be a contaminant monkey virus traced back to the Harvard researchers own laboratory.

More than a decade earlier, in 1975, Gallo reported the discovery of a new and human HL-23 virus he cultured from human leukemia cells. Eventually, the virus was proven to be three contaminating ape viruses (gibbon-ape virus, simian sarcoma virus, and baboon endogenous virus). Gallo claims he has no idea how these animal viruses contaminated his research.16

If HIV is not related to a green monkey virus, what is its origin? On November 13, 1988, The Orange County Register devoted an entire section of the newspaper to AIDS in Africa. Several African officials were interviewed; all were adamant that AIDS did not originate in Africa. The theory "...is false and has never been scientifically proved, so why should Africa be the scapegoat?" declared Dr. Didace Nzaramba, director of the AIDS prevention program in Rwanda. The Register commented: 'From early on, scientists have speculated that the disease might have begun in Africa. Researchers in Africa tested old blood samples and said they found HIV-infected serum that went back years. In

1985, Harvard researchers, Phyllis Kanki and Myron Essex, announced the discovery of a new virus isolated in green monkeys that seemed similar to HIV. Eventually, researchers concluded that early blood tests used in Africa were not reliable, and Kanki and Essex said their blood tests probably had been contaminated and that their results were invalid. But the perception of an African link was established.

Media Disinformation

With the publication of *And The Band Played On* in 1987, the media became obsessed with author Randy Shilts' *Patient Zero* story. In the popular, award-winning book, a young Canadian airline steward named Gaeton Dugas is portrayed as the promiscuous gay man 'who brought the AIDS virus from Paris and ignited the epidemic in North America'. Shilts, who later died of AIDS, never explained where or how Dugas got his infection.

After a year of swollen lymph nodes and a rash, Dugas was finally diagnosed with AIDS-associated 'gay cancer' in June 1980 in New York City. What Shilts probably did not know is that when Dugas was diagnosed in 1980, over twenty percent of the Manhattan gays in the Hepatitis-B experiment were HIV-positive. This 20% infection rate was discovered after the HIV blood test became available in 1985, and after the stored blood at the New York Blood Center was retested for HIV antibodies (JAMA, Vol. 255, pp. 2167-2172, 1986). Remarkably, these gay men had the highest recorded incidence of HIV anywhere in the world for that time! Even in African populations, where AIDS has been theorized to exist for decades, or even millennia, there were never reports of such a high incidence of HIV in 1980.

Shilts' sensational *Patient Zero* story quickly became 'fact'. Even the AMA-sponsored American Medical News (October 23, 1987) fell for the ludicrous story, claiming that Dugas 'may have brought AIDS to the United States'. The media continue to promote unlikely stories about the origin of AIDS, always avoiding discussion of the idea that HIV came out of a laboratory, and always pointing the finger to black Africa.

Despite the denial of the Times regarding the laboratory creation of new AIDS-like viruses, it was common practice during the early 1970's for virologists to alter animal viruses by inserting them into other animal species and into human tissue cells in culture. Experiments performed at Harvard in the mid-1970's by Max Essex and Donald Francis (two of the best-known AIDS experts) produced AIDS in cats with the feline leukemia retrovirus. In addition, a decade before the outbreak of AIDS in the U.S., Robert Gallo was engineering cancer-causing retroviruses and studying the effects of viral mutants and their ability to suppress the immune system. A full description of Gallo's animal retrovirus research activities dating back to 1967 is chronicled in *Emerging Viruses, AIDS and Ebola: Nature, Accident or Genocide?* by Dr. Leonard Horowitz.

Secret and Covert Biological Warfare Research

It is difficult, if not impossible, to determine the truth about global biological warfare capabilities and their possible effects on world health. The American taxpayer is kept ignorant about U.S. chemical and bio-warfare programs. Scientists involved in bio-warfare research are sworn to secrecy and silence. Thus, 'classified' and 'top secret' medical experimentation continues to be promoted by powerful government agencies, such as the CIA, the CDC, the Department of Defense, the military, and other institutions.

Recent revelations of horrific radiation experiments conducted on unsuspecting U.S. citizens during the Cold War years up until the 1980's have shocked the nation. Some of this research was conducted at the most prestigious medical institutions in our country. None of the perpetrators have been brought to trial. In light of these revelations, it is inconceivable to think that leading AIDS scientists would be unaware of the connections between their institutional research and the bio-warfare establishment.

Strange and unprecedented diseases have mysteriously appeared in various parts of the world. The peculiar Persian Gulf War Syndrome sickened over 50,000 vets who served in Desert Shield/Storm. Their illnesses have been largely dismissed by health experts as due to 'psychological stress', even though there is evidence that this new disease is contagious and sexually-transmitted. Nevertheless, government health officials remain silent on these issues.

A few scientists insist that some cases of Gulf War Syndrome are related to biological warfare agents. Dr. Garth Nicholson and his wife Nancy, formerly scientists at the M.D. Anderson Cancer Center in Houston, have discovered in the blood of some sick reservists a new infectious microbe (a mycoplasma) that has part of the AIDS virus spliced into its genetic material! The Nicholsons say, "The type of mycoplasma we identified was highly unusual and it almost certainly didn't occur naturally. It has one gene from the HIV-1 virus – but only one gene. This meant it was almost certainly an artificially modified microbe... altered purposefully by scientists." (National Enquirer, April 2, 1996).

By censoring certain aspects of AIDS history, particularly the origin of HIV, we allow dangerous medical experimentation to continue. The New York Blood Center is now testing a new vaccine made from a 'harmless' canary-pox virus that has been genetically engineered to carry parts of HIV, the AIDS virus. The Center is recruiting HIV-negative gay men by funding Project Achieve, an organization designed to test and sign-up young men for the new vaccine experiment. Homosexual men are lured into the program by posters that feature cute, multi-ethnic gay boys. According to Timothy Murphy of HX magazine, there is a waiting list for the Center's vaccine experiment.

The enigmatic Dr. Szmuness has been erased from AIDS

chronicles. His name does not appear in Shilts' *Band*, nor in Mirko Grmek's *History of AIDS* (1990), or in Laurie Garret's massive tome on emerging viruses, *The Coming Plague* (1994). Although his untimely death went largely unnoticed in medical journals, he was remembered and honored on May 11, 1984, by a small coterie of medical power brokers and distinguished scientists who convened at a landmark symposium in the U.S. capitol. The meeting entitled 'Infection, Immunity, and Blood Transfusion' was sponsored by the American Red Cross.

Paying tribute to Szmuness were top government scientists in AIDS and cancer research, the most well-known researchers in animal experimentation, the heads of the most prestigious biomedical establishments in the country, and the chief executives of drug companies tied to genetic engineering, vaccine production, and biological warfare research. Dr. Robert Gallo, who had announced the discovery of the AIDS virus to the American public three weeks earlier, was one of the most distinguished attendees.

There is an ominous link between cancer and AIDS, between animal experimentation and the genetic engineering of viruses, between biological warfare technology and drug companies, between gay experiments and AIDS, between vaccine programs and the contamination of the nation's blood supply. Why else would all these people from diverse areas of science be attending this high level government conference?

There is also a connection between Szmuness' gay experiment and the outbreak of AIDS that cannot be denied. This connection is not coincidental or a paranoid fantasy. It is time for a serious study of the link between covert biological warfare research and the initial outbreak of the 'gay AIDS plague'. Ignoring evidence pointing to AIDS as a man-made disease makes a sham out of AIDS education.

Copyright: Jon DePew

THE CORAL CASTLE CODE
Jon DePew

I have discovered the secrets of the pyramids, and have found out how the Egyptians and the ancient builders in Peru, Yucatan, and Asia, with only primitive tools, raised and set in place blocks of stone weighing many tons!
~ Edward Leeskalnin, (1887 - 1951)

Coral Castle is a phenomenal multi-ton structure in Homestead, Florida, in the U.S. Built single-handedly by Edward Leedskalnin between 1923 and 1951, it is both a phenomenal feat of engineering and a work of creative genius that has baffled scientists, engineers and scholars.

Some of the more incredible of the structures at the Coral Castle complex are; an obelisk monolith 40 ft tall and weighing nearly 30 tons, a rocking chair weighing three tons that can be rocked using one finger, and a spiral staircase made from one piece of stone that leads to a subterranean refrigerator, but perhaps the most spectacular of these is a huge nine-ton revolving door. Precisely aligned with the stone's center of gravity, it is so perfectly balanced that it can easily be pushed open using one finger. Today's engineers using advanced technology would be hard-pressed to duplicate this... so how on earth did a short man weighing only 100 pounds, working alone and using only simple tools, quarry, cut, trim and assemble over 1100 tons of dense coral blocks, and interlock them with exacting precision without the use of mortar?

Edward Leedskalnin claimed to have re-discovered the laws of weight, measurement, and leverage, and stated that these laws *"involved the relationship of the Earth to celestial alignments"*. Beyond these sketchy explanations, he didn't say much. Ed was a private person who was very secretive about his method of operation; working only at night. He could sense when people would sneak around at night trying to catch him at work and, at such times, would stop his work and would continue only after they left. Nevertheless, Ed's neighbor reported seeing Edward 'singing to the stones with his hands placed on their surface', and another witness claimed to see coral blocks floating through the air 'like hydrogen balloons'.

The only written records Ed left to posterity are five booklets, which are available from the Coral Castle gift shop. His first, *Magnetic Current,* was published in 1945. For many years people have searched within them for clues to the secret of how Ed built his Castle. In 1994, Jon DePew cracked the code.

For information about Jon DePew's work, visit: www.coralcastlecode.com

Coral Castle: www.coralcastle.com

When I was seven years old, my grandfather died and I inherited a box of coins he had collected through his life. Out of all of them, there was one coin that I felt really attached to and I carried it with me everywhere I went. My parents told me I'd better not, or one day I'd lose it. I didn't listen. One day, when I was about 10 years old, I was playing in the mountain forest near my home with friends. The next morning I was going through my pockets looking for my coin... to my horror it was *gone.* I'd lost my favorite 'magic coin', and I was devastated. Not knowing where the coin came from or what it symbolized, I felt I had no way of finding another one like it. Years passed. I still held on to this memory and the constant torment in my brain of what the symbol on the coin represented. I thought the answer to this might lead me to find another one someday. In my search, I recognized the same symbol in many ancient references as the

Solomon's Seal

'Seal of Solomon'. When I went to Coral Castle for the first time, at the age of 28, and saw this same symbol carved in Ed's coral pieces, this intrigued me no end.

Coral Castle was first known as Rock Gate Park. It was built using the sacred knowledge of our ancients, and contains the principles of construction that follow principles revealed in many ancient

Picture courtesy of Coral Castle

temples, architecture, and paintings, etc. There are many examples throughout the world, for example; Solomon's Temple, and the Great Pyramids in Egypt. Their principles of construction follow the natural laws within all of nature's manifestations. That's why it is called 'divine proportion' – they are aligned and in tune with the cosmic constructions.

Edward Leedskalnin was born on August 10th, 1887, in Riga, Latvia. He came from a family of 'stone masons'. He moved to Florida in 1918 to a town called Florida City in the Miami area, and lived there until around 1936, when he decided to move to a different location. Ed had already begun his coral/mason works at the Florida City site and, incredibly, he moved everything he had already finished along with him to the new site, which is known today as Coral Castle.

Whenever I have a curiosity about something I'm interested in I can't rest until I look into it with more depth, so I read Ed Leedskalnin's books. His descriptions and writings about science being off-track and not quite right in its perceptions of energy (and life in general) rang very true for me personally. I also studied not only Ed's work, but also many wonderful individuals from our history that have been ignored with similar important messages – including John Worrell Keely, Nikola Tesla, and Emmanuel Swedenborg.

After years of experiments, I was researching magnetic energies and began running physical magnetic experiments of my own design. One late night in May 2004, I discovered a wonderful magnetic resonance principle inspired by a visual phenomenon that I had always taken for granted; the cascading visual banding pattern seen in a spinning spoke rim of a bicycle, which cascades one way, then the other way. This is a visual display of magnetic propagation and the polarity domains of magnetic energies – a visual phenomenon representing the 'laws of harmony', which is a mathematical law of energy and its natural inherent harmonics. The visual patterns I discovered in these experiments had bands that were at certain angles, just like the 'flower of life'

Edward Leedskalnin's Magnetic Current

message of the ancients! At that moment, I realized that the two curves on the cover of Ed's book, *Magnetic Current* were a clue... the key to opening the most sought-after mystery of the world.

By connecting the nodes (tips) of those curves like puzzle pieces, it revealed that *sacred geometry represents magnetic currents!* There is no other piece of information throughout all of history that exceeds this one. This is what 'squaring the circle', 'law of the triangle', 'golden ratio', 'golden mean', 'golden rectangle', and 'divine proportion', etc., is really all about! Those 'curves' that Ed Leedskalnin left for us on the cover of his book represent this base formula or 'unit' of energy, which is two individual magnetic currents and the neutral particles of matter. The mathematical formula to this energy is the value of *pi* or 'phi' because of specific 'cosmic vibration rates' that our system is held within. Human beings and every other living manifestation are immersed or contained within those vibration values – *everything* in nature will have the 'inherent value of *pi*' built into it because of this fact.

In his book entitled *A Book in Every Home,* Ed cryptically wrote that his 'Sweet Sixteen' refers to a "new one" – *not* a sweetheart! To me, 'Sweet Sixteen' represents the perfect 'harmony' before a strong impression changes it forever. 'Sweet Sixteen' represents 'energies in harmony', which is also represented by a circle

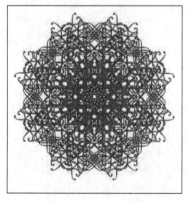

divided by 16 perfectly spaced neutral divisions *(pi).* My physical experiments and my visual *Blueprints to Energies* magnetic patterns reveal this message.

The complex patterns built from those two curves at my website and in the illustrations you see here all have the attributes of phi/sacred geome-

Copyright: John DePew

tries inherently built into them. This should now make it easy for people to see what all of our ancient sacred geometry really represents. To some trained mystics it is obvious – to others, whether untrained or experienced, it is not. Buddha, among many other avatars, was trained and guided people in these ancient studies. Jesus was also a trained mystic who also taught his disciples about the 'divine proportion'. This is what the *Da Vinci Code* is *really* about... *not* what the author of the book has claimed.

Every single formation or structure has its own magnetic field design that binds it together and keeps it in its shape. Any manifestation of nature owes its existence to energy, and vibrations of energy, from its 'base' level. This discovery represents that fundamental 'base' level. Present science seems to study higher levels of manifestations such as the atom. They need to take it further down to the 'base' – the things that form and hold the atoms together. These patterns of two magnetic currents are the fabric that holds everything together in our universe; including the atoms themselves... this is what builds an atom into a structure. The 'base' is *three things that unite as one whole working/living system.*

'Static pressures' (without the spark) is that base complete system or substance. Science already plays with all the parts of static but they do not combine them into one working/functioning unit. The three fundamental attributes of magnetic/static fields and/or charge are;

1. Positive magnetic currents
2. Negative magnetic currents
3. Neutral line or gap that separates both magnetic forces - 'The Zero'

The way particles receive their charge will dictate the inherent attributes they will display (one of the three charge attributes mentioned). We are comprised of these three energies. Our cells have a centered positive charge which is revitalized when we breathe (lungs are the charging system for the centers of our cells). The outer rim of our cells are negatively charged and vitalized by the food and water we eat and drink. The vibrations of the center positive charge are different than the negative vibrations – one vibration will be high, one vibration will be low. They must follow the natural resonant combinations to keep in harmony. Each vibration level (rate of vibration) has a specific polarity dominance assigned to it by nature's 'laws of harmony'. These vibration polarities are switching back and forth as alternating magnetic currents. This is why everything is in constant change (matter breaking down and building up). The Coral Castle Code represents the same principle of magnetic propagations and or principles of the functioning of all cells. Nature displays it in everything that 'is'.

*

Ed Leedskalnin said the electron theories were wrong. Electrons are really *both* of the individual kinds of magnetic substance. Science says energy is cancelled when positive and negative connect – Ed Leedskalnin believed that science is mislead by this false principle; only north and south whirling against each other can run – they run in a screw-like twisting motion (vortex motion).

Development or growth in nature is by means of centrifugal forces. The vortex motions are throwing out north and south individual magnets – the magnets that are lost are instantly replaced... all that is lost is gained back instantly. North and south come back to their own kind of magnet, rejoining the individual perpetual orbits.

Magnetic energy flows through everything, but each and everything allows different amounts of it. Magnetic currents flow through metal easier than the air. The metal is *not* the magnetic substance – it just holds more magnetic current flowing through it than anything else. Sunlight is caused by the obstruction of magnetic currents. For earth, the air is the obstruction that illuminates our planet. Ed said, *"Today, yesterday's sunlight is the neutral particles of matter"*. The changes of seasons are really the change or pulse of two magnetic currents. This is what gives us our reoccurring axis tilt, or precession. Ed said the currents are always strongest at summer's end.

Ed Leedskalnin learned for himself that science was mistaken about the movements of our earth and sun. He said he was 'defooled' by building his own rock telescope and sundial that revealed to him the true paths of the earth and sun. The sundial utilized the inverse curvature of the Earth. The 30 ton, 25 ft tall rock telescope is aligned to the North Star and also casts a shadow that points in and out of the north-east opening of the Castle complex during sunrises and sunsets. This north-east opening is positioned or 'timed' to the sun's magnetic path. I believe it is also aligned with the Solstice on June 21st.

There are some illustrations from Frater Albertus (the Rosicrucian alchemist) on my website that show the true earth and sun orbits, and also show that Earth will be in a neutral zone of magnetic influence in the year 2012. This could be a very interesting time period for the earth and sun. If the tapping of the earth into the sun were to happen it would be at that point. In my experiments, that's when that type of charge interaction occurs. I have no way to say for sure what will happen. I'll be very curious to see what does occur at that crossroad or equilibrium point. Basically, visualizing it, the Earth will be positioned right in the center of a Yin

Ed's Polaris Telescope (picture courtesy of Coral Castle

Yang Pattern of galactic magnetic propagation. The earth is dominantly negatively charged and the sun is dominantly positively charged, but each have both kinds of magnetic energies that they utilize and function with. These energies are in constant interaction/communication with each other. From my experiments, if a particle charge is switched it will slam into/'tap' the center, then switch back to a repelling orbit. If I only switch the charge once, it will remain repelling until it decides to 'nibble' and 'tap' by its own choice. This 'tapping' activity is very akin to the particles eating/nibbling in order for a new dose of energy. The cells in our bodies do the same. In our solar system, this 'center' is the sun. It is quite possible the earth can periodically 'tap' the sun and then be ejected back out with another force field after its ejection. The same goes with the sun and its magnetic attachments in our galaxy.

*

To realize and accept that sacred geometry represents two magnetic currents and the neutral particles of matter is a huge message for the world to absorb. To me, there is nothing more important than this realization. The individual magnets are what hold everything in this universe together. It is the vibration levels that the ancients referred to as Spirit. This is how all matter is manifested into its present state of being. There are only three things the whole universe needs to have for all its majesty – North Pole magnets and South Pole magnets orbiting neutral particles of matter (starlight).

This discovery leaves me with no doubt that our ancestors had advanced knowledge of energy... and there is a ton of evidence. In fact, they have passed down the blueprints for us to find in their architecture and designs that we have all taken for granted for centuries. For example, the tri-spiral is indicative of the code.

Places like Stonehenge and Newgrange are storehouses of

energy. To me they are akin to Ed's Coral Castle complex as a whole. These places are designed to complement the harnessing/steering and concentration of Cosmic Energies. Energy is distributed all over the globe – there are specific propagations of magnetic currents. These ancient complexes complement and utilize those natural propagations of magnetic energies.

Using the same energy that the ancients did, Ed was able to move the large blocks of coral that built the Coral Castle complex, but I have not tried this myself. On a small scale I can display the mechanism of these same principles of anti-gravity or opposite/same charge interactions and what they can do. I can make salt or sand shoot out of an invisible fountain of animal magnetism (magnetic substance). I can show many wonderful insights of these principles on a small scale and also have many of my own hard-earned discoveries that reveal these laws of harmony. I've entitled one of my inventions the 'Equilibrius Grid'. This is a demonstration of expanding magnetic fields of resonance and a fundamental unrecognized principle of neutral magnetic distribution. It is the zero point everyone is chasing and misunderstands. This particular discovery has so many new unrecognized attributes for scientists to explore that I couldn't name them all here... it's a science of its own! I find something new in almost every experiment with my Equilibrius Grid.

THE HEALING TECHNOLOGY OF SOUND
Jonathan Goldman

The true sound of healing is Love.
~ Sarah Saruah Benson

Jonathan Goldman is an international authority on sound healing and a pioneer in the field of harmonics. He is author of *Healing Sounds, Shifting Frequencies, Tantra of sound* (co-authored with his wife Andi), winner of the 2006 visionary award for "best alternative health book", *The 7 Secrets of Sound Healing,* and his latest book - *The Divine Name,* (Hay House). Jonathan presents healing sounds seminars throughout the world. He is director of the Sound Healers Association and president of Spirit Music, inc. in Boulder, Colorado. A Grammy nominee, Jonathan has created numerous best selling, award winning recordings including *The Divine Name* (with Gregg Braden), *Reiki Chants, Ultimate Om, The Lost Chord,* and *Chakra Chants* – winner of the visionary awards for "best healing-meditation album". He is a lecturing member of the International Society for Music Medicine. Website for Jonathan: www.healingsounds.com. Website for the Sound Healers association: www.soundhealersassociation .org. Website for the Temple of Sacred Sound: www.templeofsacred-sound.org.

One night, probably around 1979, I was playing in a rock and roll band in a club at the seaside town of Marshfield, Massachusetts. I was nearly 30 years old and had been performing profes-sionally for close to 13 years, playing lead guitar and singing. That night, as I was looking out at the audience, I became aware that an ambience of negativity and violence was exuding from the club and I had the sudden realization that it was being enhanced and amplified by the music that I was creating.

Within a couple of weeks, the question of using sound for healing began to sink into my psyche. I attended a workshop on using sound and music for healing given by a woman named Sarah Benson. Holding a quartz crystal, I was placed in the middle of a circle while everyone in the circle chanted my name. I was 'transported' inside an amethyst pyramid and I remember a green light flowing into me. After the chanting had stopped, I finally came back into my physical body and opened my eyes, thinking, 'I've got to find out more about the sound work', and that was my first initiation into sound.

When I first began to research the uses of sound and music for healing, I came across a number of different books that talked about rock and roll as being, for want of a better word, 'the devil's music' or 'bad' music, and I stopped playing for a number of years until I had a major revelation that you could not simply take any one genre of music and say that it was 'good' or 'bad'. Some of the greatest and most love-filled music on the planet is by The Beatles – how much greater song can you have than *All You Need is Love*? How much greater a statement can you have than 'And in the end, the love you take is equal to the love you make'? Every type of music, depending on the time, space and the need of the individual, can be healing. Every type of music, depending upon who made it and the energy that they had when they made the music, will have different effects. This is especially true when you contemplate the need of the individual who is receiving the music. Do they need music that will relax them or would music to stimulate them serve them better? It is my belief that if your intention is pure, depending upon the time, the place and the need of the individual, any type of music can be healing.

Many years ago, I was working on my first book. I had a stack of paper probably a foot high from all different scientists, spiritual masters, and teachers and I was trying to understand how sound actually worked as healing. I was in a state of intellectual angst, because few of the scientists and the spiritual teachers who used sound were in agreement with each other. Spiritual master A might use a particular mantra to resonate a particular chakra while spiritual master B might use a very different mantra to resonate that same chakra. Scientist A might use a particular set of frequencies to resonate one organ while scientist B might use a completely different set of frequencies for that same organ and yet they all seemed to be claiming success. I remember sitting there with my head in my hands trying to figure out how this could be, when I distinctly heard a voice say, *"It is not only the frequency of the sound that creates the effect, it is also the intention of the person creating the sound that creates the effect"*, and I wrote down these words: 'Frequency + Intent = Healing'. This may be one of the most important formulas that I've ever come across. It may help provide a unified theory of not only sound healing, but perhaps of almost everything in the universe. I've slightly altered this, since, to come up with another formula which is basically this: 'Sound + Belief = Outcome'. This simply means that our belief is so powerful that when coupled with the sound we create, it helps create the outcome of what we experience with the sound. These seem to be very important aspects – neither one of them by itself is more important than the other – the frequency of the sound we create is as important as is our belief or our intentionality that we tone upon the sound. Intention is the consciousness that we put upon the sound, and the two of them working together represent the working mechanism – the effect of why sound has this importance.

The basic principle for using sound for healing is this: sound as we know it travels as a wave form, which is measured scientifically in cycles per second, also called hertz (and abbreviated as Hz.). We hear a very small spectrum of sound – from about 20 Hz. to around 20,000 Hz. The higher the sound, the faster these frequencies become. Our friends in the ocean, the dolphins, can receive and project information upwards of 180,000 Hz. – that's more than *ten times* our greatest level of hearing! To us, there's nothing audible going on – but the dolphins might be exchanging encyclopedic information on different subject – perhaps various principles of Universal Peace, or perhaps the best recipe for tuna casserole! The idea that our ancient mystics and modern physicists are in agreement with, is that everything is in a state of vibration – from the electrons moving around the nucleus of an atom to planets in distant galaxies moving around their stars. Everything is in a state of vibration and if it's in a state of vibration it's putting out a sound. Whether or not we can hear the sound is irrelevant.

What is most important is that people begin to realize that sound is the original creative force. In all the different texts of all the different traditions, we find a commonality in our understanding that life, the universe and everything was created solely through the power of sound. In the Old Testament it says, 'And the Lord *said*, *"Let there be light"'*. The actual act of *saying* 'Let there be light' created light. In the New Testament is says, 'In the beginning there was *the Word*'. In the ancient Egyptian tradition, the god *Thoth* would think of an object, speak its name, and bring it into being. In the Hopi tradition, Spider Woman sings the Song of Creation and manifests life. In *Popul Vuh* from the Mayan tradition, the first men and women were given life solely through sound. In the Vedic tradition, it says, 'In the beginning was Brahman', almost echoing word-for-word the translation of St. John. So you have a commonality of understanding that everything in the universe is music and sound, or vibration – that also goes for every part of our body... every organ, every system, every bone is in a state of vibration.

When we are in a state of health, we call this 'sound health'. We are like a wonderful orchestra, playing the "Suite of the Self" and creating an overall harmonic of health. But what happens if the second violin player loses their sheet music? They begin to play the wrong notes. They are out of key and out of harmony. Pretty soon, not only does this violin player sound 'off', but the entire string section sounds 'off' and this will affect the entire orchestra. When part of our body vibrates out of tune or out of harmony, that part of the body is vibrating 'out of ease' with its natural resonance. When this occurs, we call that part of the body *dis*-eased.

I come from a family of doctors. My father, grandfather, and brother – all trained as traditional, allopathic medical doctors. I have the greatest respect for traditional allopathic medicine but, using this metaphor of the body as an orchestra, the current approach of traditional medicine is either to give the string player playing the wrong note enough drugs so they pass out, or else to do surgery – this is somewhat akin to cutting off the head of the string player with a broadsword. Both approaches effectively remove the string player from the orchestra. The bad note is removed and the orchestra is sounding better, *but you have lost the second violin player*. What if it were possible to restore the sheet music back to the string player, getting them to once again play again in tune with the orchestra? What if it were somehow possible to somehow project the correct resonant frequency to that part of the body that was out of tune, restoring it back in tune and into alignment through using the power of sound?

Not only do each of us have different 'notes', but we can shift and change our 'notes'. There are people who believe that you are born into a lifetime on a particular frequency, die on this particular note or frequency, and keep manifesting and reincarnating on the same frequency. That is not my belief system. I am very much a sonic evolutionist, if you like, I believe we can shift and change our vibratory level – that we can continue to evolve. If I thought that I was stuck vibrating at this one frequency for lifetime after lifetime after lifetime, it would be quite a bore.

On our Healing Sounds Correspondence Course, we teach people (among other things) to learn how to resonate their chakras with sound. We have had people using scientific instrumentation to find out what frequency their chakras were resonating at, and it changed from day to day depending on what activity they were involved in. Say, for example, that before you resonated your chakras you were meditating or whatnot – your frequencies, your chakra resonance, would be very different than if you were jogging, or if you were drinking alchohol, or if you had been engaged in a different activity – so I think that physical and mental activities have a correlation with our vibratory rate. Bodies can shift and change their frequencies. That being said, I think that we need to understand the fluid nature of reality and the power of sound to shift and change it. For example, after recording Tibetan monks in a studio, I went to sleep while listening to the very deep sacred growl-sound of their voices, and when I woke up in the morning I had that voice. When I demonstrated my new-found 'Tibetan Deep Voice' to a friend, Don Campbell, he said, *"Ah, that's an example of harmonic transmission."* What a great term! I think what we're talking about here is what one could call sympathetic vibration, and this is something that you will find when you're in the presence of a spiritual master. Whether or not they're making sound or not, this person is vibrating at such a high frequency level that you will walk into a room and it will immediately change your own frequency level.

With regard to the power of sound to heal and transform, there are many different devices, instruments, CDs, and other products and instruments on the market right now, but we already have the most powerful and extraordinary tool for healing. It doesn't require electricity or batteries, the owner's manual is relatively easy to use, it's free, and basically each and every one of us has one – of course, I'm talking about our voice. When you stub your toe, you usually say, "Ow!" because this is your bodies' natural way of creating balance – basically releasing stress and releasing pain through self-created sounds. They're not necessarily pleasing sounds designed to entertain people, but they can be very powerful. Have you ever stubbed your toe and not been able to make a sound? Well, I'll tell you, if you *do* stub your toe and you can't make a sound, it hurts *a lot more.*

We need to re-introduce and re-empower ourselves with the energy of sound to heal and transform. Each and every one of us can do this by using the power of the voice to massage and vibrate different parts of the body – it doesn't have to be a beautiful sound or pleasing to others. Now, I am not talking about getting up in front of an audience and singing a song, or performance art– that's entertainment. I'm talking about *entrainment.* Entrainment is an aspect of physics, whereby the vibrations of one object can cause the vibrations of another object to lock in step and synchronize with it. Learning to use your voice for self healing and transformation is an important aspect of realizing the process of shifting frequencies. It has nothing to do with having a trained voice. People say: *"Well gee, I can't carry a tune in a bucket!",* but from my experience that doesn't matter – you can even gently hum and put your body into a balance and alignment. This is called 'toning'.

A headline from the New York Times Science Section:

February 8th, 1988, said: 'Sound Shaped as a Dazzling Tool can Make, Break or Rearrange Molecular Structure and Levitate Objects.' The implications of this are astounding. When people ask me what sort of conditions can be treated with sound, I say, *"If you can rearrange molecular structure then what sort of condition can not be healed with sound, at least potentially?"*

With regard to the New York Times headline, levitation through sound is very possible – the article was about high decibel frequencies being used for levitation, but sonic levitation is a technology that I believe once was known and now is lost. It's quite possible that ancient places like the pyramids were built using sound, and that there was an interface between sound and crystals. I personally like to stay away from discussing what I call the phenomenological aspects of sound although, in truth, I've had many extraordinary experiences – for example, I was able to create light through sound in the ancient Mayan temple of Palenque back in 1987 during the Harmonic Convergence. What happens is that you can get so focused on the phenomena – the creation of light through sound – that you forget that this is really some sort of by-product... the *real* importance is to be able to generate light and love in the sound that you're making for healing.

I want to empower everyone with the realization that they too can use sound to raise their consciousness, heal themselves, and heal the planet. I believe that if we make tones and sounds throughout the planet while visualizing and feeling the energy of peace in our hearts, we can actually shift and change the energy of the world we live in. I call this process 'Global Harmonization'. Sound amplifies our prayers and meditations. This is why the majority of prayers and sacred sounds on this planet are chanted aloud.

The Internet represents what could be called the 'neural net of the planet' – it represents the mind of the planet. The global mind, or even the human mind, is a wonderful energy form, but it seems to have the ability of creating technology without sometimes asking if this technology is necessary. We need to incorporate the energy of the heart– it's the aspect of ourselves that tells us if we should or shouldn't do something if it isn't in alignment. How do you activate the heart using the Internet–the neural net of the planet? In many sacred traditions, there is the body and there is the mind, and there is an interlinking mechanism between the two, which is sound. By using sound, you can link the heart and the mind. This is why I created a virtual sacred sound temple in cyberspace – an interactive Internet healing sound temple at www.templeofsacredsound .org. People can visit the site and they will experience three different sacred toning chambers. These toning chambers have wonderful visual sacred geometries that can be viewed while hearing the voices of thousands of people throughout the planet toning an 'Om' or an 'Ah' or a 'Hu' sound. The focus of these sounds and the Temple of Sacred Sound is to activate the Global Heart and send healing energy to the planet in order to help counteract a lot of the imbalanced frequencies that are so very predominant. Technology is not going to go away, so we may as well make an ally of it, rather than an adversary.

Sound is such an extraordinary energy – especially when it's coupled with a positive consciousness. Once again, please remember 'Frequency + Intent = Healing'. Through understanding how to use sound in this manner, we can learn to resonate on a personal level, changing and raising our own vibrations. In addition, we can resonate on a planetary level, assisting the shift in evolutionary consciousness on the Earth.

4

DANGEROUS ENVIRONMENT

DANGEROUS ENVIRONMENT

*Is there a greater wisdom than nature's, which outstrips anything
that man can conceive? Knowledge of the deepest order is to be
described as that which is in accordance with nature.*
~ Sōetsu Yanagi, philosopher and writer (1889 – 1961)

When I gaze out over farmed agricultural land, I often imagine
what it would have looked like when the land was covered in
trees. I try to blot out the 'patchwork' landscape and imagine the
verdant rolling hills before they were hacked up and divided into
little pieces. I stretch my arm out and hold up my hand to cover
the pylons scarring the surface. Truly natural places are hard to
find in the natural world these days…

What we see in the world today that impacts us so greatly
represents all we have collectively manifested. We create the
environment without realizing that the environment also creates
us – it is a perpetual cycle. Simply put; if we take care of the earth,
then it will take care of us.

The powers that be, with their fear-mongering propaganda
and 'Green policies', are taking advantage of the genuine love we
have for this beautiful planet by creating false scenarios in order
to advance their agenda (which, by the way, has *nothing* to do
with creating a sustainable, just and peaceful world and *everything* to do with profit margins). Deliberately manipulating and
misleading the very people who care and who could actually
change the world is *the* most abhorrent of actions.

We need to look very carefully at all the solutions they are
proposing, to be absolutely sure we are not being misdirected.
We are told, for instance, that wind turbines are a good idea, but

we need to look again… Here in the UK, a massive expansion of around 7,000 new wind turbines has been planned over the next 12 years to meet European targets on 'greenhouse gas emissions'. More than half are expected to be built onshore – on mountains, moors and hillsides – further desecrating some of Britain's best-loved countryside.

Governments may well talk about 'carbon footprints' and try to brainwash our kids into thinking that they are killing the planet just by breathing out CO_2, but they're not prepared to put their money where their mouths are and release the free-energy technology that already exists. To do so would be the death of the oil industry and nuclear power.

In the 21st century, we are seemingly stuck between 'a rock and a hard place'. What choice do most of us have but to drive gas-guzzling vehicles and use mains-generated electricity? To live any differently in this day and age, you either have to have a lot of money to be able to afford to invest in these alternative solutions (solar panels, electric cars, etc.), or else be prepared to live a frugal existence with no technology at all. If you want to live in anything but a rectangular-shaped box, life is made impossibly difficult for you to do so, what with planning permission and other regulatory standards imposed on your every move – not to mention that land has shot up in price and we're going through a (manufactured) 'economic depression'.

To be told we need to do things differently and then make it damn near difficult for us to do anything about it should be enough to tell us that all these 'environmentally-friendly' and 'energy-efficient' policies are a charade.

If we created this mess in the first place, then it makes logical sense that we can create something better by doing things differently. So, what *can* we do? As my good friend Pat Reynolds observes;

"With our modern way of life and our need for computers, mobile

phones, Wi-Fi, electrical gadgets and communication systems, we live in an EMF (Electro Magnetic Frequency) soup and compromise our own and mother earth's energy systems. For every seemingly insurmountable problem there is an answer waiting. Ironically, one of the answers to this comes in the form of the natural and the not-so-natural mixed together to form what is known as Orgonite. Made of resin, metal and quartz crystal, it comes in all shapes and sizes and transforms EMFs back into balanced energy. It also works on buildings, nature, and people, to release, transform, and balance 'negative' energies of all kinds. Astonishingly, it even turns mobile masts into positive energy fountains. Begun by Wilhelm Reich and continued throughout the world today by dedicated individuals who 'gift' the planet, it is making a huge positive difference."

Ultimately, we need to remember and rediscover our connection with the earth; to have consideration and respect. In order to minimize our impact on the biosphere we need to learn to live in harmony with it. This involves minimizing waste, disturbing the natural energetic flow as little as possible, and ensuring that our interactions with this earth (and everything on it) are healthy. It is human arrogance to think that we could 'save the planet'... this planet does not need saving. We need to Save Our Selves (SOS).

All the environmental campaigning in the world won't improve the situations we face today, because fighting against anyone or anything merely adds energy to the problem – it will amplify and exacerbate the situation... manifesting and perpetuating the very thing you *don't* want.

A positive solution arises when we come from a different perspective – going all-out *for* the earth by putting a well-grounded foot down and stating our intent. For instance, writing letters to companies telling them you DO want to buy natural soft drinks is far more effective than saying you DON'T want them to produce drinks laced with aspartame. Although it seems that you're saying the same thing either way, these are two *very different* approaches – one produces more of what you don't want and the other manifests what you do want.

It's curious that we readily know what we don't want, but if someone asks the question, *"What do you want?"*, we don't often know the answer. Handy-hint: take a look at what you don't want, then turn it around and focus on the opposite. In this way, we will transform the planet... by holding the vision.

CODEX ALIMENTARIUS:
Big Pharma & Big Farmer – Making Sickness Compulsory
Ian R Crane

*Almost all the latter part of my life has been spent unlearning the
nonsense I learned in my youth.*
- **Geoffrey Higgins, Cambridge Educated Bible Scholar
(1771-1834)**

*The most common of all follies is to believe passionately in the
palpably not true. It is the chief occupation of mankind.*
- **H L Mencken, Journalist, Essayist, Satirist (1880-1956)**

An ex-oilfield executive, Ian now lectures and writes on the
geo-political webs that are being spun; with particular focus on
US Hegemony and the NWO agenda for control of global
resources. Prior to his retirement from the corporate arena, Ian
enjoyed a career of 25 years in telecommunications and international oilfield services, a career that provided the opportunity

to live & work in the U.K., Continental Europe, the Middle East & Houston, Texas.

Over the past seven years, Ian has given literally hundreds of presentations on the anomalies between the physical evidence and the official version of events for both 9/11 and the London Bombing of 7/7.

More recently, Ian has focused his efforts on raising awareness of the Codex Alimentarius; the UN agenda to eradicate Organic Farming and to destroy the Complementary & Alternative Healthcare industry; an agenda driven and financed by the corporatocracy of Big Pharma & Big Farmer.

Ian is the founder of The Alternative View events - bringing people together to advance awareness and facilitate discussion of Political, Scientific and Spiritual alternatives without constraint by Consensus Reality and/or Received Wisdom.

I can absolutely identify the moment when things started to change for me, and that was in 1991. I was one of the first civilians to go into Kuwait after Gulf War I with a small group of fellow oil field workers. We were there to take a look at the physical and human logistics that would be needed to address the fires that had been lit; supposedly by the retreating Iraqi forces. As we were driving around the southern oil fields in Kuwait, it became very evident to me that the physical evidence did not support the official version of events, being that the fires were started by the Iraqis. The Iraqi government denied this, but that was never reported in the media in the West. What I saw were a multitude of dead Iraqi troops around a number of the burning wells – it looked to me as though they had been killed trying to *defend* the wells.

When I happened to make this observation, a few days later a guy in American battle fatigues sought me out and basically told me that I needed to keep my mouth shut. What he actually said was: *"I've bin hearin' you've been castin' some aspersion about who set them wells alight. That's the kind of thinkin' that can get you into a whole lot of trouble!"* And as he turned to walk away, he said, *"What the fuck's the matter, Ian? Aren't we paying you enough?"*

As it happens, I got on with the job. We did what needed to be done. The fire-fighting that was coordinated by the oil industry was really amazing – there were people from all over the world, people of all nationalities working as one to achieve one objective; to get the fires under control and then clean up the country. It was a massive team effort. There was no place for the ego, because no one individual could put those fires out by themselves. It was actually quite an experience to behold.

By the late 1990's, I had become disenchanted with the corporate world. I started to spend more time on the golf course, more time partying, and less time doing what I was supposedly being paid to do. I eventually left the oil industry in 1998. I did get suckered back into the corporate world for about eighteen months in 1999 but I knew that it wasn't what I needed to be doing, and that's when I really started my process of re-education – looking into alternative history, mythology, and spirituality. I was in Central America researching Mayan mythology and Mayan cosmology when 9/11 went down. It rocked me because I'd been predicting for the previous six months, along with many other people, that something like 9/11 would occur. I came back to England for the first time in nearly twelve years, and spent the next six months researching every aspect of 9/11 that I could find. By March 2002, I was totally of the opinion that it was an inside job. Once you actually peel back the veneer of the official story (which was really very thin), it is quite apparent that this was a contrived event created to be a catalyst to launch the U.S. into the 'new global agenda' – exactly as described by Zbigniew Brzezinski in his book *The Grand Chessboard*, which he'd written some four years previously, where he was looking at what America would need to do to effectively establish itself as a global superpower. Incidentally, this is the same guy who nurtured Barack Obama into the White House.

I started doing some presentations on 9/11, while researching a whole bunch of other areas at the same time. Eventually, I realized that if I was going to get the 'average guy in the street' to start taking a look at the manipulation, the 'bigger picture', I needed to talk about something that was very close to everybody.

Codex Alimentarius

The Codex Alimentarius Commission is based in Rome, but there are 27 different committees dotted all around the world and chaired by different countries, all working to effectively establish global legislation with regard to all foods. What the pharmaceutical industry are doing is effectively trying to re-classify *any food that is deemed to have a medicinal benefit* as a drug.

What we have here, in my opinion, is the most evident manifestation of global legislation coming into being. It does not take into account in any shape or form national sovereignty, culture, or tradition, particularly in the case of food and medicine. This agenda is totally geared towards removing personal freedom and individual choice.

Codex Alimentarius is ostensibly a 'special interest group' that works under the auspices of the World Trade Organization (WTO) and the World Health Organization (WHO). Under the WHO you have the Food and Agricultural Organization (FAO); so what you have is Big Pharma and Big Farmer, i.e. the biotech industry, effectively colluding to maximize their revenues; that's the corporate objective. The political objective behind this is really about absolute control. Henry Kissinger was very overt in 1992 when he made the observation, *"Control the oil and you control nations; control the food and you control the people."* Fundamentally, this is exactly what is occurring. It is a conspiracy by the pharmaceutical industry, by key players in certain governments pursuing a global agenda that does not have the interests of humanity at its heart. This is what I'm trying to encourage people to see for themselves.

The whole objective of the Codex Alimentarius Commission, i.e., the corporate players behind this committee, is the abolition of natural farming and the demolition of the complimentary and alternative healthcare industry. This is so completely outrageous that the natural reaction of most people is, *"Oh, don't be stupid! That will never happen."* Hitler wrote in *Mein Kampf*, *'The greater the crime perpetrated by the leadership, the less likelihood there is that the people will ever believe that their leaders are capable of perpetrating such an event'.* That wasn't exactly original, because Machiavelli had written pretty much the same thing in *The Prince* some 500 years previously, and 2000 years before that, Sun Tzu wrote the same thing in *The Art of War*.

Big Pharma

The pharmaceutical industry is a multi-billion dollar industry. Just to put things into perspective; in 2002, the combined profits of the 'top ten' pharmaceutical companies in the Fortune 500 were greater than the combined profitability of the other 490 companies in the Fortune 500. What is driving this is out-and-out greed. Ethics don't come into it.

There's an absolutely astounding book by John Braithwaite written, ironically, in 1984 called: *Corporate Crime in the Pharmaceutical Industry*. In his research, Braithwaite was trying to understand how it was that the senior executives in the pharmaceutical industry that he met, in their homes appeared to be 'normal' family men, but the moment they went to work and sat around the board room table, it was a case of 'Jekyll and Hyde' because they were complete bastards, without an ounce of humanity being brought to bear in any of their actions or decisions. Everything revolved around profitability regardless of the impact that it had on the general populace.

It is an established and accepted fact that the pharmaceutical industry is responsible for killing more people than any other cause of death on the planet. In the U.S., for example, the official figure is that, on average, 106,000 people die every year from properly prescribed medication. In addition, another 150,000 are killed through other medical blunders. One has to smile rather perversely, because the profession that has the shortest life expectancy in the U.S. is that of Medical Doctor – mainly because they believe their own hype, or they believe the hype that is fed to them by the pharmaceutical companies.

The pharmaceutical industry hooks people on medication at the earliest possible stage of their life, because the fundamental philosophy of the pharmaceutical industry is that every human life-form is a potential revenue stream; from the moment of conception to the moment of death.

A lot of research has been done, not least by Dr. Robert Verkerk, the Chief Executive of *The Alliance for Natural Health* to show that a few decades ago, people didn't have their physical bodies assaulted by the pharmaceutical industry on the grand scale that they do today, starting with the 26 inoculations that we give our children before they even start school.

The problem of obesity that we see in children today is a combination of the pharmaceuticals that we're pouring into their undeveloped physical bodies, coupled with the absolute junk that we're feeding them. Consequently, we end up with this symbiotic relationship between Big Pharma and Big Farmer. The nutritional value of the food served up in the western world today is greatly diminished from what it was even a generation ago – and then we wonder why our children are sick or obese... but, no worries, because the pharmaceutical industry will prescribe a drug to counter these problems.

It gets worse, because we have things like Aspartame in the food chain, which was recognized as a poison by the Food and Drug Administration (FDA) back in the 1970's. It was developed by a company called Searle, which is now part of the Monsanto organization. The chairman and chief executive of Searle (*none other than a certain Donald Rumsfeld),* put a lot of money into supporting the Reagan presidential campaign in the early 1980's and after Reagan was sworn-in on the White House lawn in January 1983, they contacted Reagan and demanded that he replace the head of the FDA with another individual; somebody who was likely to be more receptive to the proposition of introducing or approving the introduction of Aspartame into the food chain. Just five months later, in May of that year, Aspartame was given approval to go into the food chain.

We know today that Aspartame causes holes in the brains of young rats. It is linked directly with hyperactivity and attention deficiency in young people. In some countries, like France, Aspartame is actually banned in drinks that are marketed at under 12's. But here in the U.K. and in the bulk of the U.S., it's freely available. But, again, no problem – no problem that we've got kids bouncing off the walls thanks to copious quantities of Aspartame being pumped into their system because we have drugs like Ritalin; and we have a crazy situation where 40% of school-age children in the U.S. are either on, or have been on, courses of Ritalin. In the U.K., in 2007, the British government spent £28,000,000 on Ritalin. This is an extremely pernicious drug – in fact, it's so pernicious the pharmacologists don't really understand how it works, because Ritalin is actually a stimulant – it has properties very similar to cocaine, but in the young brain it seems to have completely the opposite effect and effectively turns them into zombies. And, of course, this is a precursor for drugs like Prozac, which a phenomenal percentage of women in the Western world have been prescribed at some stage of their lives.

Exeter University recently published a report, having surveyed the water supply around the UK; in every city tested they were able to find traces of estrogen and psychoactive drugs like Prozac in the water supply! Obviously, the body does not absorb 100% of the drug, which is effectively being 'peed' back into the system and is not getting removed as the water is recycled. Exeter University established that where there were high dosages of estrogen and psychoactives in the water supply, it was actually making the pond-life androgynous. We must consider the possibility that this could be happening to the human race. After just forty years of the ready availability of the birth control pill, which is the blink of an eye, we can already see that these things are having an impact on our biosphere.

Fluoride is another part of the control mechanism – it is an industrial poison. It was used by the Soviets and Nazi Germans to control their prison populations. Yet most dentists will put their backs against the wall and swear blind that fluoride is good for the teeth. Have any of them actually tested for themselves or seen any irrefutable evidence of whether fluoride actually does prevent tooth decay? There have been huge manipulations of research, and this goes on all the time, of course, where people use subsets of information to support their particular dogma. But the reality is – fluoride is a control drug.

Big Farmer

Dr. Arpad Pusztai worked for 30 years at the Rowett Research Institute in Scotland. In 1998, he went on British TV and stated that under no circumstances would he ever eat genetically engineered foods, because he had been researching the effect of genetically modified potatoes on rats and discovered that it had very serious effects on the stomach lining. According to Professor Robert Orskov, one of Britain's leading nutritional experts who has worked at the Rowett Institute for over 30 years, within one day of that broadcast going out there were two phone calls to the Rowett Institute from 10 Downing Street. It was very evident that the second phone call had been initiated by Monsanto, who had called Bill Clinton, who had then called Tony Blair, who called Philip James, the director of the Rowett Institute. The following day Arpad Pusztai was fired; he was suspended and gagged by the research institute. This is a very well-respected scientist who was releasing his honest research, but because it did not reflect the corporate agenda, then it was effectively shut down.

Back in 1973, when Henry Kissinger manipulated the oil crisis of 1973, he also manipulated a food crisis with the purpose of that wiping out the American family farmer and effectively providing agribusiness with an opportunity to buy up farmland across the U.S. Soon there was a very different type of individual running the farms than the family farmer who had taken great care to protect the health of his livestock.

The biotech industry is led by Monsanto; effectively controlling about 90% of all GM foods and GM crops, but other companies are also riding on this gravy train – like Syngenta and Cargill, for example. The Monsanto drug *Posilac* artificially enhances the lactation of cows. If you look on the web, and you google *Posilac*, you will see images of seriously deformed cattle where their udders are so big they can hardly walk. Although it did increase the milk production in the short-term, it also reduced the life-expectancy of the cow. Thankfully, many farmers have now started to reject the use of the growth-hormone drugs.

The rest of the world is being told by the WTO that this stuff is quite safe and there's no reason not to import beef that has been developed using this drug. The European Union (EU) knows very well that the people of Europe would not accept genetically modified beef but as fully paid up members of the WTO, the EU are not allowed to self-determine whether or not the people of Europe should or shouldn't have access to it. Consequently, the EU pays a fine of 150 million Euros to the WTO in the form of global taxation. The global government, i.e., the UN, represented in this case by the WTO, stipulates that the EU *should* be importing this contaminated beef.

In Korea in 2008, the WTO tried to force the Korean government to accept contaminated beef, and 40,000 people hit the streets in Seoul and refused to go home until the government basically agreed that they would not bow to the pressure of the WTO and they would not bring genetically modified beef into the food chain. It's one of the reasons why the Western media demonizes the governments of developing nations for not accepting aid. Many of these nations won't accept food aid because they are scared shitless that what they're going to import is genetically modified. Once genetically modified foods find their way into the food chain or into the growth chain, then it's nigh on impossible to remove it.

The Agenda

Codex Alimentarius is a long-term agenda. We can trace it back over a hundred years into the 19th century, although the modern-day version basically came into being in the early 1960's. They set long-term goals and then develop a strategy to achieve those goals because they know that humanity doesn't like change or conflict. It's called the process of gradualism, which often means going two paces forward and then one pace back. They create agendas that will facilitate both change and conflict, often by using conflict to create the catalyst for change. 9/11 is a classic example of that.

These guys are not religious per-se; they are not constrained by what we perceive to be traditional belief systems, but they use established religions simply as control mechanisms. This is actually represented symbolically by the separated capstone which hovers above the pyramid in the Great Seal, which appears on the back of the U.S. dollar. The separated capstone with the eye in the middle, which is referred to as either the Eye of Ra or the Eye of Horus, symbolizes the knowledge and the wisdom of the few which must be kept separate and away from the masses. But who are *'they'*? Well, we can certainly streamline it down to probably about thirteen families. David Rothkopf's book, *Superclass: The Global Power-Elite and the World they are*

Making identifies the global elite as no more that six thousand people. I would suggest that it's probably even less than that. Some of them are quite brazen about their agenda – in David Rockefeller's *Autobiography*, he says, *"For more than a century, ideological extremists at either end of the political spectrum have seized upon well-publicized incidents to attack the Rockefeller family for the inordinate influence they claim we wield over American political and economic institutions. Some even believe we are part of a secret cabal working against the best interests of the United States, characterizing my family and me as 'internationalists' and of conspiring with others around the world to build a more integrated global political and economic structure – one world, if you will. If that's the charge, I stand guilty, and I am proud of it.'*

There is no question that certainly the Rockefellers and the Rothschilds are two of the most powerful players within this cabal, and it's very clear that this cabal has very selfish and very limited morals in terms of pursuing their agenda.

I actually think that their belief-system creates their reality, just as our belief system creates ours. At the end of the day there is no such thing as light and dark, or good and evil – there just *is*. There is stimulus and there is catalyst. Humanity is fundamentally lazy. Fortunately, for most of us, our lives aren't one continuous stream of drama and catastrophe, yet paradoxically, it is drama and catastrophe from which we learn the most. If every individual took a look at the pattern of their life, they'll see a continual stream of unexpected drama and catastrophe weaving through it; hopefully they are learning from it. If they don't, they are likely to repeat the mistake and have to go through it again and again and again, like *Groundhog Day*.

What we're finding right now is that – for reasons that are beyond Newtonian explanation – a very significant number of people are going through a personal awakening process. Carl Jung basically said this is a natural process that generally kicks in around the age of 40, but none of us knows, really, when it's going to happen until such time as that moment occurs and – *hey presto!* You're in for a hell of a ride. In the Biblical texts this was known as 'metanoia', which has been mistranslated as meaning 'repentance', but what it actually means is having an opportunity to fundamentally change the way we think and to fundamentally change the way we see the world. Indigenous peoples have always recognized this. In the West, we would call it a 'mid-life crisis', but amongst indigenous peoples it's called a 'mid-life opportunity'. In many indigenous communities, an individual is not invited to be an Elder until they've been through this process. When people in the UK started to experience this 20 or 30 years ago, their families would rally round them and say, *"Come on, man! Get a grip! Keep a stiff upper lip!"* Instead of being allowed to go through this tremendous experience, it would effectively be shut down before it had even had a chance to get started. Fortunately, there is a growing awareness of this process; it's been very well documented thanks to the likes of Carl Jung, Stanislav Grof, Ram Dass, Richard Alpert, Stuart Wilde, Robert Anton Wilson, and hundreds of others who have shared the subsequent knowledge and understanding that they've gained from their own experiences. There's absolutely no reason today for people to feel that they're going crazy. But, let's recognize that it can go all wrong without the right support; if an individual is unable, for whatever reason, to integrate the experience then they can turn into delusional narcissists. Obviously in extreme cases, that's when some people declare themselves to be the messiah.

Rudolf Steiner said in a series of lectures that he gave in 1917 entitled, The Fall of the Spirits of Darkness, *"It will be considered a sign of illness for anyone to arrive at the idea of any such thing as a spirit or a soul. People who think like that will be considered to be sick and – you can be quite sure of it – a medicine will be found for this... Taking a 'sound point of view', people will invent a vaccine to influence the organism as early as possible, preferably as soon as it is born, so that this human body never even gets the idea that there is a soul and a spirit."*

That sounds outrageous, but Zbigniew Brzezinski, wrote a book in 1969 called *Between Two Ages – Americas Role in the Technotronic Era* which clearly says, '*The challenge for governments in the future will be to prevent man from effectively discovering his true self. And keeping humanity locked in consumerist materialism'*. Now, this is a guy who himself was in his early forties at the time. He's now in his eighties – he's been a part of the 'inner sanctum' for pretty much all of his adult life and here he is spelling it out in words of one syllable. It's very difficult to get hold of this book now; you can still get second hand copies of it.

Don't underestimate the Brotherhood; they certainly have a role to play here. It is a multidimensional, multifaceted game to these guys and humanity are their pawns. This is a very complex situation – that's why the study is called 'deep occult geopolitics'. Unfortunately for these guys, and fortunately for humanity, there's an increasing number of people who are wizening-up to the deep agenda, and are prepared to share their research and encourage others to take a look for themselves.

The big difference between the way in which we try to get people to see what's going on is that we don't try to tell people that we know *everything* that's going on (I'm sure in most cases that we're still missing a trick), but what we do is we encourage people to take a look at things for themselves; to step outside consensus reality and received wisdom. This is part of the process of metanoia. I gotta tell ya, that pretty much over the last twelve years I've been effectively re-learning everything, because when the realization came that everything I thought I knew was a complete crock of shit, and the evidence was actually *showing* me that it was, I had a choice to either say, *"Okay, fuck it. I'm not interested and I just want to spend the rest of my life playing golf"* (which was certainly an attractive option) or, *"Hang on a goddamn second! Am I really comfortable with the fact that humanity is being treated effectively as cattle by those who believe themselves to be superior to the rest of mankind?"* I guess that, at the end of the day, everybody makes their particular call. And you can judge for yourself what decision I took.

I want to encourage people to do their own research. I would be mortified if anybody ever simply regurgitated something they'd heard from me. What I try to do is sow seeds with people so that they will do some research themselves and come to their own realizations. There's a distinct disengagement between what we're being told and what we're finding out to be the truth.

We can change things by educating ourselves and taking the appropriate steps to ensure that we're not putting this crap into our own bodies, which means identifying our own food sources. Now, I'm very fortunate in that where I live in South Devon I am surrounded by organic farmland. My local shop is an organic farm shop. The water that I drink comes from a Dartmoor spring – I know the guy who bottles it, and the same guy delivers it. Now that's not to be a zealot on the subject because the likelihood of eating organic food in the average restaurant is slim to none, so I'm not suggesting that people must live the life of a recluse, only ever eating food that can be sourced, but most of us can control 80 or 90% of what goes into our bodies. We can take that responsibility. It's the same with health – one of the reasons the pharmaceutical industry is becoming even more aggressive in its attempt to get control of natural remedies is because people are beginning to recognize that complimentary and natural health is a far better way to remain healthy; it's more about prevention than it is about cure. Whereas the allopathics of the pharmaceutical industry are not about cure, they're about keeping people in the revenue stream. It's one of the reasons that I have a presentation called *Making Sickness Compulsory.*

I'm not saying that the pharmaceutical industry doesn't have a positive role to play – it does. There's no question that there are times when pharmaceuticals are extremely important. My issue is with the total lack of ethics employed by the pharmaceutical industry. Very few industries are whiter than white, but the pharmaceutical industry, in my opinion, absolutely leads the pack in terms of total lack of ethics.

Ultimately, businesses that are not ethical will fall by the wayside – but that won't happen overnight. In the first instance, *we*, as individuals, have to take responsibility for ourselves and our actions. Then hopefully we can encourage people, once they have taken the time and the trouble to educate themselves, even if they only manage to persuade one other person to look at what's going on, then they will have done very, very well indeed.

CHECK THE EVIDENCE, FIND THE TRUTH
Andrew Johnson

To acquire knowledge, one must study;
but to acquire wisdom, one must observe.
~ Marilyn Vos Savant, Writer

Andrew Johnson grew up in Yorkshire and graduated from Lancaster University in 1986 with a degree in Computer Science and Physics. He has mainly worked in Software Engineering and Software Development for most of the last 20 years. He has also worked full and part time in lecturing and tutoring (at a College of Adult Education). Now he works for the Open University (part time) tutoring and assessing students, whilst occasionally working freelance on various small software development projects. Andrew is married and has two children.

Since 2003, Andrew has given presentations and written and posted a number of articles on various websites about 9/11, Mars, Chemtrails and Anti-gravity research, whilst also

**challenging some of the authorities to address some of the data
he has collected.**
Website: www.checktheevidence.com

I've been interested in UFOs ever since, at the age of 9 or 10,
when coming out of a youth club I used to go to, I saw some star-
like objects circling one another. So, even from an early age I
knew that there was something to the UFO phenomena – it
wasn't people messing about and trying to make money or fool
people, even though there was still obviously some of that going
on. So the scene was really set for me at an early age...

One of the first things I researched when I joined the
"broadband Internet revolution" was the 1980 Rendlesham
incident, where an unidentified flying object had landed outside
the Bentwaters military base in the UK. I'd been aware of this
story for a long time and it's a very well-documented case... there
are a lot of official denials over it. My interest in the case led me
to further UFO research and eventually, in 2004 I met Larry
Warren – the security policeman who witnessed the landing.
Finding out about Steven Greer's Disclosure Project was a big
step for me in realizing that not only was the UFO-thing serious;
it was *very* serious...

In 2001, Greer organized a press conference in Washington DC
at the National Press Conference Club. There were 21 witnesses
present, testifying to their involvement in the UFO issue. Captain
Robert Salas said that he would be prepared to take an oath
before congress and swear that, in 1967, he had been in a capsule
underground at one of the minute-man missile installations in
North Dakota when he received a report from the 'top side' of the
base that an unknown object had come over the silo – at which
point, all his missiles became unlaunchable. This happened at the
height of the Cold War, so these things had to be primed and
ready to go at a moment's command. The common thread
between his testimony and the incident at Bentwaters was the

involvement of nuclear weapons. Bentwaters' nuclear weapons were *also* de-activated by a craft that flew over the base. That information didn't 'come out' until a lot later, but that's what happened…

Apollo 14 astronaut Edgar Mitchell also gave some testimony to Steven Greer's Disclosure Project, regarding his knowledge of people who knew of alien bodies being recovered from "crashed craft". Mercury astronaut Gordon Cooper's story is particularly interesting, because he said that he filmed an object landing at Edward's air force base in 1955. His film was taken away from him – it became classified information and he never saw it again, but he tells us that this story is true. The fact that we had never heard about this really shocked me, frankly. We've had hundreds of UFO programs over the years yet they'd never covered his story. As I realized that things were being hidden, I started looking further into other areas right across the board.

One of the big connections that Steven Greer's Disclosure Project made for me was between UFOs and the energy issue. He talked about this in 2001 at the press conference that I mentioned earlier, when he said that the reason we don't know the truth behind the UFO phenomenon is *not* because of aliens – but it has everything to do with energy. If we come to realize that craft are flying to earth from elsewhere in the galaxy and they're not using coal or petrol or gas, fossil fuels and nuclear energy… that they're using 'something else' – then we're eventually going to say, *"Why can't we have some of that?"*.

Chemtrails... *I Didn't Vote for Them!*

I first found out about chemtrails while browsing the web. Although I'd looked at the information and I already knew at that point that there was something going on. The clearest indication to me yet that it was happening literally right over my head was in June 2005, when I looked out of my window one evening and I saw a tic-tac-toe grid of aircraft trails in the sky.

I know enough about physics, about water condensation and vapor pressure, to know that this grid was a physical impossibility. I knew that it wasn't a realistic proposition that regular passenger planes were making the trails because you don't get air traffic flying in such a short space of time to make a grid – *it just does not happen...* this was a *design*. That grid pattern was a trigger point for me, and I started doing a bit more investigation into what was going on.

In February 2007, I was watching the aircraft overhead while my kids were playing at a local park. I had my camera with me and I filmed some video for about 15 minutes over a period of two and a half hours. In those 15 minutes of film which was taken, I filmed *42 aircraft* – and that's just the ones I filmed... I didn't catch them all, because I was looking after the children! The digital camera time-stamped all the clips, so that I could prove categorically that these planes were there at that time. I take a scientific approach and measure and date things, to make sure that all the data I collected is verifiable.

I've also done some time-lapse photography, which is very easy and inexpensive to do these days – all you need is a webcam.

You point it out of the window, run a program on your computer (which you can download online for free), leave it running for however long you want to, and then convert the footage into a 'movie'.

By June 2007, I had put together a 20-page report of my own analysis on chemtrails, including photographic and video evidence. 20 people who were also concerned about chemtrails endorsed my report, requesting that the issue be properly and honestly investigated. I posted this report on the internet and I sent it to Greenpeace, the World Wildlife Fund (WWF), the Department of Transport (DoT), Department of Environment (DoE), the Royal Air Force (RAF), and I also wrote a press release and sent this press release out to the media.

I didn't get a response from the RAF, I didn't get a response from Greenpeace. The WWF sent my report *back* – they said they didn't have the resources to investigate it. I *did* get a reply from Roger Worth at the DoT, whose response was, *"There is simply no evidence of unknown aerosols being covertly introduced and to claim otherwise is distorting the facts."*

This is the typical response you get when you're challenging the established status quo. Mr. Worth did, however, send me some useful information about a Professor Ulrich Schumann who'd written a report for the Institute of Atmospheric Physics based in Germany. Schumann's report about aircraft contrails was 26 pages long (the last six pages were references).

Schumann's report only contained about two pictures (there were no photographs of 'grids'). My report essentially had far more 'raw data' – I didn't reference other people's studies much and had used my own data that I could verify as being accurate. In my humble opinion, my report was of a higher quality than his in terms of scientific data... yet he works for the Institute of Atmospheric Physics, so who's going to be listened to?

I've come to the conclusion that non-governmental organizations like Greenpeace can't do anything because they take the official line that these are just aircraft contrails and so they're all banging on about carbon footprints and global warming, which has nothing to do with anything when you actually look at the data. CO2-based global warming is a fiction. There is so much other data which is hugely more significant. If a scientist who wanted funding for a project were to apply for a research grant for studying the squirrel population in Northern Scotland, for example she/he wouldn't get it – but if she/he applied for a research project into the *carbon footprint* of squirrels in northern Scotland, then they'd get their funding! 'Carbon footprint' has become a mantra now… it's everywhere – you see written on the side of buses, 'this truck has a lower carbon footprint'. That is the way that people get programmed to believe it, and it's relentless.

The following six points prove that we're not seeing aircraft trails – anyone who repeatedly says that we are and doesn't look at the other data is in denial.

1. Visibility of Trails on Satellite Photos

The mass of water vapor contained in a standard contrail would be tiny and certainly not observable from 150 miles up in space – yet as Jeff Challender observes, we can see the trails on many satellite photographs. When I took the video of the 42 aircraft in February 2007, someone I know was able to track down a satellite photo of Britain on that day – there isn't an exact time correlation but it's the same day and we can see the linear trails on this satellite picture.

2. Time of Trail Persistence

People will dispute this figure to the death but the vapor trails from aircraft should NEVER persist for more than about 2 minutes – even in ideal conditions. This can easily and clearly be demonstrated from the time-lapse footage, which you can view online (e.g. YouTube). A chemtrail does not even behave like a cloud formation – it does not 'billow' – it forms, spreads out and then 'fades away'. Clouds will billow and re-form as more water vapor moves around and the cold air mixes with the warm.

4. Irregular Pattern of Appearance

The number of trails seen simultaneously at a given time is variable. The frequency of the appearance of trails does not bear any noticeable relationship to levels of civilian air traffic. It is not possible to have such a high level of civilian or, for that matter, military air traffic (even during an exercise) which would generate my previously-observed number of trails (42 planes flying over a small area in 2½ hours). If it *were* civilian air traffic, then you should be able to observe a relatively steady pattern of trail appearances – like every Monday there's a certain number of flights in every direction, every Tuesday, etc., but it doesn't follow a pattern. You can have the same weather conditions prevailing but you don't get the same trail patterns from day-to-day – instead, you get different trails, different directions, and different amounts of trails. I have even been sent a sequence of pictures of a plane making a chemtrail *circle*.

5. Height of Appearance of Trails

With repeated observation, some chemtrails can be seen at much lower altitudes than any persistent contrails should ever appear at – this can be observed from the apparent size of the plane in the sky. For example, contrails are normally seen to form when planes are so high in the sky that it is difficult to make out the color or any salient features the aircraft may have. You can barely see the engines and you can see this little dot of a plane with the trails going out behind it. I have also observed persistent trails from aircraft in lower-level cloud contrails, where you can see the color of the plane, and the engines. Sometimes you can even see a chemtrail forming *below* cumulus cloud. A contrail doesn't form below cloud at such a low level.

6. Broken Trails

In many cases, instances of 'broken' trails are seen, and these 'breaks' are also persistent. If the trail was a contrail, a break in it would indicate that the engine had momentarily stopped burning fuel. Clearly, this would not make sense... you can't be flying along switching your engine on and off to stop the trail coming out – you're either going to get a continuous trail or you're not going to get one at all. The broken trails could also indicate there were very small-scale localized variations in air temperature or moisture level – but this would not happen as air temperature and pressure does not vary enough over a few meters to influence contrail formation this way. In some cases, the 'breaks' in these trails seem to be deliberate – perhaps to form some kind of grid or arrangement of a pattern.

The Missing Planes

If somebody says that, *"These trails are caused by ordinary aircraft"*, then surely we must be able to find out what they are... whether they're Easy Jet or British Airways flights, for example. Surely there is a database of flights in these days of supposed international terrorism? Somebody somewhere should have logged all these flights so that they know where the plane has come from and where it's going, because every flight has got to have a flight plan. So I wrote to my local airport (East Midlands Airport), the Civil Aviation Authority, and the Department of Transport – I gave them a date, time, and geographic location and requested information under the Freedom of Information Act about what particular flights had gone over at that point at that time.

The Civil Aviation Authority wrote back to me and said, 'No, we don't have any information about this – we don't know what these flights were because we don't deal with flights that come in above 30,000 feet'. In other words, unless you fly at below 30,000 feet, they're not interested – they don't deal with it... which was a bit of a surprise to me. They suggested that I contact the National Air Traffic Service, which I did – and that was just a weird experience... all I got was a reply about some event in California somewhere which was nothing to do with air traffic!

East Midlands Airport also replied, but *they* said that unless the flight is below 15,000 feet (?), as far as they're concerned it's out of their airspace and they don't need to worry about it, which is fair enough when you've got a busy airport.

So, from a data point of view, I've got people telling me that this is civilian air traffic but nobody seems to be able to provide any evidence that it is – we can't get information about the flight numbers or the airlines that these planes belong to from official sources.

I myself haven't tried to study and identify the planes specifically, but a friend of mine has – he's a bit of an 'aircraft-spotter', and has seen the KC767 military planes leaving chemtrails, as well as the KC135 which is a military tanker plane. Of the latter, he writes: *'It is powered by 4 engines, so unless the plane in question was only using 2 engines that particular afternoon whilst traveling at high speed, the nature of these two thick milky-white lines being released from the aft section of the aircraft is of great interest. To my amazement, a 747 crossed paths closely below the KC135 in question whilst I was observing the latter through binoculars – with the 737 leaving **absolutely no contrails** whatsoever'.*

I've got several videos of two aircraft in the sky where one's leaving contrails and one isn't. If it's down to atmospheric concentration of water vapor and temperature, etc., that doesn't happen... they either both leave contrails or they don't.

Climate Manipulation

I started to look into Wilhelm Reich and his work with 'Cloudbusting' and weather modification and began to collect evidence that the weather is actively being modified. I'm now totally convinced that the weather is categorically without any doubt being modified to quite a large extent. I suspect, although I can't prove it, that this is one of the primary reasons that chemtrails are being put down... to help with weather modification and weather control.

In 2008 when we had all the flooding in the UK, I was very suspicious because we didn't just get one or two, not even *three* weeks of continuously bad stormy weather – but around *eight weeks*. Hull and other places were flooded badly. It was almost as if these places had been specifically targeted. They were trying to promote the idea that the climate is now changing – that because we were a threat to the climate, the climate was now a threat to us.

People are getting fed-up with the big use of 'Big Agra', with Monsanto, etc. selling 'GM'-crops. What an increasing number of people want to do is have their own smallholdings and grow their own food. *However*, if you can control somebody's ability to grow food by controlling the weather, then you can control them. They want to control the food supply by introducing GM crops. If they can sell crops that are weather-resistant to damp conditions to farmers, then why *wouldn't* they manipulate the weather?

We already have the technology that allows us to extract energy from the environment without burning any fuel... without creating any pollutants at all. Quite a number of 'garage inventors' are experimenting with free energy devices – people like John Beddini, John Searle, Stanley Meier, *and various other people that I could probably give you the names of.* This technology works in various ways.

Unfortunately, some of that technology was used on 9/11 to destroy the World Trade Center. A lot of people are not aware that weather control was part of the 9/11 operation. That day, a category-three hurricane was closest to New York City, - 'Hurricane Erin', at 8am in the morning – we can show the unusual path that it took and there's no question about it. Dr. Judy Wood has shown that the barometric pressure and wind speed measured at JFK airport were constant throughout the day of 9/11, and that normally doesn't happen.

The 9/11 research that I've done has taught me how information is managed. People are given certain information to disclose – about UFOs, perhaps, and then as they build up their credibility, they become a source where people go to for information. People can then easily be 'managed' perhaps through mind control, threats, or bribery or even just feeding them selected information.

Free energy is real but it's already been weaponized. The ruling elite, or whoever they are, know all about this and they've known about it for a long time. They've got the technology and all the rest of us have basically become hostages to the lack of this technology. That's why we're in the dreadful state that we're in.

I think Chemtrails change the electrical properties of the atmosphere which is what enables them to control the weather, because they're using some type of 'field-effect' technology to control the weather. People have said that chemtrails have got barium and aluminum in them, and there does seem to be some evidence of that from collecting water samples. These metals are not good for human health. We know, for example, that if you go to the hospital and you have an x-ray you are given a 'barium meal', so we know that barium must have a special property, otherwise you'd have a copper meal or an iron meal or something. You're given a barium meal because it has properties that make it "radio opaque". It may be that it has an immunological suppression effect – in other words, whatever is coming down in these chemtrails is stressing our immune system. It's probably immunosuppressive, which makes us sicker, so we go to the doctors more, and we spend more money on drugs, etc... that would be my guess as to what is happening. I favor that as an explanation to chemtrails releasing bacteria or viruses, although that could well be happening, too. Apparently, these black projects are often dual-purpose – for example, 9/11 was obviously a dual-purpose exercise.

Everything going on in the world right now involves pushing people into a box of control – the 'credit crunch', ID cards, chemtrails, 9/11; the whole lot... it's all about taking people and shoving them into a box. You're *not* allowed to think for yourself, you're *not* allowed to breathe for yourself, and you're *not* allowed to decide on the issues for your own health which is why they are trying to control all the vitamin supplements now. It's a regime of fear – from debt to war and terrorism... from our health to the weather. If you can keep people in a state of fear, you can control them - that seems to be the primary objective.

I don't really have any idea what to do about chemtrails. It's scary that the very air that we breathe is being affected. The key factor about chemtrails is that it's a global phenomenon – it's not just in the U.S. or in Europe – it's worldwide. So, *who* has the authority to do this spraying all over the world? *Who is it?* When you look at chemtrails and you think about what they represent and what's happening, any idea that we have a democracy of any value just falls away.

Photo Credit: Katherine Proimos

HELPING GAIA AVOID THE DRAFT
Jerry E. Smith

If man can modify the weather, he will obviously modify it for military purposes. It is no coincidence that the U.S. Army, Navy, Air Force and Signal Corps have been deeply involved in weather modification research and development. Weather is a weapon, and the general who has control over the weather is in control of an opponent less well armed... The idea of clobbering an enemy with a blizzard, or starving him with an artificial drought still sounds like science fiction. But so did talk of atom bombs before 1945.
~ Daniel Stephen Halacy Jr., *The Weather Changers*, HarperCollins, 1968

Jerry E. Smith is the author of *Weather Warfare: The Military's Plan To Draft Mother Nature* (2006), *HAARP: The Ultimate Weapon of the Conspiracy* (1998), and co-author with George

Piccard (who wrote *Liquid Conspiracy: JFK, LSD, the CIA, Area 51, and UFOs*) of *Secrets of the Holy Lance: The Spear of Destiny in History & Legend* (2005). All three are from Adventures Unlimited Press (AUP). His website is www.jerryesmith.com

I first ran into the idea that my government might not be my friend during the Vietnam War. Every night on the TV, I got NBC, ABC, and CBS telling me how the war went that day – they all gave exactly the same damn story... it didn't matter which channel you listened to. Every morning, I got the British take on what had happened from the local newspaper (the only newspaper on the West Coast that had Reuters), and it was always completely different. This made me wonder... was Reuters wrong, or was I getting managed news? Of course I concluded I was getting managed news.

A wonderful book called *None Dare Call it Conspiracy* by journalist Gary Allen convinced me that conspiracy was the driving factor in human history. As he put it: *"Those who believe that major world events result from planning are laughed at for believing in the 'conspiracy theory of history'. Of course, no one in this modern day and age really believes in the conspiracy theory of history – except those who have taken the time to study the subject."*

I don't understand technology, but I'm neither a technophile nor a technophobe, I'm just not into the hard sciences. I grew up on sci-fi... between 1958 and 1972, I read somewhere around 12,000 sci-fi novels. What I read and re-read were the stories about the impact of ideas on a culture – how societies coped with new ideas or failed. What I write about now sounds like science fiction, but what was science fiction when we were in school is now in our pockets and on the dashboards of our cars! This is the 21st Century. We live in the future!

HAARP

The High-frequency Active Auroral Research Program (HAARP)

is a field of antennas on the ground in Southeastern Alaska so linked together as to work as one giant antenna. It is today the world's largest radio frequency (RF) broadcaster, with an effective radiated power (ERP) of 3.6 billion watts. It uses a unique patented ability to focus the RF energy generated by the antenna field, injecting it into a spot at the very top of the atmosphere in a region called the ionosphere. This heats the thin atmosphere of the ionospheric region by several thousand degrees. HAARP, then, is a type of device called an ionospheric heater. This heating allows scientists to induce conditions in the atmosphere, which allows them to do a number of things with the ionosphere. Controlling and directing the processes and forces of the ionosphere is called 'ionospheric enhancement'. While students and professors from the University of Alaska do the work on the ground at HAARP, a joint committee from the Office of Naval Research (ONR) and The Air Force Research Lab manages the project, which is being conducted on land owned by the United States Department of Defense (DoD).

An early HAARP document stated: 'The heart of the program will be the development of a unique ionospheric heating capability to conduct the pioneering experiments required to adequately assess the potential for exploiting ionospheric enhancement technology for DoD purposes'.

What might those DoD purposes be? Something about winning wars, eh? HAARP proponents claim it is nothing more than a simple civilian research station – which may be true, but what is it researching? It is not about understanding how the atmosphere works. That research was largely completed decades ago. It is about applying what we know to achieving military objectives. HAARP is looking for ways to weaponize the atmosphere.

This research is being conducted without adequate multidisciplinary oversight. The research itself, much less any application or technology developed from the research, has tremendous potential for environmental and human disaster. *Scientific American* noted that a dogleg in the jet stream over HAARP in 2000 resulted in a swarm of out of season tornadoes in Florida. HAARP is operating in frequencies known to have serious impacts on humans, yet there are no biological scientists involved. The European and Russian Parliaments have both demanded international oversight, and the US has simply ignored their concerns.

This is not like testing a new gun in a lab. This research is being done in the real world in real time with real natural systems and real potential for disaster - possibly irreversible disaster! The whole planet is the HAARP lab and that makes every living thing on this planet an unwitting subject of the experiment, which is a violation of the Nuremberg Code. None of us have given Informed Consent. If this is civilian science as claimed, then the international scientific community should oversee it, as the entire planet is affected. If it is military, as is clearly obvious despite official claims otherwise, then it should, at the least, have a proper multidisciplinary review panel and personal on the ground. Right now neither of those conditions are being met.

Starwars

On 23 March, 1983, President Ronald Reagan called upon *"... the scientific community in our country, those who gave us nuclear weapons, to turn their great talents now to the cause of mankind and world peace, to give us the means of rendering these nuclear weapons impotent and obsolete."*

This quest for the creation of a technology, of a weapon or weapons system, capable of making atomic war impossible was officially named the Strategic Defense Initiative (SDI). The press lost no time in dubbing it 'Star Wars', after the George Lucas movie.

That Initiative sent the United States military-industrial-scientific research community on the greatest, and costliest, weapons hunt in human history. Thousands of ideas were floated – hundreds of those were funded. Some lines of SDI research have since been abandoned. Some, however, are still being actively pursued to this day.

Not all of these ongoing developmental programs are taking place in laboratories of the military and its contractors. Some of these ideas involve technologies or applications that, as weapons, violate international treaties. Others, the use of which, would be repugnant to the ethical and moral values of the majority of Americans. In an effort to avoid public outcry, and international condemnation, some of these programs have been 'disguised' as civilian science. Like many people, I believe that HAARP is one of those. It is a sure bet that it is a ground-based Star Wars weapon system, although the people who work at it won't admit to it – and indeed, they might not even know.

Numerous studies have shown that if you inject RF energy into the ionosphere, an already electrically energetic area, you get a multiplication of the effect. The HAARP array is 180 towers with two crossed dipole antennas at the top of each tower. Each antenna has an output of 10,000 watts. Altogether that gives you 3.6 million watts, but when that hits the ionosphere it gets jacked up another 100 times and you have an ERP of 3.6 billion watts!

HAARP heats the region into which the energy is being injected (which is about 12 miles across by about two-and-a-half miles deep by about 90 miles up) by several thousand degrees to the point where the molecules are literally blown apart. If you break the bonds of a molecule it gives off a packet of energy, including a scream of ELF (extremely low frequency) radio waves that penetrate deep into the earth and sea. The United States Navy admits to having used HAARP for about 15 years to communicate with deeply submerged submarines.

This heating converts the affected atmosphere into an electrically-charged gas called a plasma. A plume of this plasma then heads out into space and keeps on going until it runs into something to stop it, which are the magnetic lines of force of the earth's magnetic field. The plume gets trapped between these lines of force and spreads out, forming a shield, just as President Reagan called for, of electrically charged particles that will disrupt or destroy anything electronic that encounters it, such as a passing spy satellite or an incoming ICBM (Intercontinental Ballistic Missile). By the way, this means every time they use HAARP they throw away a chunk of our atmosphere!

HAARP isn't the only ionospheric heater in use today. The Max Planck Institute of Germany operates one in Norway, and there's one at the big facility in Arecibo, Puerto Rico. There are two in Alaska. HAARP and another one operated by the UCLA (University of California, Los Angeles) called HIPAS (the HIgh Power Auroral Stimulation Observatory). Ionospheric heaters have been in use around the planet since the 1970s – the Soviet Union had about six of them.

The official line on HAARP is that this plasma plume goes out into space until it runs into the radiation belt, forcing it to precipitate hard radiation back to earth, which they say is a *good* thing because with the radiation in these belts reduced, spacecraft and radio signals can safely traverse them. But there has never been an Environmental Impact Study done on what happens to Earth when this radiation is dumped into the atmosphere. Indeed, the Environmental Impact Study that was done for HAARP is a total joke. It only measured the impact of the signal directly from the towers and completely ignored what would happen in and to the ionosphere, much less what the re-radiated energy from the ionosphere would do.

HAARP And Mind Control

In the 1950s and '60s Dr. J.F. MacDonald was Associate Director of the Institute of Geophysics and Planetary Physics at UCLA – who by the way are the folks who run HIPAS, Alaska's other ionospheric heater, located outside of Fairbanks, today. Dr. MacDonald was also a member of the President's Science Advisory Committee and the President's Council on Environmental Quality. He was also a member of the Council on Foreign Relations, which should ring some bells, and one of the JASONs, a military think tank at the very top of the Military-Industrial-Academic pyramid. He noted that one could use radio waves bounced off the ionosphere to induce mental dysfunction as a way to wage *covert* war!

I have been researching mind control since 1976, and so I am very much aware of the kinds of technologies that have been in use and under development. Walter Bowart's book *Operation Mind Control* blew the whistle on the CIA's mind control programs – MK Ultra, MK Naomi, MK Delta, etc. – which I detailed in my book *HAARP: The Ultimate Weapon of the Conspiracy*. The ELF that HAARP generates to communicate with submarines is at exactly the same frequency that the human brain works at. If HAARP is exactly what it says it is – nothing secret or sneaky about it – these guys could inadvertently induce mental dysfunction across half a continent and have no idea they're doing it. And if these guys *do* know what they're doing, this could be the ultimate mind control device.

In the 1950's, Dr. George Estabrooks (Chairman of the Department of Psychology at Colgate University) suggested that a small dedicated core of hypnotic technicians could be dispatched to the enemy population – for example, 100 dentists – who would hypnotize their subjects, give them specific commands, and then all that had to be done was give the command phrase to activate your 'sleeper army', turning the enemy population into your own soldiers. Of course, in the 1950's there wasn't an easy way to do that – we didn't have the technology we do today, to be able to ring every phone in a country at the same time.

These days, voice-to-skull is a proven technology – there are numerous patents on it. It's possible to put words in people's heads using a variety of technologies with radio frequencies, especially ELF. There is some evidence that the HAARP signal could be used to put emotions, possibly even words into people's minds. Estabrooks' vision could become a reality – all they've got to do is use HAARP to 'ring' every head at the same time…

HAARP AND HURRICANES

HAARP may be involved in controlling the weather over North America. In 2005, we had the largest number of named storms in history, and the largest number of category four and five hurricanes to make landfall, including hurricane Katrina. At that time HAARP was under construction. I believe that HAARP was rushed into completion – it was announced on DARPA's (Defense Advance Research Project Agency) website that it was finished in March 2006. They held the ribbon cutting in June 2007, but they finished the damn thing late in 2005 – a year-and-a-half ahead of schedule!

I believe the reason *why* they raced HAARP into completion was so that it could be used to create a hurricane shield. After Katrina in 2005, the weather pundits were saying that the 2006 weather season was going to be even worse, and I think they were very frightened of that happening again, especially during an election year.

Between 2006 and 2008 there was a stationary high-pressure dome over the Southeastern United States. Under that dome there were droughts, wildfires, and loss of life from the heat (which is why they can't admit to creating it without being sued), but as each hurricane came toward land, the dome acted like the rubber bumpers on a pinball game – the hurricane hit that high-pressure dome and bounced off, safely going back out to sea. In 2006, not a single hurricane made landfall – even though the pundits were saying it was going to be worse than 2005 season. In 2007… again, not one single hurricane. There has *never* been two consecutive years of zero hurricanes. This amazing high-pressure dome had never happened before, either – you usually get high-pressure that lasts for a few weeks… it forms, meanders around, and then dissipates. *This* high-pressure dome has formed consistently for *three consecutive years*. It's only there during the hurricane season and stays for the whole of the hurricane season. The dome itself has been getting smaller – it was huge in 2006, smaller in 2007, and smaller still in 2008.

In 2006 the weather pundits said that El Niño caused the dome, but there was no El Niño in 2007 or 2008, yet the damn dome was still there! I think this high-pressure dome is manmade. I don't know how they're generating it. My guess is that HAARP is involved in some way, but it's just a guess based on the date co-incidence of HAARP being rushed into completion early.

To add conspiracy theory on top of conspiracy theory… In 2007 and 2008, there were massive torrential rains in an area in central Texas where the government wants to build a 16-lane super-highway from Mexico to Canada as part of the NAFTA (North American Free Trade) Agreement to carry goods through what is looking likely to become the North American Union. Around 2005 the Texas state government announced that they were going to use eminent domain to take property from land-owners to build this freeway. Soon after, in 2006, the Texas Legislature passed laws making the use of eminent domain much more difficult. The next year heavy rains flooded the area. The following year, a hurricane (only two made landfall that year, both in Texas well outside the high-pressure dome parked over Georgia) walked straight down that path. It's very possible that the dome was manipulated, resized, to induce flooding in this area, as it would be much cheaper for the state to take property once it's distressed because it's under water.

Control of hurricanes was the Holy Grail of weather researchers throughout the 20th Century – from Project Cirrus in

1949 that may have misdirected a hurricane into Savannah, Georgia, to Project Stormfury in the 1960's and '70's that may have successfully reduced the peak winds of several hurricanes. If anything the desire to control these monster storms has only increased in the 21st Century and the technology to control them may indeed exist. The cover story for the October 2004 issue of *Scientific American* proudly proclaimed that Dr. Ross Hoffman and his team at AER (Atmospheric and Environmental Research) had figured out how to steer hurricanes – at least in computer models. Meanwhile a Russian company, Elate Technologies, claims to be able to create and steer these storms at will!

The most widely accepted way of modifying the weather is through a process called 'cloud seeding', which was invented in 1947 by Dr. Bernard Vonnegut (the little brother of famous novelist Kirk Vonnegut Jr.). He reasoned that a way to induce rain would be to introduce into moisture laden air microscopic particles that were very moisture friendly, that is, large numbers of water molecules would attached themselves to each of these 'seeds', called nucleating particles because the form the nucleus of a raindrop, to the point where it would become too heavy to stay aloft and would fall as rain.

Cloud seeding is used worldwide today, although it is under something of a cloud of controversy. The official position of the U.S. Meteorological Society is that if it rains after cloud seeding, you can't really say how much of it is natural and how much is artificial. All they are willing to say is that the evidence *seems* to indicate that *maybe* under certain circumstances it's *possible* that one can increase precipitation *slightly* or *possibly* prevent hail from forming. Scientists like crunchable numbers; they like to be able to quantify things. If they can't get hard numbers, they won't admit to anything.

War And Weather Control
Amazingly, the history of attempts to control the weather really

begins with the U.S. Civil War (1860 to 1864), when it was noted that great battles were often followed by great rainstorms. Now we know that this is because the smoke and dust of battle produces nucleating particles. The first U.S. patent for artificial rainmaking was granted to a U.S. Army General who had led an artillery battery during the war (on the Confederate side!). Gen. Ruggles believed that the concussions from the explosions of his artillery caused the rain, and his 'concussion theory' was patented in 1880. This means that the US Army has been intimately involved in weather modification technology literally since Day One!

The U.S. Department of Agriculture dispatched a team to test the General's theory and spent what, at that time, was a considerable sum of money – about $29,000 (which would have the buying power of about $250,000 today). The head of the team declared in his final report that, 'under the right circumstances, rain *can* be artificially induced'. This put the stamp of official government approval on rainmaking, and it wasn't long before it became 'off the shelf' technology.

In 1895, there was a drought across the Western Plains – Kansas, Okalahoma, and Nebraska in particular – and a veritable army of rainmakers showed up, each with their own various theories and secret techniques for how to make rain – and many of them did! To this day there is a certain stigma attached to being a rainmaker because of the snake oil salesman like demeanor of these men – many were sincere but a few where clearly charlatans. Dr. Vonnegut's discovery of an effective cloud seeding technology increased the rainmaker's respectability a little – and gave Uncle Sam a cool new weapon.

It is a well-established fact that the U.S military used cloud seeding as a weapon during the Vietnam War. Operation Popeye was an attempt to extend the monsoon season over Southeast Asia by cloud seeding over the Ho Chi Minh Trail in hopes of turning the Viet Kong re-supply route into a hopeless quagmire of mud. It first broke in the news in late 1971 in Jack Anderson's column in the Washington Post. Senator Claiborne Pell (Democrat, Rhode Island) launched an investigation in the U.S. Senate and called-in then Secretary of Defense Melvyn Laird, who *lied* to congress and said that it was all nonsense. Two years later, a private letter from Laird got leaked to the press in which he admitted that Operation Popeye was real and had been ongoing for a couple of years. Pell reconvened his investigation and got the Pentagon to agree to secret closed-door sessions, where they admitted that Operation Popeye had been ongoing from 1968 to 1972, that they had flown 2,600 sorties, releasing more than 47,000 units of cloud seeding material over four countries – North and South Vietnam, Laos, and Cambodia – the later two in violation of International Law. The project had a cost of about 21.6 million dollars.

Pell became what today we'd call the 'poster child' for a movement to create an international ban on using weather as a weapon. A treaty was jointly presented to the United Nations by the US and USSR in 1976 – The Convention on the Prohibition Of Military Or Any Other Hostile Use Of Environmental Modification Techniques. It was signed into Law in 1978. Prior to the United States being signatory to that convention, the U.S. federal government was spending between 40 and 140 million dollars *a year* on developing environmental modification technology and had over 700 degreed scientists working in federally-funded labs. After the U.S. signed that treaty, the budget went to zero and those jobs vanished. No, Uncle Sam did not say, *"Oops! Can't do that any more!"*, rather, the research was taken off budget and beyond Congressional scrutiny by being farmed out to civilian contractors.

Cloud seeding is now an established off-the-shelf technology available to anybody who's got the cash. When a local regional water board can afford to fund it for an entire season out of their regular budget, it's pretty cheap.

Weather Control Today

In the U.S. today, there are a number of civilian contractors engaged in environmental modification – for example, there's a private company in Fargo, North Dakota, with the hilarious name of Weather Modification, Incorporated. There are also a number of educational institutions involved in this – such as DRI (Desert Research Institute), which is a division of the Nevada System of Higher Education (NSHE). Weather Modification, Incorporated has contracted with the ski resorts in Sun Valley, Idaho, to increase their snow base and extend their operating seasons. Likewise, DRI has stations on the peaks of High Sierras to increase the snow pack, which then becomes the drinking water for California and Northwestern Nevada. The last time I looked, DRI had webcams on their mountaintop installations where you could actually *watch* the cloud seeders work in real time on your computer.

Those who are dedicated to weather modification, particularly the folks at DRI or Weather Modification, Incorporated, are very convinced that their technologies work, and work well. There are enough individuals, governments and corporations around the planet who agree that these guys are making big bucks.

While the U.S. privatized this technology, moving it from the Federal to the State and regional levels; the Soviets had a national level bureaucracy that spun itself off as a 'for profit' company, called Elate Technologies, when the Soviet Union broke up. They use a number of exotic technologies that are loudly scoffed at by the American mainstream. One of their claims is to be able to create and control at will what in the U.S. is called a hurricane, in the Indian Ocean a monsoon, and in the Pacific a cyclone. The only admitted time (in the world press) that we know that Elate Technologies whooped-up their 'big wind' was in 1998, when forest fires were burning out of control in Southeast Asia, particularly in Indonesia and Malaysia. Elate

Technologies went to those countries and told them they could create cyclones on demand that could blow out their forest fires – and Malaysia went for it! They ponied-up a never-disclosed amount of money and the Russians did indeed whip up a hurricane that blew out the forest fires. It also flattened a lot of villages and left a lot of people homeless.

If you look at what's happened around the globe since, there are other times when it appears to have been used. For example, during Gulf War II the strongest wind ever recorded in the region with the worst dust storms in 100 years, nailed the Allied advance down for three weeks. I think it's very possible that Saddam Hussein went to his old friends the Russians and asked them to buy him some running time – and they came back with, *"How much cash do you have?"*

Covert Weather Wars?

United States Secretary of Defense William Cohen said, back in April of 1997, that there were terrorists who *"… are engaging even in an eco-type of terrorism whereby they can alter the climate, set off earthquakes, volcanoes remotely through the use of electromagnetic waves…"* Is that really possible?

BusinessWeek magazine reported on 24 October 2005 that 'China has 35,000 people engaged in weather management, and it spends $40 million a year on alleviating droughts or stemming hail that would damage crops.' This army of Weather Managers promised, and delivered, perfect weather for the opening ceremonies of the 2008 Summer Olympics in Beijing. This was quite a feat because it took place during the rainy season. The Chinese held numerous Press Conferences before the Olympics to tout their weather technology and made a big deal out of the fact that they would be using a technique developed by the Russians for preventing it raining on their May Day Parade decades earlier. The Chinese have been massaging the weather over China for a decade now. North Korea, downwind of China, has been ravaged by droughts for that same decade – it is clear to me that China has been stealing North Korea's rain to water its crops, while fortuitously getting the side benefit of forcing Korea to buy Chinese food and follow China's political dictates!

In the 1960s Dr. MacDonald of UCLA wrote many articles on future weapons. In one that looked 50 years into the future he wrote: '... technology will make available to the leaders of the major nations a variety of techniques for conducting secret warfare ... techniques of weather modification could be employed to produce prolonged periods of drought or storm, thereby weakening a nation's capacity and forcing it to accept the demands of the competitor.' Are covert wars with environmental weapons actually taking place today? Many people believe there are!

According to Lieutenant Colonel Tom Bearden, what he calls 'scalar weaponry' is one of the technologies being used to modify and manipulate the environment for fun and profit. The term 'scalar' goes back to the American physicist Whittaker who coined the term in his scientific papers in 1909 and 1910. Whittaker was one of the first physicists to mathematically prove that there are more than four dimensions, which has sparked screaming debate in frontiers of physics circles ever since. At this point, most physicists agree that there are more than four dimensions to space/time, although they are still arguing over how many.

It's taken me more than a decade to grasp what Bearden says... he writes like someone from another planet and it really takes some effort to understand. Bearden maintains that the Russians developed scalar weaponry in the 1950's – in response to the U.S. getting the atom bomb, they went looking for some 'other' physics, some 'other' technology, some 'super secret science stuff' that they could use. They decided to weaponize Whitaker's work and came up with a way to inject a tremendous amount of energy into the space/time continuum around the earth and pull it out at points of their choosing. He claims that when the Soviet Union broke up, the bureaucracy responsible for this went rogue, spun itself off as a 'for profit' private company (Elate Technologies), and then sold this technology to the Yakuza – the Japanese mafia. The Yakuza used it against the Malaysian mafia, who owned the beach-front property in Malaysia that got hit by the 2004 Asian tsunami. Talk about the ultimate in drug deals gone bad!

With the question of how 'natural' natural disasters are, you have to look at each one individually and ask if science can give a plausible explanation for why it happened. For example, the undersea earthquake that set off the 2004 Asian tsunami had an unusual signature in the shockwaves. Scientists can tell the difference between the shockwaves of a natural earthquake and those of an atom bomb. This is how the 'Atomic Club' knows when there's a new member, if they set off a bomb that has the right signature.

20 years ago, India tried to join the club and they faked it. They set off a 'dirty bomb' – they mixed some atomic material with a conventional bomb so that the residue around the bomb site would appear as if from an atom bomb, but it wasn't, and the Atomic Club's scientists knew it and went 'wink, wink, nudge, nudge' to each other. When North Korea set off their atom bomb recently, there was a great deal of debate as to whether it was real or not. The signature of the undersea earthquake that set off the Asian tsunami had the signature of an atom bomb – not an actual earthquake... which indicates that it may have been an induced event as opposed to a natural event. Possibly induced with electromagnetic (radio frequency) waves such as Secretary Cohen said terrorists could do.

Global Warming And Agenda 21

Global warming is a scam. Al Gore and company's hysteria about climate change has nothing to do with the environment and everything to do with behavior control. If global warming is something caused by human behavior, then they can create a world government with police powers to stop that behavior. That's what they want. This is because they believe our consumer driven lifestyle is wrong and must be stopped. The mantra is that North America consumes 80% of the world's resources, but produces only 20% of those resources. This is seen as a crime against Humanity, and they feel compelled to stop us – for our own good of course. Two of my favorite quotes come to mind: sci-fi writer Robert A. Heinlein, said, *"Never trust an altruist"* and, more to the point, humorist and magazine editor H. L. Mencken wrote, 'The urge to save humanity is almost always a false front for the urge to rule.'

The United Nations (UN) funds the Intergovernmental Panel on Climate Change (IPCC). The IPCC's governing panel is composed of UN bureaucrats and agenda driven (activist) scientists. Since its last report was issued nearly 300 member scientists have quit in protest because the report misrepresented their findings – but you won't find Al Gore mentioning that little inconvenient truth!

The 1992 Earth Summit in Rio was an official meeting of the United Nations, where the document that is currently driving the UN into the 21st Century was created and signed into law as a binding resolution. This document is *Agenda 21* and it is the official Agenda for the 21st Century. This resolution, sponsored by, promoted by, and enforced by the United Nations, has created an ever-growing UN bureaucracy for 'sustainability'. It was signed by 172 nations, with only the US abstaining (Vice President Bush refused to sign). When Al Gore became the VP one of his first official acts was to sign *Agenda 21* for the US.

Sustainable development really means *no* development – it is all about changing behavior in the first world and preventing behavior in the third world – and don't forget the lovely side benefit of someday imposing a carbon tax, i.e. revenue stream, the life blood of government.

Agenda 21 called for the creation of an Earth Charter – intended to be a declaration of fundamental values and principles for creating a just, sustainable, and peaceful global society... yada, yada, yada – the preamble, if you will, for a new global constitution for the global government that would replace the UN with a bigger, badder Big Brother. The drafting of the text for the Earth Charter was overseen by a Commission, convened by Maurice Strong, who called the Rio Earth Summit, and Mikhail Gorbachev – now here's one for you, Gorbi, a 'former' hard-line Communist, was tasked by the UN under *Agenda 21* to write a new environmental *moral code* to build their new and improved Super UN on!

The Earth Charter was completed in March 2000 and launched in a ceremony at The Peace Palace in The Hague, Netherlands, on 29 June 2000. Virtually all of the environmental community has since signed it, including more than 5,000 NGOs (non-governmental organizations), but a single government has yet to sign it. What nation would sign it, knowing that in doing so they acknowledge the end of the Age of Nations?

Conclusion

What I see happening in the 21st Century are several competing dynamics. At the super-state level we have eco-communists, like Al Gore and Mikhail Gorbachev, trying to create a true world government that would effectively abolish the nation-state as we know it. As global warming plays into their hands they may actually be exacerbating the heating to gain political strength.

At the national level we have individual powers, like China with North Korea and the US with Iraq, elbowing each other for wealth and resources. And at the 'gun for hire' level we have corporations, scientific organizations and criminal syndicates playing with the environment for fun and profit. Some operations, like HAARP, are somewhat in the open, others are covert.

Regardless of openness or lack there of, this environmental mischief puts the cross-hairs of unseen and unthinkable weapons on all of us.

In 1969 Dr. MacDonald wrote: 'Our understanding of basic environmental science and technology is primitive, but still more primitive are our notions of the proper political forms and procedures to deal with the consequences of modification'.

It would appear that the gap between our understanding of environmental science and technology and our ability to grapple with this knowledge as a body politic has changed little in the intervening decades.

Photo credit: Sue Quatermass

BEYOND ECOLOGY
Peter Taylor

A human being is part of the whole called by us universe, a part limited in time and space. We experience ourselves, our thoughts and feelings as something separate from the rest. A kind of optical delusion of consciousness. This delusion is a kind of prison for us, restricting us to our personal desires and to affection for a few persons nearest to us. Our task must be to free ourselves from the prison by widening our circle of compassion to embrace all living creatures and the whole of nature in its beauty. The true value of a human being is determined by the measure and the sense in which they have obtained liberation from the self. We shall require a substantially new manner of thinking if humanity is to survive.

~ Albert Einstein (1879 – 1955)

During his varied career, Peter Taylor has lectured widely in Universities, published papers, acted as an advisor to various governments, the EU and the UN, and followed the rule of science whilst at the same time studying and training firstly in yoga, then shamanic practice. The latter has taken him to many teachers. He was initiated by the legendary Himalayan yogi, Babaji, and has taught yogic practice and spiritual training focusing on the healing power of breath. He has also worked with Native Americans and neo-Druids and leads an international shamanic *Ghost Dance* project. He is currently working on an integration of the scientific and shamanic world views in a book provisionally titled *Shamanic Ecology*.

Peter studied Natural Sciences at Oxford University, graduating in 1970. For a few years he indulged a passion for mountains, deserts and jungles, crossing the Sahara and climbing the Eiger, meeting many peoples from all levels and cultures, and eventually returning to Oxford to do research in Social Anthropology. In 1978, he left the University to set up his own research group, aiming to provide scientific and legal support for communities threatened by dangerous and polluting development. His group became heavily involved in the nuclear issue, energy policy, and ocean pollution (his autobiography *Shiva's Rainbow* ends with the sinking of the Rainbow Warrior). Peter was glad to move on in the mid-1990's to more creative conservation work in wildlife and forestry. He published *Beyond Conservation: a wildland strategy* in 2005 and set up a network of pioneering land managers called the Wildland Network. In the last few years he has looked very carefully at climate issues and has a new book just published *Chill – a reassessment of global warming theory*. There is a DVD of his climate analysis by the *Holistic Channel* and his ecological work can be accessed at www.ethos-uk.com

In the mid-seventies when I was living in North Germany, there was a proposal to build a massive nuclear fuel reprocessing plant a couple of miles away. Being a trained ecologist, I was listening to these guys in smart suits talking about how the radiation would be below certain levels, and I was thinking, 'Hang on... you're telling me you *release* radioactivity into the environment?' (I was very naïve in those days). I asked a few awkward questions and got in touch with the local university at Bremen and talked to some physicists there who were radically anti-nuclear and were working against that centralized, elitist, white-coated... almost a priesthood. Part of their concern was that the people heading the company were old Nazis. We were appalled by the idea of a plutonium factory in Germany run by the same guys who, in the seventies, had been engaged in clandestine nuclear programs in places like Chile and Argentina. We mounted a very powerful campaign and prevented it from being built.

For me, then, it was a revolutionary awakening to the forces that were at work. For example, when we organized an occupation of a French reactor site, the military came in and gassed us. It became very stressful for my wife, who had married someone who was a writer and a bit of a hermit, to suddenly find herself plunged into an intensely dark and stressful existence. After a while, we headed to Oxford, England – my intention to build a more secure future for us as an academic.

While in Oxford, the British Government announced that they were going to build an identical plant at Windscale in Cumbria (later renamed Sellafield). I managed to get hold of the plans for the operation and realized they would be discharging thousands of times more nuclear waste than the German plant. They were already discharging vast amounts of radioactivity into the Irish Sea. It was a real shock, and I became very engaged in opposition. Although I was connected to the Green movement – what was known in those days as the Ecology Party (a small group of us actually drafted the Ecology Party Manifesto in Oxford), I was really quite surprised that none of them were interested in radioactive discharges... they were all looking at economics and energy strategies.

By the early eighties, I'd set up a small but very strong group of engineers, scientists, sociologists, and lawyers (Political Ecology Research group). We were very effective and in one case discovered that they had lost supplies of a particular gas and came very close to a major nuclear incident which would have certainly matched the scale of Chernobyl. The more we found out the worse it was... I became quite obsessed with it, which completely destroyed my marriage. After we found out that there had been some incidents at the plant where they had contaminated the sea, we collected data from along the coastline and eventually forced a public enquiry. Greenpeace became interested in the discharges from a marine perspective and sent boats out there.

It was horrible, in many ways. We were heavily locked in battle on all fronts – discharges, reactor safety, reprocessing plutonium, nuclear weapons testing, chemical discharges... the whole deal. They were concerned that because we knew what was going on, we had information that could be used for terrorist groups, like the IRA. Around that time, when we realized that the forces we were up against were actually strengthened by our opposition, we also realized we were under 'psychic attack'. We had to rapidly learn about a whole other dimension of reality as it applied to the political world. This couldn't have happened if I hadn't had a grounding in yoga and martial arts, as this was an area I'd read about that we suddenly were being faced with. At that point, we collectively started to distance ourselves from the battle.

It's a bit like dealing with the Roman Empire – there's no point in trying to think you can overthrow the whole Empire... you can maybe safeguard your own little patch as best you can, and eventually the whole thing will transform through its own processes. I realized that during the battle, I had completely lost track of my own creative power by continually reacting to someone else's agenda. What I could've been doing on a creative level is the big question, and I didn't wake up to that until pretty much 1990's, when I then became engaged in the conservation side of things.

We had some successes... we certainly contributed to cleaning up the ocean. Eventually the government capitulated, threw their hands up and said, *"We agree with you guys – this industry needs controlling"*, and they brought me in on an advisory basis in 1985 for a couple of years. It wasn't until about 1992 that we finally tied it up through a legal process with the UN. It cost 'them' many billions in terms of things they could no longer do or invest in – such as cheap options for disposing nuclear waste at the bottom of the ocean, and all manner of things in relation to chemicals and the chemical projects they were planning.

Moving on to a More Creative Life

I still maintained my conservation work, and I wanted to do something really creative that would stretch me. I'd been trying to persuade the Countryside Agency that one of the problems with the whole approach to the countryside was that there were no means for people to visualize the changes being proposed, whether it was new forests or wind turbines or whatever. My children were getting heavily involved with computer games, where they would go into these mythical landscapes, and I thought of doing something like that in relation to visualizing the future of the countryside. I looked for a computer modeler and, quite by chance, I found a 3D computer animator in Glastonbury (Richard Fraser) who developed mythical landscapes in his spare time. Eventually the model started to look like Shropshire and East Anglia instead of something out of Tolkien! We built these models, where you can 'fly' into them... you can design your own houses, and factories, and turbines and you can put them wherever you like. We were the leading visualization specialists at that time.

However, expertise with models led me back to critical antagonistic work (old habits die hard!). In 1988, environmental modelers had raised an industry probably worth I'd say twenty or thirty million dollars. As soon as it was taken up by the UN, the whole thing took off – by the turn of the century, something like two billion dollars a year was spent on computer modeling and during the final stages of writing *Beyond Conservation*, and looking more closely at climate and biodiversity issues, I suddenly realized they had used virtual-reality computer simulation to create a whole world. Meanwhile, little money was spent on actually monitoring the environment itself – not just the temperature, but studying cycles of past temperature change, which you have to infer from proxies in ice, icicles, stalagmites, ice fields, sediment structures, tree-rings, etc. The nitty-gritty science, which is very time-consuming, was in comparison very neglected.

I already had a little knowledge of the science. In 1996, the Countryside Agency were concerned as to what the implications of global warming might be for them, and asked me to review a report they had commissioned from Professor Clayton's team at East Anglia University (which was the top climate science research group). My advice to them was, *"Don't believe what their model is telling you."* It was entirely linear. There wasn't a single reference in the whole report about the oceans and the North Atlantic conveyor system – if you warm the North Atlantic, you'll hit some kind of tipping point, where you could shift the whole circulation of the Atlantic... it's happened before in geological time. If that happens, paradoxically, in the 'warming world', Britain could be as cold as Halifax, Nova Scotia, which would be Northern Europe's natural climate if it weren't for the trajectory of the Gulf Stream, as we're on the same latitude.

In 2006, a unit in Southampton studied data over a fifty-year period, where there was a 20% slow down of the circulation from 1942 to 1992, and a twelve-year period, where there was a drop of 30% between 1992 and 2004. I contacted them and I said that 20% over fifty years and 30% over twelve years is an exponential decay – we're looking at a complete shut-down of the Atlantic conveyor by 2015. The experts said, "You can't combine those dates", but it wasn't at all clear why not, and the answers are complex and uncertain. Basically, you can't plan on the assumption that within fifty years we're going to have a climate rather like Northern Portugal. You've got to plan for a robust system that's resilient to change in any direction – it could get colder... it could get warmer, drier, or wetter. That's a lot different than trying to work to a prediction. Personally, I would send working parties to Sweden – they have to cope with extremes... very dry summers and very cold winters. They don't grind to a halt when they get a few inches of snow! We need to look at their transport system, their agriculture system, housing, habitation... the whole deal.

On these issues I developed a visual presentation for The Countryside Agency and presented to all the other government agencies. The slides looked really beautiful – they were very diverse and covered all the possible scenarios... what the landscape and rural life would look like if we carry on without any consideration for community, for sustainability of social and cultural values, landscape values, and biodiversity. If we had to source all of our energy potentially from renewable power, we'd have mega-turbines on every single hill, we'd have barrages on the estuaries and small hydros buzzing on every stream, and 15% of agriculture would be needed to produce fuel for power stations. It would completely transform the countryside.

I showed them the so-called 'S4 Scenario' (derived from a Royal Commission study), where the first objective is to reduce demand by 50% and only then develop small-scale production of power in a completely decentralized grid. The maximum size for a biomass (like woodchip) power station would be around two megawatts. They would sit on the edges of villages or towns, or in clusters around the edges of a large town. They're low-profile small stations which blend into the landscape. Wind turbines, if you have them on land at all, are small-scale – they don't intrude on the landscape. The huge turbines are all off-shore, far enough out not damage the scenery. The biomass stations are fuelled by short-rotation coppice – willow or poplar, grown locally, and it's tractored in from a few kilometers away – there's no need to build any new infrastructures like bypasses, because you're not dealing with any heavy transport.

With this Sustainable Scenario, there was also massive investment in new solar technology – solar roofs, tiles, walls, and micro-generators in every home, about the size of a refrigerator, which would generate electricity and heat from a fuel cell. The technology was just breaking then, but it's now commercial. The scenario would require massive amounts of money because all of these renewable sources are many times the cost of even fossil fuels at the current price. This is the price you'd have to pay for sustainability, for not destroying the very thing that's worth living for. But in order to explain that you need to be able to visualize it, and that's what my work began to do.

I delivered this visualization presentation at an inter-agency meeting to people like Scottish National Heritage, the Environment Agency, the Countryside Agency, and the Countryside Council for Wales, and I said that if the Atlantic shifts then we'll get plunged into a cold scenario. We'd have frozen rivers during the winter, for example, and I showed some pictures where I'd had some fun turning these landscapes into winter, deep-freeze scenarios, as well as flooding the whole of East Anglia and looking at the changes there. At that point, the Environment Agency climate expert stood up and questioned the professional integrity of our team for even considering a cold scenario, saying, " *It's well-known that the UN have said there's no possibility of a cold scenario. It doesn't need to be considered, not for 200 years.*" When I asked if she had seen the figures for the speed at which the conveyor is changing, she had not. I explained that if it's a linear progression then it *would* take 200 years, but having seen the data, I told her it could be exponential. It's a classic example of scientists just following authority and not looking for themselves.

That was the last contract I had with the Countryside Agency. It was too controversial for them, but I recall, a couple of weeks later, the BBC *Horizon* program interviewed oceanographers from the top institutes in the States, who said that this could indeed happen in a matter of decades.

The Use and Abuse of Computer Models

The visualization models I developed are an artistic dimension of computer modeling aimed at helping communities. In contrast, the climate models are all about justification of policy and are constructed with box diagrams, algorithms, formulas, and so on... you don't really *see* anything. Because of my familiarity with and previous critique of modeling, I also understood the ways in which models could be 'tweaked'...

When I was on a British government commission to review the science of the dumping of radioactive waste in the ocean, the Ministry of Agriculture, Food and Fisheries (MAFF) were already the lead authors of a major UN review, so I naturally insisted that we had a copy of the first draft – a document about an inch-and-a-half thick – and I made sure I was really familiar with it. In between the first and the final draft of the MAFF-led assessment being delivered to the UN, Scandinavian ministers were pressuring the British government because they had discovered evidence of radioactivity moving from the Irish Sea across to Denmark and Norway and they were, naturally, concerned about their fisheries.

When I got hold of the final draft, I was astounded. In the first draft, their argument was that the radioactive material would sink into the sediment in the mid-Atlantic, and either stay there or move slightly north with the currents up as far as Greenland. This bottom water is pretty isolated but there was a possibility that they had built into their first model, caused by a phenomenon called Shear transport – that the down-flow from the Arctic would accelerate the radioactive materials flowing in a counter current, upwards, so the contamination *could* surface in the Norwegian Sea. Of course, the final published model had abandoned the Shear transport phenomenon. Instead, the radioactivity now turned around, and took 500 years before it surfaced *in the Antarctic* where there's been no political concern about fisheries.

When I delivered this news of a revised model to the floor of the UN and said, *"This is blatant manipulation of the models for political reasons"*, that spelled the end of the dumping program. The British government and MAFF never forgave me for that! My last piece of work in this area was in 1993 when I published scientific papers critical of the UN's failed system of protection (relating to toxic waste as well as nuclear waste). I gave some indication of how to avoid the same kind of mistakes recurring but it is clear from the climate debacle that they still haven't learned.

Whenever there is strong political resistance to considering certain scenarios there is likely to be major interference with the science. Any scientific data that runs counter to computer models of the preferred policy is then passed off as controversial or uncertain. In climate projections, the UN believes that their models are accurate to within 95%. When you look at the models you find that that's rubbish. The models are deeply uncertain in key areas. If you go into the working groups where the real scientists are active, these levels of uncertainty are acknowledged. There is actually no consensus in the IPCC on what causes climate change – only that the temperature has increased.

The early models were saying that we might hit trouble in around 2050 and 2100 if we double carbon dioxide levels. At that time, I had accepted the whole carbon dioxide issue completely. You naturally assume, and everyone tells you, that carbon dioxide is a greenhouse gas, so it's bound to get warmer. I thought I'd have a look, just to see what was going on, because it just didn't make sense- many things predicted for 100 years hence were already happening. I was also concerned about the remedy proposed for the sickness – nuclear power, biofuels and endless arrays of wind turbines.

Having realized that the carbon dioxide model could be wrong, I spent weeks in the British Library trying to track down the original physics that programmed the computer models, and I couldn't find it. Even the UN report explaining their carbon dioxide model (which was probably the most difficult document I've ever had to get hold of – I've only ever seen one copy anywhere) doesn't say anything about the original physics and doesn't even contain the original references.

I wouldn't have been able to persevere with climate research without the internet (not now running a research group), though even then it is galling the number of times I've located a crucial paper that the journal want $30 online to access – and this is work that has already been paid for by the public in taxes! I then have to track the authors, find out if the paper is downloadable directly from their personal website and, if it isn't, then I e-mail and ask if they will send me a copy. Now, that could take me a whole morning… so, although the internet has its uses, it can be very frustrating.

I was deeply shocked during this research by what I found. I had no idea that a great deal of substantive science had been published in the peer reviewed literature on the potential effects of the solar, electric, and magnetic field on climate. *I had no idea!* Natural cycles are very powerful. I've been studying them since, and I'd say they're driving 80% to 90% of the changes that we see.

The most crucial scientific data was published in 1997 by the Danish Meteorological Institute. It was ignored by the third meeting of the IPCC in 2001. If they were really concerned about what was driving the climate, scientists would have looked at this new data and taken it seriously. But, of course, that's exactly what they *don't* do that because it goes against everything they've ever said. And contrary to a good scientific education, they are incapable of seeing and more of saying that they might be wrong. Maybe there are sociologists somewhere who are looking at what scientists get up to who, and who do have words for this syndrome. For myself, I'm quite happy to go out there and say, *"This is what I think is happening and I might be wrong"*, and I'm willing to look at any argument that will show me I'm wrong. That's true science.

The problem is that institutional pressures and prior commitment work against such open mindedness. With management structures in major institutions (including environmental groups like Greenpeace, Friends of the Earth, the Environment Agency, the Countryside Agency, and so on), the human resources experts, the PR people, accountants, and anyone else who's got a position on the board of directors of whatever institute you're dealing with – they are more concerned with managing a business than in truth or science. What happens is they put pressure on whoever is representing the science. The policy maker wants a single, certain answer – i.e.; 'What are you certain about?', 'We want one answer... we don't want alternatives', 'We don't want to know that you might be wrong'. If you say to a policy maker, and this also applies within governments, *"Sorry this area is indeterminate. It's uncertain, and it's actually not possible to know"*, then they won't give you any money. If you say, *"Well, quite a lot of this kind of change is natural, which you can't really do anything about, and it's also very difficult to predict"*... then they also won't give you any money.

All of these forces and pressures operate within the IPCC and within all the institutes that contribute to it, and so gradually, over time, the uncertainty and the caveats get removed. It depends a lot on the political environment – sometimes it works in their favor to listen to those scientists who say, *"Look, the science is uncertain"* but fundamentally, there'd hardly an institute worldwide that's standing out (two that I know which study the Arctic). I could maybe find three or four scientists on each continent who are outspoken and qualified, and so maybe you're looking at twenty worldwide. These people are mostly meteorologists, sedimentologists, Arctic scientists, and oceanographers. The professional meteorologists are probably the strongest contingent of the dissidents.

Christopher Monkton, now in the House of Lords, has been giving climate scientists a really hard time. I learned from an article he had authored in the American Physical Society newsletter that James Hansen from NASA was the originator of the carbon dioxide model and is directly responsible for manipulating that data. He is the Director of the *Goddard Institute of Space Studies* who are one of four major compilers of world temperatures. The Intergovernmental Panel on Climate Change and (IPCC) prefer to use them and they consistently produce higher figures than any of the other four.

Christopher Monkton was pointing out something that I'd heard of in the very first meeting of the IPCC. One senior meteorologist had objected to Hansen's model, saying that it relies, for its effect, on a water vapor amplifier. The ability of carbon dioxide to warm the atmosphere itself, on its own, is not significant. Even if you doubled the levels you would only increase the temperature by about one degree. Hansen assumed a water vapor amplifier would amplify the effects by 300%. Richard Lindzen, Professor of Meteorology at MIT, said, *"You can't assume that. Water vapor can just as easily turn to cloud."* Cloud will then cool things down... it's a negative feedback. Lindzen was overruled. He initially resigned, and then he returned to the IPCC and is still pointing this out in the working groups, but of course you never get to hear about it. It's bizarre the way he was ignored, and is still ignored.

Professor Lindzen made all these points in a documentary, *The Global Warming Swindle*. Did it make any difference? The world's press denigrated the program... they said it made loads of mistakes; unfortunately, it did make one or two. There were other motives that the program makers had, so they weren't that careful about the science. Basically, they wanted to illustrate that global warming is a way of controlling the economies of the world and preventing Third World countries from developing and exercising their birthright to ever more power stations and electricity, and I cannot subscribe to that. In my view, the whole development model has to change.

I would say that two-thirds of the critics of global warming are politically right wing. The left liberals see anyone who opposes global warming as being not only psychologically contrary and a 'denier' and whatever other labels they put on it, but they also see it as right-wing conspiracy from oil industries and corporations. Unfortunately, in some cases it's true.

When I first saw Al Gore's film, *The Inconvenient Truth*, I thought, 'Hmm, he's a dodgy character'. In my decades as a scientist I had also studied anthropology and had some shamanic training. So I dreamed into his little set-up with the help of the plant spirit medicine called Ayahuasca. Interestingly, at this time I was giving a talk at the Green Gathering in the West of England. I usually give a climate science power-point presentation, but I decided to approach it from a different angle before I went into the science... I had this big picture up at the front – a wonderful image of a snowy owl (owl 'medicine' is very good at seeing beneath the surface). I asked everyone to meditate with the owl in order to look at climate change more deeply, behind the surface. I then asked them to bring Al Gore's face into their consciousness and look 'behind him' through shamanic eyes for a few minutes. When I asked them to tell me what they saw, it was incredible. They were spot-on with their perceptions, which had everything to do with dodgy connections, finance, and power – someone even came up to me afterwards and said, *"I couldn't say this in front of everyone, but do you know about the Illuminati?"*

Al Gore is a business man. Several years ago, he set up a company called Generation Investment Management with various people that he pulled out of the banking corporations – including Goldman Sachs, which is one of the biggest global investment banks. GIM now manages billions of dollars of assets. It specializes in carbon trading.

If the U.S. government backs carbon trading (and maybe they will have by the time you read this) Al's company would clearly benefit. He was worth about two million dollars in the year 2000 when he nearly became president, and this is a significant step up from that. It would be great to think that he was a wonderful environmentalist, using his power because he cares about the planet, but I think he's been supping with the Devil and has neglected to use a very, very long spoon.

What the ayhuasca vine showed me is that the carbon issue is a magician's trick. I was told that these people want us to focus on carbon because it has a certain frequency. By focusing on that, on a deep cellular level, you're tuning-into survival and the fact that, as a human being, you are a carbon life-form, which is mutable. In other words; you're born, you live, and you die. That is why the whole global warming issue is about fear and survival and, as your consciousness tunes into the wavelength of survival and the fear of not-surviving, it's what it's *not* tuning-into that is the magician's trick. We are being distracted while the magician busily deals with the rabbit.

As you know, the main driving force is the sun. That's a different energy, with a hydrogen frequency. Hydrogen is the simplest element. In fact, the sun's energy is *dissociated* hydrogen

– it's beyond matter. The solar wind is not matter, it's a dilute plasma. As such it has the frequency of eternity (beyond destructible form), and hence of spirit and eternal life, which is life-affirming and creative. The sun and the solar wind are beyond survivalism. Many indigenous teachings tell us we are in essence solar beings. Does anyone in the climate change business, global warming, Al Gore, Sir David King, Tony Blair, Greenpeace… do they talk about the eternal spirit? Do they talk about natural cycles and how we could be facing a major destruction, like the Hopis talk about? In the face of that level of destruction, what do you do? Do you turn to carbon and survival or do you turn to the deeper teachings of spirit and love.

In this game, we have got to reach out to younger people and city-folk on another level. Conservation is fuddy-duddy… it's like Victorian stamp-collecting. I'm an ecologist, but that science paradigm isn't going to save the day – we're marginalized. Or if we fall for the carbon trick, controlled and manipulated to maintain the banking system and the power of elites.

There's a much more exciting dimension to our life which is the shamanic one, and we should be embracing that. The spirit of ayhuasca said to me, *"Look at your own life. Way back in the sixties and seventies, you were a naïve environmentalist. You really cared about the planet. You engaged in all kinds of politics, you battled and fought, and eventually came to some sort of spiritual awareness, where you had a choice of allegiance. You chose love, you chose Spirit. Al Gore had the same journey, only he's chosen a different bunch of spirit people and they are very dark."*

Whether he's fully conscious of what he's got himself into, I don't know… The one thing I learned in the 80's, is that all the top scientists, the top bankers, and the top military people have their own esoteric training. They practice their own ritual magic, their own secret religion. A lot of them pretend to be Christians – Silvio Berlusconi, the prime minister of Italy, wouldn't get anywhere if he didn't pretend to be a Christian, and if he really owned up… well, look at what happened in 1982 when a Masonic lodge in Rome, P2 – Propaganda Two, was broken open by Italian magistrates and a list of all its members was produced. All the top powers were there, including the Vatican's bank, the Freemasons, the top military, the generals, the secret police… everyone, including Silvio Berlusconi, who represented the media empires. All of these power structures got together and were hob-nobbing and sitting with the Mafia. The Vatican, the military, the police, the judiciary, and the banks have all been around for a very long time, but the 'new kids on the block' are the Mafia, who cannot be ignored because they run some of the biggest industries on the planet – gambling, prostitution, pornography, drugs, trafficking in women, and, interestingly, toxic waste disposal (which is how I know about it).

Roberto Calvi, who is the Vatican's banker, was assassinated – the story was very big in 1982 – because he was a genuine Christian, and he discovered that a billion dollars of the Vatican's money and billions of other people's money were going to finance armaments and severe political repressions in the South American regimes – the death squads, the torture squads, and the 'disappearings'. He was about to blow the whistle. He escaped to London and eventually was found hanging from Blackfriars Bridge… an elderly, portly gentleman who had allegedly crawled out onto steel gantries fifty yards over the Thames, and then hung himself so that his feet were dangling in the water and a pile of masonry and dollars were in his pockets? So these people exist, they meet, they have networks. I talk about it in my book, *Shiva's Rainbow*. It's not late night reading…

A Global Carbon Currency

The next step on from the carbon agenda is a global currency. At the moment there is competition between the Dollar, the Euro, the Yen, the Pound, etc. There is a plan for a carbon currency, and by that I don't mean that you'll have to carry around a little chink of carbon; but there'll be global monitoring, surveillance, global accounting, and transfers of vast amounts of money in relation to carbon credits. It's a complex system with which you may not be familiar, but it's already a major corruption within the EU – vast amounts of tax-payers' money has been given away and it's absurd... for example, there's a Global Environment Fund which was set up after the Rio Summit, where it was understood that to help other countries develop, we would have to pay them so they could develop 'clean' technologies. Over about ten years, four hundred million dollars (and that's only about a third of the total expenditure) went to China, yet China is awash with money, running a two trillion dollar trade surplus.

Further, the industries in China are not what they seem. Effectively, all of the industry in China over the past ten years isn't Chinese – it's Western capital, producing consumer goods for the West using cheap Chinese labor. These capitalists are running an economy that's shifting towards financial services, and the manufacturing has been relocated east – to China, Malaysia, and Indonesia, where there is no restriction on their carbon dioxide emissions. If you do a carbon footprint for Britain, not including our imports and exports, (i.e. not including the reality of the global economy) then it *appears* as though we've saved around 10% of our emissions since 1990, but if you realize that over that period we've relocated our carbon dioxide emissions to China, and then you then take account of that by carbon accounting our imports, then that figure drastically increases. Of course, the climate campaigners don't tell you about that because then they'd have to criticize Kyoto and the global capital markets.

Millions of Chinese people have been moved off their land into horrific high-rise developments that look like cell-blocks. There is terrible pollution and deprivation in these areas, and they all work in these vast industries for next-to-nothing, producing goods that we used to produce that are exported to the West at half the price. Only richer people can afford to buy European goods – cars and hi-fis, etc. – which generally cost three times the price (and last a lot longer).

The whole thing is a huge enterprise. China has accumulated a vast amount of dollars which it can't spend, and then loans that money back to western governments and banks by buying derivatives. I couldn't work out how come the whole of the global economy was collapsing in trillions when only a small percentage of people had defaulted on their mortgage. What happens is the banks provide a $100,000 mortgage to a customer who pays them $5,000 a year for their home, but that leaves the banks low on cash so they sell that mortgage to the Chinese at a discount and have got tens of thousands to play with, rather than that miserly $5,000 a year. But as soon as there is any defaulting in that market, the Chinese stop buying derivatives. And the system collapses like a stack of dominoes.

What has happened is that to keep economic growth going, Western banks have brought the lower third of consumers up a level into the housing market – that way, they're lending money to people who can't really afford to pay them back. But it increased the demand in the housing market, so the price rockets and their customers find that their homes are suddenly worth three times the mortgage. The banks then persuade them to re-mortgage, and suddenly they've got cash and can buy Porches, BMWs, cruises, a little holiday home in the Caribbean, or whatever they spend their money on. More growth in the economy.

But the economy is very dependent on mood… it's a contagion of doubt and lack of confidence which causes it to contract, and as soon as it contracts it feeds upon itself and contracts even further. The financial crash is very interesting… they've been trying to avoid this for a good couple of years, and it's as if they almost can't help themselves – it's something programmed within the system.

Their timing is incredible, because the solar electro-magnetic field has fallen to its lowest point, and the economic crash is coincidental with this. The magnetic field flickered briefly about two weeks ago as if it was going to come back up, and the markets flickered up – it was extraordinary – and then they came down again. It's well-known and well-documented that the economic cycle has a similar period to the solar cycle, which is about eleven years. Researchers, particularly at the Rutherford Laboratory near Oxford, have discovered that the solar electro-magnetic field increased by 230% over the Twentieth Century. It rose to a peak in 1990 and then it flopped. Because it's working on eleven-year peaks which are increasing in amplitude, it then dropped in the year 2000 by about 30%. The next peak is in 2012. These peaks are very important because they coincide with solar flares, which could be very damaging to satellites – hence NASA has a huge research program on trying to predict the peaks.

Theodore Landscheidt, who used to work with NASA until around 1989, predicted the pattern of these peaks in the early 80's. He also predicted the peaks of another phenomena relating to the oceans called El Nino. The dynamics of the climate is fundamentally driven by the Pacific Ocean. The Pacific is at least half the surface of the planet. If you look at the earth from a certain angle, it's all blue. 75% of earth's surface is oceans, so what happens to the oceans is vital. In Landscheidt's book *Sun, Earth, Man*, there's a chapter discussing the relationship between solar cycles and human consciousness. He said that 1990 would be the highest of the solar cycles. We're in what's called a solar Grand Maximum of the solar electromagnetic cycle. It's ramped up over 10,000 years to this peak, and it also has troughs, or cycles, in the wave – some of which can last for a hundred years.

The climate is connected to the electromagnetic spectrum. IPCC were saying that electromagnetic cycles don't affect the weather. There's a whole bunch of scientists who are now saying, *"Oh yes they do."* Basically, the stronger the electromagnetic field, the less cosmic rays get through, and cosmic rays provide a seed-base through ionizing the water vapor in the air; they provide a seed-base for clouds. More cosmic rays = more clouds. More clouds = cooler planet. Less cosmic rays = less clouds = more sunlight = warmer oceans = warmer planet. That's just about the whole story of global warming – with maybe 20% due to carbon dioxide

The climate is following a natural cycle. If you track Landscheidt's work down, which is not easy to do, the stunning thing is that he was able to predict these things using Fibonacci mathematical cycles. But this is close to Sacred Geometry, which is why mainstream science won't touch it. Sacred Geometry in this case is nothing more than the geometry of the spiral. If you look at nature in terms of spirals, circles and cycles, instead of one of these virtual reality computer models with innumerable nested boxes, straight lines, and mathematical formulas...the actual reality of nature is circles and cycles – and actually they're all spirals because they exist in three dimensions (time making sure nothing is ever repeated exactly). Computers cannot model this. He predicted, by the way, that the 21st century would become a new Little Ice Age. Global *Cooling!*

Landsheidt studied the relationship of the planets to the sun and also declared an interest in astrology – that's a no-go area among scientific fraternities who have rather a hysterical reaction to astrology, and yet Newton, Galileo, Kepler, and Copernicus were astrologers. And all the founders of the Royal Society were alchemists and magicians. It's a funny old science world, really...not at all what it seems!

A DESIGN FOR LIFE
Daniel Tatman

Our homes should not only be sustainable and cheap but have spiritual and energetic components that empower us and enrich our lives.
- Daniel Tatman

Daniel is author of the forthcoming *The Bath Mystery's.* **For more information and to order the book, visit: www.thebath-mysterys.blogspot.com**

I always intuitively understood that there was a 'higher nature' to all things. My mother, father and all their friends were 'people of faith'. My parents were basically hippy-Christians who traveled around Europe being really nice to people; part of what was called the 'Jesus Freak' movement. They were what I call 'starers'... people who would stare at a flower for hours, so I was kind of like that myself as a kid.

At the same time, growing up I had this strange background

of various interesting family figures. My great-uncle, Uncle Henry, ran gyms in the 50's and the 60's in London, in the East and West End. He trained bodybuilders, including Lou Ferrigno, the guy who was the Incredible Hulk in the 70's – and Dave Prowse, the guy who played Darth Vader. He was also connected to gangsters and other various dodgy things, and then he suddenly disappeared in the 50's and 60's; left his wife and two kids, and popped-up in America 20 years later as a major share-holder in the Singer corporation... a multi millionaire with a house on Malibu Beach worth $32 million! He suddenly had loads of money, a huge house, a 'trophy wife', and all the rest of it.

My grandfather was another interesting character; he was the CEO, the director of sales, for a company that made woodworking machinery. In his later life he was involved with a place called Mosega in Nigeria. The company wanted to build a factory and he was sent over there to do some market research and PR with the locals. The company was going to bring in workers from the next country, traveling two or three hundred miles each day to come and work in this place. My grandfather approached the company with the idea that the locals were quite an industrial people and could do the work – the company didn't agree because it would cost them too much money in the short term. He then brought groups of people from Mosega back to his little cottage in Surrey, took them to the technical college up the road to do a course in engineering, learning to operate and use these machines and to create other machines. He did this for about two or three years and helped them to get all the skills that they needed – then went back to Mosega and helped to train-up other people in the village. In the end, the whole village actually ended up working at this factory, which was really good for them because a lot of the land was being bought up by other people and they couldn't farm as well as they had done before. It was a real lifeline for them; it put money back into the local economy.

To honor my granddad because of all he had done they made him the Chief of the village; what is known as the Okakuro of Mosega, which involved a long ritual. After that, he always had bodyguards with him which was an ancient custom that had been going on for hundreds of years. One or two guys from the tribe would always be in his room or sitting outside his mosquito net watching over him always. He was the first ever white man in about three hundred years to have been honored with the title of Okakuro in that area. The last ones to attain that honor were the guys working with Dr. Livingstone when they had completely plundered Africa, and so it was quite interesting in that regard.

Because I was influenced by these characters in my life, I understood that if you put your mind to it you could do very big things – empowering yourself and living a happier life by looking at things through a different lens.

I was always interested in history, the occult, religion, mathematics, and geography – things which through the mainstream view are quite boring but if you just looked at it from a slightly different angle you could see that there was a lot of stuff going on that wasn't talked about which is really interesting. For example; the Pythagorean Theorem for working out the angles of a triangle came from Pythagoras; the head of a Greek visionary school. That whole occult doctrine is what is carried on to us when we understand trigonometry. If I had been taught this at school then I would have been a lot more interested as a child.

My way of looking at things was always trying to look at and understand the ideological or spiritual undercurrent in everything that other people take for granted. Studying theology and many world religions enforced what I had intuitively known as a child; that the real 'meat' of any topic was the idea and concept *behind* something, not necessarily in what we see or what is presented to us.

The Lowlands

I moved to Holland when I was 18 and, while I was working in a coffee shop, got to meet an investigative journalist called William Olmans, who has written many government exposés. He was very interested in architecture but in less of the metaphysical ideas – more the history of buildings and what the pictures and carvings on buildings were hinting at. One of the examples he gave me was above the main train station, Central Station, in Amsterdam – right over the doorway there are fresco carvings, and at first glance it looks like they're cherubs and children dancing... but if you look closely, you can see that they're all children in a workhouse – slave labor, pretty much – with cuts and bruises all over them. The faces of the guys that own the workhouses and the factories are honored all across the front of the building. This was a big example for me straight off, as it was something I'd looked at so many times but didn't know its history and hadn't looked closely enough at it to see what was going on.

After that, I started to get back into looking at the images that you'd see around a city, and finding out about the history and carvings on the buildings. It wasn't just a superficial aesthetic thing – it wasn't just 'glossing' or a picture on the outside of a building. The same level of deep thinking had gone into the carvings on the outside as well as to every single part of the building – from the proportions and the angles to the stone used to the layout to the way that you enter a building and progress around it. For example, museums are designed in such a way that you go in one end and move in a circular motion inside and then come out of the exit.

When I started to look more deeply into the lives of the architects who built these structures, then a whole 'can of worms' popped open. Intrigue surrounded many of those involved who paid for and designed the buildings – they were almost always involved with secret societies, mystery schools and esoteric orders.

At that point, I tried to understand the concepts behind the original builders of these neo-classical buildings that we see the world over – the banks, the palaces, the main municipal buildings, the churches, the schools, even the prisons – because they display the same two or three different types of architecture.

The very design of a city and the individual buildings within that city have a huge effect on the people within it on many different levels. There is an entrainment caused by specific geometries, ratios and proportions. As quantum science and the new alternative sciences show us, everything in existence in the universe is vibrating and everything can be denoted to a frequency. If geometries, stones, colors, and buildings can entrain a geometry and frequency to create a 'tone', this will in turn entrain earth energies, our emotions, or aspects of the psyche.

The Bath Mystery

After traveling around Europe and looking at many cities, I came back to Bath where I was born. I wanted to understand Bath, not just by looking at the architecture and dates of the buildings, but by looking at the alternative history that, as far as I knew, hadn't previously been mentioned. I think that if you are to study anything, you should have a personal connection with it otherwise you're just talking from an empty space. How am I going to talk about Washington or Paris if I don't live there and I don't interact with it? I wanted to talk about the architecture of the world by using a personal example of the city where I live to illustrate what has happened everywhere else. Bath is just a fractal of anywhere on the planet.

The most ancient origins of a place are usually denied by the authorities. This has happened virtually everywhere you go on the planet – some sort of mythical story has been invented and accepted as fact, but if you look into it you'll find that there's a completely different story there...

Based on writings from the 11th century that were changed and mistranslated, the 'official' origin of the city of Bath is put to a king called Bladud – one of the sons of Hud Hudibras, a great warrior of Troy. The mythology is that after the fall of Troy, some of the Trojans escaped and started civilization in Britain. This story was a Catholic invention to import onto the people that they were idiots before the Romans and the Latinized Saxons came here bringing civilization; that their ideas, philosophy and geology all came from a Greek/Roman source – but this was a complete lie! The oldest stories that we have about Bath actually come from the Celtic and the Brythonic people... not from the invading class or from the historians who, thousands years later, tried to create a new story to back up their religion.

Bath was a very important site for many of the mystery schools and various other groups like the freemasons and the Rosicrucians. The first King of England, King Edgar, was crowned here, which is why there have been strong connections between the royals and Bath through the generations; because they understand the heritage of the place. Many of the Orders and secret societies in Bath were very important; such as the Knights of the Bath, which is now known as the MBE; so if you're a Member of the British Empire (MBE) or a Commander of the British Empire (CBE), then you're also a member of the Order of the Bath. This was a secret society that originated here.

The rite of bathing and cleansing yourself before going through a ceremony came from this area. Before someone could become a Knight of the Bath – a holy order conferred by a king or queen – they would have to bathe; to be taken to a spring and baptized. We see this in the Gnostic tradition coming from John the Baptist. Bath was a very important ritual temple for many different cults and, before that, the Romans, Druids and Celts. It was explicitly a healing place because of the hot springs... they all utilized the waters of Aquae Sulis.

The wealth is connected to the natural land. The reason that areas were industrialized in the first place is because they had an *abundance* of resources – coal, iron, copper, oil, or gold, for example. Energetically, these places were very powerful natural geomantic hot-spots and could entrain different levels of consciousness. Areas were dedicated to the different deities, gods and principles. These sacred spaces were the first to go, and the people were then left with nothing; they became poor both socially and spiritually because the area was literally drained of energy. Whether an area is considered wealthy or poor, upper class, middle class or lower class, merely locates those who benefited from the industrial revolution and those who lost out.

Places where there are natural springs and lakes are generally regions that stay wealthy over the years because of their aesthetic beauty; both tourists and money pour through them… just like water. Places like Bath have remained wealthy because the water is naturally rejuvenating – you can't mine the water out but you can tamper with the natural flow. The natural energetic flow of the planet has been manipulated by redirecting the water, which is primarily one of its main conductors. For example, in Bath, the waters have been controlled since Roman times. They slapped Bath Abbey right next to the Roman Baths and redirected two of the streams feeding into the Baths underneath the Abbey – one of them flows under the altar and the other near the doorway. Connecting the two in this way; the Baths complex to the Abbey, will pretty much amplify the energies of the Abbey.

Natural Resonance

The ancients understood that the planet was in its optimal geomantic energetic state where everything had developed naturally, before any of the buildings were put there. They located places of resonance and healing – these were often very extreme dynamic energies – and accentuated those energies by putting their temples, cities, or little villages on these spots. The people later rebuilding these cities thought that they could tap into this knowledge in much the same way – to make their own societies run smoothly, to make business flow, etc., but also at the same time to keep people in a certain mind-state where it would be easier to control them. As the animal loving, earth respecting spirit of the ancients with their female mysteries and priesthoods warped into the male domination of the spiritual and, ultimately, the denigration of the earth as a place that held demons, we can see a slow progression from the ancient form of architecture into this modern form.

An architect learns only the proportions of a style. Somebody asks them, *"Can you build me a house in the Georgian neo-classic style, please?"* and they do so without considering the effect that it's having on the city as a whole or on the people that have to live in it. They were merely using the ideas, concepts and disciplines that they had absorbed through their training, either from university or from other architects. Most of them didn't have a clue about the origins of what they had been taught. The larger conspiracy, really, is in the ideas that get passed on without anybody questioning why. Everybody assumes that if there was something better it would already be in use, so they would just build in a neo-classical style or whatever they have been told 'works'. That's pretty ignorant when you're talking about the energetics of a whole eco system or a planet.

Our modern understanding of architecture is that we think of the physical as not being important – that it's 'just a building'. There are consequences of using sacred science without the full knowledge or responsibility that what you're doing not only affects the physical but also the spiritual or energetic realms. The shape of buildings set up what is called a 'standing wave', so if you're humming inside it, the sound bounces off the walls and folds back on itself repeatedly… it will just keep on getting louder and louder. Some of the longbarrows in Britain have what is called 'windsock geometry' (because they are higher at one side and taper down) and they create a standing wave that bounces off the back and keeps on folding in on itself. This is obviously a great discipline if you're using it in a positive way to attune to the energy of a place; on the other hand, if you're using these principles to make people get into the energy of a culture, political institution, or the army, then it can have some dangerous effects.

If the frequencies of the energetic field of the body are out of balance, you get ill. Cells forget what they're doing and start to be disruptive to the other cells. The overall electromagnetic frequency of the body is affected by the entrainment of certain geometries that encapsulate frequencies and tones. We're shown this in various different ways through cymatics – for example, if you vibrate a 'C' note onto a metal plate covered with sand, the sand will form into a particular geometric shape. Many scientists who have done this over the years now know which geometric shape is equivalent to which frequency.

Energetic Influences

The whole concept of how ghettos were built with high tower blocks facing each other was taken from the first prisons that were built. They understood how to contain a population of inmates and applied that to housing projects. They learned so much and it worked so well that they changed all the new prisons to be *like* the housing projects! It demoralized the people, took away their spirit, made them completely apathetic, and made them turn on each other. It's been used all over the world by planning agencies if they're building a large housing estate. The local Council or the government will always sell them a cheap area of land; a 'dead' area, where all the levels of the nutrients in the soil itself have gone. They then fill them with houses made with the cheapest architectural concepts and building materials they can find. The same guys making these decisions live in mansions outside the city, surrounded by trees.

If they really thought it was good, all of the wealthy people would be living in tower blocks! They understand that it's not but, at the same time, continue to create these areas for the populations that have been forgotten or economies that have collapsed, where they know they can't make money out of them. They have to keep these people content and control them, so they put them together in these little prison areas.

On the flipside, even though the guys who have these mansions are always the most powerful and wealthiest of people, and often one of the most 'educated', their mansions and castles frequently have the most horrible energies and are renowned for being the most haunted places! It makes sense on the quantum level; the individuals building that house would often be very poor and if they're working for some rich guy who's lording it over them, they're going to build it with resentment. On top of that, the wealth that has gone into supplying the raw materials to build it was more often than not built on slavery, corruption, and on all of the avarice and vice of the world.

The energy surrounding the actual building was so dark, that it's no surprise that horrible in-breeding and other sordid stuff has gone on over the years for a long time. These places have the *worst* energy for somebody who's sensitive and spiritually balanced within themselves. Yet everyone wants to live in one… it's incredible!

The stonemasons who lived in Bath and were building huge mansions outside the city lived in the city itself. If you look at their own cottages, these are incredible buildings. As they were taxed by the proportion of the building to the proportion of the windows, they knew how to get the maximum proportion of house-to-window and pay the littlest tax. But you'll also find that their houses were built using infinity numbers in the pi ratio and in the algorithmic ratio – or what are called in physics 'universal constants'. It seems they were using all of their initiated stonemasons' knowledge in their own houses. Most of these cottages were terraced and so you'd have groups of 50 people or so building that terrace with a community spirit. Even though these little cottages are very small and cramped, they've got an amazing energy... so it shows that the intent of the individual building a house – not just the person who's designing the house or the person that's living in it – also has an effect on the energy of a place.

Another thing to take into consideration is how the materials used to build a house were taken from the earth. In ancient times, the Druids would say that a stone only had power before you carved it; that when you carve it, you carve some of the natural essence out of the stone. This is why stone circles almost always were built using stones in the shape that they were found.

We can already intuitively pick up on and emulate the concepts that the ancient ancestors used in building healthy spaces in which to live. Modern scientific tools are now being developed – by using electromagnetic cameras and spectro-analyzers, we can actually get a visual picture, like an x-ray, of what the energetic field of (remaining) sacred sites and buildings look like and the way that the energy is moving round them.

A Design for Life

People in the alternative world are busy looking at the secret orders and the history of things, but we've still got a world here, right NOW, which isn't in a book or an internet site. It's right here, it's energetic and we're dynamically interacting with it.

Geophysics is the physics of the earth and geology itself. We need to apply this to where we're living, in the buildings in which we're living, and how we're living. This will have such a big knock-on effect in our individual lives – it'll give us more time and energy to help others and to create change in the world. If we can build houses that are energy sustainable (around 80 to 100% self-efficient), then we can cut our working times right down; it's an added bonus of living in a building that is holistic.

Efficiency is just the result of thinking holistically – if you're thinking holistically about a relationship, for example, fulfilling all the different parts of a person by letting them do what they want to do, then overall you're going to have a harmonious efficient relationship, but if you went into that relationship wanting to make it efficient without thinking about all the different parts of that person, it will end up being like some sort of fascist battle of wills between the two of you.

Our homes should not only be sustainable and affordable, but also have spiritual and energetic components that empower us and enrich our lives. There are many dynamic energetic influences to consider in the building of a house. We have to re-think about the way that we wire our houses; latticing the electrical wiring around a house will create an energetic cage – cutting us off from the energetics that are constantly dynamically happening outside and from the natural energies of the whole planet. If you're building a house, this problem can be resolved with a bit of foresight when you're at the planning stage; taking the wiring under the ground is a good idea, as putting layers of materials over the top dampens the adverse affects. It has to be done in a more organic and a less all-encompassing grid-like fashion latticing around you, that's really important.

Another thing to consider are the measurements you should use when building a house. Personally, I think it's a really good idea to build your proportions into it – you're basically making a fractal version of yourself; you're recreating your perfect womb conditions, which are proportioned to your body and fit you snugly. If you wear a pair of trousers or a hat, it's got to fit – otherwise it won't feel comfortable, it won't be efficient and it won't operate. When the architects of the modern world were building a mansion for a king, they'd take the measurements of that king, like measuring him for a suit, and build the house around his measurements. I think that's something that people should think about, even if they don't want to build a round house or a 'hobbit-home' and they are building a standard rectangular home.

We need a new pool of knowledge on these topics as we do with every single ASSUMED science – we can no longer take what has been left for us and run with it... this is one of the main reasons our world is in the situation it is in. The true nature of our universe (at least, on many levels) is an energetic maelstrom and, to look beyond this new age cliché, we can say that there is an electrical element to everything...

While this point seems painfully obvious; why, then, have these concepts not been relayed to the environments we create for ourselves – our homes in particular?

This is where YOU come in...

5

DANGEROUS HISTORY

DANGEROUS HISTORY

History is the present. That's why every generation writes it anew.
But what most people think of as history is its end product; myth.
~ E. L. Doctorow

Those who believe that major world events result from planning are
laughed at for believing in the 'conspiracy theory of history'. Of
course, no one in this modern day and age really believes in the
conspiracy theory of history – except those who have taken the time to
study the subject.
~ Gary Allen: *None Dare Call It Conspiracy*

There is nothing more dangerous than history used as a defense, or
history used for preaching; history used as a tool is no longer history.
~ Marcel Trudel (1921 – 2003)

History can, and should, be a fascinating exploration of the past
that helps us to understand ourselves in the present in order to be
able to make important decisions about the future – otherwise,
what is the point? The problem is that what we are taught about
the past is mostly political propaganda that, repeated over
centuries, has become accepted as fact.

I was decidedly un-fascinated by the (European) history I was
taught at school. My bespectacled teacher, Mr. Daly, read ad
verbatim from a text book for the entire lesson, reeling off lists of
countries, dates, and wars and who won them. Needless to say, I
eventually got into big trouble for reading a far more exciting
work of fiction during class...

History is mostly written by the people who won the wars.

What did the losers have to say? I suppose none of them were alive to tell the tale and, if they were, nobody bothered to ask – although I'm certain that their opinion of events would differ enormously from the victors'.

*

Ancient history is mystery. Only the intuitive and objective historian can read and heed the clues that uncover the secret pathway into a bygone age. Instead, and sadly, speculation is all too often taken as gospel, then regurgitated by scholars who don't question, or refuse to accept, contrary evidence that is right before their very eyes. This, for example, coming from a 'highly knowledgeable' guide at the ancient site of Knowth in Ireland (and I paraphrase): *"The reason why the carving on this stone is inward-facing is probably because they made a mistake and flipped it up the wrong way"*. Excuse me?! These ancient people built sophisticated temples, had advanced knowledge of earth energies and astronomy, yet they were so stupid that they accidentally flipped the stones up *the wrong way?* I have never heard such nonsense.

We, in the Western world, know little of our ancient ancestors – yet their sacred sites tell us so much. There is wisdom stored in the land. Those who re-wrote history must have realized this at some point; that the land is a depository of knowledge, because they seem to have done their level best to divert our attention from and destroy as much of the natural world as they can. Our sacred sites have been defiled; turned into tourist attractions full of disinformation, or else bulldozed to make way for housing estates and freeways. The energy at so many of these places has been dammed and diverted in every devious possible way. We have little time for quiet reflection in nature – too busy to hear what the stones or the trees have to say. As William Henry Davies wrote;

What is this life if full of care
We have no time to stand and stare?
No time to stand beneath the boughs
And stare as long as sheep, or cows.
No time to see, when woods we pass,
Where squirrels hide their nuts in grass.
No time to see, in broad daylight,
Streams full of stars, like skies at night.
No time to turn at Beauty's glance,
And watch her feet, how they can dance.
No time to wait till her mouth can
Enrich that smile her eyes began.
A poor life this, if full of care,
We have no time to stand and stare.

This is an enormously important time of awakening – the vibration of the planet is rising rapidly and pushing us beyond all literal interpretations of our world. Our own journeys inward may not be marked by fine buildings, pyramids or ancient texts, but they will most certainly be greatly impacted and sped onward by others who left us these mystical clues and signposts as they followed their own truths. Buy old maps, explore the land, and look for clues. By learning to observe what is before our very eyes and tuning-in to the land, we will gain access to the greatest library we will ever need. Ultimately, the most important knowledge is that which lies beyond any physical clues and beyond any sentences to formulate it. Whatever the ancients knew is embedded in the earth and in the mass consciousness; it is there for all who open intuitively to it. Let's not forget that we ourselves are making history for those that follow...

THE DRUIDS: Priesthood of the Ancient World
Michael Tsarion

The Druidical religion prevailed not only in Britain, but likewise all over the East.

~ Edward Vaughan Kenealy (*Book of God*)

Born in Ireland, Michael Tsarion is an expert on the occult histories of Ireland and America. He has made the deepest researches into Atlantis, the Origins of Evil, and into the Irish Origins of Civilization. Michael is author of the acclaimed books *Atlantis, Alien Visitation, and Genetic Manipulation, The Irish Origins of Civilization, and Astro-Theology* and *Sidereal Mythology*. He is the producer and presenter of the *Origins and Oracles* DVD series, which explores ancient mysteries and forbidden knowledge. He is also the producer of the *Architects of Control* DVD series, which deals with mankind's future and solutions to the humanity's current problems.

Official website: www.michaeltsarion.com

When we were kids, my dad would take us to visit old megalithic sites, for a picnic or whatever. He was an atheist but had no trouble accepting that ancient man might have been very sophisticated. He would often philosophize about it, but it wasn't until my last year at a protestant school in Northern Ireland in 1979, that it actually became important to me. My art teacher lent me a book by Jim Fitzpatrick, which contained the whole story of ancient Irish mythology illustrated with beautiful Celtic designs. It was one of the most striking books of art I'd ever seen and it inspired me to study ancient Irish history. Neither the protestant nor the catholic schools in Ireland taught this, because the ancient forefathers were looked at with suspicion by all Christians. They prefer to talk about leprechauns and banshees and other nonsense, without realizing that many secrets lie behind these tales. They hide information about the otherworld and the spiritual dimensions, as well as about cosmic upheavals and catastrophes in the heavens and on the earth.

It wasn't until I returned to America about two years later that I really started to study Irish history more deeply, by going to libraries and reading a lot of books by forgotten scholars who *did* know the truth about Britain's ancient past. This research brought out a 'feeling of conspiracy' within me. This is because the really interesting books written by the great mavericks of ancient history – Anna Wilkes, Conor MacDari, Comyns Beaumont and Godfrey Higgins – were out of print. They were expensive and hard to locate and yet they contained information that could enlighten the world. These classics describe how the tribes migrated throughout the world. They reveal what the Druids believed and how they divided their Order. They talk about the demise of the Druids, the Roman (or Atonist) campaign of genocide, the coming of Christianity, and the secret societies which appropriated the ancient knowledge of the Aryan Druids. How come not one of these masterly books is still in print?

We know that ancient man was more sophisticated than we have been led to believe – since pyramid-building, basket-weaving and mathematical systems didn't just pop-up 'out of the blue'. The only way that we can find out the truth about the ancient past is to look into the myths and legends of our ancestors who *tell* us what was really going on – that there were great earth cataclysms, there was a 'war of the gods' where super-weaponry was used, genetic manipulation was going on, and there was a conflict between the forces of light and darkness. The origins of evil lie in the past and the misuse you see of natural forces... it's all there in the myths and legends. Unfortunately, these are not treated as factual histories.

Carl Jung and Joseph Campbell, among others, went blue in the face telling people that mythology is a very deep archive of knowledge that we need to pay attention to, and yet so few people in the world bother to do so. People's sense of inner insecurity is so strong that they're going to always believe what everybody else believes. The media run from New York City will tell you to believe it, and if it's in *Time* magazine... well, then it *must* be true. People don't do their own homework anymore.

People have been so psychologically plundered in this 'war on consciousness' that they're bound to follow the particular mythology that's put before them in the Bible. People believe these lies, this total fiction, and yet our myths and legends are thousands of years older and rooted in truth. The Bible is refuted every day, showing you that it's unsustainable nonsense – they've never found a temple of Solomon or any remnants of an Israel. Every time the headlines say *'New relics found'*, they don't tell you that these could have been Canaanite, Philistine, African or Egyptian. They never tell you that the top scientists and the top archaeologists who have gone out there say there's no authenticity to these discoveries.

The greatest damage has been done to the timeline and chronology... we can't be completely sure of the historical dates that are officially given for certain lives and events. We know that the Christian idea that 'the Creation' is only 4,000 years old is obviously irrational as well as incorrect. Up until about a hundred years ago, you didn't have a choice whether you wanted to believe it or not, so we're at a very privileged time when we can now re-look at history and revise it. The Celts allegedly came to Britain in 600BC, and there's not even a consensus about *that*; whereas I'm talking about the ancient Irish – the Druids – who may go back to at least *13,000 years* BC. The word 'Celtic' shouldn't even be used to define the ancient Irish – it was first used by the Romans to describe those they considered primitive and barbaric. Why would we want to use that word today to describe the most advanced of the Irish Druids? A 'Celt' could be from Germany, Scotland, Ireland, Wales, France or Portugal, and was used to refer to almost everybody from Spain. Later on, British historians realized that the term is ambiguous, but they didn't throw it away because it's a perfect blanket term – it serves its purpose.

From West to East

The further you go back, the more you realize that we have a common homeland. The ancient Irish myths speak of four or five great continents that disappeared beneath the waves. There's no debate that these continents existed – Graham Hancock and others have gone under the oceans and taken photographs, so there can be no refutation of that fact.

Many people are familiar with Atlantis and perhaps Lemuria. They accept that according to ancient traditions, terrific cataclysms destroyed these continents and wrecked the world. Interestingly, one of the most important tasks that the Druids performed was the healing of the Earth. We know today that they were fascinated with the trees and herbs, and that they precisely positioned many of their magnificent sacred sites. In fact, after the destruction of the Druids, we find that Christian churches and cathedrals were deliberately built on top of more ancient sacred locations. It was just one more act of desecration. The Druids believed the earth had been severely wounded. We can see them as 'medics of the Earth'. They had a very important reason for positioning their megalithic sites. There was not an element of sacred geometry, astronomy, or geomancy that eluded them. When we visit a megalithic site such as Newgrange and Tara in Ireland, or Callanish in Scotland, we have an overwhelming sense of peace and stillness. There is a good reason.

I believe that the elements of civilization – like music, art and poetry and writing – didn't come from the east to the west as we are taught... they developed *right here* in the British Isles and moved to the east. The Druids were one homogenous group – they were enlighteners of the world who existed in pretty much every continent. Much like the tradition of the wandering monks in Christian times, the Druid scholars were travelers, creating colleges, temples and centers of learning in every part of Europe, and even in the East and Asia. Land bridges have been proven to exist between Britain, Ireland and Scandinavia until around 2,500 years ago. There's a strong possibility that there was also a land bridge to France. These land bridges change *everything* we think we know about history.

Caucasian mummies have been found in different parts of the world – women and men who clearly came from Britain and Scandinavia (because of the way their hair had been braided or because of the clothes they were wearing) were found in the most inhospitable reaches of China. Red-headed mummies have even been found in New Zealand, but then the Maori have always said publicly that 'the ancestors' are white Caucasian people from Europe. The Hopi Indians talk about the *Pahona*, which means 'the wise white brother from far away'. In South America it's always been admitted that white men from the 'Western lands' came and civilized them and were the ancestors of their gods. *All over the world*, you've got the same story of tall Caucasian peoples who knew how to cross the oceans and who were the Elders, and yet it's just dismissed as 'mythology'. The Smithsonian Institute and so many others massively downplay all of this and are happy to tell you about these Native groups who are the originators of civilization.

Scholars have no problem accepting that Jesus and his 12 apostles walked for thousands of miles, from corner to corner across the holy land – from Galilee into Judea and on to Syria, or that St. Peter traveled to Athens, Greece and to Rome and even up into the Northern countries on foot. Much like the tradition of the wandering monks in Christian times, the Druid scholars were travelers – creating colleges, temples and centers of learning in every part of Europe, and even in the East and Asia. Why is it so difficult for them to accept that in pre-Christian times, the Druids were also capable of doing the same thing? It's the easiest thing in the world to understand.

Pre-dynastic Egypt is many thousands of years older than they tell us. My work shows that the ancient pre-dynastic Egyptian priesthood were very much in collaboration with the Druids, if not the same order. The Scythians lived in Northern Europe. They had powerful mystery schools, most of them dedicated to language and the ancient legends. Fenias Farsa was a great scholar and mystic who had a network of colleges stretching to Egypt – his sons are believed to have even married daughters of pharaohs. In my estimation, the role of the Scythians and early Druids has been massively downplayed when it comes to Egypt.

The Egyptian Queen Nefertiti's daughter, Scotia, is believed by some investigators to be buried in Ireland's County Kerry. She is rumored to be the woman who gave her name to ancient Ireland and *Scotland*. The first pharaoh of the first dynasty of Egypt, King Menes, was reputedly buried in Knockmany, Northern Ireland, and Tea Tephi, an Egyptian queen, lies near

Tara – the ancient capital of Ireland.

Today, people believe that countries are separate and that there was no connection between the different gods and religions, and here we find that there were even *physical* connections between the people! The sons and daughters, the kings and the queens and the princesses have literally traveled between these lands.

The scholar and author Barry Fell was ridiculed all his life because he discovered old Irish *Ogham* writing in the so-called Anasazi ruins in America. It's considered a big mystery as to why the Anasazi, reputedly the ancestors of the Pueblo Indians, apparently disappeared off the face of the earth... first of all they weren't Indians, and secondly, they didn't disappear. They were traveling foreigners – people from the West temporarily ensconced in the Americas. They were probably Phoenicians, who had a connection to Scotland and Ireland. These Phoenician mariners had been to America long before the Vikings or Columbus, and stayed for long enough to help contribute to the old Algonquian language, spoken in Vermont and Carolina. It's one of the biggest (if not *the* biggest) Native American language and its closest relation is Gaelic.

Etymology, the origin and history of words, is a fascinating study. Gaelic was clearly a very early language, if not *the* first language. There's a tremendous affinity between Gaelic and a lot of European languages, Native American Indian languages, Japanese, and even Egyptian. Even in India, where you have a group of supreme Brahmans who knew their leaders as the *Druhyus* or the *Druhus*... almost the same word as 'Druids'.

The word 'door' comes from the same root as the word for Druid. The word *dru* in Gaelic comes from *doir* or *daur*. The Druids were the doorkeepers – the keepers of the mysteries of the sacred grove. At Stonehenge and other sacred sites, we can see that many of these portals look like doorways.

The ancient word for Ireland was *Eri, Are* or *Ari*, which can also be rendered Aryan. The capital of the original Aryans was *Ariland*, or Ireland – the place of the *Ari*. We still use the word today when we talk about *ari*stocracy. The difference is that the modern aristocracy today are a bunch of ignoramuses and evil-doers who don't deserve that title. The true aristocracy were the Druids, meaning the *Ari* – the pure and noble ones. It originally meant 'morally, spiritually and intellectually superior'. Later on, the word 'Aryan' was corrupted to mean literally physically white and therefore superior – that's all nonsense.

Joseph of *Ari*mathea is a smokescreen for the wise man, the Druid. Even the word 'Jesus' is based on an ancient Irish god by the name of *Esa* and *Iesa*. The Bible is full of wise men and Druids all the way back to *Sol*omon. We've got to understand how pervasive the Druidic elements and the worship of the solar religion really was.

Another word we use today is 'oligarchy', meaning 'a ruling elite of very powerful people', but the word *Oli* was the one of the names for the high Druids of Ireland – the supreme Druids and poets were part of an intelligentsia known as the *Ollamhs* or the *Oligarchy*. The ancient Druidic Bard didn't just play the harp and keep the knowledge – he was also an officiator, who decided on matters of law. That's maybe the reason why when someone becomes a lawyer, they are called to the 'bar', this perhaps origi-nating from the old Gaelic word *bard*.

Destruction of the Ancient Elders

The Druids and the Bards were murdered to a wholesale... completely destroyed. The slaughter of the Druids has always been a footnote in history. History books talk of integration between the Druids and early Christians – the official story is that Druidism in its pure form *contributed* to the birth of Christianity, as if it were an amicable transition instead of a physical genocide of amazing proportions. The slaughter of the Druids is one of the first crimes that can be laid at the door of the Crown and the

Christian church – of the Vatican.

Druids were not involved in the origin of what we know to be Christianity today – it was the Culdeans. Behind the Culdeans was a group out of Egypt known as the Atonists, which means 'followers of Aton' – a powerful but corrupt sun cult started by the famous pharaoh Akhenaton. They can also be referred to as the Brotherhood of the Snake. They were eventually expelled from Egypt approximately 1400 BC. Researchers such as Ralph Ellis, Moustapha Gadalla and Ahmed Osman have proven that these Atonists were actually the people the Bible refers to as the Israelites or, more correctly, the Judites. In fact, they constituted at least two of the so-called 'Twelve Tribes of Israel'. My work goes on to show that part of this group moved westwards to return to their ancestral homelands in the British Isles.

In Irish mythology, the Atonists are known as Milesians, after their king Mile. The Milesians, with their Scythian/Egyptian connection, worshipped the god Aton (known in Judaism as Adonai, and in Masonry as Lucifer) and were senior members of the solar cult. It was this group ensconced in Britain who was responsible for the slow demise of the Druids. They absorbed the Druidic knowledge, forming a *new* religion based on Druidic elements that was a corruption of Druidism and solar religion – what we know today as Christianity and, subsequently, Latin Christianity. In order for Christianity to arise (what's known today as Judeo-Christianity) these original masters had to die. It's very important to know about this cult because they basically control the world.

There has been an incredible program of colonialization throughout the world. Men of great violence have eradicated entire tribes and cultures in order to make sure that nobody would rise to power but who they sponsored, and we *know* this has happened... this is factual. We need to start waking up to realize the colonialism that is primarily of the mind – it's a physical thing, it's a psychic thing in which the *mind* of man is under attack by illusion and black sorcery that is very, very old and is responsible for the desecration of countries, the slaughter of nations and the humiliation of men and women from all parts of the globe.

Most people think that Christianity is just 'that stuff that comes out of Rome' and that's it. What has to be understood is that even within orthodox Christianity you have an exoteric publicly known version which everyone buys into, and then you have this hidden esoteric strain. The latter, which is basically Pagan in nature, has irritated the Latin Church for years – this is why there were so many early Christian 'purges'. Many historians and scholars were sent to research ancient Druidism and Egyptology in order to plagiarize the knowledge, but, at the same time, the Church was afraid they might 'slip back' into the old Pagan ways – that a 'neo-Druidic' element would filter into Christianity. In fact, many people would say that the Arthurian Legends are loaded with both Christian *and* Pagan motifs – the Holy Grail and Arthur and his knights are Christian concepts, while Morgan Le Fey and Merlin are old Paganism.

At many times throughout history this esoteric strain of Christianity has been at war with the official strain. Many heretical Christians were burned at the stake by orthodox Christians – the Templars were persecuted by the Church, yet they wore the cross and went on the crusades *for* the Pope. If they could do this to their own, then you can imagine what heinous violence must have ensued when they were dealing with people who were their sworn enemies.

The seed bed of the Essenes, Theraputae, Stoics, Gnostics, Bogomils and Cathars was Druidism – not Christianity as is often implied. The Essenes, who are rumored to have written the Dead Sea Scrolls, lived in a very purified way; they wore white, and were very much like the ancient Druids. When we look at some of these groups, we can easily see the Druidic remnants in exactly the same way today as you can see Christian elements in some remote outlying place where missionaries have been, because Druidism was once throughout the world – it wasn't just in Britain. Tremendous lies have been told.

Symbols of Power

It is very important not just to point out that there's been a travesty done to ancient British, Scandinavian, and Egyptian history, but to expose who is responsible, how they've profited from it, and how an entire leviathan of secret societies, churches and religions have been built upon the ruins of our ancient knowledge. There's a reason why people today are 'dumbed-down', backward, and lost – it's because the ancient Druidic symbols of power are still being used by the secret societies of the world. The original people who used it, those whose job it was to uplift the world towards the light and truth, are dead and gone. The servants of darkness stole this ancient Druidic knowledge and it's still being used... this archive of knowledge hasn't died.

The people controlling this world today *absolutely* believe in history and the power of mythology – whether it's the symbols on their military uniforms and costumes or the design of the churches. Why is the fleur-de-lys, a French symbol, found all over the royal emblems of Scotland and England? Why is the Star of David on the Ulster flag? Why is the lion to be found on royal heraldry? What's going on here? To them it's not 'just a dragon' on a Welsh flag, or just a nice 'cool' decoration – they fully under-stand what that dragon represents, they understand the ancient bloodline and the old serpent court that stretches back to the Nile and beyond in the time of Atlantis. These people are still drawing on ancient Druidic symbols and motifs and they've got an agenda that we'd better start to find out about.

Ultimately, Christianity *is* a form of Druidism – the religions are very much the same, except Christians don't know that. The Bible is a re-scripting of Druidic motifs, from Moses building the circle of twelve stones at Mount Sinai and the 'burning bush' story, to aspects of the Nativity and Crucifixion. The story of Noah is based on the first High King Nuah or Nuada of Ireland who saved his people because he was guided to build ships before a tremendous cataclysm came. King David, who played the harp and went to slay the giant Goliath, comes from an Irish myth thousands of years old – it's an old story of the sun king who killed the giant of evil with a sling.

The Druids were the first to wear a crown of thorns, roses or laurel leaves, and this symbol is used today in many corporate logos like the NATO logo, United Nations and the White House. Buckingham Palace from the air is designed to look like an Egyptian pyramid with the 'eye of Aton' at the top. Why did the British royals think of themselves as 'rulers of the waves?' Why did the greatest empires outside of Egypt arise here? The Egyptians always understood that the British Isles were the centre of the world solar religion.

The most sacred number in Druidic lore was three. Their very order was broken down into three schools – the Druids, the Bards, and the Ovates (from which we derive the words 'faith' 'fate' and 'Vatican'). In order to distinguish whether something is of Druidic origin, wherever it is in the world, if it involves the number three you can be pretty sure that at one time Druidism or Egyptian Amenism were involved. One of the Druidic symbols is the spiral trinity. Even in the Nativity you have *three* wise men visiting Jesus. Then you have the first three degrees of freemasonry, and flags that show the *tri*colour. During the coronation of the queen the 'alder man' taps a rod *three* times. The Druids knew about the secret of the trees and which wands to use at special occasions. My mentor Jordan Maxwell has always pointed out that Druids used holly wood to put people into a state of trance – and look at what comes from Hollywood today!

In America, people see the fasci symbol of the fascists on the Congress house and they never even think to ask, 'Where did that symbol come from?'. The symbols speak volumes. The symbolism of America, like on the dollar bill, of Washington DC, of the Statue of Liberty... these things come from France from the Royal families like the Bourbon dynasty and the Duke d'Orleans – these are Templar Royal families who themselves borrow the symbolism from Egypt.

The geomantic connections that exist between Stonehenge and Egypt have already been proven by people like Gerald Hawkins and have been written about for many decades. It has been discovered that a very important site in Scotland, Callaneesh, is aligned perfectly to the Great pyramid at Giza and to important constellations like Orion. The doors through which the sun enters at the winter solstice at Newgrange and the complexes around it at Knowth and Dowth, (the most important sites in Ireland if not *the* most important), are aligned to the Vatican in Rome. Of course, Newgrange is a lot older – it's at least 3 or 4,000 years BC, so who's aligning what to whom? It's quite obvious that they knew how important Ireland was and how important the Seat of the Kings were. Freeways, corporate towers and shopping malls have been placed on top of the sacred of all sites in northern and southern Ireland for decades.

There's been a reason why the stone circles and sacred sites are treated in the way that they are and why they're often made into these disgusting tourist spectacles... these super-wealthy Atonists have been sucking the energy from the land for centuries. They are also responsible for the destruction of America through the lieutenants like George Bush... they are politically aligned. It's very important to re-sacralize those places – to re-instill vortex energy at these locations.

Servants of Truth

The word 'Druid' actually means 'servant of truth'. Another word for Druid was *Druthin*. The letters *d* and *t* were inter-changeable and, through the years, it became *Truthin*, which is where the word 'truth' comes from today. The very idea that there is such a thing as 'a truth' as opposed to a lie comes from these shamanic peoples who contemplated the universe and the meaning of life.

The truth was something that was in the keeping of 'men of truth'. Not everybody was capable of keeping truth – it wasn't a matter of just *anybody* getting the knowledge and understanding. The Druids had many divisions within their order and they didn't give a damn about race, sex or creed – they cared about whether you were a spiritually adept person... whether you could be purified. They believed in becoming your own shaman, priest or priestess, by sacred initiatory and rites and rituals, which was a way of weeding-out the people who were not whole – not sacred in their mentality. These rituals are all dead and gone now, and that's why so many evil-doers have direct access to this knowledge.

Every country has had their Shamanic Elders. In every single country of the world from the earliest times, the leaders and controllers of the world have tried to sever human beings from their roots and create multi-cultural societies where nobody knows whether they are coming or going. When a man is cut off from his roots, he can be controlled. He identifies and wants a sense of belonging. His emotions and allegiance can then be co-opted. It's very important for people to learn about their traditions, and to reintegrate ancestral knowledge in a healthy way.

We can start by paying attention to our myths and legends. We have an amazing story here. We're living in an age now where we are starting to reconstruct the facts about what really *did* happen in our ancient past. The official history that's known to people is interesting, but *underneath* that... that's what the people of the world now deserve to know.

UNREPENTANT
Kevin Annett

*Kevin Annett is more deserving of the Nobel Peace Prize than many
who have received it in the past.*
~ Prof. Noam Chomsky

*The very lands we all along enjoyed
they ravished from the people they destroyed...
All the long pretenses of descent
are shams of right to prop up government.
'Tis all invasion, usurpation all;
'Tis all by fraud and force that we possess,
and length of time can make no crime the less;
Religion's always on the strongest side.*
~ Daniel Defoe, Jure Divino (England, 1706)

Kevin Annett is a community minister in the poorest part of
Vancouver, Canada, where he works and lives with aboriginal
and homeless people. He was expelled as a clergyman from the

United Church of Canada in 1997 after publicly challenging that church over its theft of Native land and its responsibility for the deaths of children in its 'Indian residential schools'. Kevin is the author of two books on genocide in Canada and a co-producer of the award-winning documentary film *Unrepentant*. For more information, visit: www.hidden fromhistory.org

Part of my job as minister in Port Alberni, was to invite people into the church, but it was also about getting to know people in the community – taking food around, doing funerals and weddings, and to counsel people. As I began to learn more about life in the Native community, they weren't too willing to share some of the bad stuff that had gone on at first but, over time, I learned more about what had happened. I wasn't trying to recruit them to come to church or anything – I was just willing to sit and listen, and I think they could see that in me... that I genuinely wanted to know what happened.

There were over 100 residential schools and over 100 day schools right across Canada. These schools ran from the late 1800s right up to 1996. Government statistics estimate that a quarter of a million children went through these schools and half of them never came back. It was a huge crime of genocide. More and more people are finally recognizing that, but for a long time there was complete denial and censorship about the whole thing.

A problem that clergy tend to have is that they isolate their feelings in order to get through a day, just to function. The more that people began to tell me stories about this huge crime that had happened, the harder I found it was to do that. I realized that I couldn't just be a minister... I had to do more than that. It made me ask fundamental questions about my culture, society, and the church.

One of the ways I helped resolve that feeling in me was to let people speak. I opened up the pulpit and held forums where people could talk and I encouraged them to speak out because I felt really overwhelmed by it. I tried to create a sanctuary where they could do that... where they could feel safe and could talk about those things and be accepted.

There was a mix of feeling among the congregation during that time – some of the older people were quite hostile, while others, who tended to be younger, were intrigued and wanted to hear more. There was a real naivety on my part because I thought the church was something different than what it actually is. I didn't think it would have the repercussions that it had.

In these small towns, people know the truth but there's a culture of denial and silence. In that silence you can function every day as long as certain things aren't brought up. The chair of the board of my church was the mayor of the town and he knew a lot of people who had worked in the residential schools. Many of these schools were open until the 1970's and 80's, so a lot of people were still alive who had worked in them. They definitely knew what had happened and didn't like the fact that I was opening up that whole can of worms.

Throughout history, all sorts of measures have been taken to gain possession of indigenous land. British general Amherst described in his diary how they used smallpox-infested blankets to depopulate the Native villages of eastern Canada.

In the late 1800s in British Columbia, about 90 to 95% of the Native population was wiped out in two generations by the smallpox. It's clear that this disease was deliberately introduced by British sailors and missionaries in native villages, using infected blankets and smallpox inoculations. You're talking massive depopulation, initially to get the land, but it's still the case today that a lot of the important resources in Canada – oil, water, minerals, timber, etc. – are still on Native land. To get easy access to these resources, it's in their interests to get people off that land... so it's profitable for them to have Native people die off and slowly drift away somewhere. When the issue of the church selling off Native land to logging companies came up, that implicated other people higher up in the church and that was when they began to move against me.

In mid October, 1994, I wrote a letter about the land deals that had gone on on the west coast and I sent it to higher authorities in the church. The chair of the board and a few of the people on the local personnel committee then called me into a meeting and gave me a warning... they basically said, "You've got to stop this stuff or we might have to can you". They were that explicit about it.

I thought it was something we could work out locally, especially since most of the people in the church were behind what I was doing. But in January 1995, right out of the blue, a fairly top official in the church handed me a letter of dismissal. The letter ordered me to undergo psychiatric treatment, although they had no evidence to show that I was in any way unstable. Even though it was a confidential letter, the church official distributed that letter to every member of my church board.

Being a small town, within the day a lot of people were saying, "The church officials are claiming Kevin's crazy and needs to see a shrink". It's always hard to refute something like that, because you know what gossip is like. It was a deliberate smear campaign to get people to back off, so that then when they defrocked me I wouldn't have any support, which is pretty much what happened two years later.

In the meantime, they immediately removed me from my job. Initially they offered me a month's pay and told me to get out of town – to move out of the church manse where I lived with my wife and two daughters. Our eldest daughter was in kindergarten and had just started school and it was the middle of the winter. They wouldn't negotiate with me at all until we hired a lawyer.

Eventually, they agreed that they would pay me and that we could stay in the house until the summer. We then moved to Vancouver and I enrolled at the University. I couldn't get work in the church – I couldn't get a job as a minister anywhere else until I agreed to psychiatric tests and 're-training'... things that were not only uncalled for, but which would have ruined my reputation.

The United Church also broke up my family by approaching my ex-wife Anne soon after I was fired, and offering to pay for her divorce if she left me. She did so, and with the help of fraudulent documents provided by the church, she won custody of both our daughters the year after I was fired. So by then I was unemployable, blacklisted, and denied daily contact with my own children. It was then that I knew from my own experience how violent and corrupt the church was, because of what had happened to me.

They began the defrocking procedure the following year – the same week that the first lawsuits began against them by Indian residential school survivors. Although I was never charged with anything, I was going through the procedure of someone under discipline.

They wouldn't even tell me the grounds for defrocking a minister, so I had no way to compile a defense. The only people that called against me at my "defrocking" were church officials, none of whom had ever seen me acting as a minister. In fact, the very officials who were firing me and putting me through this hell... a number of them had worked in the residential schools and known the people who ran it. These were senior people. I knew that they were covering themselves because they knew that they had a lot to lose if these stories ever came out.

They based a whole case against me on complete hearsay. It was the only public de-listing of a minister in church history in Canada. All the other de listings that have ever happened were done in committee, but they officially made it public and encouraged people to come and watch. It was a 'show trial' that cost them over a quarter of a million dollars. They tried to discredit me in a big way because I continued to work with residential school survivors and I also began to speak out about what had happened.

I wrote *Hidden From History – The Canadian Holocaust* while I was still going through this nonsense with the church. We then made a film based on the book, entitled *Unrepentant*, which was released for the first time in late 2006.

The film has made a tremendous impact. In June 2008, the Canadian prime minister stood up in the House of Commons and made a vague speech about how they regret what had happened in the residential schools and admitted that some children died, which was quite a thing, a real first. Some of the other party leaders even made reference to mass graves, and that wouldn't have happened a year beforehand. Frankly, I don't think there would have been that apology if it wasn't for the film and the way that it was suddenly 'out there' in the media. It really began to change things to have that story out.

The government has now set up what they call a Truth and Reconciliation Commission, but the problem is that it's very restricted and it doesn't really allow for the truth to come out. It doesn't have a mandate to do anything, it doesn't have the power to make criminal charges, and people aren't allowed to mention specific names of the people involved or any wrongdoing that happened in the schools.

In April 2008, I released to the media a list of 28 mass grave sites in former residential schools. We're now focusing on trying to get an independent inquiry going in Canada so that we can identify the grave sites – we need those graves exhumed and forensic analysis done. We've come a long way in proving what has happened through testimonies and documents but we need the forensic proof. We're also trying to get other countries to support a motion at the UN to have Canada and its churches investigated for crimes against humanity.

There's so much fear and oppression directed against Native people in Canada that the survivors who show up at the rallies and vigils we hold wouldn't be able to do so unless they knew there were non-Natives standing with them. They're able to take strength from it and it's encouraged a lot of them to come forward. On the other hand, the more that comes out, the more resistance and denial there is from the government and the churches.

Under the Indian Act, the government completely runs life on the reservations. Some of the Native chiefs who are government-funded come out and speak against the evidence of genocide coming out. They tend to be fairly hostile. In some cases, when they were in residential schools they had operated as informants – they'd 'rat out' their fellow students and were consequently given better treatment, better education, food, and they weren't as hurt as often. Those kids learned at a young age that if you collaborate with the system you get benefits from it. Quite often, these are the ones who become the chiefs. They don't want the history to come out because they're implicated.

One of the Native women I work with said, "The problem with our chiefs is that they've never dealt with their own abuse and trauma and because of that they can very easily be manipulated." If you avoid dealing with pain because you don't want to look at it, you are naturally going to resent other people who are talking about it. There's also the factor that they get paid a lot of money not to look at it, so it's in their perceived interests not to go there. They live a lifestyle around people who don't have their best interests at heart and they're not able to confront the truth.

There are almost two classes of Natives – there's the favored, educated, government-funded minority, and then there's the majority who are completely outside that system… these are the people I work with.

In Canada there were traditional chiefs, many of whom were either killed or displaced. The chiefs that were appointed by the government were not traditional chiefs – they're very much acting as civil servants of the government. They administer the money for the reservations given to them by the government, but most of it goes into their own pockets and the pockets of their families. About three quarters of the Natives in Canada don't even live on reservations – they live in the city, they live in slums, and they're in a really bad way.

For example, I deal with a lot of the younger Natives that have a big problem with drugs. A lot of the homeless people that I work with are in a situation where they've lost their land; they've lost their identity and their language. That's one of the reasons people die off, when their spirit is broken like that. There's not a lot to live for, you know? A lot of my work is with people in Vancouver who have suffered the effects of these things. Like any terrible thing that's happened in life, it's always with them.

People have to recover what they've lost and, interestingly, I've found the people who have recovered the best are those who have recovered their language. I find that a language has a link to a place and to the land... you 'come home'. There's a different way of looking at the world with your own language. People who have recovered their language have an identity again. They have healing moments in the longhouses when they recover some of their traditions – the potlatching, for example. When people are able to do that it's endless times more healthy for them than to go to a counselor and sit there and talk. It helps them with their addictions and the pain.

Also, our film has really helped because a lot of the younger aboriginal people never knew their own history. They didn't know what their parents and grandparents had gone through because it was never shared. Once they're armed with that history and awareness of why there is so much abuse and violence in their community, then they understand that because of policies and laws there were actions that were planned against their people and it explains what's still happening.

The death rate in the Native community is still 15 to 20 times the national average. There are over 500 missing women in British Columbia alone. You can definitely say that this genocide is continuing – it's just that it's invisible to a lot of communities. In most parts of the country, your 'average' Canadian can live most of their life and never meet a Native.

It's really true that knowledge is power... it gives you a sense of, 'Well we can do something about it now, we're not just helpless victims'. As they begin to recover, they start asking questions: "Who's responsible?" "Who's still profiting?" They threaten the vested interests and those people start coming down on them. That's what they go through all the time. When they try to speak, then the chiefs try to tie them up.

I have a radio program and we talk about these things over the air. The more we talk, the more people come forward. I wouldn't say that it's safer necessarily – I get threats and harassments all the time – but there are a lot of people who confirm what I'm saying now. It's harder to shut you down when you have that kind of awareness.

I knew that Christianity had been responsible for a lot of crimes against indigenous people and others, but when I saw what they were doing to me I knew that they were ruthless people. I thought, 'Well, if they could do that so easily to one of their own, they could do it even more to a stranger who they hated and they feared'. It began to make sense to me how these things could have happened... how people can profess love of Christ and his teachings and then turn round and do that to innocent children. I saw them able to do that.

That kind of cruelty, corruption, and lies said something about the whole institution for me. At that point, even if they had invited me back I couldn't morally be part of that church any more.

I had to re-evaluate everything and it helped a lot working with Native people and others just to become more of a humanist, I guess – looking for the good in anyone and not feeling the need to put a religious label on it. You don't need a church to be a Christian... it's a personal calling that starts from the inside-out.

You can't generalize about Native people because there are many different Nations and beliefs, but one thing you can say about Native spirituality is that it's not based on a creed or a set of beliefs so much as a sense of their relationship with others in the natural world... how sacred that relationship is and how it can't be violated.

One thing I hear a lot on the west coast of Vancouver Island is that they were put on earth to protect the animals, the wildlife and the trees... to be guardians of the land in that part of the world. If you had to say that this creed was their belief, well it didn't really mean anything unless they lived it every day. One older Native woman told me once that, "Christians always talk about their God, but we experience our God". It's a living thing to them – it's not just something that they preach about or go to church once a week to hear about.

When I thought of recovering my spirituality because of the trauma and shock I'd been through, the emotions that I began to feel were more a sense of awe and wonder about the world and the people in it, and maybe an awe at how terrible injustices can live alongside beautiful things that were happening to me at the same time. All these people had somehow survived this terrible torture and were still able to talk about it, and that gave me strength, too. At some point in the future I'll write a spiritual, reflective book summing up what's been going on over the last few years.

When people were beginning to talk about losing the land and their language, I certainly felt it stir an ancestral memory for me. My great-grandfather came from Ireland, and it resonates with me in a very deep way. I feel a strong sense that I need to look at my own roots and recover some of that spirituality. I think it's a knowledge inside that can be recovered.

I believe we are being 'called' back home, back to our roots, because it's a time of survival. It's time to heal and protect our mother earth, and indigenous people help us recover how to do that, I think.

THE KING ARTHUR CONSPIRACY
Alan Wilson

To know nothing of what happened before you were born
is to remain forever a child.
~ Cicero

Lives of great men remind us
We can make our lives sublime,
And departing leave behind us
Footprints in the sands of time.
~ Longfellow

'The Establishment' in Britain and the 'Taffia' in Wales have striven mightily in every way they can, legally and illegally, to obstruct, harass, denigrate, and prevent Alan Wilson and Baram Blackett's extraordinary 30-year research into British history.

Books on the researches of Alan and Baram include; *King Arthur & the Charters of the Kings, The King Arthur Conspiracy, Moses in the Hieroglyphs, The Discovery of the Ark of the*

Covenant and *The Trojan War of 650 BC*. Contact: **The Foundation of European & American Cultural Heritage, Vicarage Court, St. James', Benwell Lane, Newcastle Upon Tyne, NE15 6RS, U.K. Website: www.kingarthurslegacy.com**

I've always had an interest in history. My mother used to bring books home from the library when we were kids in those pre-TV days when people read books.

I had no interest in academics whatsoever. I wanted to go to a technical college but it wasn't possible, so I went to university instead. I got a general degree in history, economics, and in English. I later studied archeology for two years under professor Nash Williams in Cardiff, Wales, but I left in my third year to join the army. When I came out of the army in 1956, I became interested in methods and planning, which was in vogue at the time, and I became the Chief Methods Engineer and the Work Study Department Officer for 12 factories belonging to GKN – a steelworks in Cardiff employing 3400 people. My job was to make sure everybody was in the right place at the right time, with the right equipment, tools, services and instructions; and I don't mind saying I was bloody good at it!

I remained interested in history. My father bought a book; *Glamorgan: Its History and Topography* by C J O Evans, which had been printed in the mid 1930's. It was a mass of information – it listed every village in the whole county… which stones were in what field, what churches were where, when they were built, what tombs were there, etc. I would often get in the car and go somewhere and have a look at the places he'd mentioned. I casually accumulated knowledge as I collected notes and, in 1976, my colleague, Baram Blackett, suggested that I applied the same techniques that I'd used in organizing the steel industry to re-assembling what we could find of history. Our systematic and analytical approach seemed to work.

Like Mr. Magoo, like babes in the wood, we had no idea what

we were up against... We discovered that there's been a deliberate holocaust of the British nation, and we didn't even know it.
Churchill said, *"A Nation that has no history has no future"* and he's
right. Any nation clings to it's history because it's who, what, and
why we are. They've obliterated our identity – it's been planned
and it is a conspiracy; of that there is no doubt whatsoever.

The Two Arthurs

The identification of King Arthur is ancient – he existed, there's
no question about it. In fact, the royal and ancient genealogies all
identify not one, but *two* Arthurs. There's a tall carved stone cross
at Nevern church in Pembrokeshire, in memory of Howell Da
(Howell the Good) who died in 948; the only person in that area
who was ever called 'Rex' (King). One of the most illustrious
manuscripts, the Harleian 3859, which resides in the British
Museum, records extensive lists that were drawn up for the
wedding of Howell Da's son... *both* Arthurs are on it.

The Llandaff Charters are probably the best recorded
histories in Western Europe. All the land grants of the kings are
there, preserved in these cathedral records. The king is always
named, accompanied by the names of his sons and brothers and
cousins, making the grants of land. In this way, you get a rollover
of who's who right over the centuries – you can't go wrong!

There are memorial stones to members of this royal family,
naming them. They're also mentioned in the Welsh Triads
(*Trioedd Ynys Prydein*) and in the *Lives of the Saints* detailing the
lives of the noble and upper classes – you can get a huge matrix
of information from the *Lives of the Saints* and the royal and noble
genealogies, building up a 'who is who' of the entire population
of the nobility.

In Llandaff cathedral is the tomb of St. Teilo, the first cousin
of an 'Arthur of Glamorgan'; so is the grave of St. Dubricius – it
even says in the records that Dubricius actually crowned Arthur
'King'! There are stained glass windows showing King Theoderic

(Tewdrig) and his grandson who was called Arthur *(Arthwys)*. You don't put stained glass windows of cartoon figures up in cathedrals.

Arthur I *(Andragathius)* was the son of Magnus Maximus by his first wife Ceindrech. Arthur I killed Gratian, the Roman emperor, in a huge battle in France in 383. In his book, *The History of the Kings of Britain,* Geoffrey of Monmouth correctly says that Arthur goes over to France with his army to kill a Roman emperor – but he's muddled up Arthur I and Arthur II. He either doesn't realize there were two of them, or he didn't want to say. As a result of this, we reproduced the old records from the earliest extant evidence with tangible artifacts and relics in our volume *Arthur & the Charters of the Kings.* This book is a basic foundation for scrutiny and analysis.

Arthur I had a son named *Tathal* whose son was *Teithrin;* then came *Teithfallt;* then *Tewdrig* (Theoderic); *Meurig* (Maurice); then *Arthwys* (Arthur II) – a 6th generation direct descendant of Arthur I.

Arthur II's grandfather, King Theoderic, was badly wounded in a battle at Tintern fort. He wanted to be buried on *Ynys Echni,* which is Flat Holm Island on Cardiff bay. They got him as far as Mathern, meaning 'the martyred king', where they treated him there at the holy well. The same story is confirmed in the Anglo Saxon chronicles; that he was injured at the ford by a fatal blow to the head and was taken to the well where he died in 1508. They buried him at Mathern church. His bones lie in a stone coffin with a wound to his skull that confirms the story – he was dug up twice... once in 1618 and again in 1881.

Other characters from Arthurian legend can be accurately traced in the same way – for example, Bedwyr ap Pedrog is Sir Bedevir; his grave is in *Din Dryfan* in Dunraven, Castle Morgannwg... it's still there. Owen Ffindu is Arthur's brother; his grave is alongside the church at Llanhilleth, south of Abertillery – a church founded by St. Illtyd who is Arthur's first cousin. The royal Gwenevere is Gweryla – Rhain Guilda, the sister of King Meurig (Arthur's daddy).

Merthyn Wylt (Martin the Wild) and *Myrrthn Emrys* (Martin Ambrosius) are often mistakenly called Merlin – but neither of them were. Merlin was actually Taliesin, son of St. Henwg, who was dictating the life of Samson of Dol around the year 590. His grave is in West Wales in the Cardigan area – it's well-known. In an ancient 6th century poem, there are a famous couple of lines that say *'For I am Merlin and men shall call me Taliesin'*. Merlin means 'little horse' and Taliesin means 'high intellect'. The Gnostic Christian story goes that God appointed a guardian angel to look after earth and he was called *Ialdabaeth* – the 'Great Horse'. He thought he was God and rebelled and so God threw him down and appointed his son *Sabbaeth* in his place; 'Little Horse'.

In 1868, the reverend Robert Williams was asked to translate an ancient Welsh manuscript, *The Songs of the Graves* (*Englynion y Beddau*), for publication by a Scotsman named W. Skeene. He came up with, vague as hell, one-line brief notations of about 193 various ancient Welsh princes and others. Later, in 1958, W. H. Thomas gave the Rees Memorial lecture and said there are less than 70 names mentioned. I sat boggling at it for a long time... I tried every source I could think of and every dictionary I could get hold of in the libraries and could only find less than 25 names mentioned. Now, instead of the 193 brief, useless notations that were thought to be there, we've actually got 25 *detailed* locations of graves. The most famous one-liner was, *'concealed forever is the grave of Arthur'*. But it doesn't say that at all! It actually says, *'A bare, exposed place; so be it the grave of Arthur'*, and it even goes on to give you the name of the field where he is buried! All the fields in Wales had names. The owner of the field had to pay a tithe to the church – there was a book and a map and every field on the map was given a number in the book; so you've got the owners name, the person who's farming it if it's tenanted, the area acreage of the field, the amount of tithe to be paid as a tax, and the name of the field. Arthur is buried at *Caer Carradog* in *The Field of Drunken Helplessness*, which was so-named after the Saxons, who were defeated in battle and had asked for a 'peace conference' – the Welsh arrived unarmed but the Saxons had concealed their weapons. When everybody had drunk far too much, they shouted signals and each one stabbed the guy nearest to him. This history was taught in Welsh schools right until the 20th century. Of course, the English didn't like it one bit, because all the Welsh kids were being taught not to trust an Englishman.

In the 1960's, Leslie Alcock, who had *no* qualifications in either history or archeology, took the archeology department of Cardiff University out of Wales to Somerset in England, where they spent years digging up Cadbury hill in Somerset in search of Camelot. It's well known that John Leland, the King's Antiquary for Henry VIII, forged all the names all around Cadbury hill. He wanted it to *look* like it was Camelot but it isn't – it's Cadbury hill!

If you read Mallory who wrote *Morte Arthur* in 1478 about King Arthur II, he says that Camelot is in South Wales. The Welsh *Y Seint Greal*, written in 1106, also says that Camelot is in South Wales. The main residence of the Glamorgan kings is four miles from Cardiff centre at Caer Melin – Camelot (*Cu bwrd*). *Cu* means together and *bwrd* means table, so *Cu Bwrd* is the mutually together table at *Caer Melin*, which means the 'yellow fort'. Yellow Wells farm is there, so-named because of the sulfur springs. The main residence of the kings is definitely that field and that's where King Arthur would have lived. It's called Castle Field and there was a castle there in 1454 because the records plainly state that there was a wedding there. You can see the bloody field from the top floor of the archeology department!

Arthur II is a 6th generation direct descendant of Arthur I who is the eldest son of Magnus Maximus who is the only son of Chrispus Cesar who is the eldest son of Constantine the Great who descends from the holy family and from Brutus. This makes

Arthur a descendant of the holy family, according to the official genealogies of the princes of Dyfed. The English Crown has obviously got a problem because there are stacks of people walking around today who can accurately trace their descent from *Iestin ap Gurgen* (Justin son of Aurelian) – a direct descendant of Arthur II. Now, how's it going to look if you're a German king or queen of the Hanoverian line on the throne of England? When they joined England to Wales – there was no union; there was an *annexation* (it's illegal in international law by the way). They made sure that not one of the Welsh princes or nobles sat in the House of Lords, because you'd look a bit silly saying, *"I descend from William the conqueror"* if someone sitting alongside you says, *"Well, I descend from Brutus. I've got a 1600-year head start on you!"*

The last Prince of North Wales was murdered in 1282 – the last king of Glamorgan, King Morgan, was killed by the English king in 1300, 18 years later. Now, the King of England then made his son the 'Prince of Wales'; but he was Prince of Gwynedd, really, because Wales is *not* a principality, you see. There are 76 listed kings in Wales; so it's a *King*dom, not a *prince*-ipality.

Calbren alphabet

The English language doesn't derive from Anglo-Saxon German – it comes from the language of the Isinglas; the Iceni tribe of Boudicea, who were speaking the same language as the Chaldeans. The first mass migration to Britain was in around 1500 BC led by Albine, who appears to be a son or daughter of the Emperor Dungi Diocletian; the mightiest of the great third dynasty of Ur, the Chaldeans. They come from Syria – that's why in medieval manuscripts from 1100 to 1150 AD, the 'Ealde Cyrcenas' are frequently mentioned, which means 'Old Syrians'. That's also where the name Surrey in England comes from. In Homer's *Odyssey*, Ulysses asks the bailiff, *"Where do you come from?"* and he says, *"I come from the great island in the Western ocean called Syria."* (Surrey!)

Brutus got here 500BC. Wales (Khymru-land) was much larger than it is now – it took in most of the midlands of England, from Cheshire and Lancashire right up to Cumbria and Strathclyde, as well as Shropshire, Worcestershire, and Cornwall. Wales is the ever-shrinking country.

Language has played a key part in manipulating history. They've tried to destroy the Welsh language in order to destroy the records. They made it illegal for anyone in Wales to have a pen and paper in Richard II's time, and this was also done in Henry IV's time... they didn't want people corresponding with each other because they didn't want a rebellion; they wanted to keep them under control. The people who were most likely to stir up trouble more than anybody else were the poets and the bards who knew all the history, so there were many attempts to kill them.

They tried to replace every Welsh-speaking school teacher with English-speaking teachers in 1846. The objective was to get rid of the history and the records and turn everyone into 'good little Englishmen'. There's still the false idea today that if it's not mentioned in the Greek or Roman records then it must be wrong. Roman records have no interest to me other than the fact that they do support what we say.

About 100 years ago, a man in the north of England named Collingwood decided that all ancient British stone carving techniques originated in the north of England. He was a surveyor, not a historian – he knew nothing about history, but he theorized that this craft was taken over to Ireland and then the kindly Irish sent some people over every time the Welsh people wanted a stone carved. Because of this one man's unqualified opinion, where you get a stone with mixed Latin and Welsh lettering on it, it is now assumed it has been written in Latin and Irish. But the ancient Irish alphabet that they were using to translate the stones was 'invented' by a retired Colonel in about 1700, and I've got the details. Hence they're coming up with 'gobbledygook' translations that don't make sense.

Now if they say it's been written in Welsh Calbren and Latin, out comes King Teithfallt – the great grandfather of King Arthur; out comes the stone of Theodric – the grandfather of Arthur. These were Succession Stones. Unknown monks and abbots didn't make stones; royalty made stones and no-one else... you got yourself in deep trouble if you didn't. There are around 200 of these ancient inscribed stones in Wales.

There was a manuscript written in 1797 saying that the Calbren alphabet is identical with the Etruscan (Italian) alphabet of ancient Etruria and the Pelasgian of the Aegean and Asia Minor (Turkey). This was written again in 1848 by an Oxford scholar. In 1852, there was another detailed publication of the alphabet, and in 1906 it was published again.

Austin Layard dug up the city of Nineveh, capital of the Persian Empire, in 1846, and he found 25,000 inscribed clay tablets. They were sent to the British Museum in London, and some of the experts said, "Oh gosh, look! Some of the clay tablets from ancient Assyria have got the ancient British alphabet on them!"

The correct name of the Welsh is the *Cymru*. There's no such nation as the Welsh – never was. It comes from the English word 'walish', which in High German means 'strangers'. Until the last century *Cymru* was always spelled *Khumry*. The Ten Tribes of Israel were known to the Assyrians and were mentioned on their clay tablets as the *Khumry*.

In 790 BC, a king named Arazia of Judea decided to make war on the Ten Tribes of Israel. His whole army was destroyed and they tied him to his chariot, dragged him to Jerusalem (the capital city of the defeated King), pulled down 200 yards of the wall, rode his chariot through the gap and took everything from the palace. They also took everything from the temple; including the family of Obed Edom. Now, if they took everything from the temple, 'everything' would include the Ark of the Covenant. This was the great talisman of the entire 13 tribes; a box made of acacia wood, about 4ft 2 inches long by 2 ft wide by 2 ft deep, plastered with gold and with a solid gold lid about 2 inches thick. In it was placed the two tablets of stone that God had given Moses on the mountain upon which was written the alleged 'Ten Commandments'. That's the importance of the Ark. It was carried like a litter, with poles pushed through rings on either side of it. The family of Obed Edom is mentioned 14 times in the Bible as the family appointed as the guardians of the Ark. It's certain that the Ark went to Khymru-land to the city of Sumeria in about 790 – it went *north* not south.

Later, the King of Judea gave money to the Emperor of Assyria to attack Israel for him – he *paid* him to attack the other Ten Tribes. The result was that great deportations began around 740 BC and they went on certainly until 702 with four successive Assyrian emperors. In one deportation, Sennacherib said he transported 200,120 people. He was murdered by two of his sons, the heir to the throne made war with his brothers, and the Syrian empire was soon in a hell of a mess. The Book of Ezra says that the Ten Tribes headed west, through the Taurus Mountains to Turkey. They were like an avalanche – the Greeks called them the *Kimmeroi* (the *Khymru*).

The Dead Sea Scrolls were discovered shortly after the war in around 1948. Roman Catholic priests got hold of them and sat on them for about 50 years. They're all written in Aramaic on papyrus – some are complete, and others are fragments, but there are two which are written on copper. They had been rolled up and the only way to unroll this copper was to actually slice little curved segments of the roll and lay them out flat. When laid out, the copper scrolls have got rows of holes along the top and bottom that look like tear marks – clearly, they've been nailed flat to a wall at some point. I think these copper scrolls are relics from Solomon's Temple in Jerusalem. It says in the bible that Solomon put 'sheets of gold' on the temple walls. These were taken by

Shisack, the Egyptian pharaoh, when he raided the temple in about 930BC after Solomon died. His son, Rehoboarn, didn't have the money for gold, so he replaced them with copper. Doesn't it look as if somebody ripped those copper sheets off the wall and rolled them up in haste when they heard that Nebuchadnezzar was on his way to wreck the temple? The only way to preserve the scrolls was to roll them up and hide them.

In 1994, a Professor Kyle McCarter from the United States attempted to decipher these copper scrolls. He came up with a theory that some humble village scribe who spoke a local dialect and didn't write very well had written on the copper *in Hebrew*. So we've got all the skilled scholars writing on cheap papyrus and yet a humble village artisan who wasn't very clever writing on very expensive copper?!

The alphabet on the copper scrolls is neither Hebrew *or* Aramaic… it's something else. They don't know what language it is, but I can tell them – the alphabet is Calbren, the language is Khymric, and we can read the copper scrolls. The scrolls tell of the organization of the Twelve Tribes. We should get a Nobel Prize for that.

We have also translated a large sheet of bronze known as the Agnone Tablet with three inscriptions on it by using the Calbren alphabet. The first tells how there are many storms and disasters; the people are very unhappy and they leave this land under a chosen leader, following behind a 'little box that rides in a cart'. They come to another land where they settle and they are happy. This is basically describing Moses leading the people from Egypt to the Promised Land.

The second inscription tells of a second journey, where they are taken forcibly from this land and, again, they follow the 'little box that rides in a cart', and they arrive in a place to be forcibly ejected. This describes their deportation into Assyria by the Armenian emperors.

The third inscription describes how they decided in a time of opportunity to take off, and they again travel following the 'little box that rides in a cart' until they reach the sea – half of them take ships to Etruria (Tuscany), and the other half stay in the Dardanelles. 150 years later, they gathered on the island of Lemnos in around 500 BC, and sailed for Britain under the leadership of Brutus. That's a fact. In 1876, a great stone was discovered in Lemnos, plastered with Calbren writing and the effigy of a man. It tells exactly the same story as the British records – about gathering together and sailing for Britain to the 'great green island' in the oceans that is awaiting them. It's in the Athens museum, anybody can see it and the writing is Calbren and it deciphers perfectly into Khymric Welsh. So, it would appear that the Ten Tribes and the Twelve Tribes are using the Calbren alphabet in Israel and Judea. The alphabet has also been found in Egypt! A mummy was found wrapped in a 30 foot shroud plastered with Khymric writing. In 1896, John Morris Jones wrote a thesis on how the syntax and grammar of Welsh language is identical with ancient Egyptian – the Tribes and other records mention the stones of *Gwydion Gan Hebdon* upon which all the knowledge of the world is written... these were always regarded as Egyptian hieroglyphs, but we can translate them with the Calbren alphabet. There are 14,000 Etruscan inscriptions that decipher perfectly into Khymric Welsh. There is correspondence between the Assyrian emperors in Calbren on big stones. The stones right through Turkey decipher perfectly into Khymric Welsh. So do the stones in Switzerland, and then you've got it in Scotland, England, and Wales. You can track the people by the alphabet. We can prove that the Khymru are the Ten Tribes – they always said they were and the alphabet proves it.

The Discovery of the Ark of the Covenant
We knew from these records that the Ark (the little box that rides in a cart) was never 'lost' – it either went to Italy or the UK. There is the North Cardiff legend of a great wooden chest that was

buried and in this chest was a fabulous treasure. The chest was guarded by two *Cigfrangawr* which means two giant ravens. This story always intrigued me because the Ark of the Covenant is said to be a great wooden chest and is guarded by two winged, dragon-like creatures called Cherubim – not the little angels we have in modern imagination, but fearsome flying creatures. So, we decided to check it out…

Looking at the ancient Welsh Mabonogi tales, they fall into four categories – there are 12 of them. People say that these stories are disjointed… well, that's because they're four separate stories, you see. We realized that we were looking at similar versions of the *Seven Tablets of Creation* from Babylon that you can see in the British Museum; that these are creation stories. The characters in these stories aren't people – they're powers. *Pryderi* means 'anxiety' and *Pwyll* is a planet that gets destroyed. *Prothemus* and *Epithemus* are the Greek brothers; Forethought and Afterthought. One of these stories is called Sir Peredur, Son of Evrog which means 'Steel Shirt, the Son of the Hebrews'. *Steel Shirt, the Son of the Hebrews?!* We realized we were reading a coded story of the dangers to earth from wandering planets and comets. *Peredur* turns out to be the planet Jupiter and when he's off on his nightly errands going from court to court, country to country meeting barons or kings, what the story is describing is a planet moves around the sun and goes into the different constellations of the heavens. *Geraint and Enid* is the planet Mars. The 'little king', *Llassar Llaes Gyn Gwyd*, means 'Flowing Metal', which is Mercury, and *Owen* appears to be Orion. When they are mentioned journeying together, they really mean that the planets are in conjunction.

So we're being told about disturbances in the heavens – we've got four asteroid belts in two groups outside Mars and Jupiter, and two outside that. These millions of big rocks and stones hurtling around in great circles and so on; they destroyed planets, and that's what our ancestors tell us.

What history *doesn't* mention is that in 562 Britain was devastated by a catastrophe of a comet or debris from a comet hitting it. Professor Victor Clube of Oxford University's Astro Physics department says that this comet would have scattered debris like 100 Hiroshima atom bombs. The devastation must have been enormous. It meant that for seven years *minimum*, the country was virtually uninhabitable in most areas. The French records say that Ireland and Britain were on fire from end to end. Arthur withdrew his army to Brittany. The Angles and Saxons, who had small communities on the east coast, fled from Britain back to Helgeland in Holland and remained out of Britain for about 10 years – that's known. Areas of the Scilly isles also went under water, and you can see today the stone walls going across the beach under the sea. In Welsh records, there is mention that a huge area of Cardigan Bay went underwater, areas of the Conwy estuary went down, and the huge orchard ledge along the west coast of Cardiff went down – they called it 'the drowned country'. There was a great harbor at Cardiff where Arthur sailed his army out of – it's now down in the mud... you can't see it, but it's clearly shown on a map from 1858.

One of the Mabonogi tales describes how, after the battle of Mount Baden (*Mynydd Baedan* in the Maesteg valley) Arthur was going back to Camelot for the night, just north of Cardiff. Halfway back he stopped. His servant is a red man with a red beard wearing a red coat and he rides a red horse. (Incidentally, you know you've got huge white chalk horses on the hillsides in England? Well, one of them is red – and there is also a giant 'man on a horse' on a hillside in Glamorgan.)

Arthur then sits down on a carpet laid by his red servant and it's got 4 golden apples on each corner that represent stars, and they played a game called *Gwd*, which some idiots have said must have been chess – but it's in the dictionary; it means 'star knowledge'. Six riders come – three to Arthur and three to Prince Owen. Arthur is told that his men are destroying Owen's men, and Owen's riders tell him that his ravens are destroying Arthur's ravens. This is a direct parallel to ancient battles recorded; of ravens against men destroying three kings.

We realized that we were onto a solar story. Each of these six riders has a symbol either on his shield or his head – for example; a lion, serpent, and a dragon, which refer to the constellations; *Leo*, *Serpens*, and *Draco*.

If you've got three locations for three major stars you can triangulate their positions to find the 'pole star'. My colleague, Baram, pointed out a great big mound called *Blaediad* , which means 'ferocious warrior' and we looked at each other and said, "*Aaah!*" because the Egyptians, Hebrews and Arabs have a star called 'The Ferocious Warrior'; the Greeks and the Romans called it Hercules. There's another massive mound called *Twmbarlwm*, which means 'Billy goat' (Capricorn), so we'd located Hercules and Capricorn and we knew exactly where Sirius was because there's a shrine there. We were then able to find the pole star at the top of the Senghenydd valley; there's even a standing stone that marks the spot! There are *six* monuments laid out around it, and they're the six riders who are in the story.

Senghenydd valley is about four miles long and two miles wide along the mountaintop. There's a ditch and a mound called the Senghenydd dykes running along both sides – but instead of the ditch being on the outside and the mound inside defensively, the mound is on the outside and the ditch is on the inside, which indicates that it's a religious site. There is a great mound there – a short poem written on an old Tithe map says 'keep ewe sheep in this place and they get sour milk' but it's been deliberately mistranslated. What it actually says is 'This is the Mound of the Queen of Heaven'. We knew now that we were on to a winner – all we had to do was to use the directions from the pole star through these other stars. We were able to draw a star map based on the 50 or 60 huge mounds all over Glamorgan and Gwent, and… *bingo!* – this is how we located the Ark. It's in an area called *Gollug*, which means 'place of worship'. It's a big massive mound – the top is clearly man-made or man-adjusted. The hill is called *Ynys y Bwl* – Bwl with a *'w'* means 'the place of the notch or the judge', but *Ynys y Byl* (with a *'y'*) actually means 'the place of the Ark'; so we're simply down to mistranslation again. We knew it was the right spot.

The ancient British had a particular way of draining underground chambers to keep them dry – we think there are possibly five underground chambers, as there are five unmistakable drain holes; bowl-shaped depressions 12 or 13 ft wide, and a downward sump filled with white stones – the only place you get them is in Cornwall… you can't get them in Wales.

At some point in history, somebody has built a stone wall right around the oval top of this hillock. If you walk up a path at the side of the hill, you come to the entrance where a hole has been broken through the ancient wall (which didn't have any gates in it… odd, isn't it?). You're then faced with the earthen mound of the hilltop in front of you, which is about 60 ft higher. We looked at this spot on the Google earth map – it not only gives you the location; north, south east and west down to each yard or two, it also gives you the height above sea level, which is 902 ft. But when you move the cursor across to the higher mound, it stays at 902 ft and it doesn't increase, so it's clear that the Google map system doesn't measure the height of man-made structures. This fits with the Welsh *Triads*, where it is told that the greatest of the labors of the Khymru was the construction of the hill of *Cyfrangon*.

We know a guy who has an immense reputation in the field of metal detecting – he was the first person to discover how to detect metal underwater. His machine will read 30 ft down, and will tell you the difference between non-ferrous metals (gold, silver, and lead), and ferrous metals (iron and steel). With his help, we have discovered a non-ferris metal object about 4 ft long and 2 ft wide; precisely and exactly the size... of the Ark of the Covenant.

*

By learning how our ancestors thought, we have followed the clues they left behind and have found many other outstanding things... there's an entry in the Anglo Saxon chronicle which says 'they' (meaning the British) gathered together all the treasures of Britain and buried them in one place and no man has ever seen them since. We know where they are. We know where loads of things are, but nobody's listening.

We have told CADW (*Baram says this should stand for 'Commission Arranging Destruction Wales'*) – they don't reply. We told the Welsh Assembly and they clearly don't want to know, either. All we're asking them to do is dig a hole – is that too much to ask? We've been trying to be friendly but it's like talking to a brick wall.

The Catholic Church doesn't want it to come out that Christianity was founded in Britain and taken to Rome, because it will 'blow them up in the air'. They certainly don't want the grave of Jesus the Nazarene to be uncovered in Wales, because then the story of the ascension, how Jesus stands on a street corner in Jerusalem and floats up to heaven on a handkerchief in a cloud of mist, is a load of nonsense. That's why they want rid of this history and that's why they don't want anybody writing about it or researching it.

The Catholic Church is going to have to eat humble pie in the end... they can eat it with me if they like. We've kept quiet about this JC thing – maybe we shouldn't have? We don't want to offend people and we weren't looking for trouble – we really had no idea. We didn't set out to find out about JC... he just 'emerged' in the research. If it's not in a manuscript, if an artifact isn't there, if it's not in a museum, or if it's not there on the ground, then we don't mention it. Everything we can say we can verify.

The worrying thing is the way the police and others have been persuaded to go after us. We have been attacked left, right and center by all and sundry. They've done everything they can to smear our names...

My colleague and his brother were walking down the street coming home at about 10pm one evening. Three police cars turned up and they were arrested and accused of a burglary that had taken place about 10 minutes earlier. A gold ring, a gold chain, and £340 had been stolen, none of which they had on them. The next morning the front-page headline read 'KING ARTHUR RESEARCH PEOPLE ARRESTED FOR BURGLARY'. They had never even mentioned King Arthur. The police had actually thought at first that they had *me* and my colleague (his brother has dark hair like mine, whereas my colleague is blond). We got a lot of bad publicity. We were in town one evening, when an off-duty policeman approached us and said, *"You'd better get down to the overflow courts tomorrow."* It turned out there were two guys on trial who had already admitted to the burglary – the materials stolen had been recovered within hours and had been in the police station safely locked away for over two months before they had even arrested my colleague and his brother. It was bedlam in the court – it was like a film! It was a hideous farce rejected by both Judge John Rutter and the jury and thrown out of Crown court. They'd set us up, but that's one of the nicer little tricks that they've done, 'cos they've done a lot worse than that. The interesting thing is that *not one word* appeared in the press – not a *word*.

In around 1990, I had cataract trouble in both eyes, so I couldn't see. The test was could you recognize another person at 5ft range and I couldn't. I was virtually blind and was waiting for an operation, so my colleague put me in a taxi and had me driven from Cardiff to Newcastle for the weekend for Christmas. When

I returned, our house was raided, I was arrested, and I was accused of stealing a car. I couldn't walk down a street at night – I went out with the dog one evening and walked into a tree! Apparently, I'd stolen a car, driven 30 miles at night to a place in South Wales, and had stolen three ancient paintings from a church that were valued at £100,000. They even had an eyewitness to me doing the theft! To cut a long story short, the man who was their eyewitness against me was waiting trial in the crown courts and he already had several other convictions and criminal records. So we did a 'James Bond'; we had people in restaurants (because he liked to go to restaurants) with tape recorders. We had five tape recordings of him admitting he did it and how it was all a spoof and they were trying to stick it on me. We had 18 witnesses who he had told this story to – that I was innocent. He'd had an advance from a London art dealer of over £3,000. The only fingerprints on these stolen paintings were those of the police 'eye witnesses', and there were five eye-witnesses who had seen him with the stolen paintings. No less than fourteen police authorities in England were seeking him with Bench Warrants. Our barrister went to see their barrister and said, *"Look, this is what we've got"* and that was the end of it. Now, we got massive bad publicity about that. Do you know the publicity we got when it was shown that the police were rigging us up? Again… *not one word.*

Now, you read some of our books and what we do; we're just honest – it is so outrageous it is diabolical. We've written to Prime Minister after Prime Minister, to Home Secretary after home secretary, the Welsh Secretaries, the MPs, Attorney Generals, the Law Chief Justices… we've tried everything and we get nowhere.

We've witnessed a total destruction of British histories that were known very, very well until 100 years ago. My own grand-parents knew about this history; they were teaching this in Welsh schools until 1920.

My colleague is a Geordie. My father was born in the North of England and my mother's was born in Cardiff, so neither of us are Welsh Nationalists as we have been described. We see it as a British project. It's *all* our history. They've done everything they can to destroy the ancient British heritage – not just the Welsh... but *everybody's* heritage.

If it had not been for the Arthur legend they would have got away with it, but he stood there too big, too powerful, too well-placed in the people's minds and imagination, that they couldn't get rid of him. The memory of Arthur lives on in songs and poems; its parchment in stone and in the very landscape itself. Just as the Statue of Liberty is synonymous with New York or the Eiffel Tower is a symbol of France, Wales should have a 200ft high statue of Arthur II holding his sword high in the air...

Photo courtesy of Michael A Cremo

FORBIDDEN ARCHEOLOGY
Michael Cremo

*A nation that forgets its past can function no better than an
individual with amnesia.*
~ David McCullough, American author

*History is merely a list of surprises. It can only prepare us to be
surprised yet again.*
~ Kurt Vonnegut, (1922 - 2007)

Michael A. Cremo was born in 1948 in Schenectady, New York.
His father was an air force officer, and the family lived in
various places in the US and Europe while Michael was
growing up. Michael studied foreign languages and political
science at the George Washington University School of
International Affairs in Washington, DC. He then entered the
Navy, and was sent to a weather station in Iceland. All the
travel opened Michael to new experiences and ways of looking
at the world.

Michael is author of *Forbidden Archeology, The Hidden History of the Human Race, Forbidden Archeology's Impact,* and *Human Devolution.* These and DVDs of his work can be purchased from his website: www.mcremo.com. Other websites are: www.forbiddenarcheology.com and www.humandevo lution.com

When I was a young man, I wanted to find my own path of truth. Through the teachings of Bhaktivedanta Swami (one of the teachers of George Harrison of the Beatles and the founder of the Hare Krishna movement) I became interested in studying the ancient Sanskrit writings of India – particularly the histories, which are called the *Puranas.* In those books, I learned that human civilizations existed on earth for vast periods of time going back many millions of years, all the way back to the very beginnings of history of life on earth. This was something different than I had learned from my teachers at school and university. I thought, "If there's any truth to what these ancient writings say, there should be some physical evidence to back it up." So then I began looking through modern text books on archaeology, history, and anthropology.

In those books, I only found evidence supporting the current theory – that humans like us came into existence about 100,000 years ago, having evolved from more primitive ape-like ancestors. But I decided to go beyond the textbooks. I began looking into the original reports published in scientific literature by individual researchers – archaeologists, geologists, paleontologists and others – and I was very surprised to find that many scientists *have* actually discovered evidence to support extreme human antiquity... it's right there in the original scientific reports but is simply not mentioned in the textbooks. This evidence takes the form of human bones, human footprints, and human artifacts many millions of years old. I have documented this extensive evidence for extreme human antiquity in my book *Forbidden Archeology.*

I tried to explain to myself why this evidence is present in the primary scientific literature (original scientific reports) and yet is absent from the secondary literature (textbooks)... the only reason why, that I could see, is a process of knowledge filtration. Evidence that supports currently dominant theories passes through this intellectual filter, therefore it's mentioned in the text books, whereas any evidence that radically contradicts these accepted ideas is filtered out.

It's not necessarily a conspiracy to suppress truth. It is something a little more complex. In many cases, those doing the knowledge filtering don't think that they're covering up true facts – rather, they think something must be wrong with this evidence simply because it contradicts the theory of evolution. . In one sense, it's human nature. If, for example, I love somebody and someone tells me something bad about the person I love, I wouldn't want to believe it or accept that it's true and I may even become angry with the person who tells me. Today's scientists are very much in love with their theories – like Darwin's theory of human evolution, for example – and when they hear things that contradict the theory that they love, they don't want to believe this evidence.

In another sense, it has something to do with power. If one group of scientists has a monopoly in the education systems and scientific institutions as the supporters of evolution do today, then they don't want to give up their position. Scientists who support the Darwinian theory have managed to convince governments in most of the world to outlaw any alternatives to evolution in their national education systems. For example, last year the Council of Europe passed a resolution asking all the European governments to exclude alternatives to Darwinism from their education systems, and in the United States every time an alternative is proposed, scientists who support evolution have used the power of the state to exclude these alternatives. Scientists like to talk a lot about intellectual freedom – Galileo, for example, proposed an alternative understanding of the solar system a few centuries ago and the Church, through its influence in the governments, was able to suppress his teachings. Today, now that scientists have considerable influence over governments, they are using that influence to exclude alternative ideas. If they thought about that very carefully, they would realize that one of the main principles of scientific investigation is the idea of academic freedom – the ability to propose new ideas on the basis of new evidence. There can of course be disagreements about the alternative ideas and the evidence that supports them. But one party in the debate should not be able to use government to exclude ideas it does not agree with.

Devolution

After people read my book *Forbidden Archeology*, they began to ask the following question: If you have so much evidence that contradicts the evolutionary explanation of human origins, then how do you think the human species came into existence? I answered that question with my latest book, *Human Devolution: A Vedic Alternative to Darwin's Theory*. In that book, I propose that we need new answers to the questions "Who am I?" and "Where did I come from?" The goals that we set for ourselves individually and collectively depend on the answers that we give to these questions. The supporters of Darwin's theory of evolution, through their government-enforced monopoly in the education system, have had the power to dictate to all of us the answers to these questions. Darwinists would say we are simply machines made of matter, so it's no surprise that our goals, individually and collectively, within our human civilization have today become extremely materialistic. Most people seem to think that the main purpose of human life is to produce and consume more and more material things. This overproduction and overconsumption is one of the leading causes of our environmental crisis. Darwinists tell us that not only are we material machines but we are also material machines in competition with each other. I think this is one of the main causes of the intense levels of conflict that we see in human society – among individuals, nations, and religions. It is also one of the main causes of our worldwide economic crisis. Some people, in their desire to win the economic competition, have become too greedy, and everyone suffers from it. These are just some of the effects that the Darwinian theory of human evolution has had on human society and values, and if we're going to change this we have to come up with new answers to the questions, "Who are we?" and "Where did we come from?"

Today most scientists believe that matter is the primary thing – they believe that everything comes from matter, including consciousness. They believe that consciousness is just a temporary byproduct of chemical interactions in the brain. When the chemicals cease to interact, there is no more consciousness. So for these scientists it is only matter that really exists. But in my book *Human Devolution* I propose that *consciousness* is the primary substance. Matter doesn't produce consciousness. It cannot produce consciousness. Rather, it can simply cover or limit consciousness temporarily. We didn't evolve up from matter – we *devolved* from the position of pure consciousness. I think we should be putting more energy into developing the resource of consciousness and less energy into fighting about control of material resources. If we all understood that we're *not* material machines in competition with each other, if we under-stood that we're all beings of pure consciousness who come from the same source, that we're all part of the same family, that we're all related to each other, this would reduce the level of conflict, economic inequality, and environmental destruction that we see in the world today.

If we go back to the ancient wisdom traditions – whether we're talking about the Egyptian tradition, the Chinese tradition, the traditions of South America or the ancient Greeks and the

Romans – we find in none of them the idea that human beings evolved from ape-like creatures. Generally, we find in all of these systems that the human body is produced by higher beings. It's important to understand that a human body or any other kind of body is a vehicle for the conscious self. In its natural state a conscious self has no need for a material body. It has its own form. For example, as human beings we are naturally meant to live on the land. If we want to live in an alien element like water we need a special kind of vehicle that will allow us to do that – we'd need a submarine or a diving suit, produced by intelligent engineers who understand that if human beings are going to exist under the water they need a specialized vehicle that will allow them to do that. As beings of pure consciousness, when we leave the realm of pure consciousness and come to the world of matter we need a vehicle that will allow us to exist and function in the world of matter and these vehicles are our bodies. Just like any other vehicles, they are manufactured by intelligences who understand that if a conscious self goes into the world of matter it's going to need a vehicle.

We can see that there are two kinds of personalities in this world – those who are using their human vehicles to exploit and dominate matter, sometimes very violently. They struggle for the control of material resources like oil and gold and things like that. On the other hand, there are those who are using the human vehicle to try to understand and develop the resource of consciousness. They tap into the inner sources of happiness, and are able to live lives of voluntary simplicity, thus reducing their level of material consumption to environmentally sustainable levels. They also recognize that all others are also beings of pure consciousness, coming from the same source. They feel an intimate sense of relationship with all living beings, and do not become easily involved in destructive competition. We have to decide, each of us, which type of personality we're going to be. Are we going to become more and more deeply involved in conflicts with others to control material resources, or are we going to try to understand we're all beings of pure consciousness... we're all related?

I believe that time really does go in cycles and that human civilizations have come and gone over these vast periods of time. The Greek philosophers – Plato and Aristotle – also believed that. There are times when, in the course of these vast periods of time, the human species does disappear from the earth, but the earth is then repopulated from the higher levels of the cosmos.

Practically every culture that has ever existed in this world has had the idea that we're part of a whole cosmic hierarchy of beings – we don't exist alone in the cosmos. There are higher beings. I believe that such beings actually do exist. I'm not just talking about ordinary humans like us existing somewhere else on some other planet, but beings that actually exist at higher levels or higher dimensions of the cosmos.

The Evidence

One reason I proposed an alternative to the current evolutionary theory of human origins is that there were cases of archeological evidence that showed that humans like us have existed for far longer times that the current evolutionary theory allows. The thing that most impressed me was that there were so many of these cases in the scientific literature of the past 150 years. We're not talking about a few; we're talking about a *huge* body of evidence that contradicts the current theories of human origins. There were *hundreds* of cases... enough to create my 900-page book, *Forbidden Archaeology*. One of my favorites is the California Goldmine discoveries...

In the 19th century, gold was discovered in California. Miners were digging tunnels into the sides of mountains – like Table Mountain in California, and the Sierra Nevada Mountains. Deep inside these tunnels of solid rock, the miners found human bones and human artifacts that, according to modern geologists, date back to the early Eocene period and are about *50 million* years old. This is really quite astonishing because, according to modern theories, human beings capable of making artifacts like that didn't come into existence until about 100 thousand years ago – this would be before the time of the first apes and monkeys, even. These discoveries were reported to the scientific world by Dr. J.D. Whitney, who was the chief government geologist of California. His report was published by Harvard University. These discoveries were made by a *prominent scientist*, reported in *professional scientific literature*, and yet they are *never mentioned in any modern text books!* The scientist most responsible for the knowledge-filtering in this particular case was Dr. William Holmes – an anthropologist working at the Smithsonian Institution in Washington, who said, "If Dr. Whitney had understood the theory of human evolution, then he wouldn't have published that report". In other words, if the facts didn't support Darwin's theory of evolution, then the facts had to be put aside – and that's what happened.

Some of the artifacts from the California goldmines are still in the museum of anthropology of the University of California at Berkley. A few years ago, I was a consultant for a television program called *'The Mysterious Origins of Man'*, which was shown on NBC – the largest American television channel at that time. During the filming of this program, I told the producer, Bill Cote, to visit the museum at the University of California in Berkley, but the museum officials denied him permission to see and film the artifacts. Nevertheless, we were able to find some photographs that were taken by Dr. Whitney in 19th century and we used those instead. It was interesting that when Darwinist scientists of the United States found out that NBC were going to broadcast the show, they tried to stop them from doing it.

A more recent case that I find fascinating is the case of Virginia Steen-McIntyre – an American geologist who was involved in dating an archaeological site called *Hueyatlaco* in Central Mexico.

Some American and Mexican archaeologists were excavating the site and found human artifacts that could only have been made by humans like us, not by any kind of 'ape-man'. They called a team of geologists to date the site – four of the latest scientific methods to date this site were used – and they concluded the site must be at least 250 thousand years old. The archaeologists said, *"That's impossible!"* as the human beings capable of making these artifacts didn't exist at that time according to their theories, and they refused to publish the age of the site. Virginia Steen-McIntyre independently published the site's age in a scientific journal, but then found her career in geology was finished because she had dared to publish something that contradicted the Darwinian theory of human evolution.

In South Africa, miners discovered some interesting round objects made of hematite, which is a kind of iron ore and semi-precious stone. These round metallic objects were found in layers of solid rock that are over two *billion* years old. Their most interesting features are the parallel grooves that go around the center of each object – some of them have two of these grooves, some have three. We showed them on *'The Mysterious Origins of Man'* but before NBC would agree to film them, we had to give them to an independent company of metallurgists for examination. They couldn't explain how these objects could have formed naturally in the layers of the earth, especially with the grooves that go round the center of each object. This suggests that they had to have been made by someone with human-like intelligence in the very, very distant past.

There are many cases that have come to my attention since the publication of my book, and I'm working on another book that I'm tentatively calling *Forbidden Archeology II* to present this new evidence.

We now have evidence that humans existed during the same time as the dinosaurs – human footprints were found alongside dinosaur tracks at a place called Glen Rose on the Paluxy River in Texas, America. The principal researcher, Dr. Henry Morris – a Christian Creationist, published a book in which he claimed that human footprints were present alongside dinosaur tracks. After more careful study, he concluded that the human footprints were just dinosaur footprints that had been eroded to somehow *look* like human footprints, and he published a retraction of his original claims in *Nature* – one of the world's prominent scientific journals. Because he had withdrawn his claims, I became a bit skeptical about the case. Later, an archeology student at a university in Texas wrote to me asking if she could help me with my research, so I asked her to go to this site in Texas. She spent a couple of weeks there and participated in some new excavations where more human footprints were found. She studied them very carefully and said that as far as she could tell they were footprints of human beings like us. On the basis of these new reports, I'm going to include this case in my next book as evidence that humans existed at the same time as dinosaurs.

I've recently been to Russia investigating a case. A former Russian Naval Officer showed me a piece of amber that he found on a beach in Latvia. Now, the amber in that region formed about 30 million years ago – of course, amber is formed from the liquids that come from trees and hardens into a kind of semi-precious stone. Sometimes scientists find interesting things in amber – for example they have found fully-preserved 30-million-year-old mosquitoes and flies. In this particular piece of amber, this gentleman claimed to have found a piece of cloth, which is very interesting. He showed me some microphotographs of this, and you could plainly see that there's some kind of woven fabric inside this piece of amber. This is amazing because, according to standard history, the weaving of cloth is something humans started doing only about 10 or 15 thousand years ago.

There's another piece of evidence related to the discoveries in Mexico that I mentioned, in the same region of the *Hueyatlaco* – some human footprints have been found in layers of solidified volcanic ash, and scientists from the University of California at Berkeley have dated this layer of ash as being over one million years old. Of course, they concluded that the footprints can't possibly be genuine, because according to their understanding of things human beings of our type – anatomically modern humans capable of making footprints like that – came into existence only between 100 and 200 thousand years ago in Africa. According to the current theories, they also don't think there were any human beings in North America until about 20 thousand years ago, at most. They believe that Siberia and Alaska were connected by a land bridge about 20 thousand years ago and that humans came over that land bridge. The evidence that humans existed in Mexico about one million years ago is impossible for them to accept, and so they think that the dating rules out the possibility that the footprints are those of human beings. I say; the footprints are there, they're definitely human, and if the geological studies show that the layers of rock in which the human footprints are found are one million years old, then what a *real* scientist should do is revise the theory in line with the new facts. I think this is what should really be done. The footprints near Hueyatlaco show that humans like us existed a million years ago.

There are two kinds of ways to learn about the past – one is by digging in the layers of the earth to find whatever we can find there, but that's very limited. A lot of the technological tools we use today won't preserve for very long in the archaeological record – for example, I've got a laptop computer sitting on my desk here… well, what if one hundred million years ago there were people that had laptop computers? Then you have to think, well what's a laptop computer going to look like after millions of years? One thing to consider is that plastic starts to decay after about 50 to 60 years. Museums are having a problem preserving things made of plastic – even in museum conditions it sometimes decays completely, so if we have plastic objects sitting outside exposed to the elements... well, after a few hundred years, or a few thousand years they are going to dissolve. But what about the metals in the computer? One reason we consider gold to be very valuable is that it doesn't oxidize – very few metals are like that. Most metals will also oxidize. Something made of iron will rust away. After 100 million years you might not find very much left of a computer, but a stone tool will last for hundreds of millions of years without changing very much. So that is one reason why most of the evidence we have encountered takes the form of stone implements. People using advanced technologies might have existed at the same time, but that kind of plastic and metal technology does not preserve very well over vast periods of time.

Another way to learn about the past is to study the records left by the ancient civilizations. For example, the ancient Sanskrit writings speak of spaceships called *vimanas*. In these vehicles, they would not only travel from planet to planet but from dimension to dimension in the cosmos. They made their space-ships with mantras, by sound vibration, by manipulating subtle energies. They also had advanced weapons resembling our modern nuclear weapons, and were able to tell time by measuring the movements of atoms.

Today, if we want to make a spaceship we have to mine metals, we have to refine the ores of these metals in factories, we have to bring all these materials together in another factory and build it. These ancient civilizations had advanced technologies, but they appeared to have made more use of subtle energies than we use today. This may be why very little evidence of advanced technologies has been preserved in the layers of the earth.

KING JESUS, KING ARTHUR, AND THE
EGYPTIAN TESTAMENT
Ralph Ellis

He that hath ears to hear, let him hear.
~ Matthew 11:15, 13:9, 13:43 ~ Mark 4:9, 4:23, 7:16 ~ Luke 8:8,
14:35.

Ralph Ellis was trained in mineral surveying and computer
science, but after several years in the industry he decided to
retrain as a pilot. Ralph has always had a distinctly lateral,
open-minded view on history and religion, which has allowed
his research to proceed unhindered by historical preconceptions and doctrinal dogma. Ralph has written six books so far,
which purport to explain every last facet of Western religious,
political and social history. Surprisingly, despite the radical
nature of some of Ralph's claims, they are all supported by
historical fact and make a great deal more sense than Church
dogma ever did.

Ralph is author of many books, including; *King Jesus, Eden in Egypt, K2: Quest of the Gods, Cleopatra to Christ, Scota: Egyptian Queen of the Scots, Solomon: Falcon of Sheba, and Thoth: Architect of the Universe.* His books are available from his website: www.edfu-books.com

I have always had a long-term interest in religion. My father wasn't religious but he was a bit of an amateur historian, so we probably visited every major church and cathedral in Britain and quite a few in Europe as well. As a child, I had a very independent view of what I thought history and religion should be so I never considered what I was told as being the absolute truth. I started my own little quest when I was 14, and wrote a small thesis on the life of Jesus, which I included in one of my first books *Jesus, Last of the Pharaohs.*

I use 16 different Bibles in my research. My biggest boon is a computer Bible which will give me the text in different languages, as there is no one particular Bible in the original language... for example, if you're looking at the New Testament there are about four different Greek versions, and there are Greek, Latin and Hebrew versions of the Old Testament (the Tanakh). When I look at each of these to see how they compare, in no way do they actually agree with each other. I don't think that the Hebrew was the original language either, as I believe the foundation of Hebrew is ancient Egyptian. These biblical figures *came* from Egypt – Joseph was Prime Minister of Egypt and Moses was an Egyptian prince and army commander, which could not be possible if they did not speak Egyptian. So many words are identical in both languages that it is my contention that Egyptian is the original 'parent' language. Therefore, if we want to understand the Tanakh properly we need to look at it in Egyptian.

For example, one particular section describes Jacob's brother, Esau, as 'red and hairy' and he drank some 'red soup' and therefore he lost his inheritance. This doesn't make any sense at all in any language but Egyptian. The primary meaning of *djesret*, which also means 'desert', is not 'red soup' or 'red and hairy' – it is actually the red crown of Lower Egypt, which is the inheritance that [Prince] Esau obviously lost. Everything in the Bible is a play on words, and is metaphorical in some sense. It's full of parables from end to end.

Who Was Jesus?

Many people believe that Jesus was a figure of mythology. It's as though someone has written a story about events taking place on a different planet, because everything in the Bible is missing from historical records. I never believed that from day one, which is why I started this research... Here we have one of the most detailed histories of ancient times, passed on through the generations, and Jesus himself, the most influential person of the last 2000 years, can't be found in historical records? I discovered that he is not 'lost' if you know the true era and location in which things happened. Basically, the dates have been changed. If you move the era forward from AD 30 to AD 60, as is mentioned in Hebrews VII, he suddenly 'appears' as Jesus of Gamala; the leader of the Fourth Sect. We've a pretty good clue that this guy is the biblical Jesus because he was described as being the leader of a 'seditious mob of fishermen'. The symbol of the fish is, of course, the symbol of Christianity.

Jesus of Gamala was a very influential figure – he was a prince who owned a castle and governed the city of Tiberias, which is a very different story to the one we have been given. We're not talking about paupers and carpenters here... we're talking about rich influential people, but isn't that ever the way? We don't write a history about Joe Bloggs down the road – we write a history about Princes and Kings! All of these important people in the Old Testament were all Kings of Israel. Moses was a Prince of Egypt, Joseph was Prime Minister of Egypt – these were the people with power.

Let's face it – if you wanted to create a new story for a new religion, you could do an awful lot better than the Old Testament. It's a terrible story of duplicity, intrigue, battle, genocide, child murder and God knows what else. During the Exodus, they killed every man, woman, child and donkey in the city of Jericho! This is one of the main reasons why I believe that both the life of Jesus and the Bible itself are genuine history; and the Egyptian streak running through it makes it more than likely that if Jesus was a leader, a king as he was proclaimed, then he was a king with an Egyptian heritage.

Jesus is also referred to in the Book of Acts as the 'Egyptian False Prophet'. During life, Pharaohs of Egypt were regarded as reincarnations of Horus; in death they would have become the reincarnation of Osiris, therefore we can see the parallel between the life of Jesus and the resurrection story of Osiris. Egyptian mythology and religion is where Christianity comes from.

The New Testament has nothing to do with Jesus; it wasn't written by him and is not his story – it was written by Saul (St Paul) who I believe (and have proven) was actually one and the same as Josephus Flavius, the First Century's premier historian. Jesus and Saul-Josephus were actually contemporaries and Jesus was at the height of his power in AD 60 – in a sense, the Bible was

Jesus, the Warrior King

a battle fought with words. Saul-Josephus had a completely different agenda and the resulting religion he created had nothing to do with the church of Jesus and James; it was completely and utterly different. The Church of Jesus and James was a warlike revolutionary faction – that was why the disciples were sent out to buy swords (Luke 22:36); so that they could arm themselves for the insurrection, and that's why Jesus makes this wonderful rally to arms when he says, *"But those mine enemies, which would not that I should reign over them (as king), bring them here and kill them in front of me."* (Luke 19:27). It was a rallying cry to the revolution.

There were four (later five, including Christianity) sects within early Judaea. The Fourth Sect has striking resemblances with the Church of Jesus and James in that they were slightly ascetic; they carried nothing with them but their swords, and everyone pooled the money they earned into a central purse. Judas was the man who held the disciple's purse. I identify Jesus as the leader of the Fourth Sect, which appears to have come from Persia and was closely related to the Babylonian (Persian or Parthian) Jews. Jesus of Gamala, the leader of the Fourth Sect, had 600 cavalry under his command and he was determined to bring revolution to Judaea. Jesus of Gamala was the biblical Jesus.

Exodus

The stories we have about Moses battling with Egyptian Pharaohs might suggest that he couldn't be Egyptian – but Egypt was divided into Lower Egypt and Upper Egypt... quite often North was fighting South, so the biblical story was really a tale about Moses the Pharaoh of Lower Egypt fighting against the Pharaoh of Upper Egypt. The whole of the Old Testament was a story about Kings and Princes of Egypt, specifically the Hyksos of Lower Egypt. Strangely enough, the Hyksos were called 'Shepherd Kings' and all the patriarchs in the Old Testament are known as 'shepherds'. The exodus story from Egypt is identical with the Hyksos exodus; after storms, darkness, various plagues, and a battle with the Egyptians, 500,000 'shepherds' were kicked out of Egypt on an exodus and they went from Egypt to Jerusalem... does that sound like a familiar story? It is actually the story of the historical Hyksos exodus; not from the Bible. The Hyksos exodus is identical in every respect to the biblical exodus

– the only difference is that the Hyksos exodus occurred 300 years too early; it happened in late 1600 B.C. But how many expeditions of this magnitude do we get out of Egypt?! Obviously, the date has been changed but the exodus is the same. The new era for the exodus concurs exactly with the eruption of Thera (Santorini) in about 1600 BC; which would have caused the darkness, the hail, and everything that is mentioned in both the exodus of the Hyksos and also the biblical account. Moses took a handful of ash from yesterday's hearth and it fell like dust across the whole land of Egypt (Exodus 9:8). Now, you couldn't get a better description of the long range fallout from a volcano if you tried! That's what happened – ash from the volcano at Thera spread itself across Egypt and that caused the political crisis which ended up as the exodus story.

In the first exodus, Moses sets off from Pi-Ramesse which is another name for Avaris, and traveled across the Sinai Peninsula with something like half a million people, and wanders, for no apparent reason, for forty years around the Sinai Peninsula, which is an extension of the Sahara Desert, and then arrives at Mount Sinai. You could not tramp around the Sinai Peninsula with half a million people without losing 95% of them. We need to put this story back into Egypt; into the story of Akhenaton and his brother Moses (TuthMoses).

So, what we're looking for is the great mountain, the great sacred mountain of the Jews. We get some descriptions of this sacred mountain both from [Saul-] Josephus and from the Bible and if we go through these descriptions, I think we can identify it. Mount Sinai was the largest, tallest mountain – but it was small enough that it could be cordoned off so that people couldn't touch it. It was sharp and steep and difficult to climb. It was on the edge of a desert. It had a cave inside it where god lived, and it had a black basalt pavement at the bottom of it that shone like the night sky. All those attributes apply to the Great Pyramid of Giza. Where would your sacred mountain likely be? Would it be some remote craggy peak in the middle of the Sinai Peninsula? Or would it be one of the sacred pyramids of Egypt? Clearly it would be the latter.

Let's get away from this idea that pyramids were tombs – no Egyptian mummy has *ever* been found in a pyramid. The Giza plateau was a temple complex of three 'cathedrals', and if you look at the layout of Giza; again, it's astrological. There are causeways projecting from the base of the pyramids that pointed at specific locations in the sky. The layout of the Giza plateau has been linked to the belt of Orion, the king of the stars, which was called Sar meaning 'king' in Egyptian. A title of Osiris was also 'Sar', so Moses (Osarseph) was the Sar, and we still use that terminology today; in England we call kings "Sire" – Sar. In Rome, they were called *Cea-Sar*. In Germany, they call them *Kai-Sar*. Likewise, the Persian *Shah* and the Indian term *Sahib* – these all come from the Egyptian *Sah*, which means 'the divine king'… an incarnation of Osiris.

The Great Pyramid is essentially a cathedral aligned with the cardinal points, containing a cavern with an empty sarcophagus

The Great Pyramid – Mount Sinai

inside. The central tenet of the Christian faith is the empty tomb (of Jesus) – every church is aligned east-west/north-south and the altar is a big stone box. It's an empty sarcophagus. Thus Christian churches are mimicking, in every respect, the Great Pyramid and the temples on the Giza Plateau.

In my estimation there were only five or six original pyramids; these were the pyramids of Giza and Dahshur. The rest were inferior copies made in later eras. So, of course, if you were on a migration and you wanted to go to your sacred mountain, it was bound to be one of the Giza pyramids; and that is Mount Sinai – Mount Sinai is the Great Pyramid.

The biblical texts all talk in code and you've got to be able to decipher them. One of these codes in the Old Testament is the number 40. The Israelites wandered around Sinai for 40 years; Jesus spent 40 days and 40 nights in the wilderness. Why was Solomon's reign 2 x 40 years and King David's reign 40 years? Virtually all the Judges had a reign of forty years. Why is this number 40 so important? Well, it just so happens that all of the pyramids embody mathematical functions. The Great Pyramid itself is a copy of *pi* to the nearest 2 centimeters. In fact, to be more precise, the Great Pyramid is exactly 40 times the dimensions of *pi*. All the way through the Bible when the number 40 is mentioned, what that indicates is that those concerned had been initiated into the secrets of the Giza Plateau.

The Bible specifically says that the Israelites used the Egyptian Royal Cubit as a measuring system. And is obsessive about dimensions, which you'd expect from a Masonic-type society, so they have recorded the dimensions of the Ark of the Covenant or the Temple of Jerusalem, or whatever it happened to be. Metrology was obviously of great interest to them, so they would have known the dimensions of the Great Pyramid. I can confidently say that, because we still preserve these dimensions within our measurement system today. The Imperial Measurement System is based upon *pi*. There are 1,760 yards in an Imperial mile and exactly the same amount of cubits around the perimeter of the Great Pyramid. The length of a cricket pitch, which is called a chain, is 22 yards. It all comes from the Great Pyramid and *pi*. The fractional approximation of *pi* is 22/7. Everything is based on the numerator, which is the number 22, or one chain. And if you divide one chain by 4, you get 5 ½, which is called a 'rod length'.

The Second Pyramid is a Pythagorean 3:4:5 triangle so, quite clearly this mathematical knowledge goes back a lot further than the Greeks. Strangely enough, the Station Stones at Stonehenge are perfectly aligned to yet another perfect Pythagorean triangle.

Whoever created the pyramids at Giza was saying, in a bold statement in stone, *'We understand mathematical formulae. We are extremely intelligent and we understand everything you understand in the modern era.'*

Adam and Eve

There were actually two exoduses in Egyptian (and biblical) history. There was the great exodus of the Hyksos, the Shepherd Kings, in 1600 BC, which is the great exodus from the Bible, and there was the small exodus of the 'maimed priests' and 'lepers' in the 13th or 14th century BC; the exodus of Pharaoh Akhenaton and Queen Nefertiti. These two exoduses have become conflated into one story in the Bible. The latter were called 'maimed priests' because they didn't believe in Taurus and had their strange singular god called the Aten. The brothers Moses and Aaron from the Bible were actually the historical brothers TuthMoses and Akhenaton.

The reason why we tend to think that the exodus happened in 1300 BC is because there is some confusion about the biblical role of Pharaoh Akhenaton and Nefertiti. In fact, I believe they were initially recorded as Adam and Eve; who were the 'first man' and the 'first lady' in *presidential* terms. Adam and Eve are at the *beginning* of the Bible, not in the middle, where their story should come in the era of Moses (TuthMoses) – so someone has obviously mistaken the term 'first lady' and 'first man' to be an absolute reality. Even the palace for a pharaoh was called the White House. This historical synchronicity makes more sense as to why there's a pyramid on the back of the one dollar bill, and the Washington monument is an Egyptian obelisk.

In addition, Pharaoh Akhenaton wrote a very famous hymn called *The Hymn to the Aton*, which was undoubtedly part of a ceremony that was performed at the dawn of each day, or maybe the dawn of each Sunday, because it was a celebration of the sun appearing over the horizon and illuminating the land. If you look at that hymn carefully, you can more or less see the whole of the Genesis story. Genesis is really about the dawning of the sun. When Akhenaton's hymn says 'the sun makes the animals move' someone has literally taken this to mean that God was actually creating the animals 'one by one' and so they've called it a creation epic and stuck it at the beginning of the Bible because that's where they thought it should go.

The plain of Armana, the site of the Garden of Aton (Eden)

In reality, the Genesis story is about the first lady and the first man (Akhenaton and Nefertiti) walking naked around their idyllic palace, their idyllic 'Garden of Aton' (Garden of Eden) in Armana. Almost every representation of Pharaoh Akhenaton and Queen Nefertiti either has them near-naked or naked, strolling around their gardens – these were the two naked lovebirds... the two lovebirds who finally fell from grace in the eyes of the people and were forced out of their royal idyll.

In that historical story, we have a possible explanation for the battle between Eve and the snake. The emblem of Lower Egypt was the snake. I get the impression that the biblical snake was actually a reference to Nefertiti, because she always wore the double snake *uraeus*. In the Bible she is known as *Khafa* צוה meaning 'life', and another almost identical translation was *Khia* ציה, also meaning 'life', and it just so happens that the second wife of Akhenaton was called Kia. I think that Eve was actually Kia; Nefertiti was obviously the big political figure, but his favorite wife was Kia.

The naked Pharaoh Akhenaton and Nefertiti

We know that the whole Armana enterprise ended in failure and, as there is no evidence of the royal couple's deaths at Armana, it is likely Akhenaton and Kia were forced to leave their idyll and they would have had to put clothes on at that point – another biblical conundrum fully explained! They would probably have gone north, although Nefertiti may have even stayed on at Armana and carried on as the next pharaoh, Smenkhkare (they shared common titles).

Zodiac

The primary foundation of Egyptian religion was what we would call astrology, although they would have called it astronomy because it was a science in those days. The primary preoccupation of the priesthood was watching the stars and venerating the same constellations that we know today. Their primary task was counting off the millennia via precession; that's why the Bible starts with the mythology of going on Noah's boat 'two by two', referring to Gemini. Then follows the astrological era of Taurus, because within Egypt we have the great era of the Apis bull, which comes to an end just as Abraham comes on the scene. This is why we have an iconoclastic clash in the biblical texts, with Abraham and Moses wanting to eradicate bull worship because the constellations had changed; it was no longer the Apis bull (Taurus) who was dominant in the night sky, but Aries and so the era of the Shepherd Kings had begun – the Hyksos kings of Lower Egypt. This is where we have a clash between pharaohs: the Upper Egyptian pharaohs had not changed their religion and had obviously forgotten why they were tracking the stars, as they were still worshipping the Apis bull; but the Lower Egyptian pharaohs, the Hyksos, were known as 'Shepherd Kings' because Taurus had given way to Aries in around 1800 BC; which, again, is in coincidence with the exodus story, for the Old Testament patriarchs were all known as 'shepherds'.

After the eruption of Thera (Santorini), 'someone' was obviously to blame for this great traumatic event and this need for a scapegoat precipitated a civil war between the 'shepherds' and the 'bulls'; and that's why, if we look into the Old Testament and the stories about Joseph, I think we can find some verbatim transcripts from that original argument way back in 1600-1700 BC – actual conversations have lasted into this era and are still with us today. When Joseph came down to Egypt just after then eruption of Thera in around 1500 BC, he brought his family down to Egypt (after being kicked out during the Hyksos exodus), he is bringing his family back down to Egypt and they have to meet the pharaoh. Jacob says to his brothers, *"And it shall come to pass, when Pharaoh shall call you, and shall say, what is your occupation? That you shall say, your servants' trade has been about <u>cattle</u> from our youth even until now, both we, and also our fathers: that you may dwell in the land of Egypt; for every <u>shepherd</u> is an abomination unto the Egyptians."* (Gen 46:33-34)

But what does this mean? It is nonsense and it doesn't make any historical or agricultural sense whatsoever in either in Greek, Hebrew *or* English, unless you know the context, and the real context is astrology; we are not talking about sheep and bulls, we are talking about Aries and Taurus, which tells us that the standard imagery of the zodiac that we are familiar with today existed in Egypt in 2000 BC. Joseph confirms this when he says that the Twelve Tribes of Israel, the twelve rods of the Tribes, and the twelve disciples of Jesus are all based on the twelve signs of the zodiac. Furthermore, at the Last Supper table with the twelve disciples around it; you have Jesus, the son of God, at the center of the table with the twelve disciples around the outside – just as we have the sun surrounded by the twelve constellations.

When Alexander the Great invaded Egypt and became Pharaoh, he adopted and wore the two horns of a ram and became a Shepherd King after he had been told about Aries being the dominant constellation. The last incarnation of the Shepherd King was Jesus himself who was born as the Lamb of God: he was born under Aries. But the reason why Jesus was *so* important is that he was born at the end of the 'great month'. During the precessional year which lasts 26,000 years, we have a precessional month for each sign of the zodiac, for each constellation. Each constellation lasts about 2,000 years and it just so happens that when we came up to the birth of Jesus there was a change in the precessional month between Aries and Pisces – we 'zeroed' the year at that point because a new precessional month had started; this was to mark the years of precession *not* the birth of Jesus.

So, Jesus was born as a Lamb of God, born under Aries, but he became the Fisher of Men because we changed to Pisces at that time. Traditionally, within the New Testament, 'bread' means knowledge. Giving the disciples bread is giving them knowledge. And this is made perfectly clear in several of the parables that Jesus talks about. Similarly, the fish represents Pisces. So when we have the feeding of the 5000 with loaves and fishes, it literally means feeding the five thousand with the knowledge of Pisces.

King Jesus

So, where did Jesus come from? His history goes back to Cleopatra and Julius Caesar, who were supposed to have had a son called Caesarion; but just before Caesar was murdered by Brutus and his comrades, Cleopatra was actually living in Caesar's house in Rome and after he had been murdered Cicero wrote a series of letters which alluded to the fact that Cleopatra was pregnant and that her life was in danger, so she returned to Egypt. The question is: what happened to this pregnancy? Cicero alludes to the fact that she may have miscarried, but I don't think that is necessarily so – the other reason that this child would have disappeared from view was if it was a girl. A girl could not become Emperor and Cleopatra wanted a son, so that he could become Emperor of Rome and she would then be secure; a dowager queen. Instead, Cleopatra maneuvered herself into marrying Mark Antony and they had two children, Alexander Helios and Cleopatra Selene (whose names mean 'sun' and 'moon'). Cleopatra and Mark Antony were finally killed by Octavian Augustus, who took Cleopatra's children and they were brought up in the Royal Court. We then move on a few years and Octavian has some problems on his borders and he needs to placate some of these rebellious rulers, so he gives his old friend Jubba II, the King of Mauritania, the daughter of Cleopatra as a diplomatic bride. Octavian had an even bigger problem on his eastern borders with the King of Persia (Parthia), Phraates IV. Rome had already lost two battles with Phraates and his predecessors – they had lost several legions in battle, which was unheard of for the Roman army. Octavian, wanting to placate Phraates, comes to a somewhat diplomatic conclusion and, according to historians, he gives Phraates a prostitute by the name of Thea Muse Ourania. But if Octavian had really given Phraates IV a prostitute, he would have declared war on the Roman Empire! But, no – Phraates was most impressed with his 'prostitute' and he makes her his Chief Wife and when she has children he eventually makes her sons heirs of the whole Persian (Parthian) Empire. So why was Thea Muse such a diplomatic catch for Phraates IV? Why was she greater in status than Cleopatra Selene, the daughter of Queen Cleopatra? There are many reasons for thinking that Thea Muse was the long-lost elder daughter of Queen Cleopatra and Julius Caesar.

Thea Muse Ourania became Queen of Persia (Parthia), but she was not satisfied with this and poisoned her husband and married her son, to inherit the throne herself. It was an Egyptian custom for the pharaohs of Egypt to marry a sister, father, or a very close family member – this was just standard practice to keep the bloodline pure. Clearly this was not a Persian custom because Thea Muse was subsequently exiled from Persia for this transgression. So, in AD 4, they go to the borders of Syria and Judaea and what then follows comprises the complete biblical scenario – all of the central tenets of the New Testament...

In the Gospels we have a story about an important couple who were linked to 'shepherds' (i.e.; of the Hyksos royal line), who were on the move for some reason, wandering around in Judaea or the borders of Judaea in a state of some poverty, where they had a baby boy... a prince who was visited by the Persian Magi. But why on earth would the Persian Magi be interested in a Judaean boy being born in Judaea? The Persian Magi were not only the priesthood of Persia – they were the 'king-makers'; they sought out and proved the next King of Persia, so what they were doing hanging around the stable of Jesus when he was born? It doesn't make a lot of sense, does it? However, in terms of the exiled aristocracy of Thea Muse Ourania, the exiled Queen of Persia, it makes every sense. They were of the Persian royal family and they *would* have been visited by the Persian Magi because, notwithstanding any of the problems that the parents had had, their child was nevertheless a Prince of Persia – a possible heir to the throne of Persia (Parthia).

In exile, this royal family were looking for land to start a new empire, so they struck a deal with one of the Herods of Judaea. (Often within the New Testament and within Josephus there is some confusion because there were many 'Herods'). Persia was the biggest threat that Rome had, and so the royal family agreed to protect Rome's eastern border and, in return, were given some land, tax free. This is why when you go through the New Testament, verse after verse after verse is about taxation. Similarly, the biggest bugbear the historical Fourth Sect had was taxation – they refused to be taxed either by Jerusalem or by the Romans. In the New Testament, a 'publican' is a tax collector. Many of the Gospel parables have something to do with taxation and absentee landlords; that is what caused the Jewish revolt because the Fourth Sect were not about to be taxed, and Jesus was the leader of the Fourth Sect.

This new city state was called Gamala, and it lay along the borders of what we would call eastern Jordan and eastern Syria. It was known as the Kingdom of Ourania, which means 'the Kingdom of Heaven'. So when it says in the Bible that, 'You will inherit the Kingdom of Heaven', they are not talking about something spiritual up in the sky – they are talking about a physical tax-free kingdom that had been established in Syrio-Judaea.

This family was primarily based in Palmyra – an oasis border village, slap bang in the middle of the desert on the borders of the Roman and the Persian empires. This was one of the major caravan routes for trade going between the two, but suddenly in the 1st century it went from being a small village to one of the largest Roman cities. Nobody knows why. They say it was because of trade, but the village had been there for centuries and had never grown until then. The reason why it became such a big and influential place, I believe, is because it was the primary power-base of Thea Muse Ourania. Initially, I thought that, like the biblical story says – they were downtrodden, exiled, with no money and finding a stable the only place to stay for the night.

However, on second thoughts, I realized that, no; Thea Muse left Persia on her *own* terms. She took with her 200 courtiers and 600 cavalry. (No wonder there was no room at the inn in a small, desert village!) Remember that the historical Fourth Sect of Judaea, the Babylonian Jews, also had their own private army of 600 cavalry... quite clearly this was the same story – about Thea Muse Ourania, who came from Babylon (Persia). The royalty of Lower Egypt were the ancestors of the Jews, and were considered to be Jews themselves. Josephus, for instance, says that the Jews were the Hyksos Egyptians, and Strabo's description of Jerusalem was that the majority of people in the Temple were Egyptian, so there was a big connection between the (Lower) Egyptians and the Jews. Hence this royal family who were being thrown out of Persia would have been known as exiled Babylonian Jews.

Therefore, rather than being absolute paupers I think that these exiles also took with them half the Persian treasury, which is why Palmyra suddenly sprang from being a village into being the most influential town in the Roman Empire; they had so much money that they could buy whatever they wanted.

There is a lot that links the Palmyran story with the Judaean story and part of that comes from the Talmud; which a wonderful historical resource... but everything is written in code. It transpires that Palmyra was very influential in Judaean politics, as the Palmyrans were one of the few people in the East who could be considered Jewish as of right.

Then we come to Queen Helena, who was probably a daughter of Queen Thea Muse Ourania – a Princess of Palmyra. She and Queen Helena are really important in this quest, because Helena saved Judaea in the famine of the A.D. 40s. It was also Queen Helena who donated all the furniture for the Temple of Jerusalem, including the great candelabra; the great *menora* which was made of solid gold, which was finally taken as booty by the Romans in A.D. 70 and was imaged on the great triumphal arch of Titus in Rome. The son of Queen Helena is also quite important in this quest because his name was Izates in the Persian, but his colloquial name was Izas and I think from here we see a possibility for the biblical Jesus being a son of Queen Helena.

The Talmud also mentions Jesus and Mary and various characters from the Bible on numerous occasions, but the Christians won't tell you this because what it says doesn't fit in with their dogma. A classic example is Mary of Bethany – it's been conclusively shown by Robert Eisenman, the eminent theologian, that the Mary and Martha in the Talmud are actually the Bethany sisters from the New Testament. Throughout religious history, numerous commentators have said that Mary of Bethany is actually a pseudonym for Mary Magdalene; the 'prostitute' who famously wiped Jesus' feet with her hair. Note the title of 'prostitute' once more, just like Queen Thea Muse. However, in the Talmud Mary (Magdelene) was said to be the richest woman in Judaea – she had a daily perfume allowance of something like 400 dinari; she had a palace in Jerusalem with a carpet that went from her palace into the Jerusalem Temple, so that her dainty little feet didn't get dirty. This is Mary Magdalene, the richest woman in Judaea, whose husband is called Jesus (of Gamala). Now, isn't that a different tale to the one we are normally peddled?

In addition, Mary purchased the high priesthood for Jesus (of Gamala), and it cost 75 liters of silver – an enormous amount of silver coinage. Being high priest was a highly prestigious position, both secular and religious, because the incumbent became 'de facto' king – he controlled all the tax income in Judaea, as well as the army.

Jesus and his followers were Gnostics, and if you translate 'Gnosticism' into the Latin, it becomes *scientia*, or what we would call science. He was a prince. He owned a vast palace and would have had courtiers, court astrologers, and *magi* from Persia.

Relating this to masonry, the basis of masonry is Gnosticism. After Grand Lodge was set up in 1717, they subsequently set up the Royal Society, which is still Britain's premier scientific institution; and all of it's founding members were Masons. Jesus' court would have been no different; it would have been based on the seven sciences.

From this, one can deduce that one of Jesus' chief courtiers was a *magus* called Hero of Alexandria, who was known as 'the mechanical man'; he was the 'Leonardo da Vinci' of the 1st century AD and he was inventing all kinds of incredible machines. He invented the first steam turbine, a fire engine, and automatic doors... he even invented a milometer for the Roman army! He made altar pieces that sang and groaned and a flying chariot that flew across the temple using magnets. However, one of the things he particularly loved was pneumatics and hydraulics, and he made five versions of a trick that turned water into wine. It's quite obvious that Jesus used one of Hero's trick jugs for his water-to-wine 'miracle'. I've made my own 'Hero Jug' and it works perfectly – it's a simple trick based on hydraulics and pneumatics... all you have to do is cover up a hole with your thumb, and you can pour wine into one person's cup and water into the next one.

Wonderful technology came out of Alexandria and Judaea in the 1st century. We could have had the Steam Age in the 2nd Century were it not for Vespasian winning the battle for the Emperorship of Rome; and, subsequently, the Christian Church becoming the dominant religion. We could have had the Steam Age in the second century AD, and we could have had aircraft and rockets flying to the Moon in the 3rd century AD... so we have lost nearly 1700 years of technological advancement, all because Jesus lost the battle for the Empire.

One of the thrusts of my books is how history can affect the future. If we allow another backward, Dark Ages religion to come along and stifle the scientific revolution that we've had over the last three hundred years, we could go back to square one again, and that would be disastrous because the same fossil-fuel energy supplies that we have used for our advancement will not be available to future civilizations – there simply won't be the resources in the ground to become a technological civilization once again. We've got to succeed; we cannot regress.

The Last Emperor

In the Talmud and Josephus' *Jewish War*, we have a story about great battle between Jesus of Gamala and the historian Josephus Flavius in the AD 60's, during the Jewish revolt which the Romans were heavily involved in. Apparently, Josephus chased Jesus and his army all around Judaea; and here we have a direct parallel with Saul (St Paul), who also chased the followers of Jesus around Judaea. No one has ever explained to me under what jurisdiction was Saul able to chase protean Christians around Judaea! Again, it looks to me that Josephus and Saul were one and the same person. Josephus was able to persecute Jesus (of Gamala) because he was in command of the Galilean cavalry, and this would explain Saul's similar exploits. It just so happens that Josephus won this war (with the help of the Romans).

But what was Jesus' primary goal? The throne of Judaea, or something much greater? The Talmud may give us the answer, for it says that the people of Jericho came out and said to this Jesus (of Gamala), *"Go up you bald head!"* (The Talmud does like to talk in riddles). In explanation, Julius Caesar was the famous bald head of that era, jokingly named because *caesaris* means 'hair' and Ceasar himself was quite bald. Likewise, to 'go up' means to 'arise', so the people of Jericho are saying to Jesus, *"Arise, Caesar!"* This wasn't just a battle for the high priesthood – this was a battle for the kingship of Judaea *and* the emperorship of Rome. Jesus wanted to become Emperor – just like grand-daddy. As he was related to Julius Caesar, Queen Cleopatra, Phraates IV, and Jubba II, Jesus was the most well-connected prince in the *whole of the known world*. Here was a prince who could possibly unite all of Persia and all of Rome and all of Egypt under one great emperonic monarchy.

We know this because the great oracle of that era, that the Romans looked to and were fearful of, was the Star Prophecy, which said that the next Emperor of Rome would be a star from the East. Now, who was born under a star from the east? To become Emperor you had to have an oracle on your side and, clearly, the next oracle was pointing towards Jesus, but he got caught up in a war against Vespasian and his son, Titus, for the control of Judaea. Vespasian won, and it was Saul-Josephus, who had become his chief translator, astrologer, and subversive spy, who was complicit in helping him become the next Roman Emperor by using the Star Prophecy (Vespasian was campaigning in the East).

After Jerusalem had fallen and the leaders of the rebellion were summarily crucified, Saul-Josephus returned from an expedition to Tekoa, only to see three of his former compatriots being crucified; Jesus of Gamala being among them. Josephus petitioned the Commander of Jerusalem (now Titus, the son of Vespasian) for these three to be taken down from their crosses. They were given medical attention but two died and only one survived. This is taken directly from the history of Judaea and is quite clearly an alternative version of the biblical crucifixion.

A very interesting event is then mentioned by various Roman commentators. Vespasian, who was still in Alexandria at that time, was looking for his oracle, his favorable portent, because three claimants to the throne of Rome had already been summarily executed and he wasn't about to stick his neck on the line unless he could be absolutely sure that he would be greeted as Emperor. The story goes that a 'King of Egypt' was brought to him who was lame in one leg, blind in one eye and had a dislocated shoulder, and the courtiers said, *"Heal him Sir, touch him and he will be healed"*. By using a standard healing trick from the

New Testament – spitting in the man's eye and rubbing his eye – the man is healed and can see again, and thus Vespasian had his oracle that would allow him to become Emperor of Rome. It just so happens that the Talmud gives a description of Jesus as being lame in one leg and blind in one eye – everyone says that is just a derogatory description of Jesus, but it is actually a post-crucifixion description of Jesus... of *course* he would be lame in one leg and have a dislocated shoulder if they had hammered a six-inch nail through his ankle and hung him from a cross-beam! The description in the Talmud matches the description of this strange person who gave the authority to Vespasian to become Emperor of Rome, and the only person who could do that was Jesus himself. This is a story about a post-crucifixion Jesus who was brought before Vespasian; and quite obviously, a deal was done – 'I will spare you, if you give me the Star Prophecy'. Vespasian then sailed immediately for Rome to claim the Emperorship.

But what to do with this dangerous rebel prince? You can't kill him – he's got too many friends. One of the reasons that Jesus was taken down from the cross in the first place was because his best friend was Berenice, the sister-wife of Agrippa II, the nominal king of Judaea, who became 'married' to Titus, the Emperor's son. Execution was out of the question, so I think they sent Jesus into exile instead, for that was the only thing they could do. But they were cautious enough to send him as far away as possible from his power base in Judaea – to the opposite end of the Empire, to Britain.

At exactly the same time in Chester in Britain, a very strange fortress, Fortress Dewa, was built by Vespasian between AD 75 – 79. It was the largest fortress in the Empire, yet it was strangely hiding away behind forests and marshes on the edge of the Empire. I think this was a Spandau prison of the 1st century AD, built specifically to hold dangerous rebel prisoners. It had its own separate society, with separate accommodation blocks, temple and bath house – no other fortress had these elements.

I definitely link this with the exile of Jesus because of what they call the Elliptical Temple, which is unique within the Roman Empire. It was a temple based on the design of the Vesica Piscis, an elliptical shape which is ubiquitous for the sign of Pisces. Of course, this was also the symbol of Jesus, the Fisher King. The temple was divided into twelve alcoves like a complete zodiac.

Jesus, in Chester, was the Egyptian warrior prince – the locals would have called him King Arturi, meaning 'King of Egypt' or, perhaps, 'King Arthur'. In *Parzifal*, King Arthur was also called the Fisher King. The line of Fisher Kings, I believe, was descended from Jesus, the first of the Fisher Kings but, interestingly, he was also called the 'maimed king' because he had a specific wound to the groin which made him infertile. As an exile, the last thing that Vespasian would want is for Jesus to be procreating more little Jesuses in the northwest part of the Empire. Undoubtedly, if Jesus was exiled they would have had to have castrated him.

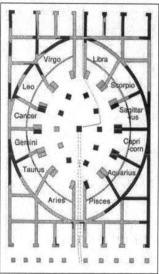

Credit: Take 27 Ltd. Dr David Mason, Peter Carrington of Chester Archaeology

Thus Jesus was not only a famous Eastern prince who became the most well-known spiritual character in the Western world, a man who spawned a billion books; his history was also the foundation for Arthurian legends and so he also became one of the most famous mythological characters in the Western world. Many a tale would have been told about Jesus' exile in the Celtic lands of the Western Empire but, following the Council of Nicaea in the fourth century and the establishment of the Roman Catholic Church, these stories would have become heresy. To say that Jesus survived the cross and was exiled to England in AD 75 would have invited a slow roasting similar to that given to Jaques de Molay, the grand master of the Knights Templar. But who could be tortured for inventing a tale about a mythical warrior king of Celtic Britain? And thus was born the legend of King Arthur, so that those with 'ears to hear' would know to the end of time that "those feet, in ancient times, did walk upon England's mountains green".

RECOVERING OUR GNOSTIC HERITAGE
Neil Kramer

A warrior is never under siege. To be under siege implies that one has personal possessions that could be blockaded. A warrior has nothing in the world except his impeccability, and impeccability cannot be threatened.

~ Don Juan Matus

Neil Kramer is a writer, speaker and researcher in the fields of consciousness, metaphysics, shamanism and ancient mystical traditions. His acclaimed website *The Cleaver* and his audio book the *Audio Cleaver* attract a discerning international audience. His essays and interviews are regularly published on cutting-edge websites, news portals and popular media networks. He is currently working on a film project. Website: www.thecleaver.blogspot.com

I was brought up with a healthy appetite for reading, which my parents instilled in me from an early age. I shall be forever thankful to them for that. In my teens, I devoured the works of Nietzsche,

Schopenhauer, Hesse, Kafka, Crowley, Tolkien, Bukowski, Jung, Huxley and Burroughs; all writers who were sincerely interested in exploring both the absurdities and profundities of life. I later gravitated to more spiritually-oriented texts, particularly focusing on Zen, The Kabbalah and Shamanism. Castaneda was a significant influence. Though I was aware from the beginning that his writings were drawn from a blend of his personal imaginal landscape and an actual consensus one, I found his words to be intensely true. You just can't sustain that kind of quality and gnosis without actually living it. One way or another, Castaneda had been transformed from an ordinary man into what we would now call a shaman. Still to this day, I find the principles and techniques of Mesoamerican shamanism to offer one of the most compelling and integral models of reality one could hope for.

As soon as was practically possible, I began to investigate the innate shamanic impulse firsthand; to 'walk the path'. I visited sacred sites across England, connected with the natural world and practiced different techniques for shifting levels of consciousness. I studied entheogens; their origins and shamanic heritage, their chemical composition, their usage and how they rekindle ancient circuitry in the mind that's been almost entirely forgotten in the smog of modern post-industrial society. Every continent has its own indigenous shamans – not just the Americas, Siberia and the Amazon region. Indeed, it was from studying the hostile suppression of shamanic traditions in Europe that I encountered the ever-present veil of historical censorship, and traced how certain dynastic elites had been quietly but decisively orchestrating human affairs for quite some time. I came to understand that an individual man wielding real universal power posed a tremendous threat to any and all systems of government.

Above all, I instinctively knew that the default position of an unquestioning and dutiful life was unspeakably deficient. I saw that the unholy trinity of (i) trading time for money, (ii) postponing living in the moment to another time and (iii) imbibing a dehumanizing prefabricated culture, have to be personally experienced before they can be properly deconstructed. Only then, when we move away from the system that is spoon-feeding us falsehoods from birth, can we see that the universe is a deeply magical place and that it is intimately bound to us. Offices, sports, nights on the town and television begin to lose their appeal. There is something infinitely more mysterious and fulfilling going on.

Path Of The Ancients

Initially, my spiritual journey was somewhat private. I would discuss some philosophical aspects with close friends and other students of gnosis, but in terms of day-to-day experience, the real inner work is, by its very nature, a necessarily individual act. I did not preach or proselytize and felt no need of an audience. In fact, I found the idea rather unpalatable. Any sharing of esoteric information or personal insights was only ever on a one-to-one basis and by specific request. Things remained this way for some time.

Around the turn of the millennium, things began to shift. The escalating war on personal freedom in England, the radical dumbing-down of the news media and later the startling events of 9/11, all combined to steer my decision to share my own personal conscious path with similar souls who were interested in making sense of what appeared to be a world spiraling out of control. Whether that was one person or a million did not matter to me. I felt this was my way of combating the disempowering falsehoods of what I call the Control System. I did not just want to criticize and condemn it, nor did I want to spearhead some kind of radical social or political reform. That would be futile. After all, the problems are not actually external to us. What I really wanted was to totally deconstruct the whole unreality construct from its very roots.

I wrote a number of essays under various pseudonyms and gave audio interviews for underground radio and podcast stations. They were well received and stimulated some very intelligent and edifying dialogue. I saw that there were a lot more people interested in the genuine issues that affect our everyday lives than the mainstream would have you believe. Finally, I decided to publish my writing on my own blog, which I named The Cleaver. This wording is a reference to a poem I wrote fifteen years ago about a psychic blade that would enable the wielder to slice through delusional thinking. It seemed rather fitting.

The Cleaver explores the alchemy of conscious evolution. Essentially, what we have come to understand as our own inner psyche must be placed in the crucible of self-awareness and reduced to its primary consciousness; resolutely dissolved into its purest form. From here, we can then cleanly and intentionally distil, shape and formulate a new, purer state of being. This ongoing alchemical process connects us with a reality that is more aligned with our own transpersonal will - our instinctive spiritual trajectory, as we might say. Within this beautiful and unified practice of being, it becomes patently obvious that we are the redeemer. There is no savior entity to wait for. We are it. We are pieces of individuated consciousness moving out from the divine source, shifting through a myriad dimensional spaces and densities, experiencing, becoming purer and finer and truly needing nothing outside of ourselves whatsoever.

Whilst it is true that few of us can entirely escape the unreality construct, especially if we have friends, families, jobs, objects, desires and beliefs that are anchored within it, what we *can* do is inoculate ourselves against its insidious psychic energy-drain by maintaining an unremitting self-awareness. I endeavor to sincerely retain a detached observance of myself in the world as well as the selves of other people, including emotions, deeds, creative expression and psychic energy flow. This is what really moves me to research, write and speak on the subjects that matter. It is the inner-knowing that there are a growing number of authentic souls who want to find a better way to live; a better way to be.

It is incumbent on all those who have sharpened their awareness to a fine edge to responsibly share their insights with those who earnestly seek the self same conscious realization. Once again, we should bring to mind that there is no absolute separation between one conscious entity and another. Only the very briefest divisions of energy manifesting into particular hard light configurations give us the impression that there are individual people and things in the world. In actuality, there are not. Acknowledging this, why on earth would we not share our deepest perceptions and knowing!?

Historical Inseparability

The English high school I attended was considered one of the best in the area. It desperately clung on to the vestiges of its own bygone glory days - prefects, the house system, blazers and ties, physical punishment, rugby and, of course, notable annual examination results. It was therefore particularly amusing, albeit not for any of the well-intended parents, that the whole thing turned out to be nothing more than a smokescreen. The reality was that it wasn't just the paintwork that was flaky.

Sadly, history was one of the most mind-numbingly tedious classes in the whole schedule. The presentation, content and student engagement was pitiful. It was perfunctory painting-by-numbers nonsense. The more unintelligent a student was, the more they loved the history syllabus. To get a decent exam result, all you needed was a good memory. Actual knowledge, analytical interpretation or any sort of meaningful historical context, played absolutely no role in the learning process. If you did happen to be genuinely interested in any of the subjects that were momentarily touched upon, you had to go to the library in your own time to approach any sort of real understanding. I remember thinking, 'My God, if this is what's going on in the good schools, what the hell is going on in the bad ones?'

A deep, reasoned and systematic exploration of both official history and alternative history only came through my own personal studies in later years. Tracing the complex roots, cultural motifs and metaphysical insights of ancient Sumer, of Hinduism,

Zoroastrianism, Mithraism, Romanism and Christianity has played a significant role in informing my research of how and why elite power structures have been so carefully preserved over the millennia.

A basic understanding of the last three hundred years of political, military and cultural history is incredibly useful in providing a contextual framework to many of the seemingly inexplicable conflicts that have shaped our cultures – such as those in Israel, Palestine, England, Ireland, India, Pakistan, the Basque Country, Spain, America, Iraq, Iran, North Korea, Afghanistan, Yemen, Saudi Arabia, Russia, Rwanda, Burma, Somalia, Tibet and countless others. It is interesting how these serious human discords get no equitable or insightful mainstream coverage, even though they continue to shape the national and foreign policies of our governments. What little TV space these wars do get involves hideous oversimplification, designed for five-second attention spans.

TV audiences are programmed not to care. People switch off their consciousness when they hear of another incidence of human massacre in Fallujah. It makes no sense. It is irrelevant to the practicalities of what is happening in the Western family home. Without real data, without the chronology of events, decisions and human narratives, five dead troops or 500 dead Iraqi citizens means nothing to most viewers. This is precisely why independent impartial accurate contextual data is absent from all mainstream news broadcasts. We are not afforded a clear view of the context in which things are occurring. The historical lens is missing. Unless people take the time to study broader perspectives and multiple sources of information for themselves, which is exceedingly rare, they are in danger of simply swallowing the imbalanced and hugely prejudiced mainstream message.

The Insurgency Of Selfhood

One doesn't need to travel very far back into history to see what lengths the Control System will go to in order to prevent the common man from attaining any measure of spiritual independence or divine gnosis. Perhaps the most staggeringly effective spell ever conjured upon humankind has been the Control System's strategy of co-opting spirituality and rebranding it as the various Abrahamic monotheistic religions of Judaism, Christianity and Islam.

Consider this... Only 227 years ago, in the apparently cultured and enlightened lands of Europe, Anna Göldi was executed for witchcraft in the village of Glarus, Switzerland. She was beheaded by the blade of a state-sanctioned executioner. This brutal killing represented the final chapter in the long tale of deranged witch-hunts that beleaguered Europe for centuries.

In 1682, in Devon, England, Temperance Lloyd, Mary Trembles and Susanna Edwards were tried for witchcraft and hanged at Exeter jail. The same year, Guenevere Damascus, her lover, and their spiritual teacher were accused of speaking in unknown languages, practicing knowledge beyond their natural abilities and acting in peculiar manners. They were burned at the stake. In 1684, Alice Molland was sent to the gallows at Exeter jail, becoming the last witch to be executed in England. In 1692, Salem, Massachusetts, 150 people were arrested and imprisoned on charges of witchcraft. 19 were hanged, one was crushed to death under heavy stones. At least five more perished in their prison cells.

Not long ago, opposing official religious doctrine on any spiritual matter or common natural law, and often simply just upsetting the wrong people, would see you branded a witch. A few allegations of supernatural powers, and in particular communication with spirits and animals, were usually sufficient to secure a guilty verdict. In every case I've looked through, the evidence against the accused was truly pitiful and in some instances quite non-existent, most data being either pure hearsay or entirely circumstantial. So why the extraordinary and lethal hysteria?

Where did it all begin?

The origins of the madness are to be found with Pope John 22nd, who in 1320 formalized the persecution of witchcraft by sanctioning the explicit prosecution of 'sorcery' in the shape of the now infamous Inquisition. This was an appalling social manipulation designed to separate man from his spiritual heritage – from his transcendent connection to the universe. It was not a theological mistake or ignorant lunacy; it was a fierce campaign to destroy all indigenous European shamanism by exploiting the supernatural fears of an uneducated populous. Though this was specifically channeled through the dominant religious apparatus, I would suggest that few, if any, of the senior religious and political leaders, knew anything about the true purpose of the coming massacres.

In 1484, Pope Innocent 8th issued a papal charter authorizing two inquisitors Kramer (no relation) and Sprenger, to systemize the persecution of witches. Heinrich Kramer and Jacob Sprenger authored the infamous treatise on witches, Malleus Maleficarum (The Hammer Against Witches, or Hexenhammer in German). So began centuries of Church-sanctioned massacres of hundreds of thousands of men, women and children. A fully intended pandemic of witchcraft hysteria swept across the peoples of Europe and across the Atlantic to America. It's hard to imagine the savage terror it brought to many rural areas in particular, with many thousands of accounts of inconceivable cruelty.

The Romanist machinery was determined to despiritualize the sacred lands of Albion. Man was pitted against himself. The unknown was setup as the enemy of the known, hurling the consensus psyche into a regressive vortex of self ignorance. Anyone who dared to express their own personal spirituality or undertake transcendental exploration was in mortal danger. The emotional fallout of this sweeping perfidy is still with us today.

Understandable, then, that any victims of centuries of irrefutable Christian/Catholic aggression would disregard the entire canon of Christian scripture as poisonous rubbish. Yet this would be a mistake. For even in what has now become a confusion of neutered allegory, we can trace the roots of something far more profound and spiritually animate.

Many are unaware that the King James Version of the Bible, the main reference work for modern Christian scholars and worshippers, was only put together, collated and edited in the 17th century – this being just one of many revisions. Every time the Bible underwent an edit throughout its several dozen editions, it was subject to the various ecclesiastical notions and changing political ambitions of the day. To put it bluntly, the authorities regularly changed it to suit their needs. So the Bible we see in our churches, schools and universities today, is not a balanced representation of the incredible and empowering spirituality from which Christianity originated many aeons ago. Of course, it is not meant to be.

The enduring veracity of truth has a habit of surviving even the most ruthless and systematic campaigns of repression and extermination. It can be good to remind oneself of this, especially when things look a little bleak.

Early European Christianity was penetrated and compromised by a bloodline of ancient Solar Cultists, who speedily diluted and edited the existing holy texts to fit their own oppressive ideologies. The formula of control is simple. First, kill those who stand up against you, then either destroy or rewrite the spiritual and cultural heritage of their people. Certain groups who had foreseen the coming genocide, such as the Gnostics, fled to foreign lands and took their sacred texts with them, in the hope of preserving their spiritual wisdom for future times. It worked. In 1945, twelve leather-bound papyrus texts were discovered in an earthenware jar in the Egyptian town of Nag Hammadi. The 52 Gnostic tractates were written in the Egyptian language of Coptic, these already likely being translations from Greek originals, so the purity of the original works has no doubt been somewhat diminished. Even so, a very different understanding of the origins of Christianity and the mythic figure of Jesus began to unfold to a modern audience as the texts first became available in an English translation in 1975.

The most explosive Gnostic material told of a lesser god who created Earth and its heavenly neighbors and who has incorrectly come to think of himself as the one supreme creator. In The Apocryphon of John we learn more about this extraordinary 'demiurge' and his underling Archons.

"Now the archon (ruler) who is weak has three names. The first name is Yaltabaoth, the second is Saklas ("fool"), and the third is Samael. And he is impious in his arrogance which is in him. For he said, 'I am God and there is no other God beside me,' for he is ignorant of his strength, the place from which he had come."

In Gnostic lore, salvation from the energetic emanations, the false world of the Demiurge, is attainable in the form of gnosis, self attained and imparted by certain redeemers, most notably Christ, a figure sent from the higher God to free humankind from the Creator God Yaltabaoth. Gnosis involves an understanding of our true nature and origin, the metaphysical reality hitherto unknown to us, resulting in the Gnostic's escape from the enslaving material prison of the world and the body, into the transcendent dimensions of spirit. However, in order to make this ascent, the Gnostic must pass by the Archons, who are jealous of his/her luminosity (soul) and who thus try to hinder the Gnostic's ascendant voyage. The Gnostics state that the Archons are 'servants of the Demiurge'. They are interpreted in the Old Testament texts as angels and demons, as indeed the Demiurge is cast as the old wrathful God, jealous and vengeful.

The Matrix trilogy of films are sleek modern representations of the principles of Gnosticism; basic coursework for any alternative researcher and student of esoteric knowledge. All the main ingredients are there in the films: the illusory world, the path of awakening, the false God (the Architect), good and bad Archons (the Oracle, the Merovingian, Persephone, Seraph, the Trainman), slick propaganda, beautiful delusions, repressive control, divine resurrection, awakening and transcendence. Look out for the quintessential Gnostic sign above the Oracle's door in The Matrix, where (in rather non-traditional Latin) we see the words *temet nosce* – 'thine own self thou must know' – translated in the Matrix as 'know thyself'.

Meet The Orbs

Sometimes, physical phenomena are thrown into one's path to accelerate gnosis, so a deeper level of information can brought into the field of consciousness. I had personal experience of this during the months of July, August and September 2009, where I had a series of encounters with crop circles and the phenomenon known as 'orbs'.

Three core events inspired me to focus on the mercurial spheres in particular. Firstly, a large crop circle appeared on the farm I was staying at in Ogbourne St Andrew (near Marlborough, Wiltshire) on the day I arrived. Secondly, through the lens of a camera, I observed a large blue orb in the crop circle in broad daylight. Thirdly, with the naked eye, I observed a white orb in my room at the farm, hovering at chest height about 8ft away to my right.

I since learned that both my orb experiences were old news in the sacred valleys and hamlets of rural Wiltshire; it was nothing special here. Previous visitors and residents (of various professional and cultural backgrounds) had also seen orbs, indoors and out, exactly where I was located, including some gliding across the fields.

Previously, I had paid little attention to orbs, being quite busy enough in other pursuits. However, I have been compelled to put experiential energy into studying them due to my own independent encounters.

My preliminary research suggests that there are two types of orbs, which I classify as follows: (i) 3D environmental particulate matter or camera lens effects, and (ii) 4D conscious entities. Most orbs are of the first 3D kind. They are composed of natural 'stuff' floating around in the air, or lens reflections – dust, pollen, moisture, rain, snow, lens flare, refracted light, etc. The second kind of orb, the 4D kind, seems differentiated from the environmental variety in that it is somehow self-illuminated and demonstrates independent movement. Whether seen with the naked eye or through a lens, they appear to absorb and/or sustain photons rather than simply reflect light from an external source. They have more substance and feel intelligent. Some researchers suggest they are conscious energy in a plasmic state.

I have observed that by cultivating a certain fusion of Alpha-Theta brain waves, it is possible to formulate a channel for consciousness to connect the human mind to the surrounding 4th dimensional architecture which enfolds us. It is from this higher dimensional awareness that we can see the 4D orbs with the naked eye, and most interestingly of all, communicate with them.

Multiple independent studies suggest that the orbs 'naturally' use local energy systems in order to provide for visible manifestation. This has been repeatedly detected by researchers using EMF meters (measuring electromagnetic fields), the spherical form itself being a natural expression of many pure energy bodies in nature, at the micro and macro level (the prime example being a sun).

In mid-September 2009, I was part of a small group who traveled to a beautiful rural hill top in deepest Wiltshire, endeavoring to connect with the orbs through a series of conscious experiments. The location was well away from any light pollution, roads or human activity. It was also 'charged land' – that is, with natural subtle energies flowing through it, free from the ravages of industrialization, with many areas probably remaining relatively untouched for hundreds of years. Perfect for analyzing the subtleties of this decidedly elusive phenomenon.

We captured both types of orbs in our photographs - environmental and 4D. Of special interest to me, was the fact that during an intentional meditation, the orbs seemed to specifically respond to what I was doing.

Over four separate sessions outside, we observed orbs in and around the trees, some brighter and denser than others. Inside, under regular electric light bulbs, we observed a further five orbs, which according to one of our party, is rather unusual. Outside again, after placing my hands on a telegraph pole, I concentrated on the air above me, and dozens of orbs appeared to congregate around me. When I concentrated my attention onto the wooden pole itself, a form that resembled an iridescent dragonfly appeared. As my eyes were shut, only the photographer captured the incident. The camera was some way off, and the anomalous object was distinctly self-illuminated, rather than just reflecting light from the flash. The final meditation exercise proved most intriguing of all. As I shifted to a deeper meditational state, phasing brain patterns from Alpha to Theta, I formed a triangular dhyana-yoni mudra (meditation hand form). As I did so, three large orbs appeared over my head, forming a triangle that suggested they knew exactly what I was doing/projecting. It felt like there was a definite intelligence moving around us, adapting its behavior according to our conscious actions.

So what are the orbs? I feel that what we are seeing are 'slices' of fourth dimensional intelligent entities. This is more fully comprehended if we move down a dimension. For example, an entirely two dimensional observer could only ever see a slice of a three dimensional object - it would only ever perceive 2D slices of a tomato, rather than the entire red sphere of the whole 3D structure itself, which it does not have the dimensional perspective to handle. Similarly, we can only see 3D components of fourth dimensional objects, as we are firmly anchored in the 3D. So the 2D observer gets slices of the 3D, and the 3D observer gets spheres of the 4D. We call those spheres 'orbs'. They are a pure, single point energy reference for a structure that stretches outside of itself and is not restricted by the same apparent laws of time and space that we are. This is why they blink in and out of space, just as many authentic UFO craft appear to do. They are not moving *through* space, they are jumping directly from one point to another – quantum relocation, without physical movement.

Uncharted Territory

Many humans gravitate away from the apparently unexplainable phenomena of life because they associate the unknown with discomfort. Psychologically speaking, this is sometimes referred to as cognitive dissonance, that is, a feeling of uneasiness derived from encountering an idea that opposes the customary consensus paradigm.

In shamanic terms, we could say that a certain degree of personal power, or psychic energy, is required to more purely experience the sublime truth and untold magnificence of reality. Without that power, the instinctive impulse is to simply turn back when we reach a boundary marker. This is what most people do when they come across something weird. Things that lie outside the consensus belief systems are either ignored, ridiculed or feared. In some emotionally charged individuals, we often see a very visceral transmutation of fear into hate. This is a severe mental aberration that has no place on the sacred path. Its presence can be clearly traced in fundamentalist religious structures which all seem to share a rigid intolerance for that which lies beyond the doctrines and dogmas of their ontologically absolute scriptures. With such extreme polarization, millions of souls may perish with the simple stroke of a pen. Even in more enlightened societies, the basic principles of human spiritual transcendence are firmly discouraged in the individual, as these things belong to the realm of God, which is not the business of mortal man. Only officially nominated theologians may ponder such things, within certain parameters of course. Quite ridiculous isn't it?

For the above reasons, and many others, we see that the earnest seeker of truth and pure reality often finds himself standing alone and outside the comfortable certainties of the hive. Evidently, this must occur if he is sincerely committed to the sacred path of authentic being. Classical tales of transcendental spiritual journeys are replete with such symbolism.

One must understand hive mentality before one can be rid of it and become an intellectually and spiritually sovereign being. In the modern era, we can say that the mainstream is the way of the hive. Perceive the hive as a medieval city within defensive walls. What goes in and what goes out is controlled by official guards operating under strict orders. All access to information, goods and services is meticulously regulated by the rulers of the city. As a citizen living within the hive, the knowledge that is available to you has been edited, spliced and diluted before you get anywhere near it. You have no real idea about what goes on outside the hive. Many hive-dwellers believe that those outside the hive are plotting its downfall. After a few generations of living in the hive, the general citizenship (a) has become accustomed to obeying hive law, (b) cannot remember what came before the hive and (c) cannot imagine what might be a better alternative to life in the hive.

Up until the end of the 17th Century, the hive was a literal and physical reality for many. Feudal society, characterized by the legal subjection of the majority of the population to a hereditary landholding elite, reigned for many hundreds of years until it was finally brought down by the peasant class who decided that a lifetime of enforced slavery was unfair and inhuman. Stories of bloody revolts and uprisings (by no means limited to just peasants) fill the history books. It was a long and bitter struggle to change society with 330 years of separate revolts over France, Estonia, England, Catalonia, Hungary, Slovenia, Germany, Sweden, Croatia, Finland and Russia, officially ending with the Swiss Peasant War of 1653.

In the face of this massive social disintegration, the elites realized that a shrewder system of control was required to keep man from realizing that he can and should be governing himself. The subtle shift from overt to covert control was manifesting and it was to be the sanctified dominion of religion that would take the laws out of the hands of the common man and seemingly pass them to God himself. The Christian church, having systematically slaughtered millions in a series of military campaigns lasting 250 years (aka the Crusades), was now set to become the new standard bearer of the hive's sociological, moral and spiritual edicts.

The Church austerely decreed and upheld hive principles, on every issue under the sun, from commerce to sexuality, from art to science, from taxation to war. The state was inextricably linked to the Church and failure to give allegiance to God (the Church) and the King was punishable by death. These were the good old days for the Control System. If they didn't like what you said they'd take you away, chop your head off and stick it on a spike at the city gates. Individuals, groups, countries and whole continents were subject to the destructive tyranny of a single belief system.

In today's secular society, the Control System has once more transferred the hive reins. This time, they have been passed from the Church to corporations; the mega-corporations that own the governments, military and media, and even *these* super-powerful entities are merely executing the plans of higher masters. Researching these dark realms, one must be exceedingly careful.

There is a distinct class of alternative researcher that exhibits a consuming fetish for dramatic revelatory disclosure. Unconsciously vampiric, these individuals are easily identified by the energy vacuum they leave in their wake; a low pressure drag destabilizing any nearby high frequencies. They are the doomsayers. Quite unable to escape their own gravitational pull, doomsayers monotonously resonate the low apocalyptic vibrations of scarcity, upheaval, pestilence and havoc. They cannot help themselves.

Through understanding the basic dynamics of consciousness, how it moves, contracts, transforms and expands, we can infer that doomsayers have no real interest in raising consciousness, otherwise they would not proclaim their black prophecies so freely. Certainly not without first balancing such an unmitigated energy drain with the sharing of deeper wisdom and higher dimensional awareness. The doomsayers appear confined to deal only in the 3D, the world of mind, of thought-form and illusion, all tightly choreographed by the unobserved egoic mind. No light or wisdom. They are gullible black marketeers, unwitting assets of the Control System. I resist the temptation to name these conduits of numbness; they make themselves stand out.

Psychic equilibrium is important on the path. It is critical to understand that information alone is not enough. It is a mistake, for example, to concentrate all one's energies exclusively on the unveiling process. To specialize solely in matters of exposing conspiracies is tantamount to spiritual self-harming. Endless conspiratorial digging serves only to repeatedly confirm the existence of the Control System. No solutions, just problems. Many powerful minds have had their spiritual advancement hindered, and in some cases terminated, by succumbing to this negative vortex. On the flip side, disregarding the unveiling altogether can lead to the rather unfortunate space bunny syndrome; where previously evolving minds liquefy into self-contained escapist fantasy worlds where everything is always bouncy.

Being The Vessel

Perhaps the single most important piece of information that I could share with someone new to my work would be this; contemplate replacing the concept of *believing* with the concept of *holding*. It's hard to drop a belief but it's not hard to drop something you are merely holding. Similarly, a belief can be a heavy thing to carry around, whereas something that is just held, without believing in it one way or the other, remains as light as a feather. No egoic investment = no weight.

Is belief necessary in the quest for wholeness, gnosis and integration? Is it a valuable tool for research and exploration? Though I still fall into the linguistic habit of saying *"I believe this"*, or *"I don't believe that"*, I have in fact ceased to believe or disbelieve anything. I just stopped doing it.

This applies equally to possessions of the non-physical kind. Beliefs are personal possessions. With no beliefs to carry, the speed, fluidity and expansion of the warrior's spirit is greatly enhanced.

Fear transforms one's own inner darkness into an external enemy. Appropriated beliefs can conjure this false adversary into being. At super dense levels, ordinarily quite invisible to the isolated mind, we are imaginatively complicit in the existence of such demons and their elaborate conspiracies. It is only by going within, into the unfathomable depths of one's own mysterious caverns, that we can identify and disperse the stagnant energies that fuel this counterfeit foe. This is the game of the grand spiral.

Everything that is, vibrates. Each different configuration of vibration creates a form, and we give names to those forms. They are what Lao-Tzu called 'the ten thousand things'. All the stuff of the world… trees, cars, oranges, iPods. Some things are not 'things' as we ordinarily think of them – like awareness, fascination, fear, love, joy and melancholy – but they are, all the same, forms within the illusion… vibrations within the matrix.

Physicist David Bohm said, *"Dividing the universe up into living and nonliving things has no meaning… Even a rock is in some way alive… for life and intelligence are present not only in all of matter, but in energy, space, time, the fabric of the entire universe."*

The universe is seeking to bring deeper and fuller consciousness into itself. All energy configurations, all entities – animal, vegetable and mineral – contribute. This is the main game. The 2012 dimensional shift is another evolutionary augmentation in the divine cycle. It is upon us right now. The 21st December 2012 is the top of a bell curve on a graph – it isn't a switch being thrown, it is the apex of an energy potential.

This is what the Control System really doesn't want you to think about. It undoes a lot of the hard work they've put into containing your thought. They'd much rather see you carrying banners around central London or downtown New York, shouting anti-NWO slogans and giving out pamphlets, or ranting on radio shows. They love that.

Want to unplug from the matrix? Want to fight the NWO? Want to become an authentic divine entity? Then let nothing be a barrier to your own spiritual growth and transcendence. Work on yourself and be committed. Display the spirit of the impeccable warrior in every moment. Seek wholeness not fragmentation. Understand that the only thing that is real is your conscious experience. Do not resist change. Make change become your change. Outdo them at their own game.

The spiral of creation is not static; it is a living, evolving, emergent system of extreme creativity. Hence, gnosis is a moving target. Walking its path is a nomadic life. When night falls, you pitch your tent. In the morning, you pack it up, put it on your back and start walking again. Don't pitch it anywhere permanently.

Words can darken the mind (the third eye portal, deep blue light). The heart is harder to deceive (the heart portal, green light). Words of integrity and intent can be felt. Their energy resonates clearly.

Deep inside the ultrasoup of undivided energy, there is no differentiation between one form and another. All temporarily discrete components of the universe are facets of ourselves, of each other. In the face of every personal challenge, in both suffering and joy, the truth of this should be brought to mind.

The integral growth of consciousness is not measured in volume, it is measured in resolution. The number of humans who understand what is occurring will perhaps always necessarily be few. Not all configurations of consciousness are ready to upgrade the bandwidth so radically. Not all are meant to. Furthermore, the Earth possesses a rich and diverse spectrum of consciousness – the human expression is but one of them. There are others. Many timelines, dimensions and destinies to unfold.

For those who choose to cast off the shroud of inertia, those souls who would rather live outside the city gates, the privilege of the outsider is unbounded discovery.

6

THE DANGEROUS CORPORATION

THE DANGEROUS CORPORATION

*As long as we go out and buy stuff, we're at their mercy. We're at the
mercy of the advertiser. And, of course, there are certain things we
need, but a lot of the stuff that is bought is not needed. We all live in a
little village. Your village may be different from other people's villages,
but we are all prisoners.*
~ Patrick McGoohan (1928 - 2009)

*If the American people ever allow private banks to control the issue of
their money, first by inflation and then by deflation, the banks and
corporations that will grow up around them (around the banks), will
deprive the people of their property until their children will wake up
homeless on the continent their fathers conquered.*
~ Thomas Jefferson (1743-1826)

*You just can't leave it up to the media – to TV, to magazines, to MTV
– to feed you life. It's somebody's corporate fiction.*
~ Jeff Buckley (1966-1997)

Shopping is unnatural, but we all do it! I have to admit that it
feels good sometimes. The trouble is, I often buy things I don't
really need. I've lost count of the number of times I nip out for a
pint of milk and return home laden with 'buy one, get one free'
(BOGOF) offers. (They want us to BOGOF and I wish *they* would
BOG OFF!) The economy thrives on 'happy shoppers' who can't
resist a good bargain. Who doesn't? Most of us struggle as it is to
pay the bills…

At this point, I'd like to share some confidential information with you regarding my financial earnings. This may come as a surprise, but for every one of my books sold via a bookstore (internet or otherwise) I get around 50 British pence, which is currently around 80¢. The larger multinational companies can buy my book direct from the distributor for more of a discount than I get! This is not my publisher's fault – they're not making any money, either. *So who is?* Certainly not those directly involved in writing and publishing...

If we're going to change the material world we have to hit them where it hurts – in the wallet! This involves us shopping consciously, which is a whole different ball game – it takes twice as long reading all the labels on the packets, for a start, after which I put most things back on the shelf without buying them. It's a full-time job (as Mr. Bush once famously said) *"putting food on your family"*. Shopping consciously also involves buying things that are locally-sourced whenever possible, and to stop buying cheap electrical goods from overseas! Easier said than done...

We have been so conditioned to think that we need things that never even existed up until a couple of years ago. There were no mobile phones until very recently. There were no laptops. There was no internet. Going back even further (a bit before my time, but not much) there was no TV. How on earth did human beings cope without all these 'things'?! The most important things in life are not things.

You may wonder how law and shopping are connected – read on, and you will find out. Law is based on commerce and is there to protect corporations. What we often think are 'public services' are really functioning businesses; my local police station and county council, the schools my kids go to... pretty much *every-thing* is listed in *Dun and Bradstreet* (a database of all trading companies/businesses worldwide). Law and money are inextricably linked. Businesses make money if we break their laws; for example, banks make a lot of money by charging us when we go overdrawn, and libraries make money by charging us when the books we borrow become overdue. The council charges us if we park where we shouldn't or if we've overstayed our time; I have direct experience of this… I pulled into a disabled parking space on the ground level of a multi-storey parking lot that runs alongside a bus depot to wait for my son to come home from school. His bus was due any minute. Feeling tired, I closed my eyes for the briefest of moments and suddenly felt that something 'wasn't quite right'. When I opened my eyes, lo-and-behold, there's a traffic warden staring at me (with some menace, I might add). *"Show me your disabled parking badge!"* he barked. When I explained that I didn't have one, he said, *"I'm going to book you."* Just like that. I'd only been there a moment and hadn't even got out of the car (technically, I wasn't even 'parked'), so I sensibly decided that the best course of action was to drive away before he could issue me with a ticket. I told him I was leaving and he then tried to obstruct my exit from the parking space by standing behind me, until I politely asked him to move. Two days later, I had a phone call from my local police station. A lady constable stifled a laugh as she explained that she was calling about the 'incident' in the multi-storey – *the traffic warden had actually accused me of deliberately trying to reverse over him!* I don't think he can be that popular because, when I explained what had happened, she dropped the matter immediately – didn't even ask me to go down to the station. I thought that was the end of the matter, but no… a few weeks went by and I received a letter from the County Council asking me to pay for the parking ticket that I was never issued with! After a couple of smart replies (with help from a friend with a law degree), I never heard from them again.

Legal matters are designed to be as befuddling and confusing to anyone but lawyers themselves. This is because they have their own language (no, *really!*) called Legalese. If you don't believe me, go look it up. A word can mean an entirely different thing in Legalese; for example; the word 'must' in English means 'you have to' but in Legalese it means 'you can if you want'.

If we realize that the 'must' is really a 'may', then we 'must' also realize that we have the power to say, *"No"*. Having said that, I personally feel more empowered when I throw open my arms and say, "*Yes!*" to life. It's far more interesting...

Picture credit: Daniel Miller

CORPORATE CORRUPTION –
The Way it Changed the World, and How to Combat it
John Perkins

For you see, the world is governed by very different personages from what is imagined by those who are not behind the scenes.
~ Benjamin Disraeli, 1st Earl of Beaconsfield and twice Prime Minister of Britain (1804 - 1881)

As Chief Economist at a major international consulting firm, John Perkins advised the World Bank, United Nations, IMF, U.S. Treasury Department, Fortune 500 corporations, and countries in Africa, Asia, Latin America, and the Middle East. He worked directly with heads of state and CEOs of major companies.

John Perkins's classic exposé of his former life, *Confessions of an Economic Hit Man*, spent over 70 weeks on the New York Times bestseller lists and is published in more than 30 languages. His follow-up New York Times bestseller, *The Secret History of the American Empire*, provides a plan for creating a sustainable, just, and peaceful world, while his latest book, *Hoodwinked*, describes the deep underlying causes of the current economic crises and provides a blueprint for change. He is the author of *Shapeshifting, The World Is As You Dream It*, and other books on indigenous cultures and personal transformation; a founder and board member of Dream Change and The Pachamama Alliance, nonprofit organizations devoted to establishing a world our children will want to inherit; and has lectured and taught at universities in many countries. Websites: www.johnperkins.org and www.dream change.org

I was an economic hit man for ten years. As Chief Economist for the Boston consulting firm of Chas T. Main, it was my job to identify third world countries that had resources our corporations covet, like oil – and convince that country to accept a huge loan from the World Bank or one of its sisters. But the money wouldn't actually go to that country. Instead, it would go to our own corporations to build big infrastructure projects in that country – power plants, industrial parks, highways... things that would benefit a few rich families in that country as well as our corporations, but not help the majority of the people who are too poor to buy electricity, don't have the skills to get jobs in industrial parks, and don't have cars to drive on the highways. The country would be left holding a huge debt – one so big it couldn't possibly repay it. Then, the Economic Hit Men would go back to that country and say something like, "Listen, you know you can't pay your debts – so, give us a pound of flesh, sell your oil real cheap to our oil companies, vote with us on the next critical U.N. vote, send troops in support of ours to somewhere like Iraq. . .".

On the few occasions when we failed (and I talk in my book about how I failed with Jaime Roldós, the president of Ecuador, and Omar Torrijos in Panama) – *then* the Jackals go in, and they either overthrow governments or assassinate the leaders who we haven't been able to corrupt. Assassinations are very effective at breaking the spirit of a country – the two Kennedy brothers, Martin Luther King... a lot of other people, good people, in the anti-Vietnam movement were either assassinated or put in jail. In Latin America, Salvador Allende of Chile and Manuel Noriega of Panama were also taken down. On the few occasions when the Jackals *also* fail, like in Iraq – *only then* does the military go in. That's really how we built this empire in a very subtle and clandestine way. A lot of people have no idea that the lifestyles we lead in the United States and throughout much of Europe come at the cost of the terrible exploitation of other people.

As an EHM, I was patted on the back by Robert McNamara, the president of the World Bank, and I was asked to speak at Harvard and other prestigious universities. What I was doing wasn't illegal... it met the tests of all the Macro economic models that I was taught and that were being promoted at business schools that said 'if you invest all this money in infrastructure you will have economic growth'. In fact, you usually *do* – but what the models *don't* show is that the gap between rich and poor usually increases, only a relatively few of the people in the upper classes benefit, and the majority of the population suffer as a result.

Being an EHM offered a very attractive lifestyle. I was getting to travel around the world and see countries that I really wanted to visit, flying first class, staying in the best hotels and eating in the best restaurants... things that I'd never done before in my life. I grew up pretty poor in rural New Hampshire, the son of a schoolteacher, so it was very enticing and I had a lot of power – I had several dozen highly-skilled employees working for me. I was like so many people who have jobs with big corporations that they know are doing bad things – they earn a good living, provide their children with excellent homes and education and enjoy many other benefits, and so they find ways to justify that their company really is trying to do good work. It was *easy* for me to justify that what we were doing was the right thing, because the economic models and business schools said it was the right way to do business.

I was young – in my twenties – and I was pretty naïve but, because I'd been a Peace Corps volunteer in Ecuador in South America for three years, I was not as naïve as many others in my business. The World Bank says that its mission is to use power to get rid of poverty, but I began to see that it was doing exactly the opposite.

Over that period of ten years – during the 1970s – I increasingly began to understand that what we were doing in the world was not only dangerous and immoral, but ultimately destructive and self-destructive. I returned to the Shuar in the Amazon, where I had been a peace corps volunteer, and I said, "I want to help you save your rainforests... to save your world", and they said, "Well, if you want to do that, don't come here and try to change us because we're not the problem; you're the ones destroying these things... it's your oil companies and your lumber companies and most of all it's your *dream* that is causing all the destruction. You know, the world is as you dream it. You have had this dream of big buildings, lots of cars, and heavy industry and your dream has come true but now you're beginning to understand it's turned into a nightmare. So, if you want to help us save our rainforests and our way of life here, go back to your people and help them change their dream."

After that, I came back to the United States and created a nonprofit organization that eventually became *Dream Change*. Out of a Dream Change trip to Ecuador in the early '90s the Pachamama Alliance also came into existence, and I still serve on the board of both of those organizations. They're pretty phenomenal nonprofits that are aimed at changing the dream of our people in the North and at the same time helping the people of the South save their forests or fight their legal battles against oil companies and others who are encroaching on their territories.

During the 1990s, I was doing non-profit work with the Mayans of Central America. An ironic and interesting aspect of this whole situation was that I was a consultant for Stone & Webster, one of the largest U.S. engineering corporations in the world at that time, who wanted to build a geo thermal project at a sacred Mayan site. I understood that if they went ahead with this, there would be a lot of trouble – the Mayans would strongly object to it, there would be protests and people would probably be killed – so I convinced Stone & Webster not to move forward with the project. In that particular case, I was able to do both sides a service. But there I was, riding around the streets of Guatemala City with Stone & Webster's Guatemalan partner – a very, very wealthy person who the Mayans considered to be evil. We had a car up front and a car behind ours filled with bodyguards – essentially protecting him and me from the very people I was *also* working with in my other life in the non-profit world.

*

People often ask if there was a particular incident that convinced me to stop being an EHM. The answer is "yes." it happened like this… I took a vacation in the Virgin Islands on a sailboat in 1981. Late one afternoon, I anchored off St. John Island. I rowed the dingy ashore and climbed to the top of a hill, to the ruins of an old eighteenth century sugar plantation. As I sat there and watched the setting sun in this very idyllic location, I suddenly realised that the sugar cane plantation was built on the bones of thousands of slaves. Then I understood that the whole hemisphere was built on the bones of millions of slaves. And *then* I was struck by the fact that I, too, was a slaver – that what I was doing in the world was every bit as much breeding slavery as those who had gone into the jungles of Africa and dragged the African people out in chains. Today's slavery takes a different form, but it still meets the definition of slavery. At that moment, I made the decision that I would no longer do this – that I couldn't live with myself any longer if I continued; so I went back to Boston and quit my job.

I started writing what eventually became *Confessions of an Economic Hit Man* shortly after quitting, in the early '80s – I interviewed other economic hit men and some jackals to get their stories and, as a result, I was contacted and threatened. I took the threats very seriously… I had seen what jackals can do to people. By now, I had a young daughter and a wife and I was very worried about harm being done to any of us. At the same time, Stone & Webster offered me a legal bribe of about half a million dollars. The chairman of the board took me out to dinner and made it very clear to me that they would not ask me to do much, but if they paid me this money they certainly wouldn't want me to write the kind of book that I was writing. I took the bribe and I gave a lot of that money to causes I believed in – it assuaged my guilt to help organizations that were working to assist the people I had 'screwed'. I did not write the book that I wanted to write until much later. When I finally did, I wrote it in secret and took the completed manuscript to a publishing company. At that point, it became my 'life insurance policy'. I knew that the jackals understood that if something suspicious happened to me, my book sales would skyrocket.

There have been many times in my life when I've been physically in danger and fearful, beginning when I was a Peace Corps volunteer in the Amazon, crossing rivers in precarious baskets hanging from thin ropes, navigating white waters in dug-out canoes, and hiking through unexplored jungles. Later, I was in Guatemala where there were battles going on with the Guatemalan Army – which incidentally was supported by U.S. military aid. I've practised martial arts for years, which has taught me about courage. I had a third-grade teacher named Mrs. Schnare who encouraged me to stand up to a bully and it stuck with me all my life. The Shuar teach that if you run into something in the forest that you're afraid of, like a jaguar, the worst thing you can do is to turn and run – it'll run after you. You've got to confront it. The same is true whenever we are tempted to avoid things that frighten us. Always confront your fears, don't run away from them. To flee from something you're afraid of is, in the end, self-defeating. I think that's extremely important and a great lesson for our culture today.

For the first time in history, every human being on the planet is challenged by the same crises. It used to be that Indonesians faced a tsunami and Florida faced hurricanes and San Francisco faced earthquakes, but today we're all facing climate change, diminishing resources, increasing food prices, economic turmoil, species extinctions, and the prospects for violence and terrorism that result from the sad fact that roughly half the world's population lives below the poverty level. We're all facing these crises and we all know it, because we're all communicating with each other via the internet and cell phones. This is a time that requires courage, which is about overcoming those fears and moving into them and doing something to change, to create a better world… one that is sustainable, just, and peaceful for all people everywhere.

Our time is one that requires a very shamanic approach, a type of shapeshift that every shaman I've worked with has taught. When there's fear we also must realize there is *opportunity*. When we move through our fears – not foolishly, but with awareness, intent, and commitment – then we also move into a higher level of consciousness.

*

We have entered an era when corporations rule the world.

Previously, certain nations like the United Kingdom, the Soviet Union, the United States had tremendous amounts of power at certain times, but the situation has changed; no one nation is really in control – the real empire-builders today are the big corporations, what I call the 'corporatocracy'. Nobody gets elected to a major political post in most countries without their support. Just in Washington D.C alone there are 35,000 lobbyists, most of them paid for by corporations. The corporatocracy also control the press – either through direct ownership or advertising budgets. We're really very much at a time in history that I think is analogous to when the city states became nations. The nations are losing their importance and the *real* geopolitics is driven by these massive corporations – you might envision them as huge clouds that circle around the planet... they're not stationary in any one country. They don't adhere to any set of laws that's unique to any particular country, and they pick and choose which laws they want to follow. They'll strike partnerships with the Chinese and the Taiwanese, with the Israelis and the Arabs, with the Russians, the French, or the English... whoever suits their interest at the time. They don't recognise any borders.

When something like a tsunami hits Indonesia and other parts of Asia, aid immediately pours in that is altruistic – water is shipped-in and tents and medical facilities and so forth. Billions of dollars are invested in these countries to help them get back on their feet – but what we're *not* told is that a great deal of this money goes to helping big corporations gain a foothold where they never had one before, rather than helping the people that really suffered from the tragic event. For the most part, those development funds go toward building big hotel and restaurant chains, huge fishing and agri businesses, and other corporative industries instead of putting that money into rebuilding the 'mom and pop' bed and breakfasts, the local fishing fleets and restaurants, or the small farms that were destroyed. That's a tragedy… it shouldn't happen. We *allow* it to happen, and one of the reasons I write the books I write is because we must let people know that these things go on and they must stop. No longer can we tolerate this. We *must* stand up to them, we *must* create a better world – we can't wait for someone else to do it.

Big corporations are driven by one single goal: to maximize profits regardless of the environmental and social costs. As consumers, we must convince them to change this goal. We must send out the message that they can maximize profits but only if they do so in environmentally and socially responsible ways.

I'm hopeful that Barack Obama is going to help expose a lot of these things – I think he *is* aware of them and I think he realises that the American people need to understand more about what's going on… I certainly hope that's the case, but I think it would behove Obama to be *extremely* careful where he goes and how he shows himself, because there's no question that there's been a terrible history of assassination in our country.

This world is controlled by big corporations, there's no question about that – but the big corporations are totally beholden to us, the consumers. They can't exist unless we buy their goods and services, and we must understand that the global market place is democratic. We the people, the consumers, have to take responsibility. There will be no more sweatshops if no-one buys anything made in sweatshops. It's as simple as that. If none of us ever again purchases a gas-guzzling car or inefficient appliance, there will be no more of those. The market place is democratic – by the way we choose to shop and sometimes by the way we *don't* shop at all, we decide which corporations are going to make it and which ones will have to change and which ones will fail. Up until now, we've told these corporations that we want to buy goods for the least expensive price possible and at the same time we want a high rate of return on our investments, on our stock. These corporations are basically doing what we've demanded them to do and we've essentially said to them, "We don't care if our t-shirts or our sweaters are produced by slaves in sweatshops, we don't care if rainforests are destroyed in order for us to get cheap oil – we just want these things to reach us at the lowest possible price." It's time now for us, the consumer, the 'average citizen', to turn this thing around.

We have to shop consciously and in a way that has an objective of creating a sustainable, just and peaceful world for every life-form on this planet – for our children, our grand-children and all future generations to come. We need to under-stand that in this shrinking and highly interdependent world, no child growing up in the United States can hope to live in such a world unless every child in every country has this same expec-tation – and it is realized around the planet.

Picture credit: Dean Warner

A SHORT GLIMPSE AT COMMERCE
Winston Shrout

I went to a doctor once, and said, "Doc, every time I lift my arm like this, it hurts!" The doctor said, "Well, don't do that anymore!"
I went into the bank, and I told the banker, "Every time I go into debt it hurts!"
And the banker said (yes, you guessed it), "Well, don't do that anymore!"

Winston Shrout lectures under the title of *Solutions in Commerce* in the United States, Canada, UK, Australia, and New Zealand. *Solutions in Commerce* produce DVD recordings of all of these presentations, which have had a wide circulation. While he does not say that he has *all* the answers, he has developed some workable solutions that have aided many when dealing with the debts they labor under. For more information, visit: www.wssic.com

My first exposure to commerce came about eleven years ago. I heard the word 'claim' mentioned in a lecture, and started to study that word. One thing led to another and, slowly, the world of commerce opened up to me. To my good fortune, I happened onto some very learned men in that area, and my learning was started on a solid foundation.

I have been a student of the scriptures and the gospels probably all of my life and so when I started to look into commerce and the way the world is run I saw many parallels. Commerce is not a copy of the gospels, nor is it the opposite – but it is a *mirror image* which is more or less the gospel inside-out.

I believe that the King James Version of the scriptures was probably at the insistence of Sir Francis Bacon, who was involved with the secret societies of Europe. He put in place a man named Robert Fludd as the man who would oversee the translation of the scriptures. Robert Fludd was, at that time, the Grand Master of the Priory de Sion who were closely affiliated with the Knights Templars. Most of your City-of-London-type commerce evolved out of the banking system that was established by the Knights Templars. Hence the focus of the translations under Robert Fludd was the doctrines of banking.

Sir Francis Bacon was also closely aligned with John Dee. John Dee was a former master of the Priory before Fludd. He was at court under Queen Elizabeth I as an astronomer, astrologer and alchemist. He was also in the spy service, and his designation was 007. There was a certain agenda that was being worked on by all those characters and that purpose spilled over into the 'New World', into what we call North America today. It appears that they were trying to establish the New Jerusalem, and that their intention was to work toward the return of the Messiah at the appropriate time. Many of the efforts that were being undertaken by such men were for that purpose.

If you trace the history of Sir Francis Bacon, you'll find out what his genealogy is... and it's not exactly as it appears. He was most likely the son of The Virgin Queen, Elizabeth I, but was raised in another family for certain political purposes. I believe that Sir Francis Bacon was also writing under the pseudonym of William Shakespeare. The word 'shakespeare' is itself a play on words. Spear Shaker was the mythological character Pallas Athena, considered highly by the secret societies. The symbol of royal 'Britannia' is based on Athena.

The King James Version, then, which bases itself on the ancient scriptures, tended to teach the principles of commerce. If a person reads and understands the parables, the principles that are contained therein, then commerce is fairly simple to understand. Many of the indications in the King James Version about how to deal with debt are very much slanted toward how we can deal in commerce – for instance, what's been called The Lord's Prayer. It actually appears in King James' twice, with somewhat different wording. In one of the versions, when the disciples ask Jesus, "How shall we pray?" he instructs them, among other things, to 'forgive us this day *our debt*, as we forgive *our debtors'*. Now, the word 'debt' is a word that strictly appears in commerce – scripturally, it is called 'sin', and what it indicates is a liability that arises from some action that had been taken. Jesus is indicating that when we pray or when we plead – for instance, to the court – that before going in we should certainly forgive our debtors, because it would be improper to go before the court and before God and ask for some remedy or some forgiveness of debt if we have not forgiven our brethren.

There is the parable of the man who went before his master to whom he owed a debt. He asked the master to forgive his debt, which the master did. The man, after having been forgiven, then went after the people who owed *him* and tried to extract on the debt. When the master found out about it, he took some pretty serious actions against that party.

In another parable, a man who was going to go and see the master over his debt immediately took all the debts that were owed to him and wrote off half the debt. When he went in to his master to pray or plead for a forgiveness of his debt, the master was aware of what he had done and was very lenient upon him.

Paul said in the New Testament, "For all have sinned and come short of the glory", but he could have said, "For all have gone into *debt* and come short".

Any system of government or of practice, in order to be successful has to abide by Natural Law or it's doomed to failure. Commerce goes back to what's known as the Law Merchant Law which is Substantive Law related to the Common Law of Merchants, which is good law based on natural principles. There are many versions and varieties of Common Law – Anglo-Saxon Law, British Common Law, and so forth. The colony of North America decided to adopt British Common Law and that was their practice.

Over the centuries, Law Merchant Law has evolved from the use of gold and silver into the use of a negotiable instrument – paper money, bills of exchange, promissory notes, etc. People would be well-served to make a study, because one of the presumptions of Law Merchant Law is that if someone is using these instruments, which includes almost everybody, then the Law of Merchants considers them to *be* a law merchant and they had better act properly when using those things. These negotiable instruments are actually only what would be called *Quasi* Law – the word 'quasi' basically means 'as if' – so Quasi Law is 'As If' Law… it's *not* the law but it acts 'as if' it were. Law Merchant Law is very strict and unforgiving and so people using these negotiable instruments must understand what they're doing. If they don't, they will fall victim to their ignorance and have no-one to blame but themselves.

Quasi Law evolved into a system of codes and practices that were embodied in the Uniform Commercial Code. The purpose of *that* was to standardize commercial practices across the globe to cut down all litigation or misunderstanding – regardless of what language a merchant is dealing in, the Uniform

Commercial Code prevails. What essentially has happened is that the Law Merchant Law, which was Substantive, has turned to Quasi Law under the Uniform Commercial Code. If you go back in history several hundred years ago you'll see that, since then, the volume of commerce has greatly increased. The Uniform Commercial Code and Quasi Law have facilitated that amount of commerce now that it can speedily be done virtually over the internet and other electrical facilities.

*

We have steadfast natural occurrences upon which we can *rely*. When the sun goes down at night, I go to sleep with the full confidence that on the morrow the sun will come up again. Commerce relies upon the confidence of the people in the system. If commerce were unreliable or helter-skelter, no-one would do it. Law Merchant Law is the law of contract and is very exacting. If a contract is broken or in breach, then the Law of Merchants will simply get rid of that merchant – they will not do business with them.

All law is based on contract. Unless there's a contract or a covenant or some sort of other agreement made, there is no law. One of the educational points that we make in our Solutions in Commerce is simply to tell people, "If you're in a contract then you must abide by the law of that contract". The Law is put in place as a remedy for breach of contract. If you abide by your contracts then what's called The Law has absolutely no effect on you, because you are honorable and abide by your contracts. However, if you break or breach your contract, then The Law is the remedy to mend the breach.

If you've gotten into a contract erroneously, or fallen victim to adhesion or an implied contact, then we also try to teach how you can deal with those things.

There's a book that you can find on the internet that I have shown in many of my seminars called *Invisible Contracts* by George Mercier. I would highly recommend a study of that book. Even though The Law uses terms and phrases you might not understand, you can always go back and re-write the contact.

Admiralty Law, believe it or not, goes back to the story of the Garden of Eden. Whether it's a real story or an allegory – *that* we can judge for ourselves... I believe the lesson we learn from it is the important part. It appears that God had placed a man and a woman into a particular situation and given them instructions as to how to conduct themselves while there, warning them of the consequence of not complying with God's Law. Now, they went ahead and broke the commandment and so God was under the necessity at that point of destroying them. Rather than destroy them at that time, he removed them into another jurisdiction – another venue (a *re-venue* or revenue that seems to affect us greatly, even to this present time) or Law forum... what we call today the Admiralty Law. Under the Admiralty concept we would be involved in a reorganization bankruptcy, which means we can reorganize our debt in an effort to resolve it. In the scrip-tures, we call this resolution and reorganization 'repentance'. When God took Adam and Eve out of the jurisdiction of God's Law, because of their 'sin' (debt), he put them into reorganization so that they would have time to resolve the consequences of their debt, providing them with an opportunity to resolve the debt in an equitable manner.

When Adam was cast out of Eden, it was called Pass Over in that he 'passed over' the law which was given in Eden (which is still celebrated today in some forms of worship), but Adam was wise and got a promise from God that there would be a way back. So, God contracted with Adam that He would provide a Pass Thru. This Pass Thru is the basis for the New Testament or New Contract. Jesus, the Messiah, is the Pass Thru, and since the New Contract was pre-paid by Jesus' sacrifice on the cross at the start of the contract (unlike the shedding of the blood of John the

Baptist at the end of the Old Contract) we live in Grace under that New Contract. The New Contract is by operation of law, whereas the Old Contract necessitated execution of law... hence animal sacrifice, etc. This is exactly how the modern nations in the world operate their commerce under 'bankruptcy reorganization' or repentance.

The genesis of Admiralty jurisdiction, form, and venue is from that time. Since God put Adam and Eve into Admiralty jurisdiction, men devised among themselves another system which they called their Common Law. Common Law may or may not align itself with God's Law. If the Common Law is in conformity to God's Law, then all is well and will work smoothly. If not, then there are problems. For instance, most Common Law is execution of law and has no 'mercy' built into it. In that case, it would be obvious that the Common Law is Old Testament law and denies the 'grace' of the New Testament. Without 'grace' (or time to repent), a practitioner of Common Law could never realize the benefit of the Pass Thru, but would be forever cast out of Eden with no way to return. 'Forgive us this day our debts, as we forgive our debtors' has no place in Common Law.

Admiralty Law is enforceable by military means, which means 'under force of arms'. If there are problems with commerce, then under Admiralty and under force of arms, those contracts can be enforced militarily. For instance, how many wars have there been during my lifetime? These wars were not fought upon principles, they were fought upon commerce. War is a commercial enterprise.

If I have a contract with my brother and we cannot reach equity, for instance, if my brother is more powerful than I am, I might go hire a mercenary – someone who had more guns, more soldiers – to go deal with the situation. Of course, I would have to pay them part of the results of the conquest. Piracy differs from theft, as it is a legitimate practice of commerce and Commercial Law. For instance, in 1776 in North America, when the colony was at war with King George – that, of course, was strictly a commercial war. King George was, among other things, trying to impose the Bank of England currency on the colony and they weren't having any of it. During that war, there was a Frenchman by the name of Lafayette – a sea captain of great renown. George Washington, who was the commander of the continental army of North America, made a deal with Lafayette. He gave him a letter of marque and reprisal so that Lafayette could go and catch any British vessel that he came upon on the open sea. When Lafayette conquered that vessel and took the prize then he was required to split a certain portion with George Washington in the name of the United States. People generally think of a pirate as someone who flies the skull and crossbones flag called the 'Jolly Roger'. That emblem came from the Knights Templars – it's one of their battle flags.

In 1925, the United States government commissioned the army corp of engineers to survey North America. Those survey stakes are still in place... I've seen some of them here in the Western States. In the 1990s, the government commissioned the United States Coast Guard to go back and resurvey North America. The army corp of engineers determines sea level to be the high tide mark of the ocean as it encroaches upon the land so that 'zero' is set at sea-level. For instance, the highest point in North America is Mount McKinley, which is 20,320 feet above sea-level, but when the United States Coast Guard came in and did a resurvey, they made the *highest* point in North America at sea-level – therefore, all of the land is now below sea level according to their survey. By putting all of the land 'under water', consequently Admiralty prevails over all the land, thus it operates in commerce. (The movie *Waterworld*, starring Kevin Costner is entertaining and also very educational.)

You'll notice that one of the parables in the New Testament had to do with Jesus walking on the water. A 'perfect man' (i.e. a man who abides by all his contracts in commerce) can walk on top of the water and will not sink into it as Peter did.

Benjamin Franklin used to say, "Neither a lender nor a borrower be". If a person could take up that motto and try to live by it, the difficulties will slip away. The bulk of what I have tried to work through with Solutions in Commerce is to find ways to deal with and resolve the debts that people seem to be encumbered with. Constant worry and stress work a distress on the immune system of people causing sickness in the body. People don't understand the ramifications of going into debt and have no knowledge of how to resolve the problems. One of my personal practices has been to avoid debt, and so sometimes it's easier for me to make observations because I'm outside the system looking into it. Perhaps it's a little bit easier for me to see solutions when I don't have so much of a burden to deal with.

Commerce is a very broad subject and a student of the things that I'm trying to put across should not have more confidence than they're actually able to demonstrate. Many times, people will get a little bit of knowledge and think they have the whole thing when they don't have enough information to accomplish what it is they're trying to do. My advice (if I can give advice) is to do a great deal of study. It would be a smart thing for people to get as broad a view as possible rather than listening exclusively to what I have to say.

*

I am not sovereign. A sovereign is a party who is not susceptible to liability. As far as I know, the only sovereign is God and we may only attempt to become *like* Him. It is said that the Queen of England is sovereign, but that is absolutely not correct. At the very best, the Queen can claim to be a 'defender of the faith'. We also have parties who claim to be the 'vicar of Christ'. None of those parties can claim sovereignty because they are *not* God.

Recently, I was talking to some of my friends in Canada and

they pointed out to me that Queen Elizabeth was portrayed on their coins as wearing a crown, but after 9/11 when the twin towers were destroyed, all of a sudden a coin came out with the queen *not* wearing a crown. It demonstrated the vulnerability of the Queen. Why, suddenly after 9/11, did her image on the coin *not* reflect that sovereignty?

Queen Elizabeth and that family line are technically usurpers to the throne. There is a difference between the *anointing* of a king or queen and *coronation*. A coronation is accomplished by appointment from the Vatican. An anointing brings forth a Messiah. Messiah or mssh means 'anointed one'. The founding fathers in the colonial days in North America realized that King George was not the rightful heir, so George Washington and Ben Franklin sent word to the man who they knew to be that party, which was Bonnie Prince Charlie of Scotland. They asked him to take up the monarchy but he refused on the basis that he had no male heir. At that point, they went to George Washington (who was also of that same lineage) but he also rejected the monarchy because he had no male heir, so the founders instead established a Republic. Of course, it's devolved into something else at this point in history, but that was the genesis of what kind of government was trying to be created back in the early times. Bonnie Prince Charlie's family name was Stewart. The family name of the Queen of England is Saxe-Coburg and Gotha – *not* Windsor! The present monarch sitting on the throne in England who people consider to be sovereign is in fact a political appointee of the Vatican, who was coronate... not anointed as was King David that you find in your Old Testament, and Jesus in the New Testament.

People keep asking me what books they should study for commerce and I keep telling 'em, "The King James Version... *go back and read it!*"

AN EXTREMELY CUNNING PLAN
Robert Menard

Those who benefit from any societal mechanism rarely wish to understand that mechanism, especially if it appears to grant them power, control or authority over their fellow man, as understanding that mechanism would limit, diminish or remove that apparent power control or authority. They simply do not want to know. This is why it is far easier to ignorantly control others than it is to wisely control yourself.

~ Robert Menard

Robert Menard grew up near Windsor Ontario in a large family with six sisters. They had a small plot of land upon which his very industrious father grew tomatoes and strawberries. Apparently he spent the first year crying non-stop. The Doctor never hit him again. He was a very curious and mischievous child. Rob speaks 13 different languages and made up 10 of them all by himself. He joined the army at 18 and learned that stupid people are easy to fight and there is often little reason to fight intelligent ones. He came close to becoming a police officer, but could not reconcile throwing people in jail for marijuana offenses. His favorite color is purple.

Websites: www.thinkfree.ca and www.worldfreemanso-ciety.org

I was a stand-up comedian for ten years. I was motivated to study the law because, like many people, I suffered an injustice at the hands of the people in the government. As a result of that, I kind of lost a bit of my 'funny', but I also realized that I was wasting my talent talking about the banal and trivial stuff just to make people laugh so they could forget their problems; but then it didn't really help them with their problems at all.

So, I conceived and started a website called Think Free, along with Robert Christie, Clint Mitchell and a couple of others, for the purpose of disseminating the information that we were learning about the law.

I like to use comedy when I'm bringing information to people – if I can make it funny, they're more likely to be receptive to the information. *You can't let the bastards get you down!* Humor is also the most effective way to empower yourself and to disempower the authority figures you're dealing with. They want you scared of their authority and if you laugh and ask them questions – well, they don't like that... not one little bit. I don't want to piss people off and I try to avoid it, but if I have to choose between making them angry and abandoning my beliefs... well, they're going to be in for a little bit of a disappointment.

Anger is like a poison to the mind – I don't think it's possible to truly think properly and find your remedy if you're angry; it clouds your mind, clouds your judgment, you're going to miss a lot of information that otherwise you wouldn't and which you need. If I thought that anger would serve me then I would use it, but I've never found that it does. Being nice to people isn't just 'woo woo'; it's almost a tactical thing.

Learning law and learning about yourself and your place in the universe go together. One of the big problems that people make is they believe that once they have knowledge of the law they're suddenly going to be free and I don't believe that's really the case... I think that freedom comes from your heart and then the knowledge of the law kind of follows. It's not that you learn the law, create some documents, then you become free – you realize you *are* free then you learn what documents you need to inform people of that. I don't see how one can claim they're free if they're ignorant. There's no freedom in ignorance, but there's no sense knowing what the law is if you can't apply it, and if you know how to apply something but you don't know what it is you're applying, then there's no use in that, either.

The World Freeman Society

By looking at what we're facing, what the problems are, and applying the knowledge of who we're facing, what they fear, and analyzing it from there, you see the pieces fit together. When you're putting a puzzle together you see how the pieces fit together but first of all you've gotta lay it all out and flip it all over and find the corners, find the edges. There is a process.

For me, finding one of those corners was moment when a judge was reading my letter head in court, and part of the letter head referred to the fact that I'm the director of the Elizabeth Ann Elaine society. When she got to that, she refused to speak further and it put a huge break on her words. I said, "Continue; you're not done, keep reading" but I could tell she was kind of nervous and she then said, "No, that's enough" and put it down. So, like a pig can smell a truffle, I knew that there was something there to dig at...

People in the Law Society were a little bit unhappy with me and tried to use unlawful means to get cops with guns forcing unlawful court orders at me. What they have been known to do in the past is that, even though you might be proven innocent in court or be found at least 'not guilty' in court, they still use as much force as possible as a means of punishment in bringing you to court. You effectively get 'thumped-out' just on your way to court, and if they lose they don't care... you still got 'thumped-out' and they delivered a message. I was examining what a remedy would be and, clearly, we've got to get these people with the guns, the cops, on our side doing our bidding or we could be at their mercy. There are two ways to do that – one is to get them to agree, and the other is to bring a stronger force to bear. I didn't want to do the latter, but the problem with getting them to agree is that they only follow court orders. Since I saw that the existing courts weren't going to do it because they're not ours – they don't belong to us – then I saw the need for the *creation* of a court.

The court in existence is a de-facto court belonging to the Law Society. Analyzing all the existing courts through history, the one thing that they share is that they've all had a Society; an actual society that you could name and define who were members. When I looked at other people who had tried creating courts and had ended up in jail, I saw that they were unsuccessful because they were not acting within a structured societal framework within which they could claim their lawful protection that such a thing provides. Societies provide a huge amount of protection in the eyes of the law.

A society is a number of persons united together by mutual consent in order to deliberate, determine, and act jointly for some common purpose.
~ John Bouvier *A Law Dictionary*, 1874

I don't believe that a Society exists unless you can name it. One of their biggest tricks is that they've got us thinking that we live in a Society. They talk about the society all the time; they say 'it's for the good of Society' and your assumption is that *you're* a member of that Society and that they're talking about you and yours – but the fact is that they're *not* talking about yours... they're talking about theirs. All I'm trying to do is give people who think that they're a member of a functioning Society the evidence that they are *not* a member of *any* society, let alone a functioning one.

In finding a few more corners and edges and putting it all together, the picture started to become clear; I came up with what I call my 'Cunning Plan' – to form the World Freeman Society. Essentially, the goal of creating it is so that we can create our own courts where we can bring the existing courts in and have them face charges if we need to. Once we have our own courts, then we can ensure 'this and that', which the existing peace officers must obey. In order to justify that court we must have a society, which involves a roll – a means of identifying a number of people, a means of communicating and determining and acting for a common goal and, finally, a common goal.

For example; if I had a Society of people from across the world, where people were actually enrolled and we had a newsletter, and we existed only for dancing monthly; that would be enough to create a court. We could operate on a charter that says: 'we dance freely and in peace to bring abundance to the world'... whatever you want to define it as. Who's going to say you can't do it? What can anyone do to stop you? Fundamentally, what it all boils down to is that if we can show them that we have a roll, we have a newsletter, and we're acting and doing something positive on a monthly basis – right there you've got enough to claim the right to create a court.

Never underestimate the power of dance! Being a 'freeman on the land' requires remembering who we are as human beings and finding that place of joy where no government agent can touch it. If you dance, you will generally find that place. They can't come and tell you that you must dance 'this way' or 'that way'... you get to do whatever you want when you're dancing, and this helps awaken you to your place in the universe and the fact that no-one has a right to govern you without your consent.

I realize that people don't want to come to the World Freeman

Society just to be able to dance and say, *"Oh, I'm dancing and now I'm free!"* – they want information; the knowledge of the law and how to deal with it, so we're creating a system that gives them that as well. One of the key parts of the World Freeman Society is Freedom School – a place where people who are home-schooling can go for resources and support, but also where (because I don't think we should stop learning when we get to a certain age) *anyone* can go and learn just about anything. Let's say if I wanted to develop better communication skills, for example, I'd be able to go there and find a teacher and take a one-month course. What we're looking at eventually is the largest online free university in the world; that's what we're aiming for.

The World Freeman Society is already growing in leaps and bounds. There are chapters of the Freeman Society opening up in the British Isles, New Zealand, Australia, Canada, the US, Holland, and Greece – essentially we're going to be claiming different areas in different places... anywhere where there's common land, we've got a right to seize it and go claim it and then start using it.

There are certain laws of human interaction that are just as powerful as the law of gravity; there are certain laws that cannot be denied. The rest of it seems to be a system of regulation for the purpose of control so that they can extract money and they seem to rely on generating conflict to do that. When we say no to the conflict, their ability to control starts evaporating very quickly.

To a certain degree, any Society needs a constitution, a charter, or a body of words that people can point to and say, *"These are the words that you can judge me by. This is what you can use against me and, if I fail, then these are the tools we use to achieve equity and find remedy."* It's got to be something that a kid who's 12 years of age can understand, recognise, and know when he's crossed the line. The World Freeman Society would go through a legal determination process to judicially determine 13 key points, but really everything only boils down to about three:

don't harm another human being; don't damage property; and don't use fraud in your contracts. That's why part of the World Freeman Society is a promise of peace and in our Charter you agree to recognize that. Of course, people do fuck up – you're not judged on whether or not you fuck up, you're judged on whether or not you can pick yourself up and make amends.

One of the problems we face today is the contraction of the existing money supply and the refusal to issue credit, which results in economic meltdown and collapse. It stagnates our ability to interact and yet we still have tools, we still have our backs, we still have our knowledge and our brains, but suddenly people can't work because the bankers are simply shutting off the tap.

The World Freeman Society will have our own form of exchange, so we make our own money that is suitable for use in any Freeman Valley that we operate. People can still use whatever means of payment they want in or out of it; we're not going to say, *"You're a member of this society so you can only use this"* – that's not what we're about. The means of exchange that we establish within our society is only going to address a need that exists... not to create control.

You would go into a bank and write a promissory note saying something like, *"Okay, this year I intend to work a 30-hour week for 40 weeks and I'm going to be charging $25 an hour for my services. Here's my promise."* You make and decide your own promise, you decide how much you need, and you determine your ability to repay. Your ability to repay is a function of how many hours you intend and pledge to work and how much you will be asking for your efforts. Then we print up the money with your face on it in the denominations that you want. You put it out into circulation and after a year you have to demonstrate that you have fulfilled your promises to your community, to your fellow man, to yourself, and to the universe, and you bring us back the money that we lent you *but it can't have your own face on it...* it has to be other money that you've circulated and used. If you meet that obligation with the evidence that you did use it properly, we're going to do the opposite of any conventional banking system... we will only take back 90%, so you keep 10% and then the money supply grows, but I see no problem with that if it grows at a rate that demonstrates the energy and effort that people have put in.

I don't see giving people millions of dollars because they intend to *employ* others – that's not the way to do it. They've got to find their own passion and riding on the backs of others is not the way to do it. That's the purpose of freedom... if you're not finding and riding your passion, then I mean, what the hell are you doing? I want people to realize that their dreams are the first step to creating their reality.

There's a growing consciousness awareness of the universe; of the unity of Spirit, so there's going to be much less need for systems that are designed for the resolution of conflict. When we don't want to be in conflict anymore the systems that presently make a lot of money are going to become irrelevant. Since the people in power control them and gain their relevancy by the control of these systems, they don't like it when we start waking up to a certain spiritual outlook that makes their conflict ludicrous.

I walk down the street, take the bus, fly on planes and what-not just like everyone else. There's no sign on me or anything... the only difference is that if the cops stop me and try to enforce statutory restrictions on me then I know how to put them in their place so they don't. Cops used to laugh at me and now they're finding it less humorous and a lot of them seem to run once they realize who I am.

There are those who are awake and there are those who choose to continue sleeping. All you can do is try to wake them up by having fun. Let them be the ones to ask, *"What did you do? How can I do this, too?"*

THE AUTHORITY HOAX
by Mary Croft

Imagine how people will interact with each other when they know they
cannot harm another person, place, condition or thing without
harming themselves. Imagine the difference when people, everywhere,
accept the divine truth: as they give, so shall they receive.
~ Don Alejandro Cirilo Perez Oxlaj

Mary grew up in Toronto, Ontario, and moved to Hermosa
Beach, California, where she ran on the beach and worked (as
little as possible) as a Registered Nurse. After a decade, she
moved north to Petaluma, California, where her two boys,
Colin and Casey, were born. Over the decades, Mary has
remained fascinated by the power of the subconscious mind
and all disciplines of energy and frequency healing. She also
moved, against her will, to Roswell, New Mexico, for the
challenging experiences without which she would not have
had the material to write, upon moving to Canmore,
Alberta, her book: *How I Clobbered Every Bureaucratic Cash-*

Confiscatory Agency Known to Man... A Spiritual Economics Book on $$$ and Remembering Who You Are. **This can be downloaded from her website, and you can read subsequent, related articles on her blog at: www.spiritualeconomicsnow.net**

The Trust Account

In my internet article, *The Authority Hoax*, I wrote: '*The only thing you need to know about laws – codes, rules, regulations, statutes, by-laws, ordinances, constitutions, policies, legislations, laws, bills, acts, and even case law – is that they have nothing to do with you. The USA and CANADA, Inc., along with all other corporations (STATE OF CALIFORNIA, PROVINCE OF ALBERTA, etc.) have a Policy Manual, just as SEARS has a Policy Manual for employees. Unless we work for SEARS, their Policy Manual does not apply to us.*' The head servant of the mansion's kitchen staff put up a Notice which reads, 'No Refrigerator Raiding: 11 pm to 7 am'. Does the mistress of the house think that this applies to her? The only 'laws' by which we are bound are Nature's laws and our conscience.

For years, I was on the fence between wanting to know who I am and behaving accordingly so that I didn't have to play the commerce game, and wanting to know how to play the game so that I could win the game. It always seemed as if we were getting closer to the answer, but the investigation was interminable. Most researchers continue to look outside, rather than looking to themselves, recalling their experiences, and remembering who they are. It seems that, for all the riding 'madly off in all directions', all their various, personal agenda come down to only this: we are all tired of being controlled.

I notice that those who search legal land for the answer, albeit to no avail, still do learn much in the process and wind up wanting to sell their information because, "*I put a lot of time and effort into this and I'm not about to give it away.*" But, isn't the reason that they did all this research because they wanted to do so? Now they want people to *pay* them for what they chose to do? The only information worth having is that which will allow us access to the Trust account. The very act of their charging their fellow man evidences that they do not know this, not to mention the dishonor, i.e.; they do to others what the banks are doing to all of us.

Due to all this 'learning', so many researchers have a penchant for wanting to utilize their information and this is what gets them into trouble. They write too much and they say too much – all because they want to be 'right' in thinking that years of study were not spent in vain, so they tend to take on the task of settling public matters, by acting as the liable party, instead of making the public servant do his job. The one who creates the liability, i.e. the public, must provide the remedy. Balancing their books is *not our job*. They work for us.

People who do not have this valuable information, paradoxically, are very willing to sell and tell what they purport to know. But, if we cannot figure this out by ourselves, it is no good to us. No one can tell us how to know who we are. To become free and to feel free is not a process… it is a realization.

I have received hundreds of emails from people who criticize me for not telling them how to implement what I wrote in my book. If I had included a 'how to' in my book, it would have been outdated by the time it hit the internet. I am stunned by the number of people who missed seeing, in my preface, '*I do not, cannot, and will not tell anyone what to do*'. The title of my book is 'How *I* Clobbered…' not, 'How YOU Can Clobber…' I wrote the book to expose the fraudulent banking system and I did certain things to prove it. My book was simply and only a heads-up so people could think about conducting their commercial affairs accordingly and begin to experiment for themselves. I put the book on the internet free of charge. It offers only hints for you to realize who you are, which is all any of us need to know.

Of these hundreds of requests for 'what to do', not one ever asked me about the latter part of my book – 'remembering who you are'; the part about energy – which is all there is. In whatever we do or say, what matters is our energy and the attitude from where we behave, so my 'telling' someone what to say or do is worthless. Becoming free requires 'remembering who you are', so when you come across websites or seminars, just remember; those who sell and tell don't know, and those who DO know cannot tell. 'Knowing' is a private matter and one cannot make it public. The minute it becomes public, the win can no longer stand as a win. I had to look to myself. Accurate answers come effortlessly, from within.

In one of my snits of frustration, recently, I packed it all in (as I do episodically) and read Gregg Braden's book, *The Spontaneous Healing of Belief – Shattering the Paradigm of False Limits*. He reminded me of what I have known for decades – that we can create... in fact, that's all we *can* do. We don't do anything *but* create. We create every aspect of our life experience. If we really knew who we are, we would not be dabbling in any of this commercial investigation, particularly, because every bit of energy we hand over to those who seem to be running the planet only strengthens them. What we want to do is turn away from them and look to ourselves. Why fight someone else's creation when we have our own creating to do? We've already created them as they are; now, we must create something that will override that. As long as we are giving them our time, attention, energy, and emotion (which is what keeps them alive), those whom we most want to convince that we know who we are know that we do NOT know who we are by the very fact that we are involved with them and their silly 'policy manuals'. Dealing with agents, at their level, proves that we believe that the illusion of their authority is real and, ergo, the reality of ours is not. We ought to have nothing to do with them, other than to be sure they keep their word, honor their oaths, and do their jobs. Servants must always be monitored, lest they overstep their position.

If we knew who we are, we would have nothing to do with them. This includes their 'medicine', their 'schools', their 'law', their 'churches', their 'media', etc. – ALL designed to keep us from knowing who we truly are. Somehow, they know this; hence, every time we converse with them, frequent their places of 'worship', argue over 'payment', read their 'newspapers', go to their 'courts', follow or resist their "orders", attend their 'classes', visit their 'doctors', etc., they know that we do not know who we are and they treat us accordingly. If we knew who we were, we would be minding our own health, educating ourselves, conducting our own spiritual development, and not deferring to them for anything.

*

I simply cannot even imagine the enlightened beings of this planet poring over law books, writing paper, learning what to say in court, filing documents, attending seminars, paying for the latest process, etc. in order to get out of a situation which they know, in their hearts, simply does not involve them. They know who they are. I have concluded that, as long as we are still investigating any aspect of the commerce game, those who control it have us where they want us – IN the game, which they control, by THEIR rules, which apply only to them. I suspect that the less we know about their game, the better off we are. That is their business, not ours – and simply becoming very clear on who we are and acting accordingly is what will get us out of this ludicrous mess. I feel as if I have arrived, which is why I am writing this... now.

I could always sense what was wrong when I heard the latest and greatest information because it was complicated and the documents involved were egregiously long and legal. I always said, *"If it isn't simple, it isn't accurate. If most people cannot grasp the concept, then it isn't accurate. If it involves knowing the policies of the Psychopathocracy, then it isn't accurate."* Consequently, I knew that I would know the truth when it showed up because it would be simple – something that we could all see and grasp (if we truly remembered who we are) and it would have nothing to do with any corporate policy manual.

So, whilst reading Braden's book, the penny dropped... I remembered who I am. I clearly saw all I need to know about how to handle the public. There is a Trust, evidenced by the NAME; my parents granted the original value, the Province of Ontario registered it, so it is the Owner and Trustee, all public servants are Agents for the Trustee, and, the Trust/NAME itself is the Beneficiary-in-fact. The entire game of Commerce is played for the beneficiaries. Needless to say, the public isn't about to create a game which doesn't benefit them, so, 'beneficiaries' includes them. My parents granted the original value to the NAME/Trust, via their signatures, and, over the years, I gave it value, via my labor. I cannot be involved in commerce so I use the NAME/Trust in order for me to function in a society which is based upon commerce. Think 'Monopoly®™' We require a token to play, and the only money is that within the game.

I guess it is human nature to try to get out of doing one's job, yet, since I stand to lose, it would behoove me to ensure that the servants serve not only themselves but also me. I hold all public Trust corporations in trust, and, if an agent becomes 'un-trust-worthy', e.g.: if he neglects his fiduciary duty and pretends that I am the Trustee – the one responsible for settling and adjusting the Trust's accounts – then, I am obliged to remind him of his oath of office, wherein he has sworn 'to serve and protect' me and my rights. It is the trust owner, trustee, and agents who have a job to do – not I. Since their debts are their business, not mine, and, since the one who creates the liability must provide the remedy, they are the ones required to settle all charges against the Trust. If they refuse, then they are in violation of public policy and the criminal code and I would be obliged to lay claim against them for Breach of the public Trust and Breach of Oath of Office.

Will we soon lay claims against doctors for Breach of their Hippocratic Oath wherein they swear: *"I will... never do harm to anyone"*? Taking down some of the medical mafia might move 'medicine' out of its present position of the #1 cause of death on this continent.

Maybe we ought just to say that we do not choose to be recognized through the Name and unless they can prove that we are required to be or that we are a Trust or a Name, why are they trying to get us to pay a debt that belongs to the public, particularly when we cannot 'pay', there is no money and we are not even permitted to play the game, let alone incur debt. The charge is against the Trust; who is the Trustee? Not us, so, who is the one required to settle the account? They have the wrong party. We wish we could settle it for them yet we do not have access to the account; we cannot take from it; we can only give value to it. Haven't we done that, already? How could they have set up, for example, a credit card, if we didn't give them the value up front? Now that they have created debt for that account, aren't they the ones liable for the remedy, for setting off the debt, for balancing the account? This has nothing to do with us.

Whoever created the debt is the one responsible for settling it, yet, they will do everything to try to make us liable. But why would anyone willingly go to court? A place where we were not invited, where we have no standing, where our chances of prevailing are almost nil, where we are not being compensated for our time or effort for a charge which has nothing to do with us, and for which the agent for the Trustee, not ourselves, is not only already in the court but also the one legally obliged to settle the account for the Trust/Name? I heard that one judge, upon hearing a fellow lament that he is not the Name, ask, *"Well, if you're not the Name, why are you here?"*

Why have we been doing the servants' work for them?

Because they tricked us into believing that we are responsible for balancing the books of the Trust (the name of which we have continuously been told is our 'name' and is not), for which we are NOT Trustee, and we forgot to question this, all because... we had yet to remember who we are.

The Solution: Nothing We Could Ever Have 'Found' – We Had to 'Arrive'.

The only thing in existence in the universe is energy. Knowing how to make that work for us is all we need to know. The only way we can make energy work for us is to know who we are.

Studying rules to a game which appears to be made up and controled by 'them' is a waste of time. There are only a few things we need to know about 'them'. Our experience of them exists for the same reason that our experience of anything exists – because we created it. We created 'them' and our experiences with them, in order to discover who we are. Our experiences of 'them' are solely for the purpose of our spiritual evolution, which happens to entail challenging ourselves to discover the truth about our power. This is all an illusion and we are simply here to observe our conduct which will reveal the degree to which we realize our all-powerful nature. The reason we cannot win by finding a solution within their rules is because that would ruin the game. We have forgotten that it is OUR game. Our only rule is: we can't win until we remember who we are. It's a Catch 22. We can't win because we don't know who we are but as soon as we remember, the game ceases to exist. Therein lies the win because the game was designed for us to discover ourselves and, when we do, its over.

We created antagonists solely for the drama since 'they' appear to be sub-plots to the main plot which is the drama of observing ourselves. I've noticed that many emails I receive report some form of theft of our basic rights. The most righteous of the writers complain of the new 'laws' which restrict our choices of healthcare. Did it ever cross their minds that this might be good news? If we can't have these 'health products', I guess we'll have to; realize who we are, learn that there is nothing outside ourselves, and, go about healing ourselves. Whenever I hear about this sort of thing, I always take a look at it from another perspective. When I worked at Banff hospital, someone complained that "The Province is no longer going to pay for ....." (some procedure). Nurses were angry. I told them that this is good news because this is pushing people to take responsibility for their own health. Medicine or Naturopathy or whatever... they are all external and no matter what 'the Province' does or no longer will do, they are forcing us to get it through our skulls that we can create perfect health all by ourselves. We do not need anything or anyone for the things in life which we have been programmed to believe that we can obtain only from the 'professionals' – teachers, doctors (allopathic or otherwise), ministers, lawyers, etc. Haven't we learned, yet, that none of them is as good as our own intuition, which is our connection to Spirit? Those who send out this sort of news do not know who they are and, maybe, are as threatening to our realization of our personal power as any other well-programed bureaucrat. The mere fact that some have made distinctions between allopathy and naturopathy tells me that they do not see the distinction between looking within and looking without.

Putting our time, attention, energy, and emotion into trying to correct something which 'appears' to be outside ourselves is what David Icke calls 'combing the mirror'. If we look into the mirror and can only anticipate a 'bad hair day', combing the mirror will not get us out the door any sooner. The only way to change anything that is going on in the mirror is to change the source of the reflection. We are that source.

Knowing who we are is the only thing that will allow us to change how we conduct ourselves which is the only thing that will alter the reflection. Responding to a situation any time but in the here and now will not work. This means that we cannot pre-empt the future and we cannot correct the past. Neither exists. The only thing we can do is respond in the moment. Intending to un-do what we have done in the past, or write documents to stave off potential difficult situations in the future, will only demonstrate to those whom we use for the purpose of discovering where we measure, on our enlightenment scale, that we have not become acquainted with our own unlimited power. If we had, we would not be dallying in affairs which have nothing to do with us. Only in the moment can we deal with what is occurring right now. Our point of power is in the now and any conduct which takes us out of now – into either the past or the future – will not serve us.

I always wanted to pave the way for an easier life and the only thing that I experienced was constant preparedness; I forgot to live in the here and now and, noticing that I have lived nearly six decades, I realize that much of that time has been spent either trying to un-do, balance, make up for my mistakes or prepare for the next situation so that I wouldn't make any more mistakes. I hated getting 'life' wrong because my ego's drug of choice, to cause me to feel 'wrong', was 'regret'.

In case you haven't noticed, our society does not allow for mistakes. We are either threatened not to err or punished if we do. Since the best way to learn is to fail, it behooves us to 'fail fast'. Only then, can we be open to success.

Success is going from failure to failure without any loss of enthusiasm. – Winston Churchill.

Yet, we all live in fear. We actually are not permitted to experience the most efficient way to learn, without severe emotional, not to mention physical, mental, and spiritual repercussions. Our society is designed to keep us from venturing out, experimenting, throwing caution to the wind, because we are kept in fear of making mistakes. Society discourages us from 'living'. We are punished if we don't either make amends or correct our ways. The entire court system, which came from the ego mind, is based upon this.

All the 'attorney wannabes' are studying the rules of a game they cannot win because, if they could actually win, they would no longer need or want to play it. After I jumped out of an aeroplane, I didn't need to do it again. If you know you can do a thing, you don't need to do it, yet we all must do that which we think we cannot do. It seems as if what we all think we cannot do is to state, on the spot, whatever is necessary to empower ourselves to prevail, in the here and now. I always said, *"I'm better on paper."* What does this tell you? That I didn't trust myself to conduct myself, in the moment, in a manner which demonstrates that I know who I am and that I am capable of demonstrating the love and power that I know I am.

So, people are still digging in the same pit, year after year, with only slight tributaries, instead of surfacing to look around to see that the solution is in the here and now and can be only in the here and now.

You can't plan a miracle. – Philippe Petit.

Their intent, as mine, was to set up a situation so that we could not fail. This is an impossibility because, since each of us is the creator of our own circumstances, there could never be a 'one-size fits all'. Where one might prevail, by saying the right thing in order to get out of a tight spot, the same words coming from the mouth of another might land him in jail. Therein lies the solution which is the miracle. If we simply BE who we are and act in the moment, we'll create whatever we create, yet, all the while knowing that the circumstance that we create is precisely for our own information which is: to observe where we are on the 'I know I am all love and all powerful' scale.

It seems we have come full cycle. We began by saying, *"That's not my name."* A dozen years ago, that landed me in jail, but that is only because, although I was acutely aware of what I was not, I had only a flicker of an idea of who I was. My friend once said of me, *"Mary may not know what she wants, but she sure knows what she doesn't want!"* Well, knowing what I didn't want didn't assist me in knowing what I want or even knowing where to look. It has been a long road, yet I have learned a couple of things. Observing something we resist will only empower it because 'resistance' is an extremely powerful energy and we will find ourselves at the effect of it. We cannot argue with quantum physics/mechanics. This is why those who are sending fear-filled emails will experience precisely what they believe; however, those of us who chuck them into the trash will not. Nothing exists without my observation – so, if I put my attention elsewhere, those things cease to exist... in my universe. If you continue to observe them, they will continue to exist in your universe.

So, does 'apocalypse' mean 'horror show' or 'unveiling'? It means 'unveiling' or 'revelation' to me, so this is what I will get. In my observation, I will be able to know the entire truth of this universe. If you believe the word means 'hell and damnation', end of the world, natural disasters, you will experience precisely that... your option.

When you change the way you look at things, the things you look at change. - Wayne Dyer

In his book, *Fractal Time*, Gregg Braden says that what 2012 will be depends upon how we choose to respond to all that occurs. We play a role in the creation of the shift of World Ages and nothing will be 'happening to' us. If we choose to respond with love, strength, and balance, the next World Age will be one of peace. I suspect that even if you choose from fear and you opt for greed, comfort, and profit, those of us who want the new World Age to be one of love and peace, will, with the strength of love energy, override your desire, so, if you can't beat us – and you can't – then consider joining us. In other words, it will take only a few of us to create what we want. You who want disaster cannot prevail.

We won't ever know what works until we try, but there is nothing to try. There is no paper which will circumvent what we are avoiding because the minute we file it, they (whom we created to do so) suddenly know that we *don't* know who we are and they ignore the paper because why would they honor any paper we write when the very writing of it evidences that we don't know who we are? Has anyone ever received any worthwhile answers to questions we post to them? I think that it is alright that we know how they operate, as long as we do not let them know that we know.

Have more than thou showest; speak less than thou knowest. – William Shakespeare.

In other words, never fire their laws back to them because that appears as if we think they matter. We make the illusion real. I think if we write anything, the less legal-land crap we include, the more effective it will be. All we have to let them know, right here, right now, in the moment, is, *"I don't know your business but I do know it isn't mine."*

If we were courageous, had no fear, knowing that all of life is our creation of circumstances to measure our fear, we would jump in and deal with the alleged consequences. The only way to be in control is to be willing to be out of control; if we are willing to die, we cannot die. If we had no fear, we could be who we are. Whatever occurred, we could simply include, just because we would know that we can never die and it would all be just part of the movie. Who lives like that?

The movie, *Man On Wire*, proves that Philippe Petit lives like that. This is the man who walked on a wire between the Twin Towers of the World Trade Center in 1974. When he walks a wire in a place that the local constabulary considers 'illegal', he gets arrested. He's been arrested over 500 times in his career. (This causes me to wonder what I have been doing with my time.) He does not see these arrests as something that ought not to be. His arrests are just the finale to his theatricals. He tells us that we must 'exercise rebellion'. He handles every situation in the 'now'.

When we are forced to handle a situation, we must handle it in the here and now. If the situation is on paper, we must handle the situation as close to 'now' as possible, which ought to be considered as 72 hours because the ones to whom we are responding will consider that 'now' (they are fictions... what do *they* know about 'now'?) In other words, our tactics change with each situation. At the moment the Name is 'charged', I think we ought to let them know that we do not consent to being recognized through the Name. I can provide the Statement of Birth as proof that the Name belongs to the province and a declaration that I have nothing to do with it. My signature is not on it. This is their business, not mine.

However, in a case where the public already has our cash, we must conduct ourselves properly in the moment. This means that we tell them, as soon as possible, that the fruits of our labor have ended up in the public as a tax, which is in violation of public policy and so we ought to file for a tax return (return of the tax). Since it is ALL tax, we can go to our receipts. I would just put it all into a cover letter, put the NAME and the amount to be refunded on a 'tax return' form, sign it, and beg their pardon if I haven't done this properly and, if they please, tell me what I can do to correct it – which forms to use, etc. Again, this is their business, not mine. I don't mind assisting them, but I ought not to be expected to do it alone.

"Whoever creates the liability must provide the remedy." We have all heard it and seem to have forgotten it. So, whoever charges, creates the debt, or sends the bill is responsible for discharging, settling the debt, and balancing the books. Since all debt is created on paper, all debt can be discharged with... other pieces of paper. This has nothing to do with me since it is impossible for

me to create any liability because I do not, will not, and cannot operate in commerce. Since those in the public must know this, I think a gentle reminder is all that is required.

Again, since we live in the 'now', in fact, *must* live in the 'now', we cannot pre-empt today for the future and we cannot explain tomorrow for the past. Our point of power is *now*, in the moment. There is no other time and living in the past or future is only disempowering. Do not handle anything which does not require 'handling' RIGHT NOW. Remember Occam's Razor: eliminate non-essentials. The procrastinator's oath is, *"Never do today what can be done tomorrow"*. However, that suggests that one is living for a 'to-do list' and not living in the now and doing whatever shows up next in life, which is all we are ever required to do. I admit, living life by the motto, *"Be Here Now"* is a facer. The ego mind so loathes it.

I often imagine this scene: Someone... cop... anyone... asks for ID. If we produce 'identification', we admit to being the Name and, immediately, we become the liable party because, then, they know that we do not know who we are. THAT is what makes us liable – our not knowing who we are – nothing else. *"Do you have ID?"* ID!? *"Identification."* Of what? *"You!"* Well, you're looking at me. *"We need to see something that identifies you."* Well, nothing is identical to me so what is it you really want? *"Who are you?"* Who are **you**? *"We need to know who you are."* I am who I say I am. *"Who do you say you are?"* I am you, and if you don't know that, then you don't know who you are, so why would I discuss anything with someone who doesn't know who he is?

You can see where this might escalate... If you have any ID with you, which I do not recommend, it might be a good idea to carry the Statement of Birth – the document your parents signed, along with a Declaration stating that you do not consent to be recognized through the name on the document plus, maybe, an addendum, generic to any agent who might need to know. It is our responsibility to remember who we are. The instant that we do, all this will come to a screeching halt. The disappearance of the universe is contingent upon our remembering.

FREEMAN OF ENGLAND
John Harris

I will not be pushed, filed, stamped, indexed, briefed, debriefed or numbered. My life is my own.
~ **Patrick McGoohan (1928 - 2009)**, *The Prisoner*

John Harris is the co-founder of The People's United Community. Website: www.tpuc.org

All my life I have questioned things. As a child, I always bucked authority if I felt that the authority was wrong and I did suffer because of this. I also made quite a lot of friends! I drifted through life, really, up until a few years ago when I became a carpenter.

9/11 was a definite trigger-point for me. While I was working on a local job one day, I was given a film about 9/11 called *Loose Change*. It didn't register at first, but the second time I watched it,

I noticed something interesting – that a camera shook in a building. Something had obviously exploded with such magnitude and force that it brought those buildings down. I looked into the 'official story' of what had happened, but the unofficial story was far more interesting and seemed nearer the truth.

I decided to start a website called *The People's United Collective* (TPUC), which focused on 9/11 and 7/07 (the London Bombings). The website evolved and as we started to question how and why the people of this island are suffering under what seem to be very draconian measures being employed by parliament, councils and all the different elements of the society we live in.

I believe in my heart that you evolve with the information that you're given. Your mind-set changes. I know it sounds absolutely bizarre but, a lot of the time, I don't think about things… I allow things to happen *by realization*. At every stage in the information that I came across, there was some sort of recourse I could see. One of these was to visit Buckingham Palace with an affidavit to the Queen, saying, "*I am removing myself from your system*". I used an ancient law – article 61 of the Magna Carta (1215), but eventually realized that the Magna Carta actually created the society we live in.

After that, people started to contact me, telling me about Constitutional Law and Common Law and other wonderful things that I just couldn't grasp but, for some reason, I started to retain certain parts of this information and so I looked at different aspects of law. After a period of time, I got heavily involved in trying to understand the history of this country – from the kings and queens to the development of law.

I drew a timeline on a small piece of paper that grew to be 6 foot wide and 8 foot deep. I was stood on it one night with my husky (who liked to run about on it as well… I could never get him off the bloody thing!) and the penny dropped. Because I was stood above it and I had it all laid out in front of me, I could actually see it in front of my eyes... I suddenly realised that what I could see was *history repeating itself* over and over again.

As I looked at it, I could see that *none of it applies to a human being* – nothing at all! This is going to sound absolutely crackers, but the truth is; we have a 'person' attached to us via our birth certificate. Anything that has a title before the name – including Mr, Mrs, Ms, Master, Sir, etc. – refers to the status, the legal character of a 'person' or a 'thing'. Vicar, bishop, archbishop, etc. are also titles, so they're 'persons' – they're not human beings. Westminster Abbey is a registered corporation, would you believe? There's nothing in this country that's not. The United Kingdom plc was dissolved in February 2008 and now it's the United Kingdom Corporation *ltd*. Her Majesty is one of the leading figures within the Crown Corporation – but Her Majesty Queen Elizabeth is also a title; therefore she is a 'person', *not* a human being.

When I had sent that affidavit to Her Majesty, without knowing what I was doing at the time, I actually wrote my name in capital letters. So, in effect, what I did was send an affidavit (a Common Law document from a human being that's referring to a 'person') *to* a person. So, I'd actually unintentionally started the process of sacrificing my 'person'.

I'm not talking about an out-of-body experience or anything like that, but it was like I had 'stepped out' of this 'person' and became a man again, a human being, and *then* looked at what actually applied to me as a *man*. Not as this persona, this mask, or the personality of this person... *me as a human being.* Stepping outside of my 'person' was like seeing the world through a different set of eyes. I looked back on the world and I could see that everything that we live in is just an illusion. The 'person' sees a world in a different way – a world where money is valuable... you have to have this and you have to have that. You, your Self, the human being, realizes that money isn't worth anything. The only reason it works is because everyone believes it's real. The only way the system is propagated and maintained is because we use the stuff every single day. If the government decided tomorrow that money doesn't exist and now we're going use buttons instead, everyone would laugh but when they went to buy their next loaf of bread they would go and look for buttons to pay for it with.

I started to look more in-depth at the legal world. A lot of this involves the bankers, the bankers' attorney and the private sector. Shakespeare actually wrote in one of his plays, *The Tragedy of King Lear*: 'Keep... thy pen from lenders' books, and defy the foul fiend'. He was basically saying, *'never, ever borrow money from these fiends'*.

The Hidden Meaning of the English Language

All the clues have been left there. If you actually define the word 'society', it means 'the socially dominant members of a community'. We live in a world controlled by the socially dominant. There's a two-tier money system, there's a two-tier law system, and there's a two-tier community. When people say there's a New World Order... that, again, is just a creation. What's actually happening is that the socially dominant just want to maintain their social dominance. That's all it is. The only way they can do that is to enslave the people – the 'unwanted necessity' – because without them nothing in their world works. *Nothing.* The working people of any country are the engine of that country because if they stopped doing what they're doing, everything would grind to a halt.

If we wanted to solve this problem once and for all, all everybody in any country has to do is not go to work *for one day*, not buy anything *for one day*, and not use any services *for one day*. That's it. That would sort this problem out, because the country would just seize-up. Believe me, these people don't do anything unless you actually create a problem that they start to suffer from – when the food's not on their table because the lorry's not delivered it, when the fuel's not in their car because the lorries have not delivered it...

Of course, they make sure that doesn't happen by enslaving that engine with fear, and the fear is the lack of this make-believe product. I believe that fear resides in the brain because you only start fearing something when you start thinking about it. If we don't think about it in the first place then we won't fear it! The fear is that we believe that everything we've got is valuable and that's the materialistic, egotistic world, which works on 'status'. They've manipulated that one word because in their society, if you've got money, a big house, or a big car, then you've got status.

If you break the word 'status' down, it actually means 'the legal character of a person or thing' – it's actually *telling you* it's about something that doesn't exist. A character does not really exist. It goes back to Shakespeare again, when he wrote, *'All the world's a stage, and all the men and women merely players'*.

They've just created a legal world of illusion – it does not exist, it's all fiction, and it's so complicated that we would never ever understand it. The trouble is that once the genie's out of the bottle, it's very hard to get that genie back in again. I'm now suffering the effects of trying to live my life without money, and this world is geared-up so we can only live by money because that's the only way they can control the workforce, the slaves. The word 'slavery' itself means 'the principle part of any work force'.

As I started to look into Statute Law and the language that they use, I realized that it's exactly the same all over the world – what every Statute *really* means is 180 degrees in the opposite direction. Basically, the Acts become Statutes; the Statutes are enacted under and enforced by Statutory Instruments; and Statutory Instruments are a legally-created written contract. It's all Contract Law but it's *not* Law – it's a farce. It's a fallacy because Law only exists if it has morality. A Statute is not Law because the actual definition of a statute is 'the legislative rule of a society given the force of law by the consent of the governed'. Note that it says *'force of* law' it doesn't say *'it's* law'. And it's 'by the consent of the governed' and so, by definition, if you *don't* 'consent' it doesn't receive the 'force of law', so that means it doesn't exist – it's not real... it's just policy.

The word 'policy' relates to politics, which is the administration of a government, which is policy. Police officers are 'corporate policy enforcement agents' who are there to enforce fictitious statutes under statutory instruments and maintain that they can get the 'person' to do it. A police *man* or woman is something different... these are the human beings who uphold the law, serve and protect, and never deny or delay right or justice to any individual. Most of the police men and women that I talk to don't realize that there is this difference... they really don't. I always try to talk to the human being, *not* the person. Sometimes you can get through to the human being, and sometimes you can't... it depends how indoctrinated they are.

There are only two laws that actually exist – never cause harm to anybody or anything; and never cause loss to anybody or anything. That covers all eventualities... and that's Common Law. In Common Law to 'confiscate' from someone means 'to take from someone unlawfully which is rightfully theirs'. Now, as a corporate enforcement agent, a police officer can say, *"I'm going to confiscate that from you"*. By fooling the human being into representing the 'person', he will get your name and your address (which means he's contracted with the 'person', not you as a human being) and now he can apply a Statute Law against you, which is the Law of Confiscation. If that human being had maintained that he was a human being, the police officer could never confiscate because he would be committing a crime.

They've fooled us with words. When you 'submit' an application of 'registration', to 'submit' means 'to bend to someone else's will' and 'application' means 'beg', which implies that you know what you're begging for and that you know you're about to hand over authority of whatever you're trying to register. When you register something, you're handing over the title ownership of whatever you are registering to who you are registering...

When you 'register' your child, that child is now 'owned' by the corporation United Kingdom. We have a mandatory schooling system – you can only take your kids on holiday when *they say*, and they will fine you if you take them during term-time instead of the summer holidays. We have mandatory vaccinations. This is why when you don't look after 'their' property, they send in the Social Services plc. to take your children away. The Social Services are a registered corporation; they are a public limited company that basically makes money by stealing children to pay the shareholders. That's how it's done.

When you 'register' your car to the DVLA, which is a trading name of the Department of Transport (DoT) corporation, they send you back a Registered Keepers document – so you're the keeper, *not the owner*. That's why when you don't put tax on *their* vehicle, they can come and take *their* property and crush it. It's simple how it works... it's just that we've been completely duped.

Our language has been completely and deliberately messed-up. We say words that are not needed. Have you ever spoken to someone and there's just something about the way they speak that agitates you? It's all to do with the vibration of the sounds we're producing when we say a word, and we've been taught to pronounce words wrongly. If you take the *e* the *n* and the *w* out of any word, what is left actually gives you a clue... when you take the *n* out of the word 'mind', it says 'mid'. Personally, what that tells me is to 'rely on your gut feeling'. I've got this theory that the brain is just a gearbox for the body and a projector for the soul. I don't believe that there is anything achieved by thinking... nothing at all. How many people have you met and they haven't even said anything to you but you've got a 'gut' feeling that there's something 'not quite right'. And that's your natural in-built defence system – it's natural to allow your instincts to do the work, because your instincts are *you*. You don't need to be told what is right or wrong ... you already *know*.

Why do we need a leader? To lead us where? We already know where we should be so we don't need leaders – *they* are the ones who need leaders to lead us down the garden path! Interestingly, when take the '*e*'s out of 'leader', what you get is a 'lad-r'. A leader leads you to the ladder (lad-r) of social climbing. So any words that use the letters *e*, *n*, and *w* are not needed.

Sacrifice of the 'Person'

Religious people are often the hardest to get through to, because belief is the most powerful of indoctrines. I actually went into religion for about three months to learn what it does to people – I'm a very strong believer that you can't know about anything until you've actually experienced it. When people say, *"I know how you're feeling"*, if you've not suffered it then you haven't got a clue.

Whoever enters into religion is in servitude. The first of the Ten Commandments instantly puts you in servitude. You don't need to be told not to steal because if you love someone or you care for someone, then you wouldn't steal from them. They're trying to tell us something that's already inherent.

There are no gods on this earth and I don't believe that there ever have been – only men and women who *believe* themselves to be gods and that we should be enslaved to them and do as they say. The society we live in was created on the same principles as religion, i.e.; 'That's God, I'm telling you that's God, and you will worship what I tell you is God. And I will write a book that says that'. They've got a system they believe will work – they're obviously working from a coded form of something that they don't want to deviate from because they believe it's sacred. The trinity they work on; the Father, the Son and the Holy Ghost – well, you've got the Father in London (the finance capital of the world), you've got the Son in Washington DC (the defence capital of the world), and the Holy Ghost in the Vatican (the religious capital of the world). The number 3 is the concept of something sacred in numerology, which is very interesting. I use a very old form of numerology that's very simple, but it's never wrong.

They keep it hidden to make everything complicated, but what they don't bargain on are individuals who step out of the 'person'. That's all it takes. While you're still being a 'person', you're caught up in the world of complicated lives. As it says on the website: 'Truth is simple. Mankind makes it complicated'.

The belief that Jesus sacrificed himself for the good of mankind to save mankind is interesting. Jesus was basically against the bankers. It's quite possible that he didn't sacrifice *himself*... he sacrificed his *'person'*. When he sacrificed his person, he left their world because they only have control over the legal fiction, the 'person'. They have no control over human beings.

The problem is, when you sacrifice your 'person', you enter into a world that is incredibly hard because you lose all the benefits and services that you had as a 'person' – hospitals, doctors, dentists, the police... you lose *everything*. Across the world, the freeman movement is growing exponentially every day. I now know dentists and doctors who are doing exactly the same and are willing to exchange without using money – you do something for me and I'll do something for you. There is something very, very unique happening here.

Stepping out of the person is what the freeman movement is about. On the back of a t-shirt I've got it says, 'I'm not a person... I just *am*'. Unfortunately, a lot of people don't fully understand... they haven't yet realised that it's about looking on the world as 'I am who I am'. You are what you are, and that's it.

We all try to fit a criteria or comply with society in so many ways. We worry about what other people think – and we all do it... I fall into traps, because I'm still trying to get rid of my ego. It doesn't matter what people wear or what they look like or what colour they are or how they talk. This is society trying to make us comply to its rules, which are completely false – they're all imaginary.

When someone says something to us and it actually hurts us, it's because it's attacking the ego, and we've all got one of those… it doesn't matter who we are. The truth really does hurt, it's painful – but it's designed to be because it allows you to come to the understanding that it is the truth.

It's a lovely feeling to be a freeman on the land. It brings a warmth to me. I'm trying to be humble about everything. I don't want to shout at people I don't want to preach to people… I just want to say, *"Look, this is what I see – have a look at it. If it's not for you don't worry about it!"* There must be some substance to what I say because I can see it.

Everything I've gone through in my life has synchronistically led me to where I am now. No matter how bad or good those events were, I look at them and say, *"Okay, what did I learn from that?"* There is a reason for everything. Sometimes we go so far off the track that we need a good kick back onto it, but that's not punishment… that's 'tough love'.

I changed the name of the website to The People's United Community because that's what I would like us to become – a united community… even if it's just on the internet; a community that treats every single individual within that community with respect and decency and love, because that's basically what it's all about.

We need to go back to being the caretakers of this planet. That's what we were put here to do. No-one can own this planet, it's not ours… we were just gifted it to live on. No-one can really own land – we've got a right to have enough land to be able to live on and take care of adequately. Funnily enough, that's mirrored in Oodle law which is Viking Law, which actually states that land is God-given and can never be taken away. If we've got to live here, then at least let's have a decent place to live... why not? What's the problem with having somewhere great to live?

Human beings haven't got a clue how great their potential is, not yet. There seems to be something stirring. What you do with it is down to you...

AFTERWORD

Be the best. No negativity. No weakness. No acquiescence to fear or disaster. No errors of ignorance. No evasion from reality.
~ Jeff Buckley (1966-1997)

It is sometimes the hardest thing for us to do, to step beyond our learned humanness and into our essence. Thus we are given all scenarios to use as springboards into the certainty that there is absolutely nothing in all the universe, nothing at all, that is not love.
~ Pat Reynolds (www.thebluesun.co.uk)

A community is created when people join together with a common goal or purpose. Can we consider that humankind on the whole is a community? Certainly not on a superficial level – there will, perhaps, always be sub-groups bandying together at any given time for just about any purpose you can imagine, from the mundane to the exquisite. What I'm talking about here is the underlying, deeper purpose – the commonality or communality that binds us all *beyond* belief; beyond personality; beyond the perceived boundaries that exist between ourselves and everything else in the entire universe.

Nothing is worth having. By that, I mean that we will go to almost any length imaginable to secure our individual happiness; and this has got us into a whole lot of trouble both personally and collectively because, although we may *think* we know what we want in order to 'make us happy', we tend to forget the ironic maxim: 'the only thing constant is change'. As George Harrison sang, *"All things must pass"*. Hence there is nothing 'out there' that will permanently satisfy your insatiable appetite for happiness; there will never be enough. If we are to change; to heal this schismic world we live in, we may as well give up striving to be happy. There is freedom in that. When I was a kid, my dad said to me (with all good intent, bless his cotton socks), *"Do whatever you want to do in life, as long as you're happy."* As I write these very words, I have only just realized that I have found this an incredible burden to bear. It is neither practical nor realistic to have 'happiness' as your main goal or priority in life.

If you take the 'e' out of the word 'happiness' (see John Harris' story on page 460), you get 'happinss'. Paradoxically, we will be a lot 'happier' when we open ourselves to whatever we feel at any given moment by flowing with whatever 'happinss'. Everything is worth letting in, but our personal preferences tend to get in the way.

A human being is like a rainbow – black and white and all the colors in between. Tears of sadness can turn to tears of joy in seconds if we can simply recognize that we are not our feelings and simply allow them to flow *through* us rather than constantly wallowing in stagnant emotional pools. Bitterness, regret, guilt, and remorse are long-standing feelings from the murky pool of cess and ooze that causes so many human diseases and so much suffering. Holding onto anything is the ultimate death of freedom.

When a baby is sad, happy, angry or frustrated; unless they have colic or some other painful problem, there is not a trace of 'holding on' – they can switch between emotions instantaneously, each moment anew. But here we are – continually buying-into certain emotions, re-creating and re-enacting all the drama of a soap opera! This 'same shit, different day' syndrome is perfectly illustrated in the U.K's long-running TV show called *Eastenders*. (My mum went 'cold turkey' after watching it religiously for 15 years, and I am extremely proud of her!)

We are constantly faced with decisions to make that take a lot of thought and consideration, making life extremely difficult. Why? Because the mind is a complicated twisty-turny machine that does not want to accept responsibility at any cost for the choices it makes. This is actually a good thing, in my humble opinion, because what that should tell you is that IT CAN'T! It doesn't have the authority. If I tell my kids to do anything, they often reply with a defiant, *"You're not the boss of me!"* Well, it's like that. My mind is not 'the boss of me'. Your mind is not 'the boss of you', either. So who *is* the boss? I think we all know the answer to that.

The heart is simple and real and how I feel is elementary. My heart *knows* and then my mind thinks about it. Sometimes, when I know something in my heart of hearts it takes my mind a long time to 'get with it' and be brave enough to follow through with what the heart says. It can be an excruciatingly painful process. I am sometimes 'faint hearted' and cannot, will not, and stubbornly refuse to do its bidding. Our minds need to be reminded that our best interests are *at heart*.

If we no longer need to be protected from every emotion under the sun bar happiness, then the mind shouldn't have a problem with that – in fact, it will be greatly relieved of the burden, and can stop giving itself a hard time for fucking things up! When the mind becomes a servant of the heart; when we stop giving our authority to the 'powers of the mind that be', my guess is that this will be reflected in the world around us.

As many of those in this book have suggested, what we can see in the world today is a macrocosmic mirror showing us exactly what is going on within each and every one of us. We are controlled by others who give us rules and regulations and expect us to do their bidding, while denying any responsibility for our actions as a direct consequential result of the laws that they created in the first place! What that should tell you is THEY CAN'T! They do not have the authority. The solution is obvious; we take responsibility for ourselves. Again, my guess is that they will be greatly relieved of the burden, and all these countries, corporations, religions, and institutions can finally stop blaming one another for messing things up!

This takes courage and no-one said it would be easy – the shit may well hit the proverbial fan... No greater challenge have we ever to face than to allow whatever 'happnss' to flow through us without buying into the drama of world events as the whole thing unravels. It can, and must, be done. From the heart.

*

If you have enjoyed reading this book, you might like to attend an Alternative Research Community (ARC) Convention, bringing together some of the individuals in this book for a weekend of insights and discovery. The calendar of events can be found on the website: **www.arcconvention.org**

ABOUT THE AUTHOR

Karen Sawyer is a writer, artist and musician, living on the southwestern coast of Wales in the UK. Her first book, *Soul Companions: Conversations with Contemporary Wisdom Keepers – A Collection of Encounters with Spirit,* featured interviews with 45 of the world's shaman, seers, visionaries and sages. Karen organizes Soul Companions Gatherings, bringing together those featured in the book. Karen is also the founder of the ARC Convention – events featuring those in the Alternative Research Community, many of whom shared their experiences in this book. For more information, visit the following websites:

www.soulcompanions.org
www.thedangerousman.org
www.arcconvention.org
www.myspace.com/impishmusic

SELECTED BIBLIOGRAPHY

In addition to the books by the contributors featured in The Dangerous Man, the author also recommends the following;

AntiTerrorist, The. *TheAntiTerrorist Handbook*. Velluminous Press, 2009

Barranger, Jack. *Past Shock: The Origin of Religion and its Impact on the Human Soul*. The Prometheus Project, 1998

Billington, James H. *Fire in the Minds of Men: Origins of the Revolutionary Faith*. Transaction Publishers, 1999

Braden, Gregg. *Fractal Time: The Secret of 2012 and a New World Age*. Hay House, 2009

Calleman, Carl Johan.*The Purposeful Universe*. Bear & Company, 2009

Cooper, Lyz. *Sounding the Mind of God*. O Books, 2009

de Ruiter, John. *Unveiling Reality*. Oasis Edmonton Publishing, 2001

Fisher, Mark. *Capitalist Realism – Is There No Alternative?* O Books, 2009

Gardiner, Philip. *Delusion: Aliens, Cults, Propaganda and the Manipulation of the Mind*. O Books, 2009

Ghis, Madame. *Escape in Prison*. Ghis, 2009

Glickman, Michael. *Cornography: The New Swirled Order*. The Squeeze Press, 2007

Glickman, Michael. *Crop Circles: The Bones of God*. Frog Books, 2009

Grof, Stansilav, M.D. *The Holotropic Mind: The Three Levels of Human Consciousness and How They Shape Our Lives*. HarperOne, 1993

Halton, Lindsay. *The Secret of Home*. O Books, 2008

Hancock, Graham. *Underworld: The Mysterious Origins of Civilization*. Three Rivers Press, 2003

Holmes, Kylie. *Intuitive Children: Children Who See Beyond the Veil*.

O Books, 2009

Lash, John. *Not in His Image. Gnostic Vision, Sacred Ecology, and the Future of Belief.* Chelsea Green, 2006

Leedskalnin, Edward. *Magnetic Current.* Filiquarian Publishing, LLC, 2006

Lina, Juri. *Architects of Deception: The Concealed History of Freemasonry.* Referent Publishing, 2004

Maxwell, Jordan. *Matrix of Power: How the World Has Been Controlled By Powerful People Without Your Knowledge.* The Book Tree, 2003

Medhus, Elisa, M.D. *Raising Childen who Think for Themselves.* MJF Books, 2001

Melchizedek, Drunvalo. *The Ancient Secret of the Flower of Life: Volume 1.* Light Technology Publications, 1999

Pinchbeck, Daniel. *Breaking Open the Head: A Psychedelic Journey into the Heart of Contemporary Shamanism.* Broadway, 2003

Pinchbeck, Daniel. *Toward 2012: Perspectives on the Next Age.* Tarcher, 2008

Ritschl, Georg. *Operation Paradise: Effective Environmental Healing with Orgone Energy.* CreateSpace, 2007

Talbot, Michael. *The Holographic Universe.* Harper Perennial, 1992

Taylor, Eldon. *Choices and Illusions: How Did I Get Where I am and How Do I Get Where I Want to Be?* Hay House, 2007

Tesla, Nikola. *The Tesla Papers: Nikola Tesla on Free Energy & Wireless Transmission of Power.* Adventures Unlimited Press, 2000

von Daniken, Erich. *History is Wrong.* New Page Books, 2009

BOOKS

O is a symbol of the world, of oneness and unity. In different cultures it also means the "eye," symbolizing knowledge and insight. We aim to publish books that are accessible, constructive and that challenge accepted opinion, both that of academia and the "moral majority."

Our books are available in all good English language bookstores worldwide. If you don't see the book on the shelves ask the bookstore to order it for you, quoting the ISBN number and title. Alternatively you can order online (all major online retail sites carry our titles) or contact the distributor in the relevant country, listed on the copyright page.

See our website www.o-books.net for a full list of over 500 titles, growing by 100 a year.

And tune in to myspiritradio.com for our book review radio show, hosted by June-Elleni Laine, where you can listen to the authors discussing their books.

mySpiritRadio